ULTIMATE WASHINGTON

SECOND EDITION

"The book makes good on its promise to present the 'best' of the state with its careful, conscientious selection of natural and urban sights, activities, lodging and restaurants."

—*Seattle Times*

"Has a keen eye for Washington's exceptional hotels, restaurants, shops and sightseeing."

—*Milwaukee Journal*

"Written with a love for the unique beauty of the 'evergreen playground,' *Ultimate Washington* captures the intriguing Seattle music scene and leads you to the best ski areas and one-of-a-kind events."

—*Arizona Senior World*

ULTIMATE WASHINGTON

SECOND EDITION

Maria Lenhart   Marilyn McFarlane   Jim Poth
Roger Rapoport   John Gottberg   Archie Satterfield

RAY RIEGERT

Executive Editor

LESLIE HENRIQUES

Editorial Director

JOANNA PEARLMAN

Editor

GLENN KIM

Illustrator

ULYSSES PRESS   BERKELEY, CA

Published by: Ulysses Press
3286 Adeline Street, Suite 1
Berkeley, CA 94703

Library of Congress Catalog Card Number 94-61739
ISBN 1-56975-032-7

Printed in the U.S.A. by the George Banta Company

10 9 8 7 6 5 4 3 2 1

Managing Editor: Claire Chun
Project Director: Lee Micheaux
Copy Editor: David Sweet
Editorial Associates: Mark Rosen, Doug Lloyd, Kelli Hanson
Cover Design: DesignWorks and Leslie Henriques
Maps: Wendy Ann Logsdon, Phil Gardner, Mark Rosen, Lee Micheaux
Index: Sayre Van Young
Cover Photography: front cover, Terry Donnelly;
    back cover, E. Cooper/Superstock (left), G. Gehm/Superstock (right)
Color Separation: Twin Age Limited

Distributed in the United States by Publishers Group West, in Canada by Raincoast Books, and in Great Britain and Europe by World Leisure Marketing

Printed on Recycled Paper ♻

The authors and publisher have made every effort to ensure the accuracy of information contained in *Ultimate Washington*, but can accept no liability for any loss, injury or inconvenience sustained by any traveler as a result of information or advice contained in this guide.

Contents

The Best of Washington

ADVENTURES

BED AND BREAKFAST INNS

HISTORIC SPOTS

HOTELS AND RESORTS

MUSEUMS

Fort Walla Walla Museum Complex *(Walla Walla, pages 277–78)*
Maryhill Museum of Art *(Maryhill, page 297)*

RESTAURANTS

Dahlia Lounge *(Seattle, page 60)*
Wild Ginger *(Seattle, page 61)*
Shoalwater Restaurant *(Seaview, page 154)*
Sun Mountain Lodge Dining Room *(Winthrop, page 231)*
The Herbfarm *(Fall City, page 243)*
Patsy Clark's *(Spokane, page 274)*
Birchfield Manor *(Yakima, page 281)*

SCENIC DRIVES

Cape Flattery *(Page 140)*
Skagit Valley in the Spring *(Page 169)*
Chuckanut Drive *(Page 173)*
Route 20 *(Pages 222, 224)*
Route 90 over Snoqualmie Pass *(Page 241)*

STATE PARKS

Dash Point State Park *(Tacoma, page 110)*
Penrose Point State Park *(Lakebay, pages 119–20)*
Deception Pass State Park *(Whidbey Island, page 195)*
Spencer Spit State Park *(Lopez Island, page 201)*
Steamboat Rock State Park *(Grand Coulee area, page 271)*
Mount Spokane State Park *(Spokane area, page 276)*

UNIQUE PLACES

Pike Place Market *(Seattle, pages 50, 51)*
Mima Mounds *(Litlerock, page 103)*
Hood Canal Floating Bridge *(Page 126)*
Hoh Rainforest *(Olympic National Park, page 137)*
Deception Pass Bridge *(Page 196)*
Windy Ridge *(Mt. St. Helens, page 248)*
Crown Point *(Columbia River Gorge, page 294)*

Note from the Publishers

An alert, adventurous reader is as important as a travel writer in keeping a guidebook up-to-date and accurate. So if you happen upon a great restaurant, discover an intriguing locale or (heaven forbid) find an error in the text, we'd appreciate hearing from you. Just write to:

Ulysses Press
3286 Adeline Street, Suite 1
Berkeley, CA 94703

It is our desire as publishers to create guidebooks that are responsible as well as informative. We hope that our guidebooks treat the people, country and land we visit with respect. We ask that our readers do the same.

GLENN KIM.

ONE

The Evergreen State

A place of emerald beauty and scenic grandeur, Washington is the heart **1**
of a region that has long fascinated explorers and entrepreneurs, environmentalists and dreamers. This northwesternmost corner of the contiguous United States is nicknamed "The Evergreen State"—an appropriate
label for a land that boasts eight national forests. Sharing a border with
Canada to the north and Idaho on the east, Washington is divided from
Oregon on the south by the course of the Columbia River.

Water is a major force, as the Pacific Ocean batters the state's rugged
western edge and numerous rivers carve the landscape. Come to Washington and you'll discover wondrous waterfalls, glistening waterways
and verdant rainforest. You'll also find mysterious bays, sounds and
tributaries, wind-sculpted trees on wave-battered capes and inlets, gos-
samer mists on towering evergreens, icy summits that cast shadows on
pastoral valleys, bustling cityscapes with a cosmopolitan flair, warm
breezes through juniper boughs, even a powerful volcano or two.

The heavy rainfall for which Washington is famous helps keep its
vegetation lush. The drizzle and clouds that blanket the coastal region
during much of the winter and spring nourish the incredibly green landscape that grows thick and fast and softens the sharp edges of alpine peaks
and jagged sea cliffs. But there's a flip side: Over half the state (meaning
points east of the Cascade Range) is actually warm and dry throughout
much of the year.

Much of Washington remains undeveloped and there are vast expanses of wilderness close to all metropolitan centers. Almost without
exception, each of its cities is surrounded by countless outdoor recreational opportunities, with mountains, lakes, streams and an ocean within

Of the 50 states, Washington is the only one named for a president.

easy reach. It's no surprise that residents and visitors tend to have a hardy, outdoorsy glow. After all, it is the proximity to nature that draws people here.

Ultimate Washington will help you explore this diverse area, introduce you to its flora and fauna, tell you of its history. Besides taking you to countless popular spots, it will lead to unusual and unique locales. Each chapter will suggest places to eat, stay, sightsee and shop and to enjoy the outdoors and nightlife. We think you'll find Washington is a place where you can explore for a day, a week or much, much longer.

Where to Go

The number of tourists visiting Washington continues to grow as the secrets of its beauty and sunny summer and fall weather get out. Because the landscape is so widely varied, each area with its own appeal, here are brief descriptions of the regions presented in this book to help you decide where you want to go. We begin in the Seattle area, move through southern Puget Sound, the Olympic Peninsula and the Coast, northern Puget Sound and the San Juan Islands, and then to the Cascades and central Washington, finishing with the vast stretch east of the Cascades.

Seattle, recently rated the most liveable city in the United States, offers a comfortable mix of cultural sophistication and natural ruggedness. The clustered spires of its expanding skyline hint at the growth in this busy seaport, the shipping and transportation hub of the Northwest. In addition to the downtown/Seattle Center district, this metropolitan community has a number of attractive neighborhoods ideal for strolling, shopping and nightlife. Pastoral Vashon Island is just a quick ferry ride away, while east of the city center is the fashionable Lake Washington district and bedroom/corporate communities such as Bellevue, Renton, Kirkland and Redmond.

Within easy reach of Seattle, **Southern Puget Sound** is a popular day trip and a great way to get acquainted with the Washington State Ferry System. The state capital of Olympia, Tacoma and the charming little community of Gig Harbor all offer easy access to wildlife refuges. Tacoma, Washington's third-largest city, is home to Point Defiance Park, considered the best saltwater park in the state. Bainbridge Island offers art galleries and plenty of scenic beauty. On the Kitsap Peninsula is the Navy town of Bremerton, gateway to the picturesque hamlet of Poulsbo. To the north is the company town of Port Gamble,

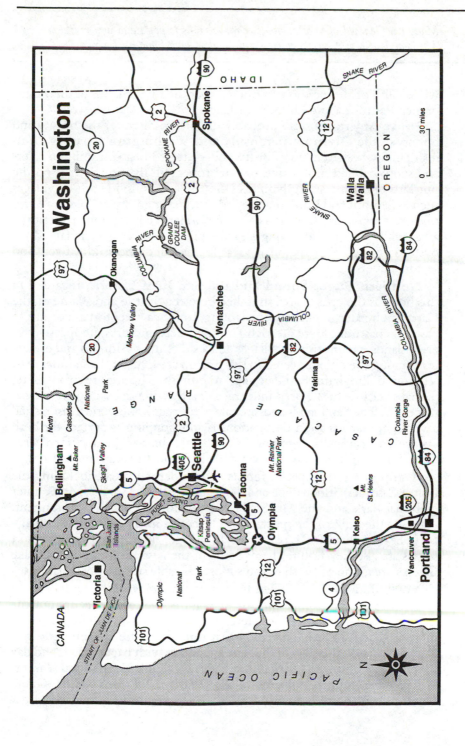

Many have learned of Washington's charms thanks to poets and writers like Theodore Roethke, Gary Snyder, Annie Dillard and Timothy Egan.

while south of Bremerton you can discover the rural charms of the Long-branch Peninsula and Hartstene Island.

Native Americans were probably the first to discover the beauty and bounty of the **Olympic Peninsula and Washington Coast**, with its lush rainforests, stretches of driftwood-cluttered beach, tumbling rivers and snow-capped mountains. Several tribes still live in the area on the outskirts of the massive Olympic National Park alongside fishing villages such as Sequim and Port Angeles and the Victorian-styled logging town of Port Townsend. On the coast, Grays Harbor is a popular maritime area, while the pristine Long Beach–Willapa Bay estuary is famed for oyster farming. This region is ideal for beachcombers, kite flyers and seafood lovers.

Northern Puget Sound and the San Juan Islands, regarded in this book as the coastal area stretched between Seattle and Blaine on the Canadian border, is entirely enchanting, from sea-swept island chains to pastoral coastline. Here are rich farming tracts, picturesque forest-covered islands, quaint fishing villages and a shoreline of sloughs and estuaries. Among the cities covered in this section are Everett, La Conner, Mt. Vernon, Bellingham, Ferndale and Snohomish. The arts are strong here, perhaps because of the preponderance of artists drawn by the area's natural beauty. The San Juan Islands are one of the state's authentic treasures and a very popular vacation destination. Island-hopping is perfect for both cyclists and campers. A region lost in time, the San Juans offer everything from plush mansions to romantic bed-and-breakfast hideaways.

A strip of national parks, forests and wilderness areas, including the North Cascades, Snoqualmie and Wenatchee national forests, Mt. Rainier National Park and the Mt. St. Helens National Volcanic Monument, make up the bulk of the spectacular **Cascades and Central Washington**. Leavenworth, a Bavarian-style village, and several small resort towns are also key features here. Some of the best are found in the Lake Chelan area, one of Washington's most desirable summer destinations.

You'll find sagebrush-filled high desert country with shoot-'em-up western towns and quiet Indian reservations scattered throughout the **East of the Cascades** zone. Here are the Okanogan Highlands, a scenic northeast Washington region that runs along the Columbia River. Rich in history, this part of the state is popular with backpackers and day hikers, who find it dryer than the Cascades. Spokane, pastoral Yakima Valley wine country, historic Walla Walla, the Palouse Hills, Grand Coulee Dam and the gateway to Hell's Canyon are also popular destinations in this region. Among other highlights are the state's original British settlement, Vancouver, which helped open the door to the Oregon Trail migration west. Other landmarks include Beacon Rock, the remote Maryhill Museum and the Klickitat River, where Native American dip net fishing remains a way of life.

The Columbia River creates a spectacular natural border between Oregon and Washington known as **The Columbia River Gorge**, a region characterized by towering cliffs, waterfalls and forested bluffs. Here you'll find tremendous opportunities for hiking, salmon fishing, and some of the best windsurfing in the country. The region can be explored by a scenic loop drive over Routes 14 and 84, or by crisscrossing the Gorge and taking time out to explore the spectacular beauty of the Cascade Locks. Watch tugboats ply the waters of the river or marvel at the natural beauty and power of the more than 70 waterfalls in the area.

Climate

Washington isn't just rain-soaked, snow-covered tundra. In fact, summer and fall days (June–September) are generally warm, dry and sunny. Overall temperatures range from the mid-30s in winter to the upper 80s in summer. There are distinct seasons in each of the primary zones, and the climate varies greatly with local topography.

The enormous mountain ranges play a major role in the weather, protecting most areas from the heavy rains generated over the Pacific and dumped on the coastline. Mountaintops are often covered in snow year-round at higher elevations, while the valleys, home to most of the cities, remain snow-free but wet during the winter months. East of the mountain ranges are temperature extremes and a distinct lack of rain. Travelers can enjoy the rivers, lakes and streams during the hot, dry summers and frolic in the snow during the winter.

The mountainous zones are a bit rainy in spring, but warm and dry during the summer when crowds file in for camping, hiking and other

SLUG FEST

The banana slug thrives in Washington's moist climate. Not quite large enough to be mistaken for a speed bump, they leave telltale viscous trails. While it's the bane of gardeners, the slug is still regarded as a sort of mascot for the state. In many souvenir shops, you'll even find plush toy replicas and gag cans of slug soup.

More than half of Washington is covered by forest.

---

outdoor delights. Fall brings auto traffic and visitors attracted by the changing seasonal colors, while winter means snow at higher elevations that provides the perfect playground for cold-weather sports.

The coastal region is generally soggy and overcast during the mild winter and early spring, making this the low season for tourism. However, winter is high season among Washingtonians drawn to the coast to watch the fantastic storms that blow in across the Pacific. Summers are typically warm and dry in the coastal valleys and along the crisp, windy coast, making it the prime season for travelers, who show up in droves, clogging smaller highways with recreational vehicles.

Keep in mind that no matter when you visit Washington, the weather is subject to abrupt change. It is not unusual for surprise snowstorms to hit the Cascades in late spring or early fall. Always bring along warm clothing when traveling in the high country.

Calendar

Festivals and events are a big part of life in Washington, especially when the rains disappear and everyone is ready to spend time outdoors enjoying the sun. Washington's larger cities average at least one major event per weekend during the summer and early fall. Below is a sampling of some of the biggest attractions. Check with local chambers of commerce to see what will be going on when you are in the area.

JANUARY

Seattle   Colorful parades take to the streets of the International District to celebrate **Chinese New Year** in late January or early February.

Olympic Peninsula and Washington Coast   A great reason to visit this region is **Centrum's Chamber Music Festival** in Port Townsend.

The Cascades and Central Washington   In addition to seeing mushing and snowmobiling contests, you'll hear carillon bells and perhaps munch wienerschnitzel at the **Great Bavarian Ice Fest** in Leavenworth. There are ice sculptures, ski competitions and dogsled races at the **Deer Park Winter Festival**. Also popular is Winthrop's **Ski Race of Methow Valley,** featuring classic and freestyle events.

East of the Cascades   The **Ag Expo/Farm Fest** in Spokane features farm-machinery demonstrations and horseshoe throwing contests. Also in Spokane, the **Northwest Bach Festival** highlights works by the German composer.

Columbia River Gorge   High school bands and vocalists perform and compete for prizes at the **Clark College Jazz Festival** in Vancouver.

FEBRUARY

Seattle   **Fat Tuesday** is a week-long Mardi Gras–style festival with a parade, arts and crafts and plenty of jazz and food. Seattle blooms with demonstration gardens and floral displays during the **Northwest Flower and Garden Show**.

Olympic Peninsula and Washington Coast   **Hot Jazz Port Townsend** brings jazz greats to the Olympic Peninsula. Aberdeen hosts the annual **Rain or Shine Dixieland Jazz Festival**, which spotlights West Coast musicians.

Northern Puget Sound and the San Juan Islands   Amateur detectives have a field day on Whidbey Island during **Mystery Weekend**, when local merchants offer clues and prizes to solve a whodunit.

The Cascades and Central Washington   Even though Bill Murray will doubtless be a no-show, you can have a great time at the **East Wenatchee Groundhog Celebration**. Or perhaps you'd prefer to join spring training at the **Winthrop Invitational Snowshoe Softball Tournament**, where participants play ball with a winter twist—in snowshoes. Winthrop is also home of the **Rendezvous Mountain Marathon**, one of the few two-day marathons in the United States.

MARCH

Southern Puget Sound   South of Olympia, you can enjoy bluegrass tunes at the **Tenino Old Time Music Festival**.

Northern Puget Sound and San Juan Islands   Enter a mussel-eating contest, watch a cooking demonstration or compare your favorite shellfish recipes at the **Penn Cove Mussel Festival** in Coupeville on Whidbey Island. The luck of the Irish will surely be with you at the **Oak Harbor St. Patrick's Day Parade**.

The Cascades and Central Washington   One of the best places to look for art in southern Washington is the **Columbian Artist Spring Show** at Longview. Snow-castle and sculpture competitions are the highlight of the **White Pass Winter Carnival**.

East of the Cascades   Indulge in rich candies, ice creams, cakes, drinks and more at **Chocolate Fantasy** in Yakima.

APRIL

Seattle   Judges under umbrellas count as contestants lure gulls in Port Orchard's **Seagull Calling Contest**. Enjoy some of the first blossoms of spring at the **Daffodil Festival Grand Floral Parade**, which also passes through Tacoma, Puyallup and nearby communities.

Northern Puget Sound and San Juan Islands   If you'd rather catch those early-spring colors in all their natural glory, queue up for the drive through the rich farmlands of La Conner and Mt. Vernon during the **Skagit Valley Tulip Festival**.

The Cascades and Central Washington   Enjoy over 40 different apple-oriented events during the 11-day **Washington State Apple Blossom Festival** in Wenatchee. Cyclists from all over the evergreen state compete at the **Lake Chelan Mountain Bike Festival**, another major event in this region.

East of the Cascades   Taste the best of local wines at the **Spring Barrel Tasting** in Yakima Valley. One of the most colorful events in the area, Clarkston's **Dogwood Festival** celebrates the coming of spring with garden tours, arts and crafts booths, music and road races.

Columbia River Gorge   In Woodland, the Hulda Klager Lilac Gardens are open for tours during the **Lilac Festival**, which continues into May.

MAY

Seattle   An international array of crafts and folktales, food, costume, music and dance is the focus of the **Northwest Folklife Festival**. **Artspring**, a popular community art celebration, features art classes, as well as dance and musical performances. Families will certainly enjoy the **International Children's Festival** where performing arts groups from around the world entertain with music, dance and children's theater. Considered one of the five best in the nation, the **Seattle International Film Festival** views more than 140 feature films.

Olympic Peninsula and Washington Coast   Sequim's **Irrigation Festival**, the state's oldest continuous event, features an old-fashioned pancake breakfast, park picnics, dance, parade and show where loggers demonstrate their skills. Many of Port Townsend's grand Victorian homes are open to the public during the **Historic Homes Tour**.

Northern Puget Sound and San Juan Islands   A salmon barbecue and beauty pageant are held in conjunction with the 85-mile **Ski-To-Sea Relay Race** between Mt. Baker and Bellingham.

East of the Cascades   The ten-day **Spokane Lilac Festival** features a carnival, bed race, torchlight parade, food booths and more. There's also a **Hot Air Balloon Stampede** with over 50 balloons in Walla Walla. The Grand Coulee Dam sparkles with a **Laser Light Show** extravaganza every night from Memorial Day through September.

JUNE

Seattle   The three-day **Philippine Festival** at Seattle Center celebrates the island chain's Independence Day and cultural heritage with music, dance, food and exhibits.

Southern Puget Sound   In Tacoma, thousands flock to **America's Largest Antique & Collectible Sale**, where you'll find everything from garage-sale knickknacks to museum quality pieces. Puyallup's **Days of Ezra Meeker Pioneer Festival**, named after one of the town's earliest citizens, celebrates the region's history and its namesake with food stands, crafts booths and bluegrass music. You'll enjoy hearty servings of strawberry shortcake and performances by Norwegian dancers at the **Strawberry Festival** in Poulsbo.

Olympic Peninsula and Washington Coast   Booths sell sausage, doughnuts, ice cream, baskets and dolls made of garlic at the **Garlic Festival** in Ocean Park (Long Beach Peninsula).

Northern Puget Sound and San Juan Islands   In addition to a range of nautical events, you'll enjoy a carnival, parade, art show and grand pyrotechnics display during Everett's **Salty Sea Days**. Traditional war-canoe races and ceremonial songs and dances are among the highlights of the **Lummi Water Festival** held on the Lummi Indian Reservation northwest of Bellingham. The border town of Blaine is home to the popular **Peace Arch** celebration.

The Cascades and Central Washington   The historic river town of Cathlamet hosts the popular **Columbia River Heritage Boat Festival**. Upcountry between Yakima and Mt. Rainier, the **White Pass Music Festival** highlights the Northwest's finest classical musicians.

East of the Cascades   Airplane buffs will love **Wings over Walla Walla**, which features an air show and displays of antique and military airplanes. Spokane takes basketball to the streets during **Hoopfest**, when over 2500 teams participate in courts set up all over downtown. Festivities also include a mini food fair, contests and special activities in Riverside Park.

Columbia River Gorge   **Sternwheeler Days** marks the return of the Sternwheeler *Columbia Gorge* to its summer port in Cascade Locks with entertainment and an arts and crafts fair. In Vancouver, the whole city turns out to celebrate **Fort Vancouver Days** with a live jazz show, chili cookoff, beer garden and historic tour.

JULY

Seattle   Kimono-clad dancers take center stage in **Bon Odori**, a Japanese festival celebrated in the International District as part of the multicultural events of **Seafair**, one of Seattle's biggest celebrations. Northwest talent is showcased in the **Bellevue Jazz Festival**, the oldest jazz fest in the region. The **Gig Harbor Jazz Festival** is a venue for big names in jazz and blues on a weekend in late July or early August. **Millstone Coffee Bite of Seattle**, the city's annual food festival, offers the chance to sample food and wine from dozens of restaurants and wineries.

Southern Puget Sound   There are competitions in bagpipe, drum and dance at Enumclaw's **Pacific Northwest Scottish Highland Games**.

Olympic Peninsula and Washington Coast   **Splash!** in Aberdeen features Indian canoe races, a grand parade and a street dance.

Northern Puget Sound and San Juan Islands   Festivities at the three-day **Kla Ha Ya Days** in Snohomish include a carnival, road race, soccer game and car show. Another winner is the music- and clown-filled **Mount Vernon Children's Art Festival** in Mount Vernon. An ideal place to celebrate Independence Day is the **La Conner Fourth of July Fireworks**.

East of the Cascades   At the **Sweet Onion Festival**, they celebrate Walla Walla's famous produce. For a foot-stomping good time, head for Newport's **Pend Oreille International Fiddle Contest**.

Columbia River Gorge   Downtown Vancouver's **International Festival** celebrates Washington's varied heritage with food, music and dance.

AUGUST

Southern Puget Sound   There's great fun at **Art in the Park** in Everett, with hands-on art exhibits for children and lots of food and live music.

Olympic Peninsula and Washington Coast   Salmon-fishing competitions, a street fair and parades highlight the **Derby Days Festival** in Port Angeles. World champions descend on Long Beach to compete in the **International Kite Festival**.

Northern Puget Sound and San Juan Islands   Many of the Northwest's finest artists display their work at top local shows like the **Coupeville Arts and Crafts Festival** on Whidbey Island. Friday Harbor is the site of the **San Juan County Fair**, with arts and crafts, agricultural and animal exhibits, a carnival and food booths featuring the bounty of the islands. Also recommended for a selection of Washingtonian art is the **Anacortes Arts and Crafts Festival**.

The Cascades and Central Washington   The **Grays River Covered Bridge Festival** celebrates a beautiful wooden span near the Columbia. Located in the shadow of Mt. Adams, the **Trout Lake Community Fair and Junior Dairy Show** is a good place to find local color.

East of the Cascades   Classic hot rods, complete with flame-painted hoods, take center stage during Yakima's **Vintiques Street Rod Car Show**.

Columbia River Gorge   The **Clark County Fair** includes big name entertainment, horse and art shows, great food and a carnival.

SEPTEMBER

Seattle   The **Bumbershoot Arts Festival** brings music, plays, art exhibits and crafts to Seattle Center. Java aficionados can get their fix at

Coffee–Fest Seattle Style, where roasters and coffee manufacturers from across the nation gather to ply their goods and demonstrate the behind–the–scene workings of the industry. "Do the Puyallup" is the catch phrase of the **Western Washington Fair** in Puyallup, one of the country's largest agricultural fairs.

Southern Puget Sound   The state's capital is the port of call for **Olympia Harbor Days**, which celebrates the Sound's maritime heritage with arts and crafts booths, tugboat races and music. See classics from an earlier age at the **Wooden Boat Festival** in Olympia.

Olympic Peninsula and Washington Coast   **Westport Seafood Festival** is the ideal place to try fresh salmon, Willapa oysters and dozens of other specialties. **Logger's Play Day** celebrates the life and times of the lumberjack in the coastal town of Hoquiam.

East of the Cascades   Broncobusting awaits at the **Ellensburg Rodeo**, ranked among the top ten rodeos in the nation. Also in Ellensburg is the **Threshing Bee and Antique Equipment Show**, which displays old steam engines and antique farm machinery. Enjoy the biergarten and German food circus at the **Odessa Deutches Fest**. Wine aficionados can tour the region's wineries and sip estate-bottled vintages at **Catch the Crush** in the tri-cities of Richland, Pasco and Kennewick. See prize-winning livestock, sample produce and local crafts, nibble cotton candy and enjoy a ride or two at the **Central Washington State Fair** in Yakima.

OCTOBER

Seattle   **Salmon Days** in Issaquah feature a salmon bake, races, live entertainment, arts and crafts and a parade. At **Festa Italiana** you'll find Italian music and food, grape-stomping demonstrations, bocce ball contests and crafts booths.

Olympic Peninsula and Washington Coast   There's plenty of seafood and entertainment along with a shucking contest at the **Oysterfest** in Shelton. Make your way through a cranberry bog and enjoy special taste treats at the **Cranberry Festival** in Long Beach.

Northern Puget Sound and San Juan Islands   A great way to get into the Halloween spirit is to attend Tillinghast's **Great Pumpkin/Scarecrow Contest** in La Conner, or visit the ghosts and ghoulies in **Mt. Vernon's Haunted Forest**.

East of the Cascades   Leavenworth is ablaze during the **Washington State Autumn Leaf Festival** complete with oompah bands and Bavarian costumes.

Columbia River Gorge   Candles provide the only light as you step back into 1845 during the **Fort Vancouver Candlelight Tours**.

NOVEMBER

Seattle   Seattle Center is all decked out with an ice-skating rink, Christmas train display and arts-and-crafts booths during **Winterfest**, which runs through early January.

Southern Puget Sound   Get into the Christmas spirit at Bremerton's **Festival of Trees**, complete with games, storytelling, carolling and, of course, Santa Claus.

The Cascades and Central Washington   The **Leavenworth Gala Holiday Food Fair** is a colorful celebration that attracts visitors from all over the state. Another of Central Washington's intriguing holiday celebration is the **Christmas Bazaar by Puget Islanders** in Cathlamet, where you can purchase locally made arts and crafts and sample Norwegian food specialties.

East of the Cascades   Yakima's **Holiday Fest**, a great place to do holiday shopping, and the Spokane **Winter Knights Snowmobile Show** both draw big crowds. Fishermen will be lured to the **Great Snake Lake Steelhead Derby** in Clarkston.

DECEMBER

Seattle   To get in the holiday mood, join the hordes of people who gather on Seattle's shoreline to watch the festively decorated **Seattle Civic Christmas Ship**.

Southern Puget Sound   **Zoolights** lend a festive spirit to the famous Tacoma Zoo from early December through Christmas. Tacoma's **Holiday Torchlight Parade and Tree Lighting** is one of the region's leading Christmas events. Also popular is the **TideFest Arts and Crafts Show** in Gig Harbor, which features fine arts and crafts for show and sale.

Northern Puget Sound and San Juan Islands   The little town of Lynden is decorated like an old Dutch community during the **Dutch Sinterklaas Celebration**, complete with gingerbread and visits with old St. Nick. **Christmas ships** cruise the Swinomish Channel in La Conner.

The Cascades and Central Washington   The Bavarian village of Leavenworth looks like a scenic Christmas card during the **Christmas Lighting Festival**.

East of the Cascades   It's holiday time down at the farm during the **Country Christmas Lighted Farm Implement Parade** in Sunnyside.

Columbia River Gorge   Stevenson's **Christmas in the Gorge** offers a tree lighting, crafts bazaar and mystery tour. Boats decorated with Christmas lights sail the Columbia and Willamette Rivers during the **Christmas Parade of Boats**.

Visitor Information

For a free copy of the *Washington State Lodging and Travel Guide*, contact the **Washington Tourism Division** (Department of Trade and Economic Development, 101 General Administration Building, mail stop AX-13, Olympia, WA 98504; 360-753-5630, 800-544-1800).

Large cities and small towns throughout the state have chambers of commerce or visitor information centers; a number of them are listed in *Ultimate Washington* under the appropriate chapter.

For visitors arriving by automobile, Washington provides numerous **Welcome Centers** at key points along the major highways. Visitors can pull off for a stretch, a cup of coffee or juice and plenty of advice on what to see and do in the area. The centers are clearly marked and are usually open during daylight hours throughout the spring, summer and fall.

Packing

Comfortable and casual are the norm for dress in Washington. You'll want something dressier if you plan to catch a show, indulge in high tea or spend your evenings in posh restaurants and clubs, but for the most part, your topsiders and slacks are acceptable garb everywhere else.

Layers of clothing are your best bet, since the weather changes so drastically depending on which part of the state you are visiting; shorts will be perfectly comfortable during the day in the hot, arid interior, but once you pass over the mountains and head for the coastline, you'll appreciate having packed a jacket to protect you from the nippy ocean breezes, even on the warmest of days.

Wherever you're headed, during the summer bring some long-sleeve shirts, pants and lightweight sweaters and jackets along with your shorts, T-shirts and bathing suit; the evenings can be quite crisp. Bring along those warmer clothes—pants, sweaters, jackets, hats and gloves—in spring

---

OBSERVATIONS OF A NATIVE

Native son William O. Douglas once wrote that visiting his favorite Washington spot, Bird Creek Meadows on the southeast shoulder of Mt. Adams, always made him feel as though he were "standing on the threshold of another world." He also observed "how badly we need high alpine meadows which can only be reached on foot, how badly we need peaks which can only be conquered by daring."

and fall, too, since days may be warm but it's rather chilly after sundown. Winter calls for thick sweaters, knitted hats, down jackets and snug ski clothes. It's not a bad idea to call ahead to check on weather conditions.

Sturdy, comfortable walking shoes are a must for sightseeing. If you plan to explore tidal pools or go for long walks on the beach, bring a pair of lightweight canvas shoes that you don't mind getting wet.

Scuba divers will probably want to bring their own gear, though rentals are generally available in all popular dive areas. Many places also rent tubes for river floats and sailboards for windsurfing. Fishing gear is often available for rent, as well. Campers will need to bring their own basic equipment.

Don't forget your camera for capturing Washington's glorious scenery and a pair of binoculars for watching the abundant wildlife that live here. And pack an umbrella, just in case.

Lodging

Lodging in Washington runs the gamut, from rustic cabins in the woods to sprawling resorts on the coastline. Chain motels line most major thoroughfares and mom–and–pop enterprises still vie successfully for lodgers in every region. Large hotels with exceptional service, lavish Sunday buffets and complete business facilities, comfortable pensiones on the European model and waterfront establishments accommodate visitors in all price ranges.

Bed and breakfasts, small inns and cozy lodges where you can have breakfast with the handful of other guests are appearing throughout the region as these more personable forms of lodging continue to grow in popularity. In fact, in areas like the San Juan Islands, they are the norm.

GRAPE EXPECTATIONS

For a long time, Washington's liquor laws were so restrictive that it was illegal to bring wine into the state; you had to buy it from state-run stores. Times have changed, and these days some 70 wineries are spread across the state, most of them in eastern Washington where the soil and climate are excellent for wine grapes. The **Washington Wine Commission** *(1932 First Avenue, Suite 510, Seattle, WA 98101; 206-728-2252) likes to remind folks that eastern Washington is on the same latitude as some of France's great wine-growing regions. The wine commission publishes a free annual guide to Washington's 85 wineries.*

More apples are grown in Washington than in any other state.

Whatever your preference and budget, you can probably find something to suit your taste with the help of the regional chapters in this book. Remember, rooms are scarce and prices rise in the high season, which is generally summer along the coastline and winter in the mountain ranges. It's a good idea to book ahead in the prime tourists season when conventions can overwhelm the lodging market in cities like Seattle. Off-season rates are often drastically reduced in many places. In general, you can get your best rates in rural areas during the week and in big cities on weekends and holidays.

Lodging in this book is organized by region and classified according to price. Rates referred to are for two people during high season, so if you are looking for low-season bargains, it's good to inquire. *Budget* facilities are generally less than $50 per night and are satisfactory and clean but modest. *Moderate*-priced lodgings run from $50 to $90; what they have to offer in the way of luxury will depend on where they are located, but they often offer larger rooms and more attractive surroundings. At a *deluxe* hotel or resort, you can expect to spend between $90 and $130 for a double; you'll usually find spacious rooms, a fashionable lobby, a restaurant and a group of shops. *Ultra-deluxe* properties, priced above $130, are a region's finest, offering all the amenities of a deluxe hotel plus plenty of extras.

Whether you crave a room facing the surf or one looking out on the ski slopes, be sure to specify when making reservations. If you are trying to save money, keep in mind that places a block or so from the waterfront or a mile or so from the ski lift are going to offer lower rates than those right on top of the area's major attractions.

Restaurants

Seafood is a staple in Washington, especially along the coast where salmon is king. Whether it's poached in herbs or grilled on a stake Indian-style, plan to treat yourself to this regional specialty often. While each area has its own favorite dishes, ethnic influences and gourmet spots, Seattle cuisine as a whole tends to be hearty and is often crafted around organically grown local produce. The city's restaurant community is particularly strong on Asian cuisine, including Chinese, Vietnamese and Thai dishes. For an offbeat experience, you might also want to try one of the city's wheatgrass bars, which serve the ultimate healthfood drink, clipped fresh and ground into a chlorophyll-laden treat. With numerous open-air eat-

Nearly all of the state's larger cities, and more than half of its population, are clustered around Puget Sound in western Washington.

eries and waterfront restaurants, Seattle is also blessed with a generous supply of coffee bars serving first-rate espresso and cappuccino.

Within a particular chapter, restaurants are categorized geographically, with each entry describing the type of cuisine, general decor and price range. Dinner entrées at *budget* restaurants usually cost under $8. The ambience is informal, service usually speedy and the crowd a local one. *Moderate*-priced restaurants range between $8 and $16 at dinner; surroundings are casual but pleasant, the menu offers more variety and the pace is usually slower. *Deluxe* establishments tab their entrées from $16 to $24; the cuisine may be simple or sophisticated, depending on the location, but the decor is plusher and the service more personalized. *Ultra-deluxe* dining rooms, where entrées begin at $24, are often gourmet places where the cooking and service have become an art form.

Some restaurants change hands often, while others are closed in low seasons. Efforts have been made to include in this book places with established reputations for good eating. Breakfast and lunch menus vary less in price from restaurant to restaurant than do evening offerings. If you are dining on a budget and still hope to experience the best of the bunch, visit at lunch when portions and prices are reduced.

Family Travelers

By all means, bring the kids to Washington. Besides the many museums, boutiques and festivals set aside for them, the state also has hundreds of beaches and parks, and many nature sanctuaries sponsor children's activities, especially during the summer months. Here are a few guidelines that can help make travel with children a pleasure.

Many Washington bed and breakfasts do not accept children, so be sure of the policy when you make reservations. If you need a crib or cot, arrange for it ahead of time. A travel agent can be of help here, as well as with most other travel plans.

If you're traveling by air, try to reserve bulkhead seats where there is plenty of room (unless you want to view a movie). Take along extras you may need, such as diapers, a change of clothing for both yourself and your child, snacks and toys or books. When traveling by car, be sure to carry the extras, along with plenty of juice and water. And always allow plenty of time for getting places.

A first-aid kit is a must for any trip. Along with adhesive bandages, antiseptic cream and something to stop itching, include any medicines your pediatrician might recommend to treat allergies, colds, diarrhea or any chronic problems your child may have.

When spending time at the beach or on the snow, take extra care the first few days. Children's skin is especially sensitive to sun, and severe sunburn can happen before you realize it, even on overcast days. Hats for the kids are a good idea, along with liberal applications of sunblock. Be sure to keep a constant eye on children who are near the water or on the slopes.

Even the smallest towns usually have stores that carry diapers, baby food, snacks and other essentials, but these may close early in the evening. Larger urban areas usually have all-night grocery or convenience stores that stock these necessities.

Many towns, parks and attractions offer special activities designed just for children. Consult the calendar listings in this chapter, check local newspapers and/or phone the numbers in this guide to see what's happening where you're going.

Senior Travelers

Senior citizens will find Washington a hospitable place to visit, especially during the cool, sunny summer months that offer respite from hotter climes elsewhere in the country. Countless museums, historic sights and even restaurants and hotels offer senior discounts that can cut a substantial chunk off vacation costs. The national park system's **Golden Age Passport**, which must be applied for in person, allows free admission for anyone 62 and older to the numerous national parks and monuments in the region. The Passport can be obtained at any national park ranger's office or park office.

The **American Association of Retired Persons** (AARP) (921 Southwest Morrison, Room 528, Portland, OR 97205; 503-227-5268) offers membership to anyone over 50. AARP's benefits include travel discounts with a number of firms; escorted tours and cruises are available through AARP Travel Experience/American Express (400 Pinnacle Way, Suite 450, Norcross, GA 30071; 800-927-0111).

Elderhostel (75 Federal Street, Boston, MA 02110; 617-426-7788) offers reasonably priced, all-inclusive educational programs in a variety of Pacific Northwest locations throughout the year.

Be extra careful about health matters. In addition to the medications you ordinarily use, it's a good idea to bring along the prescriptions for obtaining more. Consider carrying a medical record with you—including your medical history and current medical status as well as your doctor's name, phone number and address. Make sure your insurance covers you while you are away from home.

Travelers with Disabilities

Washington is striving to make more destinations accessible for the disabled traveler. For information on the areas you will be visiting, contact the **Resource Center for the Handicapped** (20150 45th Avenue Northeast, Seattle, WA 98155; 206-362-2273).

For more specific advice on traveling in the state, turn to *Access Seattle* from the **Easter Seal Society** (521 2nd Avenue West, Seattle, WA 98119; 206-281-5700).

The **Society for the Advancement of Travel for the Handicapped** (347 5th Avenue, Suite 610, New York, NY 10016; 212-447-7284); **Travel Information Service** (215-456-9603) and **Mobility International USA** (P.O. Box 10767, Eugene, OR 97440; 503-343-1284) offer general information. Also providing assistance is **Travelin' Talk** (P.O. Box 3534, Clarksville, TN 37043; 615-552-6670), a networking organization. **Flying Wheels Travel** (143 West Bridge Street, Owatonna, MN 55060; 800-535-6790) is a travel agency for travelers with disabilities.

Women Travelers

It is a sad commentary on life in the United States, but women traveling alone must take precautions. It's unwise to hitchhike and probably best to avoid inexpensive accommodations on the outskirts of town; the money saved does not outweigh the risk. Bed and breakfasts, smaller hotels, youth hostels, college dorms and YWCAs are generally your safest bet for lodging.

If you are hassled or threatened in some way, never be afraid to call for assistance. It's also a good idea to carry change for a phone call and to know a number to call in case of emergency, such as the **Seattle Rape Relief** (1905 South Jackson, Seattle, 206-325-5531; crisis line, 206-632-7273).

Foreign Travelers

PASSPORTS AND VISAS   Most foreign visitors are required to obtain a passport and tourist visa in order to enter the United States. Contact your nearest United States Embassy or Consulate well in advance to obtain a visa and to check on any other current entry requirements. Entry into Washington's northern neighbor, Canada, calls for a valid passport, visa or visitor permit for all foreign visitors except those from

The Columbia River is one of the longest rivers in the United States, meandering for some 700 miles through Washington alone.

the United States, who should carry proof of citizenship (voter's registration or birth certificate), including two pieces with photo identification. The necessary forms may be obtained from your nearest Canadian Embassy, Consulate or High Commissioner.

CUSTOMS REQUIREMENTS   Foreign travelers are allowed to bring in the following: 200 cigarettes (or 100 cigars), $100 worth of duty-free gifts, including one liter of alcohol (you must be at least 21 years of age) and any amount of currency (amounts over U.S. $10,000 require a form). Americans who have been in Canada over 48 hours may take out $400 worth of duty-free items ($25 worth of duty-free for visits under 48 hours). Carry prescription drugs in clearly marked containers; you may have to provide a written prescription or doctor's statement to clear customs. Meat or meat products, seeds, plants, fruits and narcotics are not allowed to be brought into the United States. The same applies to Canada, with the addition of firearms.

DRIVING   Foreigners planning to rent a car should obtain an international driver's license prior to arrival. United States driver's licenses are valid in Canada and vice versa. Some car-rental companies require both a foreign license and an international driver's license along with a major credit card, and may require that the lessee be at least 25 years of age.

CURRENCY   Both American money and Canadian money are based on the dollar. Bills in the United States come in six denominations: $1, $5, $10, $20, $50 and $100. Every dollar is divided into 100 cents; the $1 coin is generally used in Canada. Coins are the penny (1 cent), nickel (5 cents), dime (10 cents) and quarter (25 cents). You may not use foreign currency to purchase goods and services in the United States and Canada. Consider buying traveler's checks in dollar amounts. You may also use credit cards affiliated with an American company such as Interbank, Barclay Card, VISA and American Express.

WEIGHTS AND MEASUREMENTS   The United States uses the English system of weights and measures. American units and their metric equivalents are as follows: 1 inch = 2.5 centimeters; 1 foot = 0.3 meter; 1 yard = 0.9 meter; 1 mile = 1.6 kilometers; 1 ounce = 28 grams; 1 pound = 0.45 kilogram; 1 quart (liquid) = 0.9 liter. British Columbia now uses metric measurements.

Camping

Parks in Washington rank among the top in North America as far as attendance goes, so plan ahead if you hope to do any camping during the busy summer months. Late spring and early fall present fewer crowds to deal with and the weather is still fine.

Though much of Washington's scenic coastline is privately owned, there are a few scattered parks along the shore and even more situated inland in the mountains. It is possible to reserve campsites at several state parks from Memorial Day through Labor Day; contact the **State Parks and Recreation Commission** (7150 Cleanwater Lane, KY-11, Olympia, WA 98504; 360-753-2027) for details.

For information on camping in the various national parks and forests of Washington, contact the **Outdoor Recreation Information Center** (915 2nd Avenue, Suite 442, Seattle, WA 98174; 206-220-7450).

Wilderness Permits

Wilderness camping is not permitted in the state parks of Washington, but there are primitive sites available in most parks. Permits are required for wilderness camping in parts of the Alpine Lakes wilderness area of the Mt. Baker–Snoqualmie and Wenatchee national forests in Washington between May 24 and October 31; permits are available at the ranger stations. Campers should check with all other individual parks to see if permits are required. Keep in mind that the popular Mt. Rainier region fills up first in the busy summer months. Consider the Mt. Baker area, the North Cascades or the Okanogan as less-crowded alternatives.

Follow low-impact camping practices in wilderness areas: "Leave only footprints, take only pictures." When backpacking and hiking, stick to marked trails or tread lightly in areas where no trail exists. Be prepared with map and compass since signs are limited to directional information and don't include mileage. Guidelines on wilderness camping are available from the **USDA Forest Service** (Pacific Northwest Region, 333 Southwest 1st Avenue, Portland, OR 97204; 503-326-2877).

Boating

With miles of coastline and island-dotted straits to explore, it's no wonder that boating is one of the most popular activities in Washington. Many of the best attractions in the state, including numerous pristine marine parks, are accessible only by water and have facilities set aside for boaters.

Washington's Pacific coastline runs for 157 miles, but the state has more than 3000 miles of tidal shoreline.

Write to or call the **State Parks and Recreation Commission** (7150 Cleanwater Lane, KY-11, Olympia, WA 98504; 360-753-2027) for a boater's guide to Washington.

Water Safety

The watery region of Washington offers an incredible array of watersports to choose from, be it on the ocean, a quiet lake or stream or tumbling rapids. Swimming, scuba diving, walking the shoreline in search of clams or just basking in the sun are options when you get to the shore, lake or river.

Shallow lakes, rivers and bays tend to be the most popular spots since they warm up during the height of summer; otherwise, the waters of Washington are generally chilly. Whenever you swim, never do so alone, and never take your eyes off of children in or near the water.

Fish and Fishing

With its multitude of rivers, streams and lakes, and miles of protected coastline, Washington affords some of the best fishing in the world. Salmon is the main draw, but each area features special treats for the fishing enthusiast that are described in the individual chapters of *Ultimate Washington*.

Fees and regulations vary, but licenses are required for both salt and freshwater fishing throughout the state and can be purchased at sporting-goods stores, bait-and-tackle shops and fishing lodges. You can also find leads on guides and charter services in these locations if you are interested in trying a kind of fishing that's new to you. Charter fishing is the most expensive way to go out to sea; party boats take a crowd, but are less expensive and usually great fun. On rivers, lakes and streams, guides can show you the best place to throw a hook or skim a fly. Whatever your pleasure, in saltwater or fresh, a good guide will save you time and grief and will increase the likelihood of a full string or a handsome trophy.

For further information on fishing in Washington, contact the **Washington Department of Fish and Wildlife** (1111 Washington Street, Olympia, WA 98504; 206-902-2464; and 600 North Capitol Way, Olympia, WA 98501; 360-753-5700) concerning shellfish, bottomfish, salmon, saltwater sportfish and freshwater game fish. Ask for the department of "Fish Management."

TWO

The Washington Landscape

Washington, the northwest placeholder of the contiguous United States, **23** has enough different ecological zones to turn even the most jaded visitor into an amateur geographer. There's a wealth of dramatic scenery found here: rugged coastline, dense forests and two large mountain ranges—one young and aspiring and the other part of a dominant and established volcanic chain.

The young, low-lying Olympic Mountains, home to the only rain-forest in the United States outside of Hawaii, reign over the Olympic Peninsula, but are overshadowed by the Cascades to the east, a volcanic chain that starts in western Canada, runs down the middle of Washington and spills out over the state's southern border into Oregon. These and other geological wonders fill the state and divide it into its various climate zones. The monumental crests of the mountains trip the clouds, casting a vast "rain shadow" over the eastern part of the state. This rain shadow gives eastern Washington about 12–20 inches of annual rainfall, while the coastal plain to the west of the mountains receives some of the heaviest precipitation in the United States—over 150 inches douses parts of the Olympic Peninsula and sustains the moss-draped rainforest.

The only natural link east to west across the Cascades is the Columbia River, which acts as the Oregon/Washington border. The dry, warm flat-land climate sucks the cool ocean breezes through the Columbia River Gorge, following the snaking river into the patchwork of rolling plains, irrigated fields and vineyards of eastern Washington.

The greatest concentration of people live in a relatively narrow depression along Washington's western edge that's known as the Puget

Trough. Here, you'll find Puget Sound, speckled with the San Juan Islands—more than 170 of them in total.

Wherever you go in the state, there's an abundance of wildlife, from bears to birds, and more types of vegetation than we can do justice to in a few short pages. What follows is a brief overview of some of the highlights of the Washington landscape.

Geology

The eruption of Mt. St. Helens in 1980 was only the most recent reminder of the dramatic geological forces that have shaped this state. The Cascade Range began to rise just 20 million years ago, about the time the massive Columbia lava flow, second-largest in the world, formed the Columbia Plateau, which includes Washington and neighboring Oregon. Volcanic eruptions reached a peak about two million years ago with the formation of the Northwest's long chain of "fire mountains," part of the Pacific Rim Ring of Fire.

Volcanoes may have built the mountains, but glaciers carved them into their present form. For the last million years or so they have crept through the valleys and around the mountains, naturally sculpting the land. Within the past 10,000 years, a warmer climate has caused much of

---

THE DAY THE MOUNTAIN BLEW

The intensity of Mt. St. Helens' 1980 eruption caught many people by surprise. For weeks, there had been subtle warning signs: swarms of small earthquakes shook the beautiful and once-peaceful mountain, while bursts of steam caused clouds to form around its perfectly symmetrical peak. Residents of the mountain were ordered to evacuate, but some were skeptical or perhaps fatalistic, and decided to stay.

Meanwhile, magna rose out of the earth's core and built up under the north flank of the mountain, causing a bulge to slowly form. Then, at 8:30 a.m. on May 18, the growing bulge pushed a small section of rock down the slope and suddenly the mountain exploded with the force of 21,000 atomic bombs the size of the one dropped on Hiroshima. It powdered the mountainside and blew it into the atmosphere at about 500 miles per hour. Simultaneously, practically the whole north flank lurched down the mountain at about 200 miles per hour. By evening, ash had covered a half-million square miles in three states and the silhouette of Mt. St. Helens was left standing with a huge bite taken out of its north slope—1300 feet shorter than its 9677-foot stature the day before. Unfortunately, 57 people on the mountain or in the air above it at the time of the eruption were killed.

The Cascades' lower peaks reach over 8000 feet, while Mt. Rainier, the tallest, stretches to a dizzying 14,411 feet and, like some of its neighbors, hosts a family of glaciers.

the ice mass to melt, adding to the power of already formidable rivers like the Columbia, which has cut its way into the plateau and continental shelf. The withered remains of some glaciers can still be seen on Cascade mountain slopes, still slowly chipping away at their summits. Mt. Baker is dressed with 20 square miles of them.

Some of the state's most intriguing geology is found along the Columbia River basin. A series of volcanic eruptions, giant floods and landslides have combined to create one of Washington's most dramatic landscapes. Traveling through this region, you'll find evidence of numerous lava flows. A geological wonder, the Columbia River basin is littered with pleistocene cinder cones, submerged pinnacles, high benches and eroded scablands.

Flora

While everyone equates coniferous trees with Washington, there is much more to the flora of the region than its abundance of Douglas fir, white pine, red cedar and other evergreens. In fact, the pine-like Western hemlock with its irregular needles is the official state tree, populating the Olympic rainforest, as well as the low slopes of the Cascade mountains, and commonly growing to a height of 200 feet (some reach 300 feet). Each of the distinct geological zones hosts its own particular ecosystem. No matter where you go in Washington, expect to find yourself dazzled by such surprises as the Palouse Hills grasses in spring, the wildflowers of the San Juan Islands or the avalanche fawnlily that grows among patches of snow in Gifford Pinchot National Forest. Throughout western Washington, you'll find bright displays of rhododendron, the state flower. Hundreds of varieties, with their mass of colorful blooms in shades of pink, red and purple, are found growing wild in meadows and parks, making this species a popular icon for photographers. They also have become a cornerstone of Washington backyard gardens.

Thanks to heavy precipitation, this state is one of the greenest in America. Visit the unique rainforests of the Olympic Peninsula, where some 12 feet of rainfall annually support over 1000 species of plant life—trees, flowers and thick carpets of moss and fern. This is the place to look for swordfern, red paintbrush, glacier lily and wood sorrel. Moss-blanketed fir, cedar, maple and spruce create a majestic canopy overhead.

The rainforest is heaven for the spidery, low-lying ferns that enjoy the dank climate. Among the ferns you are likely to find here and elsewhere around Washington are bracken, oak and maidenhair. The maidenhair spleenwort, a short wiry plant with matted roots, grows in the rocky ravines. The high country houses the beautiful mountain holly fern. Up to two feet in length, this scythe-shaped plant is commonly found in cooler shaded areas. The bracken fern thrives in Washington's shaded woodlands and open fields. This triangular plant, ranging up to three feet or more in height, grows fronds all summer long.

In the moist woodlands of the coast, glossy madrones and immense Douglas firs tower over Pacific trilliums and delicate ladyslippers. Bogs full of skunkcabbage thrive alongside fields of fragrant yellow Scotch broom in a riot of color. Look for dune goldenrod, American dunegrass, coastal strawberry and rushes along the shore. Arrowgrass abounds in the salt marshes and you can also expect to find huckleberry, salmonberry and California wax myrtle.

Many different forms of seaweed commonly wash onto the seashore. The hollow tubular plants frequently found along the shoreline at low tide, in tide pools or attached to rocks are know as *enteromorpha intestinalis* (they're the ones used by beachgoing bullies to bludgeon their little brothers). Green hairlike urospora plants are frequently discovered on rocks or driftwood.

A SALMON'S ODYSSEY

The life of a salmon is a long round-trip journey from birth to ocean and back to birthplace. A salmon first enters the world in a small inland stream, where it grows for about a year before departing on its great journey. Unlike most other fish, salmon live part of their life in saltwater and another part in fresh. Salmon swim downstream to the open sea, changing their camouflage from dots for the river to smooth white for the ocean where they will flow with the currents for about two years. Then they head "home," finding the route back to their original streams by the smell of their home waters and by using the sun as a navigational reference. These fish are driven to battle ferocious river rapids, swimming upstream against the current to spawn in the same placid pools where they were born. The journey can be as long as 900 miles (to Idaho's Salmon River) and the fish often have to jump up small waterfalls to get to their mates. Ironically, after this long trip and their ritual spawning, the salmon die.

Now with many of the rivers dammed, salmon use manmade fish ladders (that look more like steps) to get back to their streams. Many salmon don't make it upstream past the huge dams, a fact that has prompted government authorities to actually truck some back to their spawning grounds to procreate and then perish.

Washington's forests contain some of the world's biggest trees, holding records in height and circumference, with fir, pine, hemlock and cedar topping 300 feet.

Bryopsis corticulans is a bright green plant with featherlike branches growing from a central tube. You'll find it attached to rocks, shells and driftwood.

In the lowland valleys, alder, oak, maple and other deciduous trees provide brilliant displays of color against an evergreen backdrop each spring and fall. Daffodils and tulips light up the fields, as do azaleas, red clover and other grasses grown by the many nurseries and seed companies prospering in the region. Wild berry bushes run rampant in this clime, offering blackberries, huckleberries, currants and strawberries for the picking. Indian paintbrush, columbine, foxglove, butter cups and numerous other wildflowers line the paths and brush the fields with color.

In the wetlands along the Columbia River and Puget Sound, tall tufts of Douglas fir and hemlock pocketed with maple and alder sprout at the river's edge and creep up the banks. In the spring, scores of violets poke out through the underbrush.

Thick groves of fir and cedar filter the sunlight, providing the perfect environment for mushrooms, lichens, ferns and mosses. As a result, mushrooming has become a favorite pastime of fungus–loving locals, as well as a tourist attraction for fine food lovers. Each spring, after a good rainfall, you can spy mushroomers sneaking off alone to their favorite gathering spot, always scanning the ground for the ultimate find: a crop of truffles, part of the mushroom family and an expensive delicacy in French restaurants. **Warning:** New gatherers should bring along an expert to decipher the poisonous mushrooms from the edible. While they will not show you their secret spots, they will steer you away from some serious health problems.

As the snow recedes, alpine wildflowers struggle to live on the rain-soaked meadows, yet a breathtaking array survive. The elegant tiger lily, beargrass, aster, fawnlily and sandwort with its small pin-wheel flowers above a mat of tough leaves, form a rainbow of colors that compliment the gray-green hillsides and decorate the rocky crevasses. Other hardy wildflowers peak through the short wiry grass and dwarf shrubs. Crowberry, red and white mountain heathers and tasty alpine huckleberries blossom and ripen in the early fall.

With the dramatic decrease in rainfall in the plateaus and desert zone comes a paralleling drop in the amount of plant life in eastern Washington, though it is still rich in pine, juniper, cottonwood and sagebrush. Flowers found here include wild iris, foxfire, camas, balsam root and pearly everlasting.

Fauna

It was the abundance of wildlife that first brought white settlers to Washington, beginning with the trappers who came in droves searching for fur. Beaver and otter pelts, highly valued in China during the 19th century, were heavily hunted. Nearly decimated colonies, now protected by law, are coming back strong. Playful otters are often seen floating tummy up in coastal waters, while the shy beaver is harder to spot, living in secluded mountain retreats and coming out to feed at night.

Fish, especially salmon, were also a major factor in the economic development of the region, and remain so to this day, though numbers of spawning salmon are dropping drastically. Nonetheless, fishing fanatics are still drawn here in search of the five varieties of Pacific salmon along with flounder, lingcod, rockfish, trout, bass and many other varieties of sportfish. Angler or not, check out the fish ladders of the Columbia River in the spring where salmon launch themselves out of the water to make it up the huge dams.

Among the more readily recognized creatures that reside in the Pacific Northwest's waters are the orca (killer whales), porpoises and dolphins often spotted cavorting just offshore. When the orca show up, the playful seals and sea lions (the orca's prey) disappear. Constantly one-upping the resident shorelife is the colony of California gray whales that migrate between the Bering and Chukchi seas near Alaska and their warm breeding waters around Baja California. Each year, you can see herds of whales passing the Washington coastline from April through June on their trip north, and again from November through December heading south. Fleets of excursion boats take whalewatchers out to wit-

---

SO, WHO GIVES A HOOT?

*The **spotted owl** has been the center of controversy in recent years, the focus of the recurring nature-versus-commerce debate. As logging companies cut deeper into the old-growth forests, which have taken 150 years or more to grow, the habitat for this endangered owl grows smaller. (These nocturnal birds need thousands of acres per pair to support their indulgent eating habits.) The old-growth forests of the Pacific Northwest provide adequate nesting spots in the protected snags and broken branches of tall trees that shelter their flightless young. Recently, old-growth forest has become increasingly hard to come by and the owl's numbers are diminishing—only about 800 pairs survive in Washington today. Some environmentalists predict their extinction early in the 21st century if logging continues at its present rate.*

Watch for the Pacific giant salamander in fallen, rotting logs; it is the largest of its kind in the world—growing up to a foot in length and capable of eating small mice.

ness these behemoth water mammals that can grow to 42 feet long, weigh over 30 tons and awe spectators with an occasional breach—where 30 tons of whale launches itself completely out of the water. Minke whales are more numerous, as are Dall's porpoises, often mistaken for baby orca because of their similar coloration and markings. Special museums and exhibits throughout the coastal zone attest to the importance of these marine animals to the region. The San Juan archipelago is an excellent place to whalewatch, thanks to three resident pods of killer whales. On whalewatching trips, you're also likely to see Dall's porpoises, splotchy brown harbor seals, bald eagles, great blue herons, cormorants and tufted puffins.

Coastal tide pools offer a closeup look at many fascinating species such as starfish, sea cucumbers, clams, oysters, sea urchins, hermit crabs, anemone, mussels and barnacles. When beachcombing along the coast, you'll find a wide variety of attractive shells. In the Puget Sound area, look for the yellow-gray Japanese littleneck clam. In shallow water you're likely to discover hairy triton, a large yellow white shell. In the same vicinity, keep an eye out for channeled dogwinkle, an inch-long yellow-brown dye shell or the bluish-white barrel bubble. Mudflat areas are a good place to find a shiny tan mollusk called the *cooperella subdiaphana* or a tiny white pear-shaped shell called carp. The brown or black *acmaea limatula* is a limpet found in rocks between tides.

Among Washington's larger creatures, of the varieties of bear living in the Northwest's remote forests, black bear are most common in southern Washington. Weighing upwards of 300 pounds and reaching six feet tall, they usually feed on berries, nuts and fish and avoid humans unless provoked by offers of food or danger to a cub. Grizzly bears, officially called *horribilis*, are much more aggressive. While extinct in California, these bears, top dog of the bear kingdom, still survive in northern Washington. Even in small numbers, this furry carnivore is a legend. Reportedly, the Lewis and Clark party shot one of these fearsome creatures six times at short range, which apparently only made the animal mad enough to get its half-ton body in motion for a half-hearted chase around the woods. Color does not differentiate a black bear from a grizzly. Some black bears can be light brown, while grizzlies can be almost black. Grizzlies, however, are bigger, have humped shoulders and wield longer claws. They are also known to be meaner and tougher.

Big-game herds of deer, elk, antelope along with moose, cougar and mountain goats range the more remote mountainous areas. Scavengers

Visit Olympic National Park and you may run into one of the colonies of marmots who reside there and are said to be the animal world's best people-watchers.

such as chipmunks, squirrels, raccoons, opossums and skunks are abundant, as well.

The coastal Johns River Habitat Management Area is a good place to look for Roosevelt elk, muskrat, weasel and river otter. An unusual animal, unique to the Olympic Mountains, is the Olympic marmot. These gregarious creatures look like a cross between a ferret and a squirrel, are slightly more curious than lazy and when they are not basking in the sun on top of the pile of rocks they call home, they are exploring and testing, whether its neighboring animals, a sibling, humans or your picnic basket.

One of the best places in the state to see deer, as well as beaver and mink, is the Columbian White-tailed Deer National Wildlife Refuge. It's located on the Columbia River near Cathlamet. At Birch Bay State Park on the coast near the Canadian border, beavers, opossums and muskrats can often be seen running along the muddy shoreline. In North Cascades National Park, you're likely to find snowshoe hare, red squirrels, bats, wolverines, mountain goats and, with luck, the elusive bobcat. Eastern Washington's Okanogan National Forest is full of porcupine, black bear and snowshoe hare. The flying squirrel also makes its rounds in the trees of this park, and is actually known more for its gutsy leaping abilities than its aerodynamics. In fact, the flying squirrel cannot "fly," but rather uses the flaps of skin that stretch from its legs to its front paws as a small set of glider wings to extend the range of its leap.

With a proliferation of protected refuges and preserves providing homes for great flocks of Canadian and snow geese, trumpeter swans, great blue herons, kingfishers, cranes and other species, birdwatchers will be in seventh heaven in Washington, one of the fastest-growing birder destinations on the continent.

Over 300 species of birds live in the Pacific Northwest for at least a portion of the year. Easily accessible mudflats and estuaries throughout Washington provide refuge for tufted puffins, egrets, cormorants, loons and other migratory waterfowl making their way along the Pacific Flyway. Hundreds of pairs of bald eagles nest and hunt among the islands of Washington along with great blue herons and cormorants. You might see red-tailed hawks and spotted owls if you venture quietly into the state's old-growth forest zones.

If you hear a rapid pounding noise, it's probably coming from the pileated woodpecker. Identified by its erect head feathers, it is the largest woodpecker in North America and the model for the cartoon character

"Woody Woodpecker." Unlike its cartoon cousin, this bird lives primarily in old-growth forests, drilling for insects under tree bark.

The Olympic Peninsula area has become a refuge for birders as well as birds. You can see both these groups in full force at Dungeness National Wildlife Refuge near Sequim. Here, you're likely to find a number of binoculars following a wide array of ducks, including canvasback, greater scaup, bufflehead and green-winged teal. The Nisqually National Wildlife Refuge near Tacoma houses thousands of waterfowl, as well as gulls, sandpipers and passerines. On the Columbia near Vancouver, Ridgefield National Wildlife Refuge has a wide range of birds big and small: widgeons, mallards, red-tailed hawks, goldfinches and red-winged blackbirds are commonly seen darting through the air. At Mt. Baker, far less crowded than popular Mt. Rainier, you'll see red-tailed hawks, bald eagles circling overhead preying on a plentiful supply of grouse, sapsuckers and warblers. In the Spokane area, Turnbull National Wildlife Refuge has a large congregation of forest birds. Bring your binoculars to spot western meadowlark, song sparrows, ducks, killdeer, great horned owls and mountain chickadees.

THREE

Washington's History

There's an intrepid outdoor spirit at the heart of the Washington population. Pacific Northwesterners feel as comfortable lying against a tree as they do sitting behind a desk. This should come as no surprise—anyone raised in a land dotted with lakes, carpeted with forests and cleaved by mountains would grow up familiar with the outdoors. But Washingtonians' love of the outdoors goes well beyond the familiar. They're unfazed by heavy rainfall—true natives leave the umbrellas in the closet—and they revel when the warm sun pokes its head through the usually gray skies. They have an immunity to the harshness of nature, but they also have a strong appreciation for it, which comes from a young tradition of explorers and fast growth, retold by living grandparents, remembered by great-grandparents and still present today—it comes from their history.

The story of Washington and the Pacific Northwest is a young one. Romanticized tales of frontier life, from fixing wagon wheels and weathering devastating storms to hunting for food and water in the yet-unsettled territory, dominate our Eurocentric textbooks. But, like other states, Washington's history can be traced back long before the arrival of the Europeans.

The First to Arrive

A popular theory today suggests that 25,000 years ago, at the end of the last ice age, the seas were 300 feet lower and a stretch of land traversed the Bering Strait. The first humans to arrive on the west coast of North

America are thought to have used this "land bridge" to walk from Asia to what is now Alaska. From there, they wandered through Canada and down into Washington in search of a warmer climate. Archaeologists have discovered solid evidence of human existence dating back 10,000 years with the find of the "Marmes Man," which are some of the oldest documented skeletal remains in the Western Hemisphere. Along with the partial remains of several individuals, Washington archaeologists, working the dig in the Marmes Rock Shelter (located in eastern Washington), uncovered many of the tools left by this ancient hunter-and-gatherer tribe.

Other, more recent evidence of human culture was found at Ozette on the Olympic Coast, the site of one of five major Makah villages. Archaeologists have unearthed well-preserved baskets, harpoons and clothing of the people who lived here an estimated 500 years ago until a mud slide, probably triggered by an earthquake, engulfed and buried the settlement. Because the slide caught the Indians by surprise, it buried utensils in all stages of use and development. While wooden and textile artifacts have often been destroyed by the region's damp climate, Ozette was beautifully preserved by the great slide. Eleven years of excavation turned up more than 55,000 artifacts, making it possible to paint a complete picture of the early Makah. This find has dwarfed all other projects of its kind and today, 97 percent of all Northwest Coast Indian artifacts are from Ozette.

These ancient people were the ancestors of the numerous Native American tribes that later populated the North American continent. Among them are the Kwakiutl, Haida, Bella Coola, Tlingit, Salish, Yakima, Nez Percé, Paiute, Shoshone, Umpqua and Rogue tribes.

The varying climate of the Pacific Northwest both provided for and dictated the lifestyles of these tribes. Those living inland, east of the mountain ranges, were forced into a nomadic existence, depending primarily on fishing, foraging and hunting game for survival, moving as the climate and animal migrations demanded. They lived in caves during warmer times and constructed large pit houses for winter camp.

The mild climate and abundant resources of the Puget Trough and Pacific coastline led to a fairly sedentary life for the tribes west of the mountain ranges. Here, they constructed permanent villages from the readily available wood, fished the rich waters, foraged in lush forests and had enough free time to develop ritualized arts and ceremonies, as well as an elaborate social structure.

Native American tribes living on the coast had a wealth of food. Their diets depended on seafood (mostly shellfish, salmon and whale) supplemented by a surplus of potatoes, a common crop for settled tribes. Materialistic and organized, these people had time to create beautiful basketry, hats and wooden whale-fin sculptures inlaid with hundreds of sea otter teeth.

Many Northwest Native Americans lived in "longhouses," wooden buildings as much as 100 feet long and 40 feet wide, which could house several families.

They were also very resourceful people, taking advantage of the malleable consistency of the western red cedar, using its wood for everything from medicinal teas and ointments to houses and canoes. The Makah, one of Washington's most developed coastal Indian cultures, used cedar so proficiently that their woven baskets could be made to hold water and their boxes were used to boil food. Cedar bark was pounded to make soft clothing and woven cedar rain hats helped to keep the people dry in the wet weather of the Olympic Peninsula.

Much of the Makah people's resourcefulness came from their religious beliefs. They took pride in efficiency, using the inedible portions of animals for household utensils so as to please the spirits of the animals who, as they believed, had given themselves up for human benefit. According to their legends, the mountains and the rivers contained great spirits and the salmon were residents of the sea who fed themselves to mankind. For these reasons, the Makah tossed fish bones back into the streams so the salmon people could regenerate to serve the hungry human race once again.

To the east, the Yakima and other mid-Columbia Indians developed an elaborate trading culture built around the region's rich fisheries. These tribes were semi-nomadic, depending on spear-hunted deer, elk, bear, rabbit and squirrel. The tribes that settled by the Columbia River depended on salmon as their main food source.

Exploration and Settlement

In the 1700s, the heads of several European nations interested in expanding their borders sent explorers to claim chunks of the Northwest coast. The explorers also searched continually for the fabled Northwest Passage, which supposedly connected the Pacific and Atlantic oceans by water. The search for the passage actually had begun much sooner. In the late 1500s, Juan de Fuca, the first recorded explorer to sail along the Washington coastline, thought he had discovered it. However, this Greek traveler, who had adopted his Spanish name as well as flag, was mistaken. What he really found was the mouth of Puget Sound, now called the Strait of Juan de Fuca in his honor.

The Native Americans supplied the potato to white settlers and taught them how to grow it successfully in this climate.

The Spanish sent out two more parties in 1774 and 1775. Juan Perez, leader of the former, was the first to describe in-depth the region's natural beauty. The other Spanish expedition, led by Bruno de Heceta and Juan Francisco de la Bodega, was much greater in number, as well as purpose. Heceta went ashore along the Washington coastline and claimed the whole Northwest in the name of Spain.

The Russians, not ones to be left out, had sent an expedition in the mid-1700s. They liked what they saw here and sent another group to follow up. Both missions were led by Vitus Bering, who quickly realized the capital potential of the land with its abundance of sea otters and beavers. The Russians moved quickly and erected a number of trading and hunting posts all along the coast, from Alaska as far south as what today is northern California. Bolstered by the prospects of a lucrative fur trade, the Russians were making their first bold move to annex the territory, either ignoring or just ignorant of Spain's outrageous claim.

Arrival of the white explorers brought many changes to the generally peaceful tribes of this relatively well-off region. There is no documentation of the Native Americans' early interactions with white men, but it is thought that Spanish explorers introduced the horse to the native tribes in the early 18th century, revolutionizing their nomadic lifestyle. The horse allowed hunters to cover much more territory, so tribes were able to remain settled for longer periods of time. By the century's end, traders were beginning to swap guns and ammunition for furs. These weapons helped make the mid-Columbia Native Americans proficient bison hunters and fierce warriors. Unfortunately, along with the horses and guns came smallpox. As early as 1775, ships arriving on the Washington coast introduced western diseases that decimated indigenous peoples who had no immunity.

Ironically, the Spanish and Russians were the first foreigners in the region, but they had started a diplomatic territorial battle that they were never to enter. Their sailing expeditions were nothing compared to England's imperialistic machine. The dominating force at the time, England flexed its financial muscle and sent Captain James Cook in 1778 to investigate the maritime fur trade. In 1792, the British commissioned George Vancouver to find the Northwest Passage and map the region, giving him extra leeway with supplies and money. He traveled the inland water routes and named every prominent geological feature after members of his crew.

About the same time, the young and independent United States started looking west. Robert Gray, an American fur trader sent by the Boston Company, explored the Washington coast in 1792 to verify its treasure trove of furry animals. The explorations took him to the mouth of the Columbia River, a discovery that later became the basis for America's claim to the territory. Many American trade companies followed the Boston Company's example and sent hunting parties west. By 1812, the United States dominated the fur trade. The Russians slowly packed up many of their outposts, distracted by the Napoleonic Wars, while the Spanish also lost interest, deterred perhaps by the English presence.

The most famous overland expedition to the west coast was started in 1804 at St. Louis by Meriwether Lewis and William Clark. Their journey, made mostly by canoe and on foot, took the 40-man party two years round-trip. Their goal was a lofty one: to study the geology, plant and animal life of the Louisiana Purchase. And even with that huge task in hand, they did more. They crossed the Rocky Mountains and headed into Washington, paddling down and charting nearly 400 miles of the Columbia River, from the foothills of the Rockies to the Pacific Ocean. In their travels, they encountered many obstacles, from rattlesnakes and grizzly bears to exposure and near starvation, yet only one man died en route. Their success was secured by good relations with the regional Native Americans. Lewis and Clark employed French Canadian interpreter Toussaint Charbonneau and, more importantly, his Native American wife, Sacajawea, who promoted friendship with the Shoshoni and kept the party on good footing with other tribes.

After Lewis and Clark returned east, a new generation of explorers headed west, convinced they could make a quick fortune in the fur trade. Perhaps the most ambitious of these enterprises was organized by John Jacob Astor, at the time the richest man in America. Eager to

---

A DEADLY MISSION

In 1836, a group of Protestant churches sent out a missionary party led by Dr. Marcus Whitman. The Whitmans settled in Walla Walla at the southeastern corner of Washington and began their mission among the Cayuse tribe. Unfortunately, their good intentions conceived ill results as many of the Cayuse became sick from the laxative remedies and garden poisons used to stave off the insects and animals. When the Cayuse came down with the measles and other western diseases, they turned on the Whitmans. Convinced that the missionaries' goals were to kill them and claim the area for white settlers, the Cayuse murdered the Whitmans and nine others on the mission site.

The detailed journals and studies kept by Lewis and Clark helped finally dispel the notion of a Northwest Passage.

monopolize the lucrative fur trade in the uncharted Northwest, he dispatched the ill-fated ship *Tonquin* from New York in the fall of 1810.

In the spring of 1811, just about the time the *Tonquin* was sailing across the Columbia River Bar, a second, overland group sponsored by Astor left St. Louis. They began by following the river route pioneered by Lewis and Clark, but then forged a new trail across the Rockies that would ultimately become part of the Oregon Trail. Among the leaders was Wilson Price Hunt, who was plagued by practically every conceivable misfortune on the journey west. Members of Hunt's party drowned, nearly starved to death, were ambushed by Indians and victimized by strange diseases.

By 1812, when this party limped into the coastal outpost at Astoria, virtually the entire *Tonquin* crew had perished in an Indian raid. A surviving crew member, in a final insane act of revenge, lured the Native Americans back on the ship, went below and lit the ship's magazine, killing everyone aboard.

The War of 1812 (in which the United States allied with France against the English) hardly affected the Northwest except for some skullduggery on the part of a British trade company. In September 1812, the remaining Astorians residing on the banks of the Columbia were visited by a party from the English-owned North West Fur Company, a business rival. These newcomers announced that a British warship was en route to seize the new American base Fort Astoria. To make matters worse, they announced that the British had just won the War of 1812. Cut off from the news that would have exposed this lie, the Astorians decided to sell off their pelts for pennies on the dollar and control of the region shifted to the British.

Once the trading companies established permanent outposts in Washington and laid some of the foundation for settlement, the missionaries came to "civilize" the Native Americans with their western religion and medicine. However, the best intentions of the missionaries often resulted in tension between the Native Americans and the new settlers. Eventually, skirmishes escalated into the various Indian Wars of the region, which started in the mid-1800s and ended by the turn of the century.

Over time, the territorial struggle came down to the United States and England. After the dust had settled on the War of 1812 (which actually stalemated in 1815), the American and British governments signed a Treaty of Joint Occupation giving both nations the right to trade and settle in the northwest region known as Oregon Country. In 1821, the two reigning British enterprises, Hudson's Bay Company and North West Company, merged and went on to set up a base at Fort Vancouver. This new regional headquarters on the banks of the Columbia exemplified the ability of the British to blend economic and political goals. Unlike Astor's ill–fated pioneers, the region's new landlords showed a deft ability to master this untamed land. Under the aegis of the Hudson's Bay Company, the British turned their Columbia River base into a prosperous trading hub, attracting Native American tribes from throughout the region.

At the same time, Dr. John McLoughlin, the chief Hudson's Bay factor who befriended American missionaries and settlers, was a superb diplomat. Recognizing the inevitability of American westward expansion, he helped smooth the way for the creation of the new Oregon Territory and the lowering of the British flag in 1848.

Homesteading, fishing, logging, ranching and other opportunities kept the flow of settlers coming. Gold was another early attraction to Washington. A small strike was hit at Walla Walla in the 1850s; however, it was not gold found in Washington that helped this state to prosper. It was the Alaska and Yukon strikes of the late 1890s that attracted droves of prospectors, most of whom passed through Washington buying supplies for their trip up north. Stage routes were established, and river traffic increased steadily. Over the next 40 years, the population expanded from 4000 to over 100,000. As the logging, fishing and shipping industries grew, railroads began pushing into the region, reaching Puget Sound in 1883. Six years later, Washington became our 42nd state and Olympia was named its capital.

THE INFAMOUS PIG WAR

Tensions left over from the War of 1812 and the not-yet-forgotten American Revolution caused friction between the Americans and British in the Northwest. The American/British Treaty of 1846 failed to properly define the border of the British territory, instead naming an unspecified "main channel" as the boundary. The Americans and British agreed to use the 49th parallel. However, this latitude divided the San Juan Islands in two, leaving the British and American soldiers staring each other down across the makeshift border. The entente was preserved until a lone British pig wandered into an American settler's garden. The American shot and killed the pig—the only bullet fired during the whole 13-year dispute, a heated diplomatic struggle for control of the islands that came to be called the "Pig War." The "war" was finally resolved in 1872 when the islands were awarded to the United States by a German arbitrator.

Modern Washington first found itself in the international spotlight when it hosted two World's Fairs in 12 years: in Seattle in 1962 and Spokane in 1974.

The 20th Century

Rapid industrial development came with the world wars, and Washington emerged as a major player in the shipbuilding and shipping industries. Expansion in lumber, agriculture and fishing continued apace. During World War II, the shipbuilding, aircraft and atomic energy industries all boomed.

Seattle became the western head of the American airplane industry with the emergence of Boeing as one of the world's largest commercial aircraft companies. Microsoft set up base here in 1975 and within a decade rose to dominate the software industry. Other companies settling in Washington included Sega Corporation, Nike and the Nordstrom corporate headquarters.

The rush of young successful companies combined with the backbone of Boeing attracted a huge influx of people. Until very recently, Seattle was expanding at a phenomenal rate. They could hardly build roads fast enough to handle the traffic. As a result, Seattle is young—from the hoards of Yuppie coffee drinkers to the development-speckled suburbs and ultramodern road system.

The early 1990s have been tough for Washington, particularly Seattle. Boeing has taken some blows, losing big contracts to McDonnell Douglas and Air Bus—and when Boeing hurts, so does Seattle. The regional economy, however, is still very much on its feet, driven by the strong computer and technology companies.

On a cultural level, many Native American tribes have proudly reclaimed their heritage. A new generation of Native Americans has gained prominence in business, education, the environmental movement and the arts. Tribal organizations are also reclaiming lands and fishing rights.

Seattle has also become the cultural center for the twenty-something generation's icon—grunge rock. Flannel-sporting musicians stomp around nightclub stages in ripped jeans shouting out what many people of this youthful genre call music. You can see the grunge influence in most bars, clubs and young Seattlites' clothing.

Tourism remains Washington's fastest-growing industry. These environmentally conscious times have bred a new generation of naturalists and Washington has become one of their favorite vacation spots. The state's lakes, rivers, forests and mountains provide ample opportunities for outdoor adventures from waterskiing to bungee jumping to simple hiking—and more and more visitors are taking advantage of it.

Washington's current challenge is to reconcile its business opportunities with its natural resources, to strike a balance between expansion and preservation that will carry it forward into the 21st century.

FOUR

Seattle and Vicinity

Rain city? Not today. Last night's storm has washed the air clean, swept
away yesterday's curtain of clouds to reveal Mt. Rainier in all its astonishing glory. From your hotel room window you can see the Olympics rising like snow-tipped daggers beyond the blue gulf of Puget Sound. Below, downtown Seattle awakens to sunshine, espresso and the promise of a day brimming with discovery for the fortunate traveler.

The lesson here is twofold: Don't be daunted by Seattle's reputation for nasty weather, and don't limit yourself to anticipating its natural setting and magnificent greenery, awesome as they may be. For this jewel on Puget Sound sparkles in ways too numerous to count after a decade or more of extraordinary growth.

The city of Seattle, squeezed into a lean, hour-glass shape between Elliott Bay and Lake Washington, covers only 92 square miles, and its population is still under 600,000. But the greater metropolitan area now boasts a population of some 2.7 million.

While most newcomers have settled in the suburbs, Seattle's soaring skyline downtown is the visual focus of a region on the move. No longer the sleepy sovereign of Puget Sound, Seattle today is clearly the most muscular of the Northwest's major cities. Its urban energy is admired even by those who bemoan Seattle's freeway congestion, suburban sprawl, crime and worrisome air and water pollution. Growth has been the engine of change, and although the pace has slowed in the 1990s, the challenges posed by too rapid an expansion continue to be topics of discussion.

Today, Seattle manages to remain tied to its traditions. It's so close to the sea that 20-pound salmon are still hooked in Elliott Bay at the feet of

In 1992, Fortune *rated Seattle the #1 U.S. City for Business;* Conde Nast Traveler *readers voted it the #5 Best U.S. Destination; and* Savvy *magazine chose it as the #1 U.S. City for Women.*

those gleaming new skyscrapers. Downtown Seattle is so near its waterfront that the boom of ferry horns resonates among its buildings and the cries of gulls still pierce the rumble of traffic. But the city's (and the state's) economy has grown beyond the old resource-based industries. International trade, tourism, agriculture and software giants like Microsoft now lead the way. The spotlight has passed from building ships to building airplanes, from wood chips to microchips, from mining coal to cultivating the fertile fields of tourism.

In the process, one of the nation's most vibrant economies has emerged. You can see that energy in Seattle's highrises, feel it in the buoyant street scene fueled in part by the locals' infatuation with espresso (you'll find an espresso bar on nearly every downtown street corner, and drive-through espresso spots in the suburbs). And there is fresh energy beneath your very feet. A "new underground" of retail shops (as distinguished from the historic Pioneer Square Underground) is taking shape around the downtown Westlake Stations in the Metro Transit Tunnel, which opened in the fall of 1990.

Civic energy has produced a glorious art museum downtown, a small but lively "people place" in Westlake Park, a spacious convention center and additions to Freeway Park. Private enterprise has added hotels, office towers with grand lobbies brimming with public art, shopping arcades, restaurants, nightclubs and bistros.

Have growth, gentrification of downtown neighborhoods and a tide of new immigrants eradicated the old Seattle? Not by a long shot. Pike Place Market's colorful maze is still there to beguile you. Ferry boats still glide like wedding cakes across a night-darkened Elliott Bay. The central waterfront is as clamorous, gritty and irresistible as ever. Pioneer Square and its catacomb-like underground still beckons. The soul of the city somehow endures even as the changes wrought by regional growth accumulate.

By almost any standard, Seattle and its environs still offer an extraordinary blend of urban and outdoor pleasures close at hand. And growth seems only to have spurred a much richer cultural scene in Seattle—better restaurants serving original dishes, added luxury hotels, superb opera and a vital theater community, more art galleries and livelier shopping in a retail core sprinkled with public plazas that reach out to passersby with summer noon-hour concerts. In this chapter, we will point you to familiar landmarks, help you discover some unique treasures and find the best of what's new both downtown and in the outlying areas.

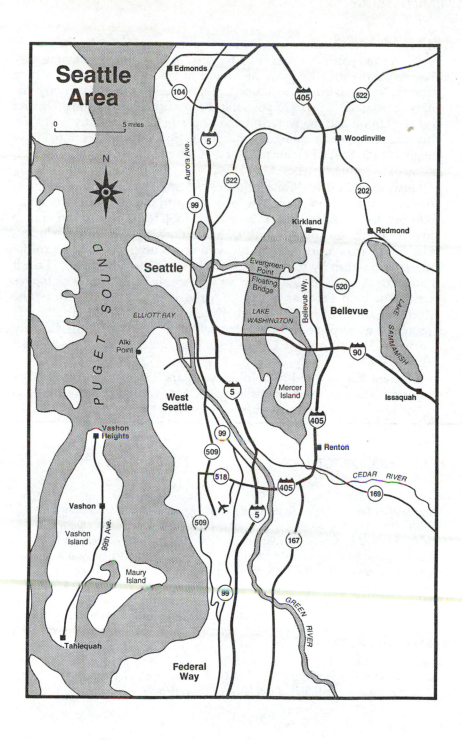

Downtown Seattle

Flying in to Seattle, the central part of this lush region looks irresistible. From the air, you'll be captivated by deep bays, harbors, gleaming skyscrapers, parks stretching for miles and hillside neighborhoods where waterskiing begins from the backyard. Seattle's neighborhoods offer a seemingly inexhaustible array of possibilities, from the International District to Lake Union and the waterfront to Capitol Hill. Eminently walkable, this area can also be explored by monorail, boat or bike. From the lofty heights of the Space Needle to the city's unique underground tour, this is one of Washington's best bets.

Downtown Seattle (Pioneer Square to Seattle Center, the waterfront to Route 5) is compact enough for walkers to tour on foot. Energetic folks can see the highlights on one grand loop tour, or you can sample smaller chunks on successive days. Since downtown is spread along a relatively narrow north-south axis, you can walk from one end to the other, then return by public transit via buses in the new Metro Transit Tunnel or aboard the Waterfront Streetcar trolleys, each of which have stations in both Pioneer Square and the International District. The Monorail also runs north-south between Westlake Center and Seattle Center. A good place to orient yourself is the **Seattle–King County Tourism Development Office** (520 Pike Street, Suite 1300, Seattle; 206-461-5840).

Pioneer Square and its "old underground" remain one of Seattle's major attractions. It was at this location that Seattle's first business dis-

---

SEATTLE'S COLORFUL PAST

Seattle offered no hint of its future prominence when pioneers began arriving on Elliott Bay some 140 years ago. Like other settlements around Puget Sound, Seattle survived by farming, fishing, shipbuilding, logging and coal mining. For decades, the community hardly grew at all. One whimsical theory for Seattle's ultimate success has it that because the frontier sawmill town offered a good array of brothels to the region's loggers, miners and fishermen, capital tended to flow into Seattle to fund later investment and expansion.

Whatever the reason, the city quickly rebuilt after suffering through the disastrous "Great Fire" of 1889. But it would be another eight years before the discovery of gold in Alaska put Seattle on the map. On July 17, 1897, the ship Portland steamed into Elliott Bay from Alaska, bearing its legendary "ton of gold" (actually, nearly two tons), triggering the Klondike Gold Rush. Seattle immediately emerged as chief outfitter to thousands of would-be miners heading north to the gold fields.

trict began. In 1889, a fire burned the woodframe city to the ground. The story of how the city rebuilt out of the ashes of the Great Fire remains intriguing to visitors and locals alike.

To learn exactly how the underground was created after the new city arose, only to be forgotten, then rediscovered, you really need to take the one-and-a-half-hour **Underground Tour** (from Doc Maynard's Tavern, 610 1st Avenue; 206-682-4646). Several of these subterranean pilgrimages are offered daily to the dark and cobwebby bowels of the underground—actually the street-level floors of buildings that were sealed off and fell into disuse when streets and sidewalks were elevated shortly after Pioneer Square was rebuilt (in fire-resistant brick instead of wood).

Above ground, in sunshine and fresh air, you can stroll through 88 acres of mostly century-old architecture in the historic district (maps and directories to district businesses are available in most shops). Notable architecture includes gems like the **Grand Central Building** (1st Avenue South and South Main Street), **Merrill Place** (1st Avenue South and South Jackson Street), the **Maynard Building** (1st Avenue South and South Washington Street), the cast-iron **Pergola** in Pioneer Square Park and facing buildings such as the **Mutual Life and Pioneer buildings** (1st Avenue and Yesler Way). More than 30 art galleries are located in the Pioneer Square area. Here, you can shop for Native American art, handicrafts, paintings and pottery.

Yesler Way and First Avenue is the heart of the district. **Yesler Way** itself originated as the steep "Skid Road" for logs cut on the hillsides above the harbor and bound for Henry Yesler's waterfront mill, and thence to growing cities like San Francisco. Later, as the district declined, Yesler Way attracted a variety of derelicts and became the prototype for every big city's bowery, alias "skid row."

The new city boomed during the Alaska Gold Rush. For a look back at those extraordinary times, stop by the Seattle office of the **Klondike Gold Rush National Historical Park** (117 South Main Street near Occidental Park; 206-553-7220), where you can see gold-panning demonstrations, a collection of artifacts, films and other memorabilia.

The main pedestrian artery is **Occidental Mall and Park**, a tree-lined, cobbled promenade running south from Yesler Way to South Jackson Street allowing pleasant ambling between rows of shops and galleries (don't miss the oasis of **Waterfall Park** off Second Avenue South on South Main Street).

For an overview of the whole district, ride the rattling old manually operated elevator to the observation level of the 42-story **Smith Tower** (2nd Avenue and Yesler Way), built in 1914.

Sharp ethnic diversity has always marked the **International District** next door to Pioneer Square to the southeast (South Main to South Weller streets, 5th to 8th avenues South). The polyglot community that

The 1980s' construction chaos caused Seattle's downtown to briefly suffer the nickname "little Beirut." Thankfully, the disruption has passed and it's peaceful again.

emerged on the southern fringes of old Seattle always mixed its Asian cultures and continues doing so today, setting it apart from the homogeneous Chinatowns of San Francisco and Vancouver, across the border in British Columbia.

Chinese began settling here in the 1880s, Japanese around 1900, and today the "I.D." as it's commonly known is also home to Koreans, Filipinos, Vietnamese and Cambodians. For all its diversity, the district lacks the economic vitality, bustling street life and polished tourist appeal of other major Chinatowns. Yet some find the International District all the more genuine for its unhurried, somewhat seedy, ambience.

A variety of mom-and-pop enterprises predominates—specialty-food and grocery stores, herbal-medicine shops, dim sum palaces and fortune-cookie factories. You're welcome to poke in for a look at how cookies, noodles, egg rolls and won ton wrappers are made at the **Tsue Chong Company** (801 South King Street; 206-623-0801). To see a variety of ethnic foodstuffs, drop by **City Produce** (South Lane Street and 7th Avenue South; 206-682-0320), a wholesale vegetable market with retail sales. The district's single major retail store is **Uwajimaya** (6th Avenue South and South King Street; 206-624-6248); it's not only the largest Japanese department store in the Northwest, but also a worthwhile experience of Asian culture even if you're not shopping.

Wing Luke Asian Museum (407 7th Avenue South; 206-623-5124; admission) offers a well-rounded look at the district's history and cultural mix with presentations that include an early-day Japanese store, historical photography and rotating exhibits on the history of Asian-Americans and their art. You'll also see paintings, ceramics, prints, sculpture and other art.

The **Nippon Kan Theater** (628 South Washington Street; 206-224-0181) is the centerpiece of the **Kobe Park Building National Historical Site** and offers occasional dramas and other cultural presentations. The park and community gardens adjacent to it offer pleasant strolling. **Hing Hay Park** (South King Street and Maynard Avenue South) is the scene of frequent festivals—exhibitions of Japanese martial arts, Chinese folk dances, Vietnamese food fairs, Korean music and the like. Its colorful pavilion comes from Taipei in Taiwan.

Beginning at the western edge of Pioneer Square, the old **waterfront** remains one of the city's most colorful quarters and what many consider Seattle's liveliest "people place." The waterfront grows more interesting by the year, a beguiling jumble of fish bars and excursion-boat docks,

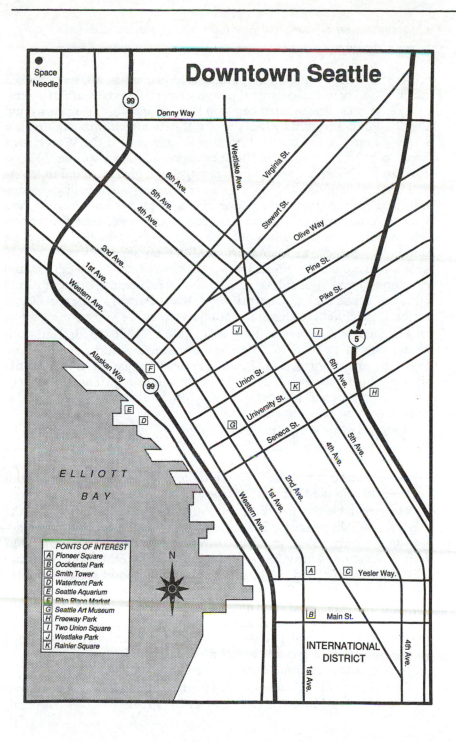

Downtown Seattle

Space Needle

99

Denny Way

6th Ave.
5th Ave.
4th Ave.
2nd Ave.
1st Ave.
Western Ave.

Westlake Ave.
Virginia St.
Stewart St.
Olive Way
Pine St.
Pike St.

J
I
5

Alaskan Way
F
99
E
D

Union St.
K
University St.
G
Seneca St.

6th Ave.
H
5th Ave.
4th Ave.
2nd Ave.
1st Ave.
Western Ave.

ELLIOTT
BAY

N

POINTS OF INTEREST
A Pioneer Square
B Occidental Park
C Smith Tower
D Waterfront Park
E Seattle Aquarium
F Pike Place Market
G Seattle Art Museum
H Freeway Park
I Two Union Square
J Westlake Park
K Rainier Square

A
C Yesler Way.

B Main St.

INTERNATIONAL
DISTRICT

1st Ave.
4th Ave.

On sunny summer days, the waterfront is the most popular tourist draw in the city.

ferries and fireboats, import emporiums and nautical shops, sway-backed old piers and barnacle-encrusted pilings that creak in the wash of wakes.

The action's concentrated between Piers 48 and 60, and again around Pier 70. Poking around by foot remains the favorite way to explore, but some folks prefer to hopscotch to specific sites aboard the **Waterfront Streetcar**, which runs from the International District to Pier 70 (you also can climb into a horse-drawn carriage here for a narrated tour). As you stroll south to north, you'll encounter a harbor-watch facility, a dozen historical plaques that trace major events, a public boat landing, the state-ferry terminal at Coleman Dock and the waterfront fire station whose fireboats occasionally put on impressive, fountain-like displays on summer weekends. Ye Olde Curiosity Shop houses a collection of odd goods from around the world, Ivar's is the city's most famous fish bar, and cavernous shopping arcades include pier-end restaurants, outdoor picnic areas and public fishing. **Central Waterfront Park** is a crescent-shaped retreat from commercialism presenting sweeping views over the harbor.

The **Seattle Aquarium** (Piers 59 and 60; 206-386-4320; admission) allows you to descend to an underwater viewing dome for up-close looks at scores of Puget Sound fish. Next to the aquarium is the **Omnidome Theater** (Pier 59; 206-622-1868; admission). This highly recommended program features the 1980 Mt. St. Helens eruption and an overview of the resulting devastation.

Across Alaskan Way is the 155-step Pike Hillclimb leading past cliffside shops up to Pike Place Market. You'll also pass some piers whose sheds have been leveled to provide public access, the last vestiges of working waterfront on the central harbor—fish-company docks and such—as well as the Port of Seattle headquarters.

The venerable market, born in 1907, has proved itself one of the city's renewable treasures. Saved from the wrecking ball by citizen action in the early 1970s, the market was later revitalized through long-term renovation. Today, the seven-acre **Pike Place Market National Historic District** and the surrounding neighborhood are in many respects better than ever. The main historic market (Virginia to Pike streets, 1st to Western avenues) now offers 400 different products in 40 categories, some 600 businesses, about 120 farmers, 225 craftsworkers and a good 50 restaurants and eateries. In all, a market experience unparalleled in the nation! To learn more, call for information (206-682-7453) or stop at the **Information Booth** at 1st Avenue and Pike Street.

One of the most valuable Pacific Northwest museums of the 1990s is the **Seattle Art Museum** (100 University Street; 206-654-3100; admission) east of Pike Place Market, designed by the husband-and-wife architectural team of Robert Venturi and Denise Scott. The five-story limestone-faced building highlighted with terra cotta and marble has quickly become a regional postmodern landmark. You'll enter via a grand staircase, but to see the collections, you'll have to ascend an elevator to the galleries. Known for its Northwest Coast Native American, Asian and African art, the museum also features Meso-American, modern and contemporary art, photography and European masters. Do not miss the superb collection of African masks.

City center, or **Downtown**, has undergone a remarkable rejuvenation. It's a delightful place to stroll whether you're intent on shopping or not. Major downtown hotels are clustered in the retail core, allowing easy walks in any direction.

One way to sightsee is to start at the south end of **Freeway Park** (6th Avenue and Seneca Street). The park's many waterfalls and pools create a splashy, burbling sound barrier to city noise. Beds of summer-blooming flowers, tall evergreens and leafy deciduous trees create a genuine park feeling, inspiring picnics by office workers on their noon-hour break. Amble north through the park, and take a short detour beneath a street overpass toward University Street (steps next to more waterfalls zigzag up to Capitol Hill and dramatic views of city architecture). Continue north as the park merges with the similarly landscaped grounds of the **Washington State Convention and Trade Center** (800 Convention Place; 206-447-5000), which offers occasional exhibits, as well as maps and tourist information.

Head west through linking landscaping that leads you past yet more waterfalls and flowers in the main plaza of **Two Union Square**. Cross

---

THE PIKE PLACE EXPERIENCE

There are so many ways to enjoy the Pike Place Market that we can scarcely begin to list them. Come early for breakfast and wake up with the market (at least a dozen cafés open early). Come at noon for the ultimate experience of marketplace clamor amid legions of jostling shoppers, vendors hawking salmon and truck-farm produce, and street musicians vying for your contributions. Come to explore the market's lower level, often missed by tourists, a warren-like collection of second-hand treasures, old books, magazines, posters and vintage clothing. Come to shop at the largest collection of handmade merchandise in the Northwest on tables set up at the market's north end. Come to browse all the "nonproduce" merchandise surrounding the main market—wines, exotic imported foods, French kitchenwares, jewelry and avant garde fashions.

Sixth Avenue and enter **City Center** on the corner of Union Street. This handsome building's lower levels are lined with upscale shops and a theater complex, bold sculptures and stunning exhibits of colorful art glass. Wander around and admire for a bit, stop for a meal or an espresso, then continue by leaving the building at the Fifth Avenue and Pike Street exit. Cross Fifth Avenue to Nordstrom. Head west on Pike Street to Fourth Avenue and turn right, shortly entering triangular **Westlake Park** (4th Avenue and Pine Street), which offers a "water wall" against street noise, a leafy copse of trees and an intriguing pattern of bricks that replicate a Salish Indian basket-weave design best observed from the terraces on the adjoining Westlake Center.

Westlake Center is an enormously popular, multilevel shopping arcade, a people place offering cafés, a brew pub, flower vendors, handicrafts and access to what's been heralded as downtown's "new underground." The marbled, well-lighted, below-street-level arcades were created as part of the city's new downtown transit tunnel. Metro buses (propelled electrically while underground) rumble by on the lowest level. Just above it are mezzanines full of public art, with vendors and shops, and underground access to a string of department stores.

Walk south on Fourth Avenue a few blocks to **Rainier Square** (4th and 5th avenues, University and Union streets) and discover another burgeoning underground of upscale enterprises. Follow its passageways eastward past a bakery, restaurants and access to the venerable **Fifth Avenue Theater**. Continue east, up an escalator back to Two Union Square and Freeway Park.

SEATTLE CENTER

*Northwest of downtown, a familiar landmark rises skyward—the Space Needle. More than thirty years after the 1962 World's Fair, the fairgrounds, long since renamed **Seattle Center**, frankly need renovating. For some time, politicians and planners have been debating what to do with the site (two miles north of the retail core between Denny Way and Mercer Street; 206-684-7200), but no firm plan has emerged. Meanwhile, locals and visitors continue to flock to the **Space Needle** (206-443-2111; admission) for the view or a meal, to summer carnival rides at the **Fun Forest**, to the **Center House**'s short-order international eateries, to opera and live theater at the center's many stages, to the wide-ranging exhibits and demonstrations at the **Pacific Science Center** (206-443-2001; admission).*

*Kids will also enjoy visiting the center's **Seattle Children's Museum** (206-298-2521) on the ground floor of Center House. The collection features a kid's-size neighborhood that includes a grocery, doctor's office, café, bus and fire engine. There's also a giant Lego room, a small lagoon for children and a drop-in art studio.*

Freeway Park—also called Ellis Park—offers five-plus acres of lawns, gardens and fountains, and is the nation's first major park to be built over a freeway.

To the south and west of downtown, surrounded by saltwater on three sides, **West Seattle** offers the finest aggregation of seaside parks and paths in town with stupendous views of the city shining across the waters of Elliott Bay. Some seven miles of roads follow the water's edge, including Harbor Avenue Southwest, Alki Avenue Southwest and Beach Drive Southwest. At low tide, there are miles of sandy strands, tide flats and a sprinkling of tidepools.

DOWNTOWN SEATTLE LODGING

Lodgings vary widely in style and price throughout the Seattle area. Downtown, there's a thick cluster of expensive luxury hotels interspersed with a few offering moderate and even budget rates.

The **Alexis Hotel** (1007 1st Avenue; 800-426-7033, fax 206-621-9009) is an elegant little haven a block from the waterfront and close to downtown stores and business centers. The 54 rooms have soft colors and contemporary furnishings mixed with a few antiques, all done in good taste. Some of the roomy suites have fireplaces. Breakfast is complimentary, and the service is unmatched in this renovated historic hotel. Ultra-deluxe.

Seattle has only one place to stay that is directly on the waterfront: the **Edgewater Inn** (2411 Alaskan Way; 206-728-7000, 800-624-0670). It began as a top-flight hotel on Pier 67 in the 1960s, later slid into decay and was recently renovated in "mountain lodge" style—meaning plaid comforters and peeled-log furniture in the rooms and an antler chandelier in the lobby. Half of the 238 rooms and suites have stunning views of Elliott Bay, West Seattle and the Olympic Peninsula. Rooms are comfortable, and the staff is accommodating. The restaurant has a fine water view. Deluxe to ultra-deluxe.

A retreat from the throngs in Pike Place Market is the **Inn at the Market** (86 Pine Street; 206-443-3600, 800-446-4484, fax 206-448-0631). The hotel, several shops and a restaurant are centered by a brick courtyard with a 50-year-old cherry tree. Small (65 rooms), light and airy, and furnished in French country style, the inn is one of Seattle's best. Rooms have views of the city, courtyard or water. Deluxe to ultra-deluxe.

Located in a former 1920s apartment building, the **Claremont Hotel** (2004 4th Avenue; 206-448-8600, 800-448-8601, fax 206-441-7140) provides spacious guest rooms converted from studio apartments. Decorated in soft tones of peach, green and blue, the rooms retain their art deco architectural details and include sitting areas with love seats and small kitchen/dining areas equipped for light cooking. Moderate to deluxe.

Hostelling International—Seattle (84 Union Street; 206-622-5443, fax 206-682-2179) is a low-priced establishment on the edge of Pike Place Market. In addition to 146 sleeping units, the bright, clean hotel has a kitchen, dining room, lounge, television room and small library. In the summer, hostel membership is required. Budget.

The **Four Seasons Olympic Hotel** (411 University Street; 206-621-1700, 800-223-8772, fax 206-623-2681) is the place to stay for classic grandeur and luxury. Priced in the ultra-deluxe range, it offers spacious, well-furnished rooms with a subtle oriental flavor. There are three restaurants, a stately marble lobby, meeting rooms and myriad amenities. The Italian Renaissance–style hotel stands in the heart of the downtown business district.

Considered a luxury hotel some 60 years ago, the **Pacific Plaza Hotel** (400 Spring Street; 206-623-3900, 800-426-1165) is now a dignified, quiet, downtown classic. Though updated, it hasn't lost its old-fashioned flavor, with windows that open, ceiling fans and traditional furniture in rather small rooms. There are 160 moderately priced rooms. A continental breakfast and morning newspaper are provided in a lounge off the multitiered lobby. The concierge is very helpful.

The **West Coast Camlin Hotel** (1619 9th Avenue; 206-682-0100, 800-426-0670), on the edge of downtown and a block from the convention center, was built in 1926 and has been renovated in recent years. The 136-room hotel has a lovely lobby of marble with oriental carpets, a

---

FOUR SEASONS OLYMPIC HOTEL

*One of Seattle's historic landmarks, the **Four Seasons Olympic Hotel** is the epitome of elegance and style, worth a peek whether you stay there or not. When the hotel opened in 1924, it was the ultimate in fine lodgings of the day. The modified Italian Renaissance brick building, on a prime downtown site owned by the University of Washington, was filled with antique mirrors, marble, Italian and Spanish oil jars and bronze statuary. Terrazzo floors were laid by Italian workers brought to Seattle for the project. The proud Washington State Hotel Association labeled its metropolitan member "a bit of New York transplanted to the Pacific Northwest."*

For years, the Olympic was the preferred site for social events, banquets, weddings and debutante balls. With time, its elegance faded, but in 1980, under new control, a $60 million renovation began. Two years later, the Four Seasons Olympic was again operating as the queen of hotels in the Pacific Northwest. It has won numerous awards, from AAA's five diamonds to first prize in Seattle's Martini Classic.

Seattle was built on seven hills: Capitol, Magnolia, First, Queen Anne, Beacon,
West Seattle and Denny, which was scraped off and dumped into Puget Sound.

restaurant and lounge on the 11th floor and a conference room on the
lobby level. Most of the oversized, classically furnished rooms have work
areas, a popular feature for business travelers. Deluxe.

Carved and gilded rosettes decorate the ceiling of the entrance roof at
the **Mayflower Park Hotel** (405 Olive Way; 206-623-8700, 800-562-
4504, fax 206-382-6997), which is connected to the retail shops of Westlake Center. Inside, there's a two-level lobby with a fireplace and quiet
conversation area on the upper level. The 1927-era hotel has been beautifully renovated, with polished woods, dark blue and burgundy room
decor, a few antiques and Oriental art objects, and original tile in the
baths. Upper-floor rooms have downtown views. There's a restaurant,
Clipper's, and a bar and lounge, Oliver's. Deluxe to ultra-deluxe.

The **Sheraton Seattle Hotel & Towers** (1400 6th Avenue; 206-
621-9000, 800-325-3535, fax 206-621-8441) manages to deftly combine the facilities of a large urban hotel with a personal touch. It has 840
rooms and suites, a highly acclaimed restaurant and a sprawling lobby
with stunning displays of art, mostly glass. The pool and exercise room
on the 35th floor have a grand view of the city with the Olympic Mountains as a backdrop. Stay in the Club Level (floors 31–33) and you'll have
private champagne check-in and a butler at your service for breakfast,
tea and evening hors d'oeuvres in the Club Lounge. The Towers (top
floor) offer the same perks as the Club Level, but with even more luxuries
and amenities. Ultra-deluxe, with several discount packages available.

For comfortable lodgings convenient to Seattle Center, the **Best Western Executive Inn** (200 Taylor Avenue North; 206-448-9444, 800-
351-9444, fax 206-441-7929) can't be beat. Deluxe-priced, with free
parking, the remodeled inn has 123 rooms and a small lobby with a gas
fireplace. There's an exercise room and spa, restaurant and lounge, and
complimentary shuttle service to the central downtown area.

Between downtown and Seattle Center is **Sixth Avenue Inn** (2000
6th Avenue; 206-441-8300, 800-648-6440), a five-story motor inn with
166 rooms. The rooms, done in crisp blue and cream, are a cut above
those in most motels. They contain blond furniture and assorted plants
and books. Those on the north and in back are the quietest. There's a
restaurant overlooking a small garden. Moderate.

The **Inn at Virginia Mason** (1006 Spring Street; 206-583-6453, 800-
283-6453) is an attractive, nine-story, brick building owned by the medical
center next door. On the eastern edge of downtown, it caters to hospital
visitors and others looking for a convenient location and pleasant accom-

---

An hour-long guided tour offers an inside look at the Kingdome sports arena.

---

modations at reasonable prices. The 79 rooms have dark-wood furnishings in a burgundy, gray and mauve decor. Two suites have a fireplace and whirlpool tub. There's a small restaurant by a brick terrace. Moderate to deluxe.

The **Sorrento Hotel** (900 Madison Street; 206-622-6400, 800-426-1265, fax 206-343-6155) is known for its personal service and attention to detail. A historic building that has been remodeled, Sorrento is on a hilltop a few blocks above the downtown area. Beyond the quiet, plush lobby are a notable restaurant and an inviting lounge. The Sorrento has been called one of the most romantic hotels in Seattle. All 76 rooms and suites have a warm, traditional, European atmosphere. Ultra-deluxe.

On a grassy hill in West Seattle, facing east toward Elliott Bay and downtown, is **Hainsworth House** (2657 37th Avenue Southwest; 206-938-1020). The impressive, Tudor-style home was built in 1906 and restored in the mid-1980s. It contains antiques, Persian rugs and lots of polished woodwork, but the atmosphere is unassuming. Guests make popcorn in the kitchen, play with the dogs and ask for scrambled tofu for breakfast if they don't want eggs. There are two well-furnished rooms upstairs; both have decks, one has a fireplace and a grand view. Moderate to deluxe.

Villa Heidelberg (4845 45th Avenue Southwest, West Seattle; 206-938-3658, fax 206-935-7077) is a bed and breakfast in a Craftsman-style home on a corner hillside. The inn has a wide wraparound porch that overlooks gardens of roses and rhododendrons. Inside, the atmosphere is comfortable and relaxed. The house features leaded glass windows, beamed ceilings and the original 1909 gaslight fixtures and embossed wall coverings. The four guest rooms are decorated in pastel florals and feature brass or oak beds and oak dressers. A full breakfast is served. Moderate.

At the southern edge of Seattle and a stone's throw from Sea–Tac Airport, the **Seattle Marriott** (3201 South 176th Street; 206-241-2000, 800-643-5479, fax 206-241-3254) is a wonderfully luxurious hotel featuring a 20,000-square-foot tropical atrium five stories high. Around it are 459 freshly renovated guest rooms. A restaurant, lobby lounge, whirlpools, health club and gameroom round out the amenities. Airport shuttle is provided. Deluxe.

DOWNTOWN SEATTLE RESTAURANTS

In a brick building near Pioneer Square, the fine **al Boccalino** (1 Yesler Way; 206-622-7688) serves some of the city's best Italian dinners. The restaurant's atmosphere is unpretentious and intimate, the antipasto imaginative (quail baked with prosciutto and cognac; beans with swordfish and fennel) and the entrées cooked and sauced to perfection. Saddle of lamb with brandy, tarragon and mustard is a favorite. There are daily specials for every course. Moderate.

Artwork is the main dish at **The Painted Table** (92 Madison Street; 206-624-3646), where each place setting features a colorful handpainted charger plate signed by a local artist and the terra-cotta walls are adorned with changing art exhibitions. The menu is artful as well, with entrées crafted with fresh ingredients provided by small local farms. Among the specialties are Dungeness crab cakes with pesto mayonnaise and jalapeño coleslaw, roasted king salmon in tarragon sauce and a variety of vegetarian dishes. Moderate to deluxe.

For a romantic dinner, try **Il Terrazzo Carmine** (411 1st Avenue South, Pioneer Square; 206-467-7797) in the Merrill Place Building. For patio diners, a cascading reflecting pool drowns out some, but not all, of the freeway noise. Entrées include *pelli di pollo valdostana* (baked chicken breasts filled with fontina cheese and prosciutto) or *lombata di vitello alla giudea* (sautéed veal chop with artichokes and sundried tomatoes). The restaurant also features an extensive Italian wine list. Deluxe.

White linen tablecloths, black rattan furnishings and loads of plants greet you at **Linyen** (424 7th Avenue South; 206-622-8181), an upscale Cantonese restaurant in the International District. In the foyer, you can check the specials posted on the blackboard, such as hot and smokey crab in a spicy sauce, red pepper beef, Linyen fishcakes with vegetables or clams in black bean sauce. Moderate.

Just a few blocks away is **Hanil** (409 Maynard Avenue South; 206-587-0464) set in the Bush Asia Center, up above a park. The interior of this Korean restaurant is filled with wood paneling, green plants and flowers. The restaurant serves great lunch specials in lovely lacquered boxes and classic Korean barbecue prepared on gas burners at your table. Barbecued chicken, pork or beef are excellent. Budget to moderate.

For great Vietnamese food at low prices, try **Saigon Gourmet** (502 South King Street; 206-624-2611). Beyond the green oilcloths and the white lace curtains, there's no decor to speak of—just hungry patrons

NORTHWEST CUISINE, SEATTLE STYLE

In the Northwest, regional cooking at its best emphasizes the bounty of fresh produce and seafood available; in Seattle, innovative chefs have turned it into a distinctive cuisine showcasing the dazzling variety of ingredients that pour in from farms and boats. Combined with fine wines from Washington's 75-plus wineries, it makes for meals that critics rave about.

Ten times more specialty coffees are sold in Seattle than in other U.S. cities, and you'll find espresso stands on almost every corner.

eager for a dish of shrimp, sugarcane and rice paper, Cambodian noodle soup or papaya with beef jerky. Shrimp rolls here are some of the best in town. Budget.

On the outskirts of the International District, you'll find **Chau's Chinese Restaurant** (310 4th Avenue South; 206-621-0006), a small, unpretentious restaurant that offers great seafood such as Dungeness crab with ginger and onion, clams in hot garlic sauce, bird's-nest scallops and rock-cod fillets with corn sauce. Choose the fresh seafood over the standard Cantonese entrées. Budget to moderate.

Hidden away is **Place Pigalle** (81 Pike Street, in the Pike Place Market; 206-624-1756). Wind your way past a seafood vendor and Rachel, the brass pig (a popular market mascot), to this restaurant with spectacular views of Elliott Bay. The dark-wood trim, handsome bar and other touches make for a European-bistro atmosphere. The restaurant makes the most of fresh ingredients from the market's produce tables. Dine on fresh Penncove mussels in balsamic vinaigrette, calamari dijonnaise, or one of the daily fresh salmon specials. The dishes are artfully presented, but the service is sometimes uneven. Deluxe.

Across the cobbled street, you can observe the eclectic mix of shoppers and artists in the Pike Place Market at **Three Girls Bakery** (1514 Pike Place; 206-622-1045), a popular hangout. This tiny lunch counter and bakery has just a few seats, but serves good sandwiches—the meatloaf sandwich is popular—and hearty soups, including chili and clam chowder. You have more than a hundred kinds of bread to choose from (the sourdough and rye are recommended). If you don't have room for pastries, buy some to take home. You won't regret it. Budget.

In Post Alley, behind some of the market shops, you will find more than just a wee bit of Ireland at **Kells** (1916 Post Alley; 206-728-1916). This traditional Irish pub will lure you to the Emerald Isle with pictures and posters of splendid countryside. A limited menu includes salmon with an Irish dill sauce, rack of lamb, Irish stew and meat pies. From the heavy, dark bar comes a host of domestic and imported beers. Irish music is piped in all the time, and live musicians play Irish tunes Wednesday through Saturday. Moderate.

This place doesn't even have a sign, but you'll know it by the pink door off Post Alley. **The Pink Door** (1919 Post Alley; 206-443-3241), with its Italian kitsch decor, is lively and robust at lunchtime. Especially good are the tubetti pasta with broccoli flowerettes in a vegetable sauce topped with parmesan, lasagna and a delicious *cioppino*. In the evening, the pace slows, the light dims and it's a perfect setting for a romantic dinner. In the summer, rooftop dining offers views of the Sound. Moderate.

Off a brick courtyard above Pike Place Market, **Campagne** (86 Pine Street; 206-728-2800) is one of the city's top restaurants. Diners enjoy French country cooking in an atmosphere that's both warm and elegant. Entrées include grilled Oregon rabbit with porcini *jus* and a rich cassoulet with duck confit, garlic sausage, pork and lamb. The simply prepared dishes are usually the best: boneless chicken stuffed with forest mushrooms, for example, or rack of Ellensburg lamb roasted with rosemary. Prices range from moderate to ultra-deluxe.

Every meal served at **El Puerco Lloron** (Pike Place Market Hillclimb, 1501 Western Avenue; 206-624-0541) includes wonderfully fresh tortillas, made by hand while hungry diners watch from the cafeteria line. The *chile rellenos* compares with the best. Tamales, enchiladas and tacos are all authentic and of good quality. There's a Mexican fiesta atmosphere in the warm, steamy room. Budget.

Tucked into a hillside in Pike Place Market, **Il Bistro** (93-A Pike Street; 206-682-3049) is a cozy cellar spot with wide archways and oriental rugs on wooden floors. Candlelight and well-prepared Italian food make it an inviting spot on a rainy evening. Several pastas are served; the entrées include rack of lamb, veal scaloppine, fresh salmon and chicken stuffed with mozzarella. Deluxe to ultra-deluxe.

On the Pike Place Market hill, **Takara Restaurant and Sushi Bar** (1501 Western Avenue; 206-682-8609) serves Japanese food in a casual atmosphere. Chicken and salmon teriyaki, fried flat noodles with vegetables and pork and sashimi on a bed of grated radish are a few of the delicately flavored, budget-to-moderate-priced dishes.

Café Septieme (2331 2nd Avenue; 206-448-1506) is Kurt Timmermeister's re-creation of the type of small Parisian café that once catered to the literati and students. This café carries plenty of reading material and turns out cups of good coffee and lattes that attract students from nearby Antioch University, as well as business folks and shoppers in the Belltown area. A favorite luncheon sandwich is eggplant with roasted peppers. Desserts include shortbread, carrot cake, a variety of cookies and other mouthwatering treats. In summer, there is a small outdoor courtyard. Budget.

Artists and others without a lot of money for eats hang out at the **Two-Bells Tavern** (2313 4th Avenue; 206-441-3050) in Belltown. Local artwork on the walls changes every two months. This funky bar with 21 kinds of beer and a host of inexpensive food is a busy place. You can always find good soups, sandwiches, burgers, salads and cold plates. Some popular choices are an Italian-sausage soup and the hot beer-sausage sandwich. Budget.

A favorite among downtowners is the **Botticelli Café** (101 Stewart Street; 206-441-9235). The small café is known for its panini—little sandwiches made of toasted focaccia bread and topped with olive oil, savory herbs, cheeses and vegetables. The espresso and ices are good, too. Budget.

Contemporary international cuisine prepared with imagination is served at the **Dahlia Lounge** (1904 4th Avenue; 206-682-4142) near the shops of Westlake Center. Bright red walls and ceiling, a neon sign and paper-fish lampshades create a celebratory atmosphere. The chef draws upon numerous ethnic styles and uses regional products to develop such dishes as roasted eggplant and garlic dip with grilled pita and green apples. Moderate to deluxe.

Padded red-and-white checked tablecloths, carpeting and an amber glow from the light fixtures give **Tulio** (1100 5th Avenue, 206-624-5500) appealing warmth. Usually packed and festive, it's a place for great food

---

SEATTLE'S STREET SYSTEM

Newcomers to Seattle often find street signs bewildering; the city is divided into several sections, each with different area designations. Here's how the system works: All avenues run north-south and are followed by a geographical indicator (1st Avenue Northwest, 23rd Avenue South); all streets run east-west and are preceded by the direction (East Ward Street, Northwest 65th Street). Exceptions are noted below.

The city's sections are:

*   **Northwest**, bounded by Puget Sound on the west, Lake Washington Canal on the south, and 1st Avenue Northwest on the east.*

*   **North**, bounded by 1st Avenue Northwest, Denny Way and 1st Avenue Northeast. South of Lake Washington Canal, the streets have no geographical indicators.*

*   **Northeast**, bounded by 1st Avenue Northeast, the Canal and Lake Washington.*

*   **West**, bounded by Puget Sound, Lake Washington Canal, Denny Way and Queen Anne Avenue.*

*   **East**, bounded by the Canal, Eastlake Avenue, Broadway, Yesler Way and Lake Washington. South of Denny Way, the avenues have no geographical indicators.*

*   **Downtown**, bounded by Elliott Bay, Denny Way, Broadway and Melrose avenues and Yesler Way. There are no geographical indicators.*

*   **South**, bounded by Yesler Way, Lake Washington and Elliott Bay and 1st Avenue South.*

*   **Southwest**, bounded by Puget Sound, Elliott Bay and 1st Avenue South.*

*   Adding to the confusion is a maze of freeways, bridges and angled streets. But with a map and some experience, the system isn't as difficult as it first appears.*

and lively conversation rather than a quiet rendezvous. Go for the specials, such as sea bass on escarole and spinach, and the desserts, which range from a rich tiramisu to delicate strawberry ice with basil. Moderate to deluxe.

Now at home in the Westin Hotel is **Nikko** (1900 5th Avenue; 206-322-4905), with a sushi and hibachi bar and private rooms for groups of six or more. Tempura, sukiyaki, sushi and sashimi are among the Japanese delicacies served. Moderate.

Original Northwest art hangs above the booths in **Fullers** (1400 6th Avenue; 206-447-5544), an internationally acclaimed restaurant in the Sheraton Seattle Hotel and Towers. The decor is plush and sophisticated and the cuisine still top quality, though there's a new chef at the helm. Monique Barbeau calls her food "globally influenced, regionally inspired." Examples are sautéed sea scallops with tempura onion rings and balsamic vinaigrette or garlic-stuffed beef tenderloin with sweet onion merlot sauce. Deluxe to ultra-deluxe.

The decor is spare and clean in **Wild Ginger** (1400 Western Avenue; 206-623-4450), while the menu is Chinese and Southeast Asian. Dark-wood booths fill the big, open room; at one end is a satay bar where skewered chicken, beef and fish are grilled, then served with peanut sauce. The wondrous Seven Elements Soup, an exotic blend of flavors, is a meal in itself. Prices are in the moderate range.

For good sandwiches, omelettes, *frittatas* and soup, consider **A. Jay's** (2619 1st Avenue; 206-441-1511) in Belltown. This deli is a place to linger over the Sunday newspaper and enjoy a casual breakfast. If you are there for lunch, try the shrimp salad—it's fresh and flavorful. Other deli items include latkes, blintzes and bagels with lox and loaded with cream cheese. Coffee is plentiful. Service is helpful and friendly. Breakfast and lunch. Budget.

Near Seattle Center and the Queen Anne district, **Thai Restaurant** (101 John Street; 206-285-9000) serves authentic Thai cuisine in a friendly, comfortable setting. There are Asian art objects and an aquarium of exotic, iridescent blue fish to look at while you wait for your order of bathing Rama (beef or pork in peanut-chili sauce over spinach) or *tom yum potek* (spicy and sour soup) or another of the menu's 60-plus items. They vary in hotness and are rich with the flavors of coconut, curry, garlic, peanuts and peppers. Budget.

At the **Space Needle Restaurant** (203 6th Avenue North; 206-443-2150), the entertainment—from 500 feet up—in either the restaurant or the observation deck is the spectacular view of metropolitan Seattle and its environs, Puget Sound, the Olympic Mountains and Mt. Rainier, the Queen of the Cascade Range, as you rotate in a 360-degree orbit.

Spend a perfect summer day at Alki Beach in West Seattle, then take in dinner at the **Alki Café** (2726 Alki Drive Southwest; 206-935-0616), where a well-rounded menu includes great salads (the wilted spinach

---

Boeing means big. The largest aerospace, electronic and computer business in the U.S. employs 103,000 people in the Puget Sound area alone.

---

and bacon is a favorite), seafood, meat, chicken and pasta dishes. Try the steak Santa Fe stuffed with bacon, feta and wild green chiles topped with tangy corn chutney. Specials of the evening are listed in the two dining areas. Be sure to leave room for dessert—a lovely fruit torte or delicious cheesecake made in the bakery. Also a popular place for breakfast, they offer hearty omelettes, french toast and a host of muffins. Coffee, espressos and lattes are good, too. If you overindulge, you can always take another stroll on the beach. Moderate.

South of Seattle, an excellent Thai restaurant convenient to Sea–Tac Airport is **Bai Tong** (15859 Pacific Highway South, Sea–Tac; 206-431-0893). Located in a former A&W drive-in, this eatery is known for its steamed curry salmon, grilled beef with Thai sauce and marinated chicken. The carpeted dining room is lush with potted plants, and the walls are adorned with photos of mouthwatering dishes. Budget.

DOWNTOWN SEATTLE SHOPPING

The oldest and loveliest structure in Pioneer Square is the **Pioneer Building** (600 1st Avenue; 206-624-1783). Here is Seattle's first electric elevator, and the **Pioneer Square Mall** (600 1st Avenue; 206-624-1164) in the basement has over 10,000 square feet of space devoted to antiques and collectibles and maintained by some 80 dealers.

Grand Central Arcade Building (214 1st Avenue South; 206-623-7417) houses 17 shops. Visitors can also enjoy drinks and baked goods at lobby tables adjacent to a brick fireplace. **Millstream NW** (112 1st Avenue South; 206-233-9719) sells Northwest sculpture, prints, stained glass and jewelry by local artisans. **Adjiri Arts** (214 1st Avenue South; 206-464-4089) has African masks, silk-screened African T-shirts and modern African art including clay sculpture and wood carvings.

For ten years, **The Prints and the Pauper** (112 South Washington Street; 206-624-9336) has been dealing in photographic art, paintings and sculptured works produced by up-and-coming Northwest artists. Prices are reasonable, and you might get a masterpiece with a signature that one day will be highly valued.

In the heart of the Pioneer Square district is the **Elliott Bay Book Company** (101 South Main Street; 206-624-6600) featuring over 125,000 titles, including an outstanding stock of Northwest books and a section for professional, business and health-science subjects. You're bound to enjoy browsing, snacking in the on-premises café or listening in on readings by renowned authors.

Seattle's connection with the Pacific Rim is legendary, and **Uwajimaya** (519 6th Avenue South; 206-624-6248) celebrates the tie with shoji screens and lamps, Kanji clocks and watches, lacquerware music boxes, goldimari ceramic pieces and Japanese, Chinese, Thai, Vietnamese, Philippine and American canned and frozen foods.

Known as an "Oriental Woolworth's," **Higo Variety Store** (604 South Jackson Street; 206-622-7572) has all kinds of small toys, bowls and sundries in the five-and-dime category. Also on hand are some more expensive articles such as hapi coats, kimonos and obi sashes.

Along the waterfront, Piers 54 through 70 are shoppers' delights. You'll love **Ye Olde Curiosity Shop** (Pier 54; 206-682-5844), a Seattle landmark where the mummy "Sylvester" presides over souvenirs, Native American totem poles and masks, Russian stacking dolls, lacquerware and Ukrainian eggs. **Hawaii Bye N' Bye** (Pier 57; 206-621-1193) is noted for its Hawaiian lace, seashells, freshwater pearls, straw hats and aloha shirts.

Called the "Soul of Seattle," the **Pike Place Market** (85 Pike Street; 206-682-7453) has been in business since 1907. Saved from the wrecking ball by citizen action in the early '70s, Pike Place is now a bustling bazaar with 600 business, 120 farmers and 50 eateries. Two of the establishments are the **Pure Food Fish Market** (1511 Pike Place Market; 206-622-5765), which ships fresh or smoked salmon worldwide, and

---

UP, UP AND AWAY

*Off Route 5 south of Seattle at Boeing Field is the **Museum of Flight** (9404 East Marginal Way South; 206-764-5720; admission), one of the world's finest aviation museums. Centered in a traffic-stopping piece of architecture called the Great Gallery, the museum is a must. In the glass-and-steel gallery, 22 aircraft hang suspended from the ceiling, almost as if in flight. In all, more than 50 aircraft (many rare) trace more than 70 years of aviation. You'll see a 1916 B & W float plane, 1917 Curtis Jenny biplane, 1929 Boeing 80-A biplane, 1932 Yakima Clipper sail plane, 1935 DC-3, 1962 A-12 Blackbird, 1968 Aerocar III (flying car) and many homebuilts.*

*The 1909 **Red Barn** houses one wing of the museum. The so-called "barn" was originally the Boeing Company's boat-building factory on the banks of the nearby Duwamish River. Later it was converted to aircraft production, the company's original plant. Since relocated several times, it now houses exhibits on Boeing's early days in the airplane business, a far cry from today's mammoth factories.*

It costs less than a dollar to ride the convenient Monorail, which zips between Seattle Center and the myriad shops of Westlake Center in 90 seconds.

Hands of the World (Main Arcade; 206-622-1696), where the specialty is ethnic jewelry, masks and home accessories such as carved picture frames and folkloric art.

In the downtown area, Fifth Avenue is Seattle's fashion street. Here, you'll find shops displaying elegant finery and accessories. **Rainier Square** (1333 5th Avenue; 206-628-5050) houses several prestigious retail establishments. **Totally Michael's** (1525 6th Avenue; 206-622-4920) has contemporary, upscale clothing. **Biagio** (1312 4th Avenue; 206-623-3842) specializes in handsome leather goods—handbags, luggage, business and attaché cases.

At the **Westlake Center** (4th Avenue and Pine Street; 206-467-1600), colorful pushcarts loaded with jewelry, scarves and imported items lend a European flavor to the 80 retail establishments here. The shops line the walkways around a four-story atrium. **Alhambra** (101 Pine Street; 206-621-9571) deals in Middle Eastern bangles, pendants and other jewelry. **Fireworks Fine Crafts Gallery** (206-682-6462) takes its name from unusual fired sculptures, wallhangings and plates. **Puzzletts** (206-223-2340) is the ultimate puzzle shop, crammed with puzzles and brainteasers. Fast foods, available on the third floor, include teriyaki, baklava, enchiladas, yogurt and quiche. **Blue Chip Cookie Company** (206-623-0301) sells good chocolate chippers.

DOWNTOWN SEATTLE NIGHTLIFE

There are many fine nightclubs in Pioneer Square, and on "joint-cover" nights, one charge admits you to nine places within a four-block radius. Among them is **Doc Maynard's** (610 1st Avenue; 206-682-4646), heavy on rock-and-roll. **The New Orleans Creole Restaurant** (114 1st Avenue South; 206-622-2563) offers jazz and blues nightly. Over at the **Bohemian Café** (111 Yesler Way; 206-447-1514) you'll find live blues and reggae Wednesday through Saturday. And at **Comedy Underground at Swannies** (222 South Main Street; 206-628-0303), comics entertain nightly.

Along the waterfront you'll find rock aplenty at **Iguana Cantina at Pier 70** (foot of Broad Street and Alaskan Way; 206-728-7071), where you can dance to deejay-spun Top-40 and dance tunes. Cover.

Unexpected Productions (The Market Theater, 1428 Post Alley, Pike Place Market; 206-781-9273) offers comedy performances and workshops in improvisational theater techniques.

Belltown, near the Pike Place Market, has lots of activity after dark. **The Vogue** (2018 1st Avenue; 206-443-0673) features modern dance music. Cover. Nearby, **Café U–Betcha** (2212 1st Avenue; 206-441-1989) offers live jazz Thursday night and deejay dance music Friday and Saturday after the dinner hour.

Crocodile Café (2200 2nd Avenue; 206-441-5611) attracts a young crowd for live alternative rock.

Showbox Comedy and Supper Club (1426 1st Avenue; 206-628-5000) features nationally known comedians. Reservations required; cover.

Dimitriou's Jazz Alley (6th Avenue and Lenora Street; 206-441-9729) is a downtown dinner theater and premier jazz club with international acts. Cover.

For satirical/comical revues, try the **Cabaret de Paris** (Rainier Square, 1335 5th Avenue; 206-623-4111). Food and drink are available. Cover.

At the **Off Ramp Music Café** (109 Eastlake East; 206-628-0232), there's alternative rock six nights a week by national and local bands. Wednesday is deejay-spun house music.

Timberline (2015 Boren Avenue; 206-622-6220) draws a largely gay crowd, with everyone enjoying country dancing. Lessons available, weekend cover.

Home of the 1962 World's Fair, the **Seattle Center** (305 Harrison Street; 206-684-7200) still offers innumerable nighttime diversions. Sharing facilities at the **Seattle Center Opera House** (along Mercer Street at 3rd Avenue North) are the **Seattle Opera Association** (206-389-7676, 800-426-1616), famous for summer performances of Wagner's *Ring of the Nibelung*; **Pacific Northwest Ballet** (206-441-9411), where the *Nutcracker* is a Christmas tradition; and the **Seattle Symphony** (206-443-4747), where the repertoire ranges from baroque to contemporary.

The **Seattle Repertory Theatre** (along Mercer Street between Warren Avenue and 2nd Avenue North; 206-443-2222) plays at the Bagley Wright Theatre, while the **Intiman Theatre** (201 Mercer Street at 2nd Avenue North; 206-626-0782) presents plays by the great dramatists.

For new renditions of classics, contemporary plays and musicals, try the **Bathhouse Theater** (7312 West Green Lake Drive North; 206-524-9108) on the shores of Green Lake.

A Contemporary Theater (100 West Roy Street; 206-285-5110) and **The Empty Space Theater** (3509 Fremont Avenue North; 206-547-7500) specialize in works by new playwrights.

DOWNTOWN SEATTLE PARKS

A well-designed 140-acre site where landscaping divides 4000 feet of saltwater shoreline into individual chunks, **Ed Munro Seahurst County Park** (206-296-2956) is just right for private picnics and sunbathing. A

For a breathtaking view of Seattle's skyline and Elliott Bay, go to Queen Anne district's Kerry Park at West Highland Drive and Second Avenue West.

nature trail and some three miles of primitive footpath explore woodsy uplands and the headwaters of two creeks. An artificial reef just offshore is popular with divers and anglers with boats. Facilities here include picnic areas, showers, playground and marine laboratory with fish ladder and outdoor viewing slots. Located on the southwest edge of Seattle at 13th Avenue Southwest and Southwest 144th Street, via Exit B from Route 5.

Seattle Neighborhoods

While downtown is the city's magnet, some of Seattle's best parks, sightseeing and nightlife can be found in nearby neighborhoods. Arboretums and science museums, lakeside dining and shopping worth a special trip are all in this region.

The six miles or so of shoreline circling **Lake Union** present an incredibly varied mixture of boat works and nautical specialty shops, street-end pocket parks, boat-in restaurants, seaplane docks, rental-boat concessions, ocean-research vessels, houseboats, flashy new condo developments and office complexes. You could spend a day exploring all the byways and funky old warehouses and oddball enterprises. The lake's south end offers extensive public access to the shore behind a cluster of restaurants, a wooden-boat center and new park.

One of Seattle's most cosmopolitan neighborhoods, **Capitol Hill** is the place to toss back an exotic wheatgrass drink at a vegetarian bar, sip a double espresso at a sidewalk café, shop for radical literature at a leftist bookstore or hit a straight or gay nightclub. If you can't find it on Capitol Hill, Seattle probably doesn't have it. Broadway Avenue is the heart of this region known for its boutiques, Yuppie appliance stores and bead shops.

Home of some of the city's finest Victorians, this neighborhood includes **Volunteer Park** (East Ward Street from 11th to 17th avenues). The park has a conservatory, lawns, trees and gardens. Be sure to head up to the top of the water tower for a great view of the region.

In August of 1994, the building that used to house the old Seattle Art Museum reopened as the **Asian Art Museum** (Volunteer Park, 1400 East Prospect; 206-654-3100; admission). This Arte-Moderne building was a gift to the city in the 1930s by Dr. Richard Fuller, who was the museum's director for the next 40 years. The museum always had a large collection of Asian art and this new museum has expanded on it. The

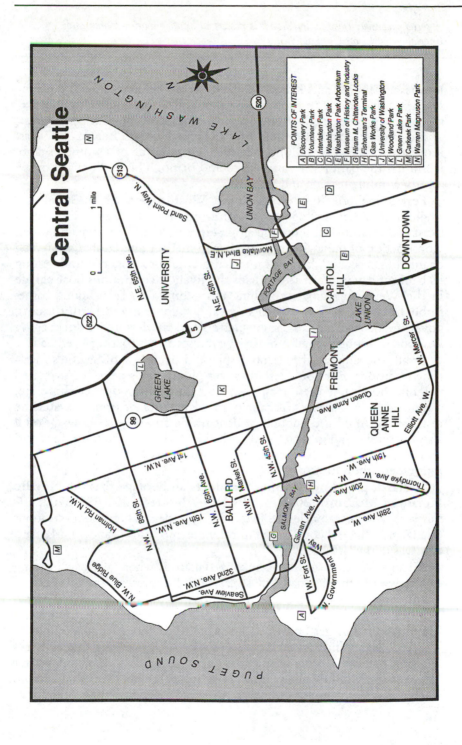

Central Seattle

POINTS OF INTEREST
A Discovery Park
B Volunteer Park
C Interlaken Park
D Washington Park
E Washington Park Arboretum
F Museum of History and Industry
G Hiram M. Chittenden Locks
H Fisherman's Terminal
I Gas Works Park
J University of Washington
K Woodland Park
L Green Lake Park
M Carkeek Park
N Warren Magnuson Park

A secret greenway close to downtown is preserved by neighboring Boren and Interlaken parks on Capitol Hill.

Japanese, Chinese and Korean collections are the largest, but the museum also has south and southeast Asian collections. Japanese folk textiles, Thai ceramics and Korean screen paintings are some of the highlights.

Nostalgia reigns in Capitol Hill's **Harvard Exit Theater** (807 East Roy Street; 206-323-8986). Once the elegant home of a women's club, it still has the parlor with a fireplace and piano. This is the place to see award-winning foreign and art films.

Few guidebooks look at the **Lake Washington Ship Canal** as a single unit. Yet it ties together a wondrous diversity of working waterfront and recreational shoreline along eight miles of bay, lake and canal. Construction of the locks and canal began in 1911 and created a shipping channel from Lake Washington to Lake Union to Puget Sound. Along its banks today you can see perhaps the liveliest continuous boat parade in the West: Tugs gingerly inching four-story-tall, Alaska-bound barges through narrow locks; rowboats, kayaks, sailboards and luxury yachts; government-research vessels; gill-netters and trawlers in dry dock; aging houseboats listing at their moorings; even seaplanes roaring overhead.

In all, the ship canal presents a splendid overview of Seattle's maritime traditions. But you'll also discover plenty that's new—rejuvenated neighborhoods like Fremont and south Lake Union's upscale shoreline, a renovated Fisherman's Terminal and a handful of trendy, waterside restaurants. Amid the hubbub of boat traffic and ship chandlers, you'll also encounter quiet, street-end parks ideal for birdwatching, foot and bike paths, the best historical museum in the city and one of the West's renowned arboretums.

Ballard, proud of its strong Scandinavian heritage, has the **Nordic Heritage Museum** (3014 Northwest 67th Street; 206-789-5707; admission), which chronicles the lives of early settlers. There are re-creations of a farm in the old country, an immigrant ship, Ellis Island, and Ballard as it was in the late 1800s.

Hiram M. Chittenden Locks in Ballard is where all boats heading east or west in the ship canal must pass and thus presents the quintessential floating boat show; it's one of the most-visited attractions in the city. Visitors crowd railings and jam footbridges to watch as harried lock-keepers scurry to get boats tied up properly before locks are raised or lowered, depending on the boat's direction of passage. Terraced parks flanking the canal provide splendid picnic overlooks. An underwater fish-viewing window gives you a clear look at several species of salmon, steelhead and sea-going cutthroat trout on their spawning migrations

(June into November). Lovely botanical gardens in a parklike setting offer yet more diversion.

Fisherman's Terminal (on the south side of Salmon Bay about a mile east of the locks) is home port to one of the world's biggest fishing fleets, some 700 vessels, most of which chug north into Alaskan waters for summer salmon fishing. But you'll always be able to see boats here—gill-netters, purse-seiners, trollers, factory ships—and working fishermen repairing nets, painting boats and the like. Here, too, are net-drying sheds, nautical stores and shops selling marine hardware and commercial fishing tackle. One café opens at 6 a.m. for working fishermen; there's a fish-and-chips window and one good seafood restaurant (Chinook's) overlooking the waterway.

The **Fremont** neighborhood is locally famous for the sculpture "Waiting for the Interurban," whose collection of lifelike commuters is frequently seen adorned in funny hats, scarves and other castoff clothing. Centered around Fremont Avenue North and North 34th Street at the northwest corner of Lake Union, the district is top-heavy with shops proffering the offbeat (from handmade dulcimers to antiques).

Gas Works Park (foot of Wallingford Avenue North off North 34th Street) occupies property that dangles like a giant green tonsil from Lake Union's north shore. Until 1956, the park's namesake "gas works" produced synthetic natural gas from coal and crude oil. Some of the rusting congeries of pipes, airy catwalks, spiraling ladders, tall towers and stubby tanks were torn down during park construction, but enough remains (repainted in snappy colors) to fascinate youngsters and old-timers alike.

"U-DUB"

Exceptional architecture, a garden setting and easy access make a campus tour of the **University of Washington** *(or U-dub, as locals call it) a highlight of a Seattle visit.*

The university began downtown in 1861; in 1895, it was moved to its present site. The Alaska–Yukon–Pacific Exposition of 1909 was held on the campus, and several of its fine buildings date from that event.

At the Visitor Information Center (4014 University Way Northeast; 206-543-9198), you can pick up a useful (and free) walking tour map. The map describes quirky bits of UW history as the hour-plus walk meanders under tall trees and past stately brick buildings. The College of Forest Resources resembles a Gothic cathedral. The Medicinal Herb Garden may be the largest of its kind in the United States. The tree-enclosed Sylvan Theater is the site of numerous trysts, plays and weddings. Fountains, ponds, a rose garden and views of Lake Washington add texture to the lovely campus.

On the south side of Union Bay, 175-acre **Washington Park** (Lake Washington Boulevard East and East Madison Street) presents enough diversions indoors and out to fill a rich day of exploring in all sorts of weather. Most famous is the **Washington Park Arboretum** (which occupies most of the park), at its best in the spring when thousands of rhododendrons and azaleas—some 10 to 15 feet tall—and groves of spreading chestnuts, dogwoods, magnolias and other flowering trees leap into bloom. Short footpaths beckon from the **Visitors Center** (Arboretum Drive East; 206-543-8800). But two in particular deserve mention—Azalea Way and Loderi Valley—which wend their way down avenues of pink, cream, yellow, crimson and white blooms. The arboretum's renowned **Japanese Garden** is especially rewarding in spring, and both arboretum and garden present splendid fall colors in October and early November.

Miles of duff-covered footpaths lace the park. For naturalists, the premier experience will be found along the three-mile round-trip **Foster Island Trail** at the north end of the park on Foster Island behind the Museum of History and Industry. This footpath takes you on an intriguing bog-walk over low bridges and along boardwalks through marshy wetlands teeming with ducks and wildfowl, fish and frogs and aquatic flora growing rank at the edge of Lake Washington.

In summer, you can join canoeists paddling the labyrinth of waterways around **Foster Island**, sunbathers and picnickers sprawling on lawns, anglers casting for catfish and trout and the swimmers cooling off on hot August afternoons.

On rainy days, the **Museum of History and Industry** (2700 24th Avenue East; 206-324-1125; admission) is a fitting retreat. It's the city's best early-day collection and pays special tribute to Puget Sound's rich maritime history, as befits any museum located next door to this vital waterway.

The **University of Washington Campus** (45th Street Northeast and 15th Avenue Northeast; 206-543-9198) borders the canal north of Montlake Cut (part of the waterway) and is a haven for anyone who enjoys the simple pleasure of strolling across a college campus. It boggles the mind to think of what awaits you on its 694 acres—handsome old

---

THE BURKE MUSEUM

*The **Thomas Burke Memorial Washington State Museum** (located on the University of Washington campus; 206-543-5590) is the oldest university museum in the West. Established in 1885, it has a notable collection of Native American artifacts. Open daily 10 a.m. to 5 p.m. There's a popular coffeehouse, the Boiserie (206-543-9854) in the basement.*

buildings in architectural styles from Romanesque to modern; Frosh Pond; the **Burke Museum** (206-543-5590) and its famous collection of Northwest Indian art; the **Henry Art Gallery** (206-543-2280) with its marvelous textiles; red brick quads and expanses of lawn and colorful summer gardens; canal-side trails on both sides of the Montlake Cut; access to the Burke–Gilman Trail; and a lakeside **Waterfront Activity Center** with rentals (206-543-9433).

A mile or so north of the ship canal, Green Lake Park and Woodland Park straddle Aurora Avenue North (Route 99) and together offer 530 acres of park, lake and zoo attractions. The star is **Woodland Park Zoo** (Fremont Avenue North and North 55th Street; 206-684-4800; admission), which since 1979 has won praise for its program of converting static exhibits into more natural, often outdoor environments. Most notable are the African Savannah, Gorilla Exhibit, the Marsh and Swamp and the Elephant Forest where you can see Thai elephants working at traditional tasks. There's also a Tropical Rain Forest, heralded as a "journey through different levels of forest," and a petting zoo. The newest attraction is the Northern Trails of Alaska, a habitat for bears, wolves and river otters that simulates trails around Mount Denali.

Green Lake Park, enormously popular with all ages and classes of Seattlites, is simply the best outdoor people-watching place in the city. Two loop trails circle the shore (the inner trail is 2.8 miles long, the outer 3.2 miles) and welcome all-comers. On summer days, both paths are filled with strollers and race-walkers, joggers and skaters, bikers and nannies pushing prams. On the lake you'll see anglers, canoeists, sailboarders, swimmers, birdwatchers and folks floating in inner tubes.

SEATTLE NEIGHBORHOODS LODGING

Seattle's neighborhoods offer several hotels and bed-and-breakfast accommodations. A bed and breakfast can be a great value, offering a casual atmosphere, homecooked food included in the room rate and personal contact with an innkeeper who usually knows the city well. Contact **A Pacific Reservation Service** (206-784-0539, fax 206-782-4036).

The **MV Challenger** (1001 Fairview Avenue North; 206-340-1201, fax 206-621-9208) is a "bunk and breakfast" on Lake Union. The opulent interior of the renovated, 96-foot tugboat is done in mahogany and oak. It has a salon with a fireplace and seven cabins with nautical furnishings. They all overlook the lake and city skyline. Captain's Cabin, the largest, includes the former pilothouse. Moderate to deluxe.

Bellevue Place Bed and Breakfast (1111 Bellevue Place East; 206-325-9253, 800-325-9253, fax 206-455-0785) is a bed and breakfast in a tony residential area on Capitol Hill. The big home, built in 1905, has three comfortable, tastefully furnished rooms that share a divided bath.

The bed and breakfast caters to a mixed gay and straight clientele. It has three parlors (one with a grand piano, one with a fireplace and dining table, where breakfast is often served, and one with a solarium). Prices are in the moderate range.

Also in the popular, busy Capitol Hill area, **Gaslight Inn** (1727 15th Avenue; 206-325-3654, fax 206-324-3135) is a moderately priced bed and breakfast with urban flair. The 1906 house is furnished with oak, maple and glass antiques. Various period styles have been effectively combined with modern amenities in the 13 guest rooms. Most have private baths, and three have fireplaces. Gaslight has a heated, outdoor swimming pool (closed in winter) and serves a continental buffet breakfast. Gay-friendly.

A mother-daughter team runs the **Salisbury House** (750 16th Avenue East; 206-328-8682, fax 206-720-1019), a quiet, dignified, gracious Capitol Hill home two blocks from Volunteer Park. Cathryn and Mary Wiese offer four crisp, clean rooms (all private baths) furnished with antiques and wicker. Fresh flowers, duvets on the beds, a full breakfast and thoughtful innkeepers make this an example of a well-done bed and breakfast. There are fireplaces in the living room and library and a refrigerator guests may use. Moderate.

Expect a friendly welcome and lots of conversation at **Roberta's Bed & Breakfast** (1147 16th Avenue East; 206-329-3326, fax 206-324-2149). The comfortable, traditional home on Capitol Hill has four rooms on the second floor and a fifth under the eaves on the third floor. There are cozy window seats, gleaming woodwork, skylights, shelves full of books, a piano and a full, meatless breakfast. Moderate. Gay-friendly.

Located on Millionaire's Row on Capitol Hill, the **Shafer-Baillie Mansion** (907 14th Avenue East; 206-322-4654, fax 206-329-4654) is a grand turreted and gabled reminder of an earlier era with its wide porches, library, formal dining room and billiards room with a copper fireplace. The gay-friendly bed-and-breakfast inn has 11 suites, all with refrigerators and televisions and most with private baths. The private carriage house was converted from the former chauffeur's quarters. Moderate to deluxe.

From the **Capitol Hill Inn** (1713 Belmont Avenue; 206-323-1955), it's an easy walk downtown and to the convention center. The Queen Anne–style home dating back to 1903 has been beautifully restored as a bed-and-breakfast inn and furnished with antiques and reproductions of Victorian wallpaper and Tiffany light fixtures. There are five guest rooms, a suite with a jacuzzi and two comfortable parlors. An abundant breakfast is served. Gay-friendly. Moderate.

On Capitol Hill near Volunteer Park in the Harvard-Belmont Historic District is the landmark **Bacon Mansion Broadway Guest House** (959 Broadway East; 206-329-1864, 800-240-1864, fax 206-860-9025), a

1909 Tudor stucco home. In addition to the two-story carriage house, which has a living room, dining room and full kitchen, there are seven rooms in the main house, six with private bath. The Capitol suite has a sunroom with wet bar, fireplace, queen-size four-poster bed, view of the Space Needle and a big bathtub. Moderate to deluxe.

A favorite of visitors to the University of Washington, both gay and straight, the **Chambered Nautilus Bed & Breakfast Inn** (5005 22nd Avenue Northeast; 206-522-2536, fax 206-522-0404) is only a block from the campus. Breezily casual, the spacious home has a family atmosphere. Games and books, soft chairs by the fireplace and an all-day coffeepot add to the homeyness. Six guest rooms on the second and third floors have antique furnishings. Four have private baths. A full gourmet breakfast is served, sometimes on the sunporch. Moderate to deluxe.

Also in the University District is **Meany Tower Hotel** (4507 Brooklyn Avenue Northeast; phone/fax 206-634-2000, 800-648-6440), a 15-story tower with 155 corner rooms. All units have views of the mountains or the lake and cityscape. Standard hotel furnishings adorn the spacious, peach-and-green rooms. Moderate.

The **University Plaza Hotel** (400 Northeast 45th Street; 206-634-0100, 800-343-7040, fax 206-633-2743) is a three-story motor hotel adjacent to Route 5, west of the University of Washington. There are 135 comfortably furnished rooms centered around a pool courtyard. Rooms on the freeway side can be noisy. On the ground floor, behind a mock-medieval English facade, are a restaurant, lounge, gift shops and beauty salon. Moderate.

SEATTLE NEIGHBORHOODS RESTAURANTS

Hearty Northwest fare with a German accent is on the menu at **Szmania's** (3321 West McGraw Street; 206-284-7305), a popular spot with an exhibition kitchen and outdoor deck in the residential area of Magnolia. The specialties include roast pheasant with a dark cherry glaze, sauerkraut with smoked pork loin and sausages and medallions of venison with grilled dates and buckwheat spaetzle. Moderate to deluxe.

Located in the Queen Anne district, **Kaspar's** (19 West Harrison Street; 206-298-0123) is an award-winning restaurant. The menu emphasizes Northwest seafood, but includes beef, pork, lamb and quail. The Pike Street Market Grill dish features an array of seafood with a ginger-butter sauce. The desserts are innovative. Moderate to deluxe.

Located in a gracious, art-filled, turn-of-the century house, **Pirosmani** (2220 Queen Avenue North; 206-285-3360) specializes in cuisine from Georgia—the one in the former Soviet Union, that is. Flavorful choices include bite-sized dumplings stuffed with ground beef and pork seasoned with mint and onion, spinach pâté accompanied by puffed cheese bread and fresh tuna wrapped in grape leaves served on a bed of roasted peppers, ground walnuts and pomegranate seeds. Deluxe.

Bicycles hang from the rafters. T-shirts are on sale in the lobby. **Cucina! Cucina!** (901 Fairview Avenue; 206-447-2782) is an open, spacious, noisy Italian restaurant with a large deck overlooking Lake Union where you can watch float planes land and take off or kayakers gently paddling by. Diners can see into the open kitchen to watch the staff making pizzas that are then baked in the woodburning ovens. One of the most interesting is spicy chicken. You will find a variety of pasta dishes, such as linguine with roasted chicken and goat cheese, seafood cannelloni, good spinach and caesar salads. Moderate.

Ayutthaya (727 East Pike Street; 206-324-8833) is a corner restaurant in Capitol Hill renowned for its Thai cookery. Small, tidy and pleasant in blue and lavender, Ayutthaya features plenty of chicken and seafood dishes along with soups and noodles. Flavors blend deliciously in the curried shrimp with green beans, coconut milk and basil. Or try the chicken sautéed in peanut-chili sauce. Budget.

Near Seattle University, **Kokeb** (926 12th Avenue; 206-322-0485) is a pleasant restaurant offering the hotly spiced dishes of Ethiopia. The finger food is eaten with chunks of a large, flat bread. The atmosphere is rustic, with an open-beamed ceiling. Budget to moderate. Dinner only in winter.

One of the world's great clam chowders is served at **Rain City Pub and Grill** (2359 10th Avenue East; 206-322-4401). That's just the start. There are other appetizers (roasted garlic plate and walnut raspberry salad to name two), a hearty chicken sandwich, a house burger and several daily pasta specials. There is also a good wine list and a compre-

---

ALL ABOARD FOR DINNER

Dining cars built in the 1930s and 1950s, refurbished in style, offer unusual views of the Seattle area to passengers who book a ride on the **Spirit of Washington**. *The train travels from Renton north for 22 miles along the east shore of Lake Washington to Woodinville. Top-quality meals at ultra-deluxe prices are served during the journey—dinners daily, and lunch and brunch on weekends.*

In Woodinville, passengers disembark for a tour of the beautifully landscaped Columbia winery. On the return journey, they enjoy dessert and coffee and watch the scenery go by. The train crosses Wilburton Trestle, the longest (102 feet) wooden trestle in the Northwest.

For information, call toll-free 1-800-876-7245 or write Spirit of Washington Dinner Train, P.O. Box 835, Renton, WA 98057.

hensive beer selection. The festive Capitol Hill restaurant has an open kitchen and a cherry-wood bar and tables, and is designed around a weather theme, complete with a sky ceiling and blue walls decorated with a rotating art display. The service is attentive. Moderate to deluxe.

At **Mamounia Moroccan Restaurant** (1556 East Olive Way; 206-329-3886), patrons sit on the floor, nestled in mounds of pillows in the dim light with music from a sitar and panpipes playing in the darkness. Dishes such as roast chicken or spicy lamb and bread arrive and then the fun really begins. There are no utensils, so diners must tear off hunks of the meat and bread and eat with their fingers. At the least, it's a gastronomic adventure, or it could be your own rendition of *Tom Jones*. Moderate to deluxe. Dinner only.

A colorful and lively Spanish-eclectic restaurant in the Madison Park area, **Cactus** (4220 East Madison Street; 206-324-4140) serves a cuisine representative of many different cultures, but mostly influenced by Spanish, Mexican and Native American food. Start with one of the most unusual items on the menu—chayote salad: grilled chayote squash on wild fall greens with Spanish cabrelas cheese and ancho chile-glazed pecans, tossed with a green apple roasted jalapeño vinaigrette. One of the more unusual entrées is mancha mantelas: boneless chicken breast and pork loin, grilled in a sauce of tomatoes, bananas, almonds and spices. Moderate.

Not too far away in a small house surrounded by gardens is **Rover's** (2808 East Madison Street; 206-325-7442), which specializes in Northwest cuisine with a French twist and is just the place for those romantic occasions. Chef Thierry Rautureau creates the ever-changing menu based on locally available fresh produce. In addition to seafood in imaginative sauces, entrées might include rabbit, venison, pheasant and quail. A good selection of Northwest and French wines is available. Service is friendly and helpful, and there is patio seating in summer. Deluxe to ultra-deluxe.

After visitors watch the ships go through the locks in the Ballard area, they stop at **Pescatore's** (5300 34th Northwest; 206-784-1733) for Italian seafood and views of the channel. For your comfort the terrace is equipped with fireplaces and a retractable awning. Choices include an antipasto platter, pizzas from a woodburning stove, Dungeness crab ravioli, shellfish stew and house-made desserts. Deluxe.

Scandies (2301 Northwest Market Street; 206-783-5080) is appropriately located in Ballard, a community with Scandinavian roots. Open all day every day, the restaurant serves such Scandinavian specialties as open-faced sandwiches (pickled herring, Jarlsberg cheese, spiced lamb), crêpe-style pancakes with lingonberries, Denmark's frickadeller (pork meatballs) and scorpa (cardamom cookies). Beers from Norway and Denmark are available in the informal, blue-and-white restaurant. Budget to moderate.

A favorite seafood place for tourists is **Ivar's Indian Salmon House** (401 Northeast Northlake Way; 206-632-0767) with its dugout canoe

---

Seattle is nicknamed "The Emerald City."

---

hung overhead and Northwest Native American longhouse-style architecture and decor. The restaurant also features views of the kayak, canoe, tugboat, windsurfer and yacht activity on Lake Union. The menu includes alder-smoked salmon and black cod, served Northwest Native American–style, and prime rib. Moderate.

When you're nostalgic for a '50s-style coffeehouse with an upbeat, neighborhood flavor, head for **Still Life in Fremont Coffeehouse** (709 North 35th Street, 206-547-9850). Set in the unpretentious Fremont district, it has high windows, a friendly atmosphere, music, great soups and generous sandwiches. Budget.

Ponti Seafood Grill (3014 3rd Avenue North; 206-284-3000), near the Fremont Bridge on the Lake Washington ship canal, has canal views and a mostly seafood menu, though there are good pasta and chicken dishes as well. Moderate to deluxe.

Also in Fremont, the popular, cheery **Trolleyman Pub** (3400 Phinney Avenue North, 206-548-8000) serves Red Hook ales made on the premises. The lunches and dinners are just right with a microbrew—chili, sausages, soups, hearty breads. Budget.

Near UW, make a beeline for the **Beeliner Diner** (2114 North 45th Street; 206-547-6313). Upbeat and lively, this is the place to go for generous portions of well-prepared all-American food: foot-long grilled hot dogs, cheeseburgers, turkey pot pie and roast chicken with mashed potatoes. Each evening there's a blue-plate special. It's a friendly café, like the 1940s diners it resembles. Budget.

Union Bay Café (3505 Northeast 45th Street; 206-527-8364) serves Northwest regional foods with a Mediterranean influence. The entrées include grilled sturgeon with roasted garlic, tomato and dill and hazelnut chicken on sautéed spinach with lemon butter. More unusual is the venison sausage with huckleberries, caramelized onions and sage. Lighter entrées are available in the simple, classic café. The appetizer list is almost as long as the regular menu. Moderate.

On a busy commercial street between the University and Ravenna districts is **Ciao Bella Ristorante** (5133 25th Avenue Northeast; 206-524-6989). The authentic Italian cuisine has been drawing raves since the little, L-shaped ristorante opened. On the menu are several classic pizzas, veal and chicken entrées and delectable pasta dishes. Chicken breast sautéed with gorgonzola cheese and fish soup with clams, mussels, calamari and prawns are flavored with artistry. Moderate.

Next door is **Guido's Pizza** (7902 North Green Lake Drive East; 206-522-5553), a funky, unpretentious place, the aromas from which send joggers across the street at Green Lake into Pavlovian salivation. You can buy pizza by the whole or slice, delicious salads and good cappuccinos. The artichoke pizza is wonderful. Budget.

SEATTLE NEIGHBORHOODS SHOPPING

The trendy boutiques of Capitol Hill draw shoppers looking for the unusual, though there are many standard stores too. On Broadway, the public art will give you a free dance lesson—just follow the bronze "Dancing Feet" imbedded in the sidewalk. Along the way, you'll see dozens of shops with new and vintage clothing, pop culture items, and ethnic wear and artifacts, all interspersed with myriad cafés and coffeehouses.

If you're in the market for a potato gun, would like to snack on Addams Family candy, crave a glow-in-the-dark squid or are searching for a popping Martian, head on over to **Archie McPhee's** (3510 Stone Way; 206-545-8344) near Lake Union, west of the university. This novelty-and-toy store offers more than 10,000 exotic items from all over the world.

In Broadway Market, go to **Urban Outfitters** (401 Broadway Avenue East, Suite 101; 206-322-1800) for casual city wear, jewelry, housewares and fashion-conscious shoes.

Close by is **Opus 204** (225 Broadway Avenue East; 206-325-1782), a small shop filled with a wondrous display of unusual and fine clothing, handicrafts, imports and gifts. **Keeg's** (310 Broadway Avenue East; 206-325-1771) has interesting home furnishings and offbeat items that make it fun to browse and shop for gifts.

Bailey/Coy Books (414 Broadway Avenue East; 206-323-8842) is well-stocked with reading material, including gay and lesbian literature.

Chocoholics can get their fix at **The Dilettante** (416 Broadway Avenue East; 206-329-6463), a combination chocolatier-café located in the Capitol

---

SEATTLE WEATHER WATCH

Historically, weather bureau statistics show that mid-July through mid-August brings the driest, sunniest, warmest weather—a sure bet for tourists, or so you'd suppose. But in the last decade or two, that mid-summer guarantee all too often has been washed away by clouds or rain. What's the sun-seeking tourist to do?

Consider September. In recent years it has brought modestly reliable weather. Or, you can simply come prepared—spiritually and practically—for whatever mix of dreary and sublime days that fate delivers. An accepting attitude may be the best defense of all in a region once described in this way: "The mildest winter I ever spent was a summer on Puget Sound."

Hill area. More health-conscious nibblers head for the **Gravity Bar** (113 Virginia Street; 206-448-8826), a full-service vegetarian restaurant with white woodwork and modern cone-shaped glass-topped tables. The extensive menu includes tofu avocado rollups, a tempeh burger, fresh spinach salad and a selection of vegetable and fruit juices. Budget.

The **Madison Park Pharmacy** (4200 East Madison Street; 206-323-6422) is popular with international travelers. A wide selection of moneybelts, world time clocks, neck pillows and guidebooks is found here.

At the **Washington Park Arboretum Visitors Center Gift Shop** (2300 Arboretum Drive East; 206-543-8800) are gardening books, cards, china, earrings, necklaces, serving trays and sweatshirts. You can also buy plants from the arboretum greenhouse.

Dominated by the UW campus is the University district, a commercial neighborhood overflowing with a vast array of retail shops. One that attracts many tourists is the **Folk Art Gallery La Tienda** (4138 University Way Northeast; 206-632-1796). Here, you'll find handpicked craft items from all over the world, including those made by 200 selected American artisans.

The largest bookseller in Washington is **University Book Store** (4326 University Way Northeast; 206-634-3400), where addicted readers can browse happily for hours. There's a huge selection of literature, technical books and college texts, as well as music and camera sections, some clothing and stationery.

Peaceable cats prowl the aisles at **Beauty and the Books** (4213 University Way Northeast; 206-632-8510). The bookstore has a worthy collection of literature, but is known for its bargain basement, where 15,000 good-condition volumes are sold at irresistible prices. They also have a solid reputation as a used-book buyer.

SEATTLE NEIGHBORHOODS NIGHTLIFE

In the Capitol Hill area, a hot venue for Seattle's burgeoning alternative rock scene is **Moe's Mo'roc'n Café** (925 East Pike Street; 206-324-2406).

Another popular spot is **Neighbors Disco** (1509 Broadway; 206-324-5358) offering progressive rock.

Capitol Hill also offers a number of popular gay and lesbian clubs and bars, including the following:

Brass Connection (722 East Pike Street; 206-322-7777) is a popular gathering spot featuring deejay dance music and occasional karaoke, lip-sync drag shows and "best body" shows. They have a gay and lesbian mixed crowd. Weekend cover.

Night Mary's (1525 East Olive Way; 206-325-6565) is a small intimate bar that attracts a gay and lesbian crowd. Cover. Because it's inside

This is a city of readers: the Seattle Public Library has the fourth-highest circulation of any municipal library in the United States.

Hamburger Mary's, a popular restaurant with a gay and straight clientele, bar patrons can order from the menu.

A 3000-square-foot dance club, **Changes Too** (1501 East Olive Way; 206-322-6356) is in an older brick building. The gay crowd rocks to deejay music five nights a week.

One of the biggest gay clubs in the area is **R-Place Seattle Pub** (619 East Pine Street; 206-322-8828). Depending on your mood, you can plunk down at the sports bar, throw darts, enjoy a music video, shoot pool, enjoy tunes from the jukebox or play a low-stakes gambling game called pull tabs.

Over in the Ballard district, you'll enjoy both the dinner and live jazz, rock or country shows at **The Backstage** (2208 Northwest Market Street; 206-781-2805). Cover. At **Conor Byrne's** (5140 Ballard Avenue; 206-784-3640), there is live Irish music on the weekends and set dancing on Wednesday night. Weekend cover.

Club crawlers also frequent the **Ballard Firehouse** (5429 Russell Avenue Northwest; 206-784-3516) for rock, reggae and salsa and **Tractor Tavern** (5213 Ballard Avenue Northwest; 206-789-3599) for a mix of rock, country and jazz.

Near the University of Washington, you'll find an array of clubs and places to park yourself at night. There are cocktail service, full dinner and shows at **Giggles Comedy Niteclub** (5220 Roosevelt Way Northeast; 206-526-5347) with music during the week and comedy on Friday and Saturday. Cover.

At the **University Sports Bar and Grill** (5260 University Way Northeast; 206-526-1489), you can dance weekends to local alternative rock bands. Popular with the college crowd, the club features big-screen television, two pool tables, an upstairs deck and darts.

SEATTLE NEIGHBORHOODS BEACHES AND PARKS

Carkeek Park (206-684-0877), a 224-acre wildland tucked into a woodsy canyon reaching toward Puget Sound, protects Piper's Creek and its resurrected runs of salmon and sea-going trout. Natural-history exhibits explain how citizens helped clean up the stream and bring the salmon back. Trails lead past spawning waters to the top of the canyon and through a native-plant garden. You'll find picnic areas, play areas and even a pioneer orchard and brickyard. To get to the park, take Third Avenue Northwest to 110th Street Northwest, turn left and follow the signs.

North of Ballard on Shilshole Bay, **Golden Gardens** (206-684-4075) has a sandy beach that swarms with young picnickers and sunbathers in summer. You can watch glorious sunsets from here. There are fire pits, a boat ramp and a public fishing pier. On the slope east of the beach, the 94-acre park has numerous walking paths under the trees.

Discovery Park offers two miles of beach trail and nine miles of footpaths winding through mixed forest and across open meadows. This bluff-top preserve (Seattle's largest at 535 acres) protects a remarkable "urban wilderness." Here are sweeping vistas, chances to watch birds (including nesting bald eagles) and study nature, the Daybreak Star Indian Cultural Center (206-285-4425) with exhibits from various tribes, four miles of road for bicycling and an 1881 lighthouse (oldest in the area). Fort Lawton Historic District includes Officers' Row and military buildings surviving from the park's days as an Army fort. You'll find picnic areas, fitness trail and a visitors center at park's east gate; information on guided walks, 206-386-4236. Located a quarter-hour drive north of downtown in the Magnolia district; the main entrance is at West Government Way and 36th Avenue West.

On Bailey peninsula, a 278-acre peninsula jutting into Lake Washington, **Seward Park** (206-684-4075) encompasses Seattle's largest virgin forest. Walking through it on one of several footpaths is the prime attraction, but many come to swim and sunbathe, launch a small boat, fish or visit a fish hatchery. It also offers a rare opportunity to see nesting bald eagles in an urban setting. The swimming beaches' gentle surf is ideal for children, and there are lifeguards in the summer. Best introductory walk is the two-and-one-half-mile shoreline loop stroll; to see the large Douglas firs, add another mile along the center of the peninsula. There are picnic and play areas, fishing pier and nature trails. The park is southeast of downtown Seattle, at Lake Washington Boulevard South and South Orcas Street.

Located on Lake Washington northeast of downtown Seattle, at Sand Point Way Northeast and 65th Avenue Northeast, **Warren G. Magnuson Park** (206-684-4075) is a 212-acre site carved from the Sand Point Naval Air Station. The park presents generous access to Lake Washington and wide views across the lake. It's a favorite place to launch a boat, swim or toss a frisbee. There are picnic areas, softball fields, boat ramp, tennis courts and swimming beaches with summer lifeguards.

Lincoln Park (206-684-8021) is the major multipurpose park for southwest Seattle, situated on a nose-shaped bluff just south of the Fauntleroy Ferry Terminal off Fauntleroy Avenue Southwest. There are rocky beaches strewn with tidepools and a network of quiet paths winding through groves of madrona, Douglas fir, cedar and redwoods. The park also offers play and picnic areas, an outdoor heated saltwater pool, tennis courts, football field and several miles of bike paths.

Vashon Island

No shopping malls, no fast-food restaurants—just natural beauty and a hometown feel. That's the draw to Seattle's neighboring Vashon Island. A mecca for artists, this 14-mile island, a 15-minute ferry crossing away from Fauntleroy dock in West Seattle, is fast becoming known as the bed-and-breakfast island. Vashon stretches south for 13 miles toward Tacoma (accessible by another 15-minute ferry from Tahlequah), creating a lovely Seattle-to-Tacoma country-road alternative to Route 5.

The Vashon Island Highway will take you fairly directly down the island, through the town of Vashon. Just south of town is the **Country Store and Gardens** (20211 Vashon Highway Southwest; 206-463-3655), where you can peruse merchandise grown or produced on the island— fruit and syrups, berries and preserves, a nursery stocked with perennials and a variety of gardening tools, natural-fiber clothing, kitchen wares and such.

Side roads beckon from the highway to a handful of poorly marked state beaches and county parks. **Point Robinson County Park** on Maury Island (linked to Vashon via an isthmus at the hamlet of Portage) is easier to find and particularly interesting, since it's next door to the Coast Guard's picturesque Point Robinson Lighthouse (not open to the public).

VASHON ISLAND LODGING

Vashon Island abounds with bed-and-breakfast inns, some of them in quaint old farmhouses surrounded by meadows and orchards. One is the **Betty McDonald Farm** (12000 99th Avenue Southwest; 206-567-4227), the former home of Betty McDonald who authored *The Egg and I* and *Onions in the Stew*. These two books wryly chronicle life on the Olympic Peninsula and Vashon Island. The six-acre farm overlooks Puget Sound and Mt. Rainier and offers two guest accommodations, a cedar-paneled loft and a private cottage both furnished with Oriental carpets, Northwest Indian print fabrics, antiques, wood-burning stoves. For nighttime reading, there are books by McDonald.

Located in an 1890s farmhouse painted blue with white trim, the **Old Tjomsland House** (17011 Vashon Highway Southwest; 206-463-5275) is surrounded by apple and pear trees and deer fields. The inn has a two-bedroom suite and a one-bedroom cottage, both furnished with family antiques and offering kitchenettes and living space. The moderate-to-deluxe rates include a huge breakfast of fresh fruit, turnovers, oatmeal, eggs and roasted salmon.

Also in a pastoral setting with resident deer, **Artist's Studio Loft** (16529 91st Avenue Southwest; 206-4630) offers a secluded cottage with a beamed ceiling, skylights, ceiling fan, kitchenette and outdoor hot tub. Other accommodations include a suite with a private entrance, French doors, cathedral ceilings, and potted palms and a smaller room decorated with Mexican tiles and wicker furnishings. The moderate rates include a continental breakfast.

The **Swan Inn** (18427 Thorsen Road Southwest; 206-463-3388) recalls Tudor England with its post-and-beam construction, leaded-glass windows and living area with baronial fireplace. Located on ten wooded acres, the inn is furnished with antiques that include romantic canopy beds with side curtains. Breakfasts are made with eggs from the inn's own chickens and herbs from the garden. Moderate.

VASHON ISLAND RESTAURANTS

Café Tosca (9924 Southwest Bank Road; 206-463-2125), in the heart of downtown, is Vashon's newest restaurant with Italian-opera posters on the walls. Entrées include calamari steak, chicken marsala, cheese tortellini in a pesto cream sauce and the very popular capellini *putanesca*, angel-hair pasta with olives, capers, garlic and anchovies in a tomato sauce. Don't forget to save room for a piece of homemade cheesecake and Italian caffe. Prices are moderate.

The old island hangout is **Sound Food Restaurant** (20312 Vashon Highway Southwest; 206-463-3565). The restaurant is known for its casual atmosphere—windows overlooking the gardens and lots of wood inside. Saturday and Sunday brunches result in long waits, but the food— whole-wheat waffles, blintzes with fresh fruit, potato pancakes, omelettes with wonderful sauces and breads and pastries from the bakery—is usually worth it. A variety of soups, salads and sandwiches of baked bread is available for lunch. Dinner entrées include a vegetable linguine, seafood dishes and a number of large salads. Desserts—sigh—come fresh from the bakery. Moderate.

Seattle North

North of Seattle, the long-time mill town of Edmonds has a lively charm and provides a link to the Olympic Peninsula. Ferries leave hourly from the Edmonds ferry landing, on a waterfront that has a recently redone beach park, a long fishing pier and an underwater park that is popular with divers. The park teems with marine life that swims around sunken structures: boats, a dock, a bridge model and others. On shore, the **Edmonds Beach Rangers** (206-771-0227) host summer beach walks.

The **Edmonds Chamber of Commerce and Visitors Information Bureau** (120 5th Avenue North; 206-776-6711) wins the prize for quaintness. It's housed in a pioneer log cabin that looks like a storybook house. Here, you can pick up brochures and a historic walking tour map that will take you past the site of old shingle mills, Brackett's Landing where the earliest pioneers settled, and numerous buildings constructed in the late 1800s and early 1900s.

The Edmonds Art Walk map points out the public artworks on display: bronze and copper sculptures, tile murals, stained glass and others.

Next door to the Chamber of Commerce, the **Edmonds Historical Museum** (118 5th Avenue North; 206-774-0900), in one of the original Carnegie libraries, has a working shingle mill model and collections of logging tools, pioneer artifacts and marine items that display the area's rich heritage. It's open Tuesday, Thursday, Saturday and Sunday; donations requested.

SEATTLE NORTH LODGING

If you're looking for upscale lodging, you're better off staying in the heart of Seattle, but for budget alternatives in Edmonds, there's the simple, comfortable guesthouse rooms at **Hudgens Haven** (9319 190th Street Southwest; 206-776-2202) and **Maple Tree** (18313 Olympic View Drive; 206-774-8420).

The **Homeport Motor Inn** (2385 Route 99, Edmonds; 206-771-8008) is a good deal as well. Guest rooms in this three-story motel are comfortably appointed and clean, with soft pastel carpets, curtains and bedspreads, and cable TV; there are even a few kitchenette and jacuzzi units. Other amenities include hot tubs and continental breakfast.

Hidden away in a little industrial complex full of shops and restaurants, the **Edmonds Harbor Inn** (130 West Dayton, Edmonds; 206-771-

---

A SIDE TRIP TO VICTORIA

*The picturesque Canadian town of **Victoria** in British Columbia combines a rich British heritage with a relaxed lifestyle. Winsome, gracious and colorful, Victoria is full of history and natural beauty, offering museums and gardens, grand old hotels and quaint shops.*

Located west of the San Juan Islands and just across the Strait of Juan de Fuca from Washington's Olympic Peninsula, Victoria is just a pleasant ferry ride away from the Seattle area and makes for a scenic day trip or overnight excursion. Whichever you choose, consider capping off your visit with high tea at the landmark Empress Hotel. (For information on getting to Victoria, see the "By Ferry" section at the end of the chapter.)

5021, 800-441-4033, fax 206-672-2880) provides basic motel-style accommodations with updated pastel decor and light wood furnishings. Sadly, none of the rooms has a view of the harbor and those in the southeast corner near the ship foundry can be noisy into the wee hours. Moderate.

SEATTLE NORTH RESTAURANTS

If you venture up to Edmonds, try **Ciao Italia** (546 5th Avenue South; 206-771-7950). This small restaurant on the main drag doesn't look like much from the outside—thankfully, the lace curtains block out most of the traffic view—but the food prepared by the robust owner/chef from Ischia (a small island near Naples) is outstanding. Best choices here include spaghetti *muruchiaro* (a garlicky seafood pasta in white-wine sauce) and *vitello alla saline* (stuffed veal like they do it in Sicily). Dinner only. Moderate.

A café and bakery, **Brusseau's** (117 5th Avenue South, Edmonds; 206-774-4166) features country-style breakfasts, homemade meatloaf sandwiches, *torta rustica*, homemade soups and a wide variety of desserts. Decorated like grandma's kitchen with calico wallpaper, the restaurant has a pleasant courtyard with planters and picnic tables. On Sunday try their oven-baked french toast made with cinnamon rolls or the sunflower walnut bread baked in custard and topped with blueberries. Budget.

Every table at **Arnies at the Landing** (300 Admiral Way, Edmonds; 206-771-5688) has a dandy second-floor view of Puget Sound and the Edmonds harbor. Chicken, steak and pasta are on the regular menu, but your best bet is to order from the fresh daily seafood list. There is a large variety of fresh broiled fish, and the clam chowder has won awards. The four-course early dinner (until 6 p.m.), available every day except Sunday, is a bargain. Moderate to deluxe.

A block from the ferry landing, **Café de Paris** (109 Main Street, Edmonds; 206-771-2350) is known for its French cuisine, served in a small dining room or on the glass-enclosed sunporch. Deluxe.

Chanterelle Specialty Foods (316 Main Street, Edmonds; 206-774-0650) has a rustic atmosphere, with wooden floors and tables and a basketry-and-fruit-crate decor. It's bright, cheerful and busy at mealtimes with patrons ordering veggie burgers, spanakopita, chili, salads and sandwiches. Moderate.

Tasters (100 2nd Avenue South, Edmonds; 206-778-7979) is favored for its consistently good and budget-priced Chinese cooking.

Kathy's Courtyard Café (515 Main Street, Edmonds; 206-778-8701), a delightful breakfast and lunch spot, has a few tables off to the side of the kitchen, but our favorites are those around the koi pond in the courtyard. Strong choices here are the broccoli quiche, croissant sandwiches and any of the fresh-baked pies, cakes and cookies along with a steaming cup of cappuccino or almond milk. Budget.

Evergreen Point Floating Bridge, the world's longest floating bridge (1.4 miles), lies across Lake Washington, between Seattle and Bellevue.

SEATTLE NORTH SHOPPING

There are a number of shops in the renovated **Old Mill Town** (201 5th Avenue South, Edmonds; 206-771-4515) worth checking out, including the **Edmonds Antique Mall** (206-771-9466), **Basketta** (206-775-1002) overflowing with baskets and windsocks and the **Old General Store** (206-771-2561) with Native American jewelry, baskets, pottery and Pacific Rim folk art.

Over 200 dealers sell their wares at the **Aurora Antique Pavilion** (2411 Route 99, Edmonds; 206-744-0566).

Seattle East

Seattle East, extending from the eastern shore of Lake Washington to the Cascade foothills, blends the urban and rural assets of this greater metropolitan region. Wineries and archaeological sites, prime bird-watching areas and homey bed and breakfasts are what attract visitors to the area.

Located south of town in Woodinville, **Château Ste. Michelle** (Route 202; 206-488-1133) is the state's largest winery with daily tasting and tours. Situated on a turn-of-the-century estate, it also offers greenswards, duck and trout ponds, experimental vineyards and frequent outdoor concerts on summer weekends.

Bellevue is the fourth-largest city in Washington, its suburban sprawl broken by two high-rise complexes of office buildings, shops and department stores. Bellevue Square (8th Street Northeast and Bellevue Way Northeast), with some 200 stores, is one of the largest malls in the state. On the third floor is the **Bellevue Art Museum** (206-454-3322; admission except on Tuesdays) showing a variety of exhibits, especially Northwest crafts and artworks.

Bellevue boasts a surprisingly diverse network of parks (206-455-6881) embedded within its neighborhoods. **Mercer Slough Nature Park** (stretching north from Route 90 off Bellevue Way) is the biggest and may be the best with some 300 acres of natural wetland habitat and ten miles of trails. **Wilburton Hill Park** (Main Street off 116th Avenue Northeast) is centered around a botanical garden of native and ornamental Northwest plants. The park covers about 100 acres and offers more than three miles of hiking trails. To see what Bellevue used to be like before the coming of freeways, commuters and office towers, stroll the short stretch of shops along Main Street westward from 104th Avenue Southeast in **Old Bellevue**.

Adults and children alike are enchanted with the **Rosalie Whyel Museum of Doll Art** (1116 108th Avenue Northeast, Bellevue; 206-455-1116; admission). Hundreds of antique and modern dolls are on display in a new, $3.2 million building that is patterned after a brick Victorian mansion.

North of Bellevue, hugging the Lake Washington shore, is **Kirkland**, with remnants of small-town charm. Pedestrian traffic is encouraged, with easy access to the lake and a one-and-a-half-mile walking/biking path. At Moss Bay, there's a public boat ramp and marina, shops, cafés and a brewery. The **Arthur Foss**, a 112-foot tugboat built in 1889, is open for tours. Originally steam-powered, the tug was given a diesel engine in 1935.

South of Bellevue, Seattle's rock legend Jimi Hendrix is buried. A caretaker can show you the guitarist's grave at **Greenwood Memorial Park** (350 Monroe Avenue Northeast, Renton; 206-255-1511).

SEATTLE EAST LODGING

Big, pink and broad-shouldered, the **Hyatt Regency Bellevue** (900 Bellevue Way Northeast, Bellevue; 206-462-1234, 800-233-1234, fax 206-646-7567) is the classiest place to stay in Bellevue. The mood is corporate, quality's high and access is convenient. The 382 rooms are painted in earth tones, and have soft lighting, contemporary furnishings and all the amenities, including room service. For a fee, guests may use the adjoining health club. Ultra-deluxe.

The **Woodmark Hotel at Carillon Point** (1200 Carillon Point, Kirkland; 206-822-3700, 800-822-3700, fax 206-822-3699) is a handsome, four-story brick structure on Lake Washington's shore. Its small scale, residential-style lobby, and comfortable bar with a fireplace and shelves of books create the ambience of a welcoming, stylish home. The 100 rooms, in pine and subdued pastels, have all the amenities: minibars, two televisions, VCR (complimentary movies), robes, hair dryers. Rooms on the lake side have panoramic views. Ultra-deluxe.

The **Shumway Mansion** (11410 99th Place Northeast, Kirkland; 206-823-2303, fax 206-822-0421) is a historic mansion with a New England flavor. To save it from demolition, the present owners had it moved to a knoll in north Kirkland, where it now accommodates guests, weddings and social functions. When a group takes over, overnight visitors can retreat to a tiny reading alcove on a second floor. The formal inn contains European furnishings, rugs out of the Orient, lace curtains and silk floral arrangements. Each of the eight guest rooms has a queen

The flavorful clam chowder at Yarrow Bay Grill and Beach Café in Kirkland won first prize in the 1992 Puget Sound Chowder-Off.

bed and antiques and easy chairs. The innkeepers serve a full breakfast on crystal and china. Moderate.

Set on three-plus acres, the **Cottage Creek Manor** (12525 Avondale Road Northeast, Redmond; 206-881-5606) has its own creek, pond and gazebo on the grounds. The English Tudor house features two guest rooms, one with a brass bed, one with an antique bed, each with its own bathroom. There's a pleasant sitting room with a piano, which guests are encouraged to play. Full breakfast included. Moderate.

The **Bear Creek Inn** (19520 Northeast 144th Place, Woodinville; 206-881-2978) is a Cape Cod house set among trees on an acre of land. There's a large rock fireplace in the living room, a patio and a deck with a hot tub. The two rooms feature country-wood furniture with oak and pine trim painted with flowered designs. Moderate.

The **Country Inn** (685 Northwest Juniper Street, Issaquah; phone/fax 206-392-1010) is a rambling wood-framed farmhouse set on five acres overlooking a lush valley. On the premises is an exotic bird menagerie and an indoor glass atrium with tropical plants and a waterfall where guests can relax with tea. Offering two guest rooms with private baths, the gay-friendly inn is furnished with antiques and displays of the owner's collector plates. The moderate rates include a full breakfast.

In a quiet wooded area southeast of Seattle is the **Maple Valley Bed and Breakfast** (20020 Southeast 228th Street, Maple Valley; phone/fax 206-432-1409; call in advance if faxing). The two-story contemporary home features open-beamed ceilings, peeled-pole railings, cedar walls and detailed wood trim. Guests like to relax on the antique furniture on the front porch. The two guest rooms are individually decorated and color coordinated. On cool nights, heated, sand-filled pads ("hot babies") are used to warm the beds. A full breakfast is served on country-stencil pottery in a dining area that overlooks trees, wandering peacocks and ponds with ducks. Budget to moderate.

SEATTLE EAST RESTAURANTS

The open kitchen at **Andre's Gourmet Cuisine** (14125 Northeast 20th Street, Bellevue; 206-747-6551) is as entertaining as the food. This restaurant offers a menu with Vietnamese specialties like spring rolls or pork with lemon grass, as well as Continental selections, such as lamb with garlic. Vietnamese chef Andre Nguyen comes with experience from some of Seattle's best restaurants. Moderate.

You wouldn't expect to find a good restaurant in this little shopping strip, but here it is. At **Pogacha** (119 106th Avenue Northeast, Bellevue; 206-455-5670), a Croatian version of pizza is the mainstay. The pizzas, crisp on the outside but moist inside, are baked in a brick oven. Because the saucing is nonexistent or very light, the flavor of the toppings—pesto and various cheeses, alone or over vegetables or meat—is more apparent. Other entrées include grilled meats and seafood, salads and pastas. Moderate.

Fortnum's (10213 Olde Main Street, Bellevue; 206-455-2033) is a welcoming little café with a bistro menu. Known for their meatloaf and homemade pastries, some entrées include fettuccine with chicken, sun-dried tomatoes and garlic, and an artichoke tart with cheese. There are also unusual savory touches like fresh ginger slices and pepper in a chicken-spinach soup. Moderate.

The best spot for a view of Lake Washington while you dine is **Yarrow Bay Grill and Beach Café** (1270 Carillon Point, Kirkland; 206-889-0303 or 206-889-9052). In the upper-level Yarrow Bay Grill, booths and tables are set against windows that extend in a wide semi-circle overlooking the lake. The Northwest cuisine emphasizes fresh fish and seafood at deluxe prices; salmon and chicken are smoked in-house. Downstairs, the more casual, lower-priced Yarrow Beach Café offers an interesting menu and a bar with Northwest wines and microbrewed beers. The bargain here at the café is happy hour on weeknights when, for $1.95, you can choose from generous portions of appetizers such as Cajun popcorn shrimp, steamed mussels, caesar salad and prawns.

Café Juanita (9702 Northeast 120th Place, Kirkland; 206-823-1505) offers the pleasures of a restaurant and boutique winery in one. In a dining room with warm beige tones and views of the surrounding woods, diners can enjoy the house's own sauvignon blanc or cabernet sauvignon (bottled under the Cavatappi label) while feasting on such entrées as fresh halibut grilled with olives, lemon and garlic or chicken breast baked with prosciutto and parmesan in a pistachio cream sauce. Moderate to deluxe.

One of the best Japanese restaurants in all of Puget Sound is hidden in the Totem Lake West shopping center in suburbia. **Izumi** (12539 116th Avenue Northeast, Kirkland; 206-821-1959) features an excellent sushi bar. Entrées are fairly standard—beef, pork, chicken sukiyaki and teriyaki—but the ingredients are especially fresh and carefully prepared. Service is friendly. Moderate.

A couple of local residents who grew up in Pakistan and Bangladesh have opened **Shamiana** (10724 Northeast 68th Street, Kirkland; 206-827-4902). The food is cooled to an American palate but can be spiced to a full-blown, multistar hot. A buffet of four curries, salad, nan and dal is offered at lunch. Dinners are à la carte and include entrées such as lamb curry with rice *pulao* or fish *tikka*. Moderate.

SEATTLE EAST SHOPPING

Domus (141 Bellevue Square, Northeast 8th Street and Bellevue Way, Bellevue; 206-454-2728) carries ever-changing design items for the home. Expect extensive selections of bric-a-brac, paintings, furniture, china-ware and some jewelry. **Fidalgo's** (172 Bellevue Square, Bellevue; 206-455-8888) has artificial flowers, plants and trees so well done they rival nature's productions. **Bellevue Square** (206-454-2431) also offers 200 other unique shops, department stores and restaurants.

One of the most elegant shops in Bellevue is **Alvin Goldfarb, Jeweler** (305 Bellevue Way Northeast; 206-454-9393). Specializing in 18-carat gold pieces crafted by an in-house goldsmith who also works with precious and semiprecious gems, this is a mecca for discriminating people who desire a one-of-a-kind item.

When you're looking for the unusual, browse through **Ming's Asian Gallery** (10217 Main Street, Bellevue; 206-462-4008), which carries Asian antiques and art, or admire the shiny brass in **Cuttysark** (10235 Main Street, Bellevue; 206-453-1265), where marine antiques are displayed.

Five miles north of Bellevue is the downtown **Kirkland Square** (215 Main Street, Kirkland), a mini-mall easily identified by its ten-foot-high clock. If you're tired of shopping, kids (and some adults) rave about **Quarters** (206 Main Street, Kirkland; 206-889-2555), where you can play such video games as Dragonslayer and Starblades.

Hunters of antiques appreciate the **Kirkland Antique Gallery** (151 3rd Street, Kirkland; 206-828-4993). Open daily, the mall has nearly 100 dealers selling antiques and collectibles.

Refurbished farmhouses, a barn and a feed store are stocked with handicrafts and artful, designer clothing at Issaquah's **Gilman Village** (317 Northwest Gilman Boulevard; 206-462-0594). Among the 40-plus shops clustered in these historic structures is **Northwest Gallery of Fine Woodworking** (206-391-4221), owned by 32 woodworkers and stocked with handicrafts such as boxes, toys, furniture, custom cabinetry and screens. **Made in Washington** (206-392-4819) handles pottery, specialty food and wine, dinnerware and wood carvings.

Satisfy your sweet tooth at **Boehm's Candies** (255 Northeast Gilman Boulevard, Issaquah; 206-392-6652), where hundreds of chocolates are hand-dipped every day. You can tour the factory (reservations are advisable; this is a popular spot) and watch the skilled workmanship that goes into making candies of this quality.

SEATTLE EAST NIGHTLIFE

Bellevue has the best pickings for nightlife in Seattle East. At **Papagayo's Cantina and Eatery** (2239 148th Avenue Northeast, Bellevue; 206-641-6666), you'll enjoy Top-40 deejay dance music. Cover.

Daniel's Broiler (Bellevue Place, 10500 Northeast 8th Avenue, Bellevue; 206-462-4662) has a jazz guitarist on Monday and piano Tuesday through Saturday, as well as a Sunday jazz showcase.

The **New Jake O'Shaughnessey's** (401 Bellevue Square, Bellevue; 206-455-5559) is a sports bar with four televisions in the lounge.

With a welcoming fireplace, the **West Coast Bellevue Hotel** (625 116th Avenue Northeast; 206-455-9444) features live piano music Monday to Friday during happy hour in the lounge.

For progressive, industrial or Top-40 music, make your way to **The Backdoor** (2207 Bel-Red Road, Redmond; 206-746-7918). There's dancing Friday and Saturday. Cover.

Good things come in small packages, and the **Village Theater** (303 Front Street North, Issaquah; 206-392-2202) proves it. The local casts here will tackle anything, be it Broadway musicals, dramas or comedy.

SEATTLE EAST BEACHES AND PARKS

Kelsey Creek Park (13204 Southeast 8th Place, Bellevue; 206-455-6885) is a 130-acre farm with an old homestead and farm animals in the barnyard. There are hiking trails, jogging paths, wooded glens, a creek and an 1888 log cabin.

A former Catholic seminary, **Saint Edwards State Park** (206-823-2992) still exudes the peace and quiet of a theological retreat across its 316 heavily wooded acres and 3000 feet of Lake Washington shoreline. Except for a handful of former seminary buildings, the park is mostly natural, laced by miles of informal trails. To reach the beach (no lifeguard), take the wide path just west of the main seminary building. It winds three-fourths of a mile down to the shore, where you can wander left or right. Side trails climb up the bluff for the return loop. Facilities include picnic areas, a tennis court, soccer and baseball fields and an indoor pool year-round. The park is located on Lake Washington's eastern shore, between Kenmore and Kirkland on Juanita Drive Northeast at Northeast 145th Street.

The 520-acre **Marymoor County Park** (206-296-2964), a roomy preserve, is a delightful mix of archaeology and history, river and lake, meadows and marshes, plus an assortment of athletic fields. A one-mile footpath here leads to a lakeside observation deck, and there's access to the eight-mile Sammamish River Trail. The 1904 Marymoor Mansion houses a historical museum, with a pioneer windmill located nearby. There's no lack of facilities, which include picnic and play areas, baseball and soccer fields, tennis courts, a model-airplane airport, bicycle velodrome with frequent races and an archaeological site. The park is located on Westlake–Sammamish Parkway (Route 901) off Route 520 at the north end of Lake Sammamish in Redmond.

Lake Sammamish State Park (206-455-7010), a popular, 431-acre park at the southern tip of Lake Sammamish near Issaquah, offers plenty to do, including swimming (no lifeguards), boating, picnicking, hiking and birdwatching along 6858 feet of lake shore and around the mouth of Issaquah Creek. Look for eagles, hawks, great blue heron, red-wing blackbirds, northern flickers, grebes, kingfishers, killdeer, buffleheads, widgeon and Canadian geese. There are also soccer fields and a jogging trail. Located at East Lake Sammamish Parkway Southeast and Southeast 56th Street, two miles north of Route 90 in Issaquah (15 miles east of Seattle) via Exit 17.

Luther Burbank County Park (206-296-4232) is set at the northeast corner of Mercer Island in Lake Washington. This little jewel presents some 3000 feet of shoreline to explore along with marshes, meadows and woods. You can tour the entire 77-acre site on a loop walk. There are picnic areas, tennis courts and an amphitheater with summer concerts. Fishing is good from the pier for salmon, steelhead, trout and bass. There's a beach for swimming, with a summer lifeguard. The park entrance is at 84th Avenue Southeast and Southeast 24th Street, via the Island Crest Way exit from Route 90.

Gene Coulon Beach Park (206-235-2568), a handsomely landscaped site at the south tip of Lake Washington, is most notable for the loads of attractions within its 55 acres: one-and-a-half miles of lakeside path, the wildfowl-rich estuary of John's Creek and a "nature islet," a lagoon enclosed by the thousand-foot floating boardwalk of "Picnic Gallery," a seafood restaurant and interesting architecture reminiscent of old-time amusement parks. A logboom-protected shoreline includes a fishing pier. There's a boat harbor with an eight-lane boat launch and ramp and a bathing beach with summer lifeguard. The park is bordered by Lake Washington Boulevard North in Renton, north of Route 405 via Exit 5 and Park Avenue North.

The Sporting Life

SPORTFISHING

Salmon is the Sound's most famous fish, but scores of other species make sportfishing a signature attraction here. A combination of migratory and "resident" stocks offer angling for Chinook and Coho almost year-round. And when salmon fishing slows, you can try your luck for some 200 types of bottom-fish that also populate these waters—colorful fellows like the Red Irish Lord and copper rock fish, as well as greenling, halibut and many varieties of cod.

The Edmonds Marina, just across the Sound, is home to the West Coast's largest fleet of charter vessels. To sign up for a Seattle charter trip (usually all day, $50 and up) call **Ballard Salmon Charters** (Shilshole Marina, Seattle; 206-789-6202); **Andy's Salmon Charters** (15254 Dayton Avenue North, Seattle; 206-365-3281); **Capt. Coley's Charters** (1053-B Avenue, Edmonds; 206-778-4110); and **All Seasons Charter Service** (Port of Edmonds, Edmonds; 206-743-9590).

SEA KAYAKING AND SMALL BOATING

In a city rich in waterways and boating, Lake Union just north of downtown Seattle offers a good sampler of small boats for rent, including sea kayaks. Novices may want to try their first paddle on the lake's calmer waters before taking to the real "sea." For instruction and rentals, try **Northwest Outdoor Center** (2100 Westlake Avenue North; 206-281-9694). Another place for kayak rentals is **Kayak Tours/Outdoors Odysseys** (12003 23rd Avenue, Seattle; 206-361-0717). For sailboats, stop by **Sailboat Rentals and Yacht Charters Inc.** (2046 Westlake Avenue North; 206-632-3302). For classic wooden rowing dories, see the **Center for Wooden Boats** (1010 Valley Street; 206-382-2628). To rent a "kicker boat" for do-it-yourself sportfishing, you'll have to leave the lake. Check out **Seacrest Boat House** (1660 Harbor Avenue Southwest, West Seattle; 206-932-1050).

SCUBA DIVING

Puget Sound's hundreds of miles of shoreline, scores of public beaches, extraordinary marine life and numerous underwater parks offer considerable opportunities for diving. But the Sound's average temperature of around 55 degrees means wetsuits are *de rigeur*, and full scuba gear is the frequent choice of divers. Of the many exciting dive spots in the area, one standout is Bracket's Landing Underwater Park in Edmonds. Numerous dive shops with equipment rentals and lessons are located around major population centers. Some of the bigger outfitters include **Underwater Sports Inc.**, with shops in Seattle (10545 Aurora Avenue North; 206-362-3310), Bellevue (12003 Northeast 12th Street; 206-454-5168), Federal Way (34428 Pacific Highway South; 206-874-9387) and Edmonds (264 Railroad Avenue; 206-771-6322); **Lighthouse Diving Centers**, with shops in Seattle (8215 Lake City Way Northeast; 206-524-1633), Lynnwood (5421 Southwest 196th Street; 206-771-2679) and Midway (24860 Pacific Highway South; 206-839-6881); and **Northwest Sports Divers Inc.** (8030 Northeast Bothell Way, Bothell; 206-487-0624). In Bellevue, **Silent World** (13600 Northeast 20th Street;

206-747-8842) is the place to go. In Kirkland, try **American Sport Diver** (12630 120th Avenue Northeast; 206-821-7200).

GOLF

Greater Seattle boasts nearly a score of private golf courses and two-score public courses. Consider **Jackson Park Golf Club** (1000 Northeast 135th Street; 206-363-4747); **Jefferson Park Golf Club** (4101 Beacon Avenue South; 206-762-4513); and **West Seattle Golf Course** (4470 35th Avenue Southwest; 206-935-5187). Some better public courses outside Seattle include **The Classic Golf Course** (Spanaway; 206-847-4440); **Capitol City Golf Club** (Yelm Highway, Olympia; 206-491-5111); **North Shore Golf Course** (Federal Way, Tacoma; 800-447-1375); and **Tall Chief Public Golf Course** (Fall City; 206-222-5911).

TENNIS

Seattle alone has some 60 parks and other sites with tennis courts, about two dozen of them lighted. The region offers nearly 600 courts at perhaps 200 sites. Given the city's unreliable weather, you may be looking for an indoor court. Try the **Seattle Tennis Center** (2000 Martin Luther King Jr. Way South; 206-684-4764).

HORSEBACK RIDING

Equestrians will find a good selection of horse ranches, riding academies and stables scattered throughout this region. One of the best places for a ride is **Bridle Trails State Park** in Bellevue (off Route 405, Exit 17;

TAKE ME OUT TO THE BALL GAME

Seattlites are solid fans of their teams. The Mariners play baseball April through September at the Kingdome (201 South King Street; 206-628-0888). Also in the Kingdome, the Seahawks football team kicks off August through December (206-827-9766 or 827-9777). The SuperSonics basketball team shoots hoops from November through April at the newly renovated Seattle Center Coliseum (305 Harrison Street; 206-283-3865). In the minor leagues, the Thunderbirds hockey team plays from September to May at Seattle Center Arena (206-728-9124).

College football takes place in Husky Stadium on the University of Washington campus (Montlake Boulevard; 206-543-2200).

206-455-7010). Crisscrossed with 28 miles of riding trails used mainly by local riders, the park has no rental mounts.

Another popular location is Tiger Mountain State Forest near Issaquah. Saddle up at **Tiger Mountain Outfitters** (24508 Southeast 133rd Street, Issaquah; 206-392-5090). Another east-of-Seattle outfitter is **Aqua Barn Ranch** (15227 Southeast Renton-Maple Valley Highway, Renton; 206-255-4618).

BICYCLING

Often praised in national media as the capital of bicycle commuting, Seattle also is friendly to the recreational cyclist. The three-mile loop around **Green Lake** is the most leisurely and rich in recreational detours.

The nine or so gentle miles between Seward and Washington parks along **Lake Washington Boulevard South** offer wonderful views of the lake. Best long-distance path is the **Burke-Gilman Trail**, stretching north 12 level miles from Gas Works Park on Lake Union, through the university campus, past lovely neighborhoods next to Lake Washington and on to Logboom Park at the lake's northern tip.

Just as easygoing as the Burke-Gilman Trail, but quite rural, is the eight-mile-long **Sammamish River Trail** beginning farther east in Redmond's Marymoor Park. It winds north past the **Château Ste. Michelle Winery** before linking with the Burke-Gilman in Bothell to create a city center to farmlands tour.

The **Alki Bike Route** in West Seattle offers six miles of shoreline pedaling—half on separated bike paths—and changing views of the city, Sound and mountains from Seacrest Park to Lincoln Park.

Pedal past Puget Sound parks, beaches and the bustling Edmonds port, home of the largest charter fleet on the West Coast, on the three-mile **Edmonds Waterfront Trail** running between Edmonds Underwater Park and Deer Park Reserve.

For a free *Seattle Bicycling Guidemap*, call 206-684-7584. For countywide information, call the King County Bike Hotline (206-296-7433).

BIKE RENTALS   Rental shops are spotted near good pedaling. Try the **Alki Bicycle Company** (2611 California Avenue Southwest; 206-938-3322) in West Seattle; **Gregg's Green Lake Cycle** (7007 Woodlawn Avenue Northeast; 206-523-1822) in the University of Washington area; and **The Bicycle Center** (4529 Sand Point Way Northeast; 206-523-8300) near the Burke-Gilman Trail.

HIKING

Nearly every park mentioned in the "Beaches and Parks" sections of this chapter offers at least a few miles of hiking trail through forest or along a stream or beach. Some are outstanding, such as Discovery Park in Seattle.

There's a visitors information center on the baggage level of Sea–Tac International Airport (206-433-5218).

DOWNTOWN SEATTLE TRAILS   For short strolls in downtown Seattle, try **Freeway Park** and the grounds of the adjoining Washington State Convention Center (.5 mile) and **Myrtle Edwards** and **Elliott Bay parks** (1.25 miles) at the north end of the downtown waterfront. Just across Elliott Bay, West Seattle offers about four miles of public shoreline to walk around Duwamish Head and Alki Point.

SEATTLE NORTH TRAILS   The **Burke-Gilman Trail** (12 miles) extends from Gas Works Park in Seattle all the way to Logboom Park in Kenmore.

The **Shell Creek Nature Trail** (.5 mile) in Edmond's Yost Park off Main Street is an easy walk along a stream. Contact Edmonds Parks and Recreation (700 Main Street; 206-771-0230) for a guide to the area.

SEATTLE EAST TRAILS   Three foothills peaks nicknamed the "Issaquah Alps" (Cougar Mountain County Park, Squaw Mountain State Park and Tiger Mountain State Forest) south of Issaquah (about 15 miles east of Seattle) include miles and miles of trail and road open to hikers year-around. Cougar Mountain Regional Wildland Park (206-296-4281) is the best bet for visitors. Call for trail maps. Another good resource is the **Issaquah Alps Trail Club** (206-328-0480), which publishes several hiking guidebooks and offers excursions, group hikes and general hiking information. One representative hike is the **West Hiker Trail**, which meanders up the foothills for stunning aerial views. Leave Route 90 at the High Point exit (the first exit east of Issaquah) and you will see the small parking lot where the trailhead is located.

Transportation

BY CAR

Seattle lies along Puget Sound east of the Olympic Peninsula in the state of Washington. **Route 5** enters Seattle from Olympia and Tacoma to the south and from Everett from the north. **Route 90** from eastern Washington goes near Snoqualmie and through Bellevue on its way into Seattle. **Route 405** serves the Eastside suburban communities of Bellevue, Kirkland and Redmond. **Route 169** leads from Route 405 southeast of Renton to Maple Valley, Black Diamond and Enumclaw.

BY AIR

About 20 miles south of downtown Seattle is **Seattle–Tacoma International Airport**, also called Sea–Tac, which is served by Aeroflot, Air B.C., Air Canada, Alaska Airlines, American Airlines, America West Airlines, British Airways, Canadian Regional Airlines, China Eastern Airlines, Continental Airlines, Delta Air Lines, EVA (Evergreen), Harbor Airlines, Hawaiian Airlines, Horizon Air, Mark Air, Northwest Airlines, Trans World Airlines, Thai Airways International, SAS, United Airlines, USAir and several smaller charter airlines.

BY FERRY

The **Washington State Ferry System** (206-464-6400) serves Seattle, Port Townsend, Tacoma, Southworth, Vashon Island, Bainbridge Island, Bremerton, Kingston, Edmonds, Mukilteo, Clinton, the San Juan Islands and Sidney, B.C. Most are car ferries. The **Victoria Clipper** passenger catamaran service (206-448-5000) operates daily trips between Seattle and Victoria, B.C. Ferry service between Seattle and Victoria on the 190-car, 900-passenger *Queen of Bandy* is offered by **Victoria Line** (604-480-5555) from mid–May to mid–September.

BY TRAIN

Rail service in and out of Seattle is provided by **Amtrak** (800-872-7245) on the "Empire Builder," the "Coast Starlight" and the "Pioneer." Call for more information on connections from around the country.

BY BUS

Greyhound Bus Lines (800-231-2222) serves Seattle. The terminal is at 8th Avenue and Stewart Street.

SEA-TAC UPGRADE

Three renovated concourses opened at Sea–Tac Airport in late 1992. Now longer, wider and brighter, they're filled with Northwest touches—rich woods, skylights, the greens and blues of Puget Sound. A selection of art, including a dramatic canoe sculpture, is on display. The $79 million project was underwritten by the airline tenants.

Parking space has increased, but for quick trips into the terminal, it's best to use the third-floor Express Metered Parking area.

You can ride Seattle buses free in the downtown area, from Battery to Jackson streets and from the waterfront to Sixth Avenue and Route 5.

CAR RENTALS

Most major car-rental businesses have offices at Seattle–Tacoma International Airport. Rental agencies include **Avis Rent A Car** (800-331-1212), **Budget Rent A Car** (800-527-0700), **Dollar Rent A Car** (800-800-4000), **Hertz Rent A Car** (800-654-3131) and **Thrifty Car Rental** (800-367-2277) and **XtraCar Discount Rentals** (800-227-5397) offers low rates and shuttle service to the airport.

PUBLIC TRANSPORTATION

Bus transportation provided by **Metro Transit** (206-553-3000) is free in downtown Seattle. Metro Transit provides service throughout the Seattle–King County area.

Waterfront Streetcar trolleys (206-553-3000) run along the waterfront from Seattle's historic Pioneer Square to Pier 70.

The **Monorail** (206-441-6038) is 30 years old and still going. Deemed transportation for the future, the Monorail was built for the 1962 World's Fair. It runs between downtown and the Seattle Center every 15 minutes.

TAXIS

In the greater Seattle area are **Checker Cab** (206-622-1234), **Farwest Taxi** (206-622-1717), **North End Taxi** (206-363-3333) and **Yellow Cab** (206-622-6500).

FIVE

Southern Puget Sound

First-time visitors to southern Puget Sound may find that it's the constantly changing geography that's the region's most memorable and striking feature. On a map, southern Puget Sound looks like a fistful of bony fingers clawing at the earth. This maze of inlets, peninsulas and islands presents plentiful saltwater access and invites days of poking around.

What nature created here, partly by the grinding and gouging of massive lowland glaciers, is a complex mosaic. From the air, visitors arriving at Sea–Tac Airport see the green-blue tapestry of meandering river valleys weaving between forested ridges, the rolling uplands dotted by lakes giving way to Cascade foothills and distant volcanoes, the intricate patterns of southern Puget Sound's island-studded inland sea.

From on high, it seems almost pristine, but a closer look reveals a sobering overlay of manmade changes. Just as Seattle's downtown is becoming "Manhattanized," the greater southern Puget Sound region is being "Los Angelesized"—with the birth of a freeway commuter culture stretching all the way south to Olympia. Some commuters even make the daily trip to Seattle by ferry from Bainbridge Island to the west (not a bad way to go if you have to commute). Farmlands and wetlands, forests and meadows, are giving way to what are often poorly planned, hastily built housing tracts, roads and shopping centers.

For the traveler, such rapid growth means more traffic and longer lines for the ferry; more-crowded campgrounds, parks and public beaches; busier bikeways and foot trails; more folks fishing and boating and clam digging. Parking can be hard to find at times, and expensive.

But don't despair. South of the heart of Seattle you'll still find a wealth of parks and wilderness, waterways and beaches. With an ample

---

Today, Tacoma is Washington's third-largest city, with a population of 177,500.

---

array of outdoor activities, southern Puget Sound serves as Seattle's back door to the wilderness.

To the southwest of Seattle, the Tacoma/Olympia region is rich in history, parks, waterfalls and cultural landmarks. Tacoma features numerous architectural gems; nearby villages like Gig Harbor are ideal for daytrippers. One of the nation's prettier capital cities (and here you may have thought Seattle was the capital of Washington!), Olympia is convenient to the wildlife refuges of southern Puget Sound, as well as to Native American monuments and petroglyphs.

Despite a lingering mill-town reputation, Tacoma, the city on Commencement Bay, has experienced a lively rejuvenation in recent years and offers visitors some first-rate attractions. Before the Alaska Gold Rush thrust Seattle into prominence at the turn of the century, Tacoma was Puget Sound's leading city. Charles Wright, president of the Great Northern Railroad, chose it as the western terminus of his railroad, and he wanted more than a mill town at the end of his line. Some of the best architects of the day were commissioned to build hotels, theaters, schools and office buildings.

Venture west of Seattle across Puget Sound and you'll find some rare treasures—such as a company town operating in the time-honored manner, a fascinating Indian cultural show, a marine-science center and inns that look like they were created for a James Herriott book. From Bainbridge Island and the other islands of southern Puget Sound west to Hood Canal, this is also a region rich in parks and natural areas. While you're here, be sure to tour the Kitsap Peninsula, explore Bremerton's Naval Heritage and check out the area's many parks.

Tacoma and Olympia Area

Located 30 miles south of Seattle on Route 5, Tacoma jealously protects its treasure of turn-of-the-century architecture in a pair of historic districts on both sides of Division Avenue overlooking Commencement Bay. The 1893 **Old City Hall** (South 7th and Commerce streets) was modeled after Renaissance Italian hill castles. The 1889 **Bostwick Hotel** (South 9th Street and Broadway) is a classic example of a triangular Victorian "flatiron."

The restored **Pantages Theater** (901 Broadway; 206-591-5894), designed by Marcus Priteca in 1918, is a classic of the vaudeville circuit (Mae West, W. C. Fields, Will Rogers and Houdini all performed here) and offers dance, music and theater productions.

Without a doubt, Tacoma's prettiest garden spot is the **W. W. Seymour Botanical Conservatory** (316 South G Street; 206–591–5330), a graceful Victorian domed conservatory constructed at the turn of the century with over 12,000 panes of glass. Inside are exotic tropical plants, including bird–of–paradise, ornamental figs, cacti and bromeliads; seasonal displays of flowers; and a fish pond with waterfall.

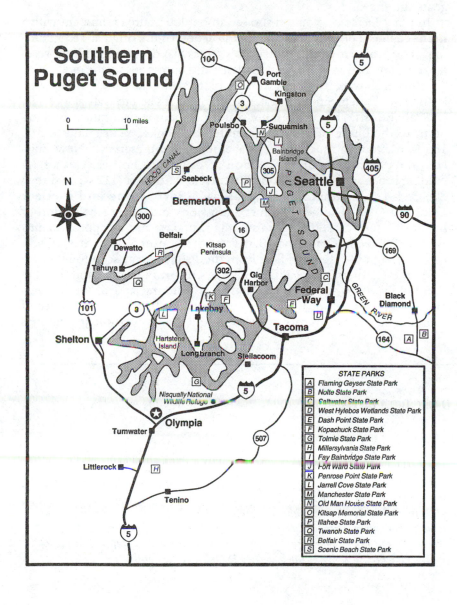

Southern Puget Sound

0   10 miles

N

HOOD CANAL

PUGET SOUND

GREEN RIVER

Port Gamble
Kingston
Poulsbo
Suquamish
Bainbridge Island
Seabeck
Seattle
Bremerton
Belfair
Dewatto
Kitsap Peninsula
Tahuya
Gig Harbor
Federal Way
Black Diamond
Lakebay
Shelton
Hartstene Island
Longbranch
Steilacoom
Nisqually National Wildlife Refuge
Tumwater
Olympia
Littlerock
Tenino

104
5
3
5
305
405
300
90
16
169
302
101
9
5
164
507
5

	STATE PARKS
A	Flaming Geyser State Park
B	Nolte State Park
C	Saltwater State Park
D	West Hylebos Wetlands State Park
E	Dash Point State Park
F	Kopachuck State Park
G	Tolmie State Park
H	Millersylvania State Park
I	Fay Bainbridge State Park
J	Fort Ward State Park
K	Penrose Point State Park
L	Jarrell Cove State Park
M	Manchester State Park
N	Old Man House State Park
O	Kitsap Memorial State Park
P	Illahee State Park
Q	Twanoh State Park
R	Belfair State Park
S	Scenic Beach State Park

The **Washington State Historical Society Museum** occupies the 1891 Ferry Museum building (315 North Stadium Way, 206-593-2830) and has a respected collection of Northwest Indian art.

A treat for both kids and adults is **Point Defiance Park** (Pearl Street off Ruston Way), set on a sloping peninsula above the south Puget Sound shore. This 700-acre urban park has an outstanding zoo and aquarium with a Pacific Rim theme. You can watch the fish from above or through underwater viewing windows. The zoo has penguins, beluga whales, polar bears, an elephant barn and a farm where city children can pet goats and sheep.

In Point Defiance, you can also see an outdoor railroad museum with a steam engine; Fort Nisqually, a reconstruction of the original 1833 Hudson's Bay Company post; a children's fantasy land; rhododendron, rose, Japanese and native Northwest gardens; and numerous scenic overlooks. A good beach walk is at the base of the bluff edging the park, heading west from Owen Beach. Since the water is swift here, it's best to walk at low tide.

Steilacoom, about five miles south of Tacoma, is a quiet counterpoint to the bustle of the city. Founded by Yankee sea captains in the 1850s, it exudes a museumlike peacefulness and preserves a New England look among its fine collection of clapboard houses. Get a self-guiding brochure at **Steilacoom Historical Museum** (112 Main Street; 206-584-4133). Don't miss the **Nathaniel Orr Home and Pioneer Orchard** (1811 Rainier Avenue; admission) and its nice collection of handmade furniture. (Open on summer Sundays and by appointment.) At the 1895 **Bair Drugstore** (Lafayette Street near Wilkes Street), you can order an old-fashioned float from the 1906-vintage soda fountain.

At the southern tip of Puget Sound, **Olympia**'s state capitol dome rises boldly as you approach on Route 5, a tempting landmark for travelers and an easy detour from the busy freeway. But this community of some 35,800 offers visitors more to peruse than government buildings

---

THE BEST BOAT-WATCHING GIG—HARBOR, THAT IS

Gig Harbor across the Tacoma Narrows off Route 16 is a classic Puget Sound small town. The community that arose around this somewhat-hidden harbor was founded as a fishing village by Croatians, Slavs and Austrians. Gig Harbor still looks like a haven for anglers, but today you're more likely to see every sort of pleasure craft here; it's one of the best boat-watching locales on Puget Sound. The tight harbor entrance funnels boats single-file past the dockside taverns and cafés where you can watch the nautical parade. Or, you can head to **Rent-A-Boat** *(off North Harborview Drive; 206-858-7341) and join the flotilla.*

One of the pioneer houses located in Tumwater Historical Park was built in 1860 by Nathaniel Crosby III (Bing Crosby's grandfather).

and monuments. Nevertheless, the capitol campus may be the best place to begin your explorations.

You can take a guided tour through the marbled halls of the Romanesque **Legislative Building** (360-586-8687) and see other buildings on the grounds—**Temple of Justice**, **Governor's Mansion** and **State Library**. The nearby **State Capitol Museum** (211 West 21st Avenue; 360-753-2580) includes a fine collection of Northwest Coast Indian artifacts.

Downtown, the handsomely restored **Old Capitol** (7th Avenue and Washington Street across from stately Sylvester Park) will catch your eye with its fanciful architecture. But most of downtown is a potpourri of disparate attractions—the new **Washington Center for the Performing Arts** (512 Washington Street Southeast; 360-753-8586), galleries, the **Capitol Theater** (5th Avenue and Washington Street) with its old films and local theater and a bit of bohemia along Fourth Avenue West.

Percival Landing (foot of State Avenue at Water Street) is an inviting, harborside park with observation tower, kiosks with historical displays, picnic tables, cafés and boardwalks next to acres of pleasure craft. For a longer walk, head south on Water Street, cross Fourth and Fifth avenues, then turn west and follow the sidewalk next to the Deschutes Parkway (or get in your car and drive) around the park-dotted shores of manmade **Capitol Lake**, which is two-and-a-half miles from the town of Tumwater.

Tumwater marks the true southern end of Puget Sound. Before Capitol Lake was created, the Sound was navigable all the way to the Deschutes River. **Tumwater Historical Park** (360-754-4160), at the meeting of river and lake, is rich in both history and recreation. Down by the river, you can fish, launch a canoe, have a picnic, explore fitness and hiking trails, watch birds in reedy marshes and see more historical exhibits. Across the river, a handsome, six-story brick brew house built in 1906 marks an early enterprise that lives on in a 1933 brewery a few hundred yards south.

Located ten miles south of Olympia are **Mima Mounds** (Wadell Creek Road, Littlerock; 360-753-3410), an unusual group of several hundred hillocks spread across 120 acres. Scientists think they could have been created by glacial deposits or even, believe it or not, giant gophers. A self-guided interpretive trail offers a close look at this geological oddity.

Howl with the wolves at **Wolf Haven** (3111 Offut Lake Road, Tenino; 360-264-4695; admission) southeast of Olympia. The 60-acre refuge shelters about 40 gray wolves. Guides give tours daily in summer and on weekends in other months. On summer weekends, visitors gather around a campfire for singing, storytelling and joining in the wolves' howls.

TACOMA AND OLYMPIA AREA LODGING

The **Sheraton Tacoma Inn** (1320 Broadway Plaza, Tacoma; 206-572-3200, 800-325-3535, fax 206-591-4105) is an elegant hotel next to the Tacoma Convention Center. The 319 rooms have a contemporary decor and most have views of Mt. Rainier or Commencement Bay. The concierge levels (24th and 25th floors) serve complimentary continental breakfast and late afternoon hors d'oeuvres. Deluxe.

On a hillside overlooking Puget Sound, **The Pillars** (6606 Soundview Drive, Gig Harbor; 206-851-6644) offers views of Mt. Rainier and Vashon Island. The gracious home has three attractive rooms, two with water views and one giving a bird's-eye look at the garden. Guests may play the piano in the large living room, relax and read by the stone fireplace, swim in the covered heated pool or soak in the covered jacuzzi. The hosts offer a warm welcome but don't intrude on their visitors' privacy. Their breakfast includes home-baked breads. Deluxe.

No Cabbages Bed and Breakfast (7712 Goodman Drive Northwest, Gig Harbor; 206-858-7797) is a comfortable, old-fashioned beach house built against a wooded hillside. It has two guest rooms, which have their own entrance and share a bath. They feature knotty-pine walls and great views of the deck terrace and harbor. A third, moderately priced room is open in the summer. The house is filled with eclectic art and interesting conversation. The innkeeper serves an outstanding breakfast. Budget.

The **Harbinger Inn** (1136 East Bay Drive, Olympia; 360-754-0389) is a restored, 1910 mansion with period antiques and a manicured lawn and garden. The living room, a first-floor porch with wicker furniture and a second-floor veranda overlook the marina, capitol building and

---

TUMTUM TUMWATER FALLS

*South of Olympia in Tumwater, follow Deschutes Parkway south to **Tumwater Falls Park** (not to be confused with Tumwater Historical Park), where the main attraction is the namesake falls, twisting and churning through a rocky defile. Feel the throb of water reverberating through stream-side footpaths. Listen to its sound, which the Indians called "Tumtum." You'll find lovely walking next to the river and plenty of history in the headquarters exhibit, including an Indian petroglyph and a monument recounting the travails of the first permanent settlement north of the Columbia River, which located here in 1845.*

the Olympic Mountains. Two of the four well-furnished rooms also have views. The owners serve a continental breakfast and lend bicycles, as this is a choice area for bicycling. Moderate.

High above Capitol Lake, on a grassy bluff with a view of the man-made lake and capitol dome, is the **Quality Inn Westwater** (2300 Evergreen Park Drive, Olympia; 360-943-4000, 800-551-8500, fax 360-357-6604). Popular with business and government travelers, it has commodious rooms with practical furnishings, a coffee shop, a lounge, a restaurant overlooking the lawns and water, and an outdoor swimming pool. Waterside rooms have the best views and are the quietest. Moderate.

Eight blocks from the Capitol, the **Ramada Governor House** (621 South Capitol Way, Olympia; 360-352-7700, 800-228-2828, fax 360-943-9349) is the latest version of a vintage downtown hotel. Its 122 rooms—some with views of the lake, harbor and Capitol building—are spread over eight floors. The hotel has above-standard furnishings, though most rooms are small, and a seasonal pool, exercise room and sauna. Priced in the moderate-to-deluxe range, it offers a number of packages and discounts.

The **Tyee Hotel** (500 Tyee Drive, Tumwater; 360-352-0511, 800-386-8933, fax 360-943-6448), three miles south of Olympia, is just off Route 5, but traffic noise is muted by walls. The 145-room, two-story Tyee has some resort amenities: 20 acres of grounds, a pool, a spacious lobby with a fireplace. The restaurant serves three meals a day, and the pastel rooms are well-furnished and comfortable. Moderate.

TACOMA AND OLYMPIA AREA RESTAURANTS

Do you enjoy good tempura? Then don't walk, run, to **Fujiya** (1125 Court C; 206-627-5319) in downtown Tacoma. Masahiro Endo, owner and chef, is a great entertainer with his knife at the sushi bar. The chicken sukiyaki is delicious. Moderate.

Sophistication and elegance describe the ambience at **Altezzo** (1320 Broadway Plaza; 206-572-3200) in the Sheraton Tacoma Hotel. There are superb views of Commencement Bay and Mt. Ranier from this gourmet Italian restaurant, located several stories above the city. Entrées include grilled pork loin chop stuffed with fontina cheese and artichoke hearts and cioppino, a hearty tomato-based stew of Dungeness crab, prawns, calamari, clams and other fresh seafood. Moderate to deluxe.

Mandarin and Szechuan fare is the specialty at **Charlie Chan's** (1009 Bridgeway Southwest, Tacoma; 206-572-3651), a family-run establishment where pictures of the owner with such celebrities as Jeff Smith (TV's Frugal Gourmet and a fellow Tacoman) are proudly displayed. Especially good are the Mongolian beef, vegetable dishes and sizzling rice soup. Budget to moderate.

One of those time-warp kind of restaurants that has had the same waitresses and clientele for decades, **Harbor Lights** (2761 Ruston Way,

---

*The 1911 **Union Depot** (Pacific Avenue and South 19th Street, Tacoma) was designed by the same architects who created New York's Grand Central Station.*

Tacoma; 206-752-8600) is where locals go for huge buckets of steamed clams, Dungeness crab, grilled salmon and other unpretentious seafood dishes. On sunny days, the best place to be is the open deck overlooking the water. Moderate.

If you've a hankering for barbecued ribs, fried chicken or catfish, try **Lessie's Southern Kitchen** (1716 6th Avenue, Tacoma; 206-627-4282). This is no antebellum mansion, just a plain, well-lighted café with good food. Just as appealing as the entrées are the greens, grits, yams, biscuits and melt-in-your-mouth corncakes served up alongside. Lessie is Southern stock herself, so you can count on this fare being authentic. Breakfast is served all day. Budget.

One of the best views in Olympia is from **Falls Terrace** (106 South Deschutes Way; 360-943-7830), through huge windows overlooking the Tumwater Falls on the Deschutes River. Start your meal with some Olympia oysters. The menu features pasta dishes, an excellent bouilla-baisse and an array of chicken, lamb and beef entrées. Desserts are more ice-cream theatrics than tasty morsels. Moderate.

Hidden across from the Farmer's Market is **Gardner's Seafood and Pasta** (111 West Thurston Street, Olympia; 360-786-8466). It is no secret to locals, who flock to this small restaurant. While seafood is the specialty here, there are several pastas that are very good, too. Try the pasta primavera. The Dungeness crab casserole is rich with cream, chablis and several cheeses. Homemade ice cream fills out the meal. Dinner only; moderate.

Patrons don't usually go for the water, but at **The Spar** (114 East 4th Avenue, Olympia; 360-357-6444) it truly is exceptional—because it comes from the restaurant's own artesian well. Once a blue-collar café, the restaurant features large photographs of loggers felling giant Douglas firs. On the menu are thick milkshakes, giant sandwiches, prime rib and Willapa Bay oysters. Budget to moderate.

Boaters, legislators, lobbyists, tourists and waterfront strollers congregate at the **Budd Bay Café** (525 North Columbia, Olympia; 360-357-6963) at Percival Landing. You can sit outside on the big deck and watch the boats come and go while you enjoy some of the specialties: fresh pasta and seafood, homemade soups, micro beers (including their own Budd Bay Ale), Northwest wines and desserts from the in-house bakery. An elaborate champagne brunch is served Sunday. Moderate.

The **Whale's Tail Dockside Deli and Espresso Bar** (501 North Columbia; 360-956-1928) is a bright little café on the boardwalk at Olympia's Percival Landing. Fast and friendly service, tasty homemade soups and sandwiches, and a fine view of Budd Bay have made this spot a favorite. Try the chunky muffins and espresso. Budget.

In a neighborhood less frequented by tourists, **La Petite Maison** (2005 Ascension Northwest, Olympia; 360-943-8812) is a charming little restaurant in a turn-of-the-century home. Seven tables fill the former living and dining rooms, with more tables on the enclosed porch. Classical music plays softly in a subdued atmosphere. Fresh Northwest foods are served, often under mild sauces. For a fine light lunch, try the homemade soup of the day with warm bread and a salad of mixed greens tossed with the delicately herbed house dressing. Moderate.

The **Urban Onion** (116 Legion Way, Olympia; 360-943-9242), known for its robust foods—omelettes, hearty lentil soup, thick sandwiches—has added some spirited touches to its menu. A dinner example is gorgonzola and walnut ravioli wrapped in spinach and roasted garlic and served in an asiago cream sauce. There are low-calorie entrées, such as the spicy chicken jambalaya as well as several vegetarian specials. The restaurant is part of a complex of shops downtown in the former Olympian Hotel. Budget to moderate.

TACOMA AND OLYMPIA AREA SHOPPING

Located in downtown Tacoma near the Tacoma Dome, **Freighthouse Square** (25th and D streets) is a historic railroad freighthouse now housing shops, galleries and eateries. Among the shops are **Lady Jayne's** (206-572-4368), a bookstore specializing in science fiction and comics; **Timber Lines Gift Gallery** (206-627-6377), which offers gift with a Northwest nature theme; and **The Silver Wreath** (206-6271650), where handcrafted silver jewelry is featured.

In the Proctor District in north Tacoma, you can find souvenirs, gifts and handmade clothing at the **Pacific Northwest Shop** (2702 North Proctor Street; 206-752-2242). Fine Irish imports are in stock at **The Harp & Shamrock** (2704 North Proctor Street; 206-752-5012). The **Old House Mercantile** (2717 North Proctor Street; 206-759-8850) offers a variety of gifts. Educational toys are found at **Teaching Toys** (2624 North Proctor Street; 206-759-9853). The **Washington State Historical Museum** (315 North Stadium Way; 206-593-2830) features gifts, jewelry, games and books.

Tacoma's best bookstores include **Fox Book Company** (737 St. Helens Street; 206-627-2223), **O'Leary's Books** (3828 Southwest 100th Street; 206-588-2503) and **Book Feire** (3818 North 26th Street; 206-759-4680).

For sportswear and outdoor gear in Tacoma, try **Sportco** (4602 East 20th Street; 206-922-2222) or the **Duffle Bag** (8207 South Tacoma Way; 206-588-4433).

In Gig Harbor, **The Beach Basket** (4102 Harborview Drive; 206–858–3008) features, of course, baskets and other gifts. Scandinavian utensils, books and gifts can be found at **Strictly Scandinavian** (7803 Pioneer Way; 206–851–5959). **Kelly's Toys & Gifts** (7806 Pioneer Way; 206–851–8697) features stuffed animals, games and handcrafted items. **Mostly Books** (3126 Harborview Drive; 206–851–3219) stocks books (you're kidding) and gift items.

In Olympia, contemporary women's clothing and accessories are found at **Juicy Fruits** (113 West 5th Avenue; 360–943–0572). **Olympic Outfitters** (407 East 4th Avenue; 360–943–1114) is housed in a restored, brick-and-metal building with a climbing wall inside and is stocked with everything from backpacking to waterskiing and cross-country ski gear.

TACOMA AND OLYMPIA AREA NIGHTLIFE

Pete's BBQ and Steak House (1602 South Mildred Street, Tacoma; 206–565–7427) has dancing every night to deejay-spun Top-40 or house music. **Christie's Lounge** (in the Best Western Executive Inn, 5700 Pacific Highway East, Fife; 206–922–0080) features live bands playing Top-40 music.

The **Tides Tavern** (2925 Harborview Drive; 206–858–3982) in Gig Harbor features live bands on weekends playing '50s and '60s rock and some rhythm-and-blues. Cover for live shows.

For Top-40 sounds in the Lakewood area, try **Leslie's Restaurant & Night Life** (9522 Bridgeport Way Southwest, Tacoma; 206–582–4118) with live bands. Also in the Lakewood area, **Leslie's Happy Days Diner** (11521 Bridgeport Way Southwest, Tacoma; 206–582–1531) has deejayed country-and-western music every night. The **Lakewood Bar & Grill** (10009 59th Avenue Southwest, Tacoma; 206–582–1196) features a deejay. Cover at all three clubs.

The **Columbia Street Pub** (200 West 4th Avenue, Olympia; 360–943–5575) offers a number of good, locally brewed beers and live jazz, bluegrass or Irish folk music.

TACOMA AND OLYMPIA AREA BEACHES AND PARKS

Northeast of Tacoma, **Green River Gorge** is less than an hour from downtown Seattle but is worlds away from the big city. The heart of the gorge covers only some six miles on the map but is so twisted into oxbows that it takes kayakers 14 river miles to paddle through it. Just 300 feet deep, the steep-walled gorge nevertheless slices through solid rock (shale and sandstone) to reveal coal seams and fossil imprints and inspire a fine sense of remoteness. State and county parks flank the gorge.

One is the **Green River Gorge Conservation Area** (206-931-3930), which includes six state parks and some 50 miles of hiking trails. Here, we highlight the two developed parks at the entrance and exit of the gorge and one nearby state park on a lake.

Flaming Geyser State Park (206-931-3930) was once a resort, but now this 667-acre park downstream from the exit of Green River Gorge offers ten miles of hiking trails and nearly five miles of riverbank. Pick up a trail map and brochure in the main parking lot. There are picnic and play areas, volleyball, horseshoe pits and kayaking for skilled paddlers; restaurants and groceries in Black Diamond. You can fish for steelhead in season (check posted regulations).

At **Kanaskat–Palmer State Park** (360-886-0148), there's lovely walking on riverside paths, especially in summer. Upstream from the entrance to Green River Gorge, the park's 320 acres offer camping, picnic areas, showers, as well as rafting and kayaking for experienced whitewater boaters. There's also fishing for steelhead in season (check posted regulations). The park is on Cumberland–Kanaskat Road off Southeast 308th Street, 11 miles north of Enumclaw and Route 410.

Surrounding Deep Lake, 117-acre **Nolte State Park** (360-825-4646) is famous for its huge Douglas firs, cedars and cottonwoods. A one-and-a-half-mile path circles the lake, taking you around nearly 7200 feet of shoreline and past the big trees; a separate nature trail interprets the forest. There's a minimal picnic area and fishing for trout, but no motorboats are permitted on the lake. You can also swim at the lake; however, there are no lifeguards. The park is on Veazie–Cumberland Road just south of Southeast 352nd Street, six miles north of Enumclaw and Route 410.

You'll share busy **Saltwater State Park** (206-764-4128) with lots of locals, nearly 800,000 visitors a year, so don't expect solitude. But among the park's 88 acres, you can revel in the fine views, enjoy some 1500 feet of shoreline and quiet woods with two miles of hiking trails. There are

---

BLACK DIAMOND

*Black Diamond (about 35 miles southeast of Seattle on Route 169) is an old coal-mining town with the odds and ends of its mining, logging and railroading history on display at the **Black Diamond Historical Society Museum** (Baker Street and Railroad Avenue; 360-886-1168), housed in an 1884 railroad depot. But the real reason most folks stop here—on their way to Mt. Rainier, the Green River Gorge or winter ski slopes—is the famous **Black Diamond Bakery** (32805 Railroad Avenue; 360-886-2741). At last count, the bakery and its wood-fired ovens produced around 30 varieties of bread, along with doughnuts and cookies.*

campsites, picnic and play areas and a concession stand. Swimming is tolerable in the saltwater tide flats at the south end of the beach. A sunken barge about 150 yards offshore from a prominent sandspit attracts a variety of fish and divers. The park is on Marine View Drive (Route 509), about halfway between Seattle and Tacoma, west of Route 5 via Exit 149.

West Hylebos Wetlands State Park (206-593-2206) offers a rare chunk of urban wetland tucked between industrialization and subdivisions. The 68-acre park provides examples of all sorts of wetland formations along a one-mile boardwalk trail—springs, streams, marshes, lakes, floating bogs and sinks. You'll also see remnants of an ancient forest, plentiful waterfowl, more than a hundred species of birds and dozens of mammals. The park is located on South 348th Street at 4th Avenue South, northeast of Tacoma just west of Route 5 and Exit 142.

Set on nearly 500 acres of forested wildland with 3300 feet of saltwater shoreline, **Dash Point State Park** (206-593-2206) manages to preserve a bit of solitude just outside Tacoma's city limits. Seven-and-a-half miles of trails ramble through mixed forest of second-growth fir, maple and alder. The park's beach is one of the few places on Puget Sound where you'll find enjoyable saltwater swimming (no lifeguard)—shallow waters in tide flats are warmed by the summer sun. Tides retreat to expose a beach front nearly a half-mile deep. There are campsites, picnic areas and showers. The park is located just northeast of Tacoma on Southwest Dash Point (Route 509).

Jutting dramatically into Puget Sound, the 700-acre **Point Defiance Park** (206-305-1000) is hailed by some as the finest saltwater park in the state, by others as the best city park in the Northwest. Here are primeval forests, some 50 miles of hiking trails, over three miles of public shoreline and enough other attractions to match almost any visitor's interests. Five

---

THE NISQUALLY NATIONAL WILDLIFE REFUGE

One of the last pristine river deltas in the United States can be found within the 3780 acres of **Nisqually National Wildlife Refuge** *(360-753-9467). The refuge's ecosystem is a diverse mix of conifer forest, deciduous woodlands, marshlands, grasslands and mudflats and the meandering Nisqually River (born in Mt. Rainier National Park). Here, the river mixes its fresh waters with the salt chuck of Puget Sound. An important stop for migratory wildfowl on the Pacific Flyway, the refuge also is home to mink, otter, coyote and over 200 kinds of birds and 125 species of fish. Trails thread the refuge; longest is the five-mile, dike-top loop that circles a pioneer homestead long since abandoned. There is also an education center. You'll find the refuge about 25 miles south of downtown Tacoma via Exit 114 from Route 5.*

The ferry to Tacoma from Vashon Island lands next to one of the city's highlights, splendid Point Defiance Park.

Mile Drive loops around the park perimeter with access to trails, forest, beach, attractions and grand overlooks of Puget Sound. The park offers picnic and play areas, tennis courts, a snack bar and concession stands, and a restaurant at the boathouse. You can fish from the pier at the boathouse or in a rented boat. The park is also known for its zoo and aquarium, particularly the shark tank. The entrance is on Pearl Street, off Ruston Way in Ruston.

Kopachuck State Park (206-265-3606) boasts lovely views across Carr Inlet toward the Olympic Mountains from its half-mile of shoreline (which also offers some low-tide clamming and fishing). Many cartop boaters launch from the beach near the park and paddle out to Cutts Island Marine State Park a half-mile away. For divers, there's an artificial reef in nine fathoms about 200 yards offshore that's designated as an underwater park. Picnic areas and campsites are available. The park is on Kopachuck Drive Northwest at Northwest 56th Street, about six miles west of Gig Harbor and Route 16.

Tolmie State Park (360-456-6464) offers a salt marsh with interpretive signs. The marsh separates 1800 feet of tide flats from forested uplands overlooking Nisqually Reach. The sandy beach is fine for wading or swimming; at low tides you may find clams. A two-and-a-half-mile perimeter hiking trail loops through the park's 106 acres. An artificial reef and three sunken barges 500 yards offshore and almost nonexistent current make the underwater park here popular with divers. There are picnic areas and showers. Located on Hill Road Northeast, northeast of Olympia via Exit 111 from Route 5.

Some 840 acres of primeval conifer forest and miles of foot trail are the big appeals at **Millersylvania State Park** (360-753-1519). But visitors also come to enjoy its 3300 feet of shoreline along Deep Lake, where you can swim, launch a small boat or fish for trout. There's a picnic area and a private resort across the lake. The park is located at Exit 95 just east of Route 5, ten miles south of Olympia.

Located 35 miles south of Tacoma is **Northwest Trek** (11610 Trek Drive East, Eatonville; 206-832-6117), a 600-acre nature preserve operated by the Metropolitan Park District of Tacoma, which provides close but safe encounters with grizzly bears and other wildlife. Walking along the five miles of trails of Northwest Trek, visitors are also likely to see bobcats, martens, wolverines, eagles and owls. In the park's Bear Exhibit, the largest in North America, grizzlies and black bears live in outdoor enclosures designed to mimic their natural habitats. There is also a Discovery Center where children can handle reptiles and observe bee and ant societies at work.

Bainbridge Island

A 35-minute ferry ride from Pier 52/Coleman Dock in Seattle will transport you to the tranquility of **Bainbridge Island** (pick up a self-guiding brochure with map, *A Downtown Guide to Bainbridge Island*, before boarding). You can easily explore the friendly town on foot, but bus service to the rest of the island is sparse and runs only during the morning and afternoon commute. You may want to bring your car to explore the island. In addition to shops and cafés, there are several art galleries, including a Gallery Walk on the second Thursday of the month.

The mile-long **waterfront footpath**, called **Walkabout**, which starts on your left as you leave the ferry landing, follows along the shoreline, over a bridge, past shipyards and hauled-out sailboats under repair to **Eagle Harbor Waterfront Park**. The park offers a madrone-shaded playground, fishing pier, boat launch and low-tide beach. Carry on to a ship chandler ("for all your boating needs") and a pair of marinas. Return as you came or make it a loop trip by walking up to **Winslow Way**, where you can stop for espresso or shop. If you tire of boutiques, step into **Winslow Hardware**, where the local folk come to chat and buy essential tools.

Bainbridge Island Winery (682 Route 305; 206-842-9463; open afternoons Wednesday to Sunday) offers a tasting room and picnic area. The Ferryboat White label is popular with visitors.

If you enjoy gardens, don't miss a tour of the famous **Bloedel Reserve** (7571 Northeast Dolphin Drive; 206-842-7631; admission). Once a private estate, the reserve has 150 acres of forest, meadows, ponds and a series of beautifully landscaped gardens. Reservations are required for a tour.

BAINBRIDGE ISLAND LODGING

Serenity and comfort in the countryside characterize **Bombay House** (8490 Northeast Beck Road; 206-842-3926), a 1907 Victorian set on a hilltop. The five-room bed and breakfast has moderate prices and a bright, cheery atmosphere. The rooms, which vary in size and decor, view the sea or the lavish flower and herb gardens.

The Beach Cottage (5831 Ward Avenue Northeast; 206-842-6081, 800-396-6081) is a complex of four cottages on a landscaped hillside above the water. The cottages have kitchens (with breakfast ingredients in the refrigerator), private decks, fireplaces and views of the Olympic Mountains, the Seattle skyline or the marina. They accommodate two to four people. Deluxe.

The town that used to be called Winslow is now known just as Bainbridge Island.

BAINBRIDGE ISLAND RESTAURANTS

Specializing in mesquite-grilled steaks and seafood, the **Island Grill** (321 High School Road Northeast; 206-842-9037) provides a pub-like setting with hardwood floors and a dark gray and burgundy color scheme. Among the popular dishes are hazlenut-encrusted halibut and linguine with smoked salmon. Moderate.

In a large Tudor house nestled in the trees is the **Pleasant Beach Grill** (4738 Lynwood Center Road Northeast; 206-842-4347). The white linen tablecloths and low lighting bespeak a comfortable island elegance. The chef specializes in Northwest seafood, but includes a couple of succulent chicken dishes, pastas and aged-beef entrées. The white fish in a curry sauce with mushrooms and red, green and yellow peppers comes recommended. Dinner only. Moderate.

What you won't find at the **Four Swallows** (481 Madison Avenue North; 206-842-3397), you can order at a standard restaurant. What you will find are exotic combinations of mouthwatering fare scribbled on a tablet in the foyer each evening. How about kiwi fruit, pears and feta cheese dipped in pine nuts and served with crackers and roasted garlic? The salads are tasty mixes of greens with flavorful dressings. Dinner only. Budget.

On a sunny day, a pleasant spot to relax with a beer and a sandwich or fish and chips is the deck at the **Madrona Café** (403 Madison Avenue South; 206-842-8339). The view from the deck above the water is always a delight, and it's only about five blocks from the ferry dock. The food is moderately priced, but high for what you get—stick with something simple and enjoy the view.

The cozy **Pegasus** (131 Parfitt Way; 206-842-3113) is a traditional coffeehouse with lots of reading material, conversation, freshly baked pastries and assorted coffees. Budget.

Walk into the **Streamliner Diner** (397 Winslow Way; 206-842-8595) and it's like stepping back into a midwestern diner. There are eight tables, a small bar and an open kitchen that serves up breakfast burritos, fried egg sandwiches, scrumptious omelettes and buttermilk waffles. Lunches include soups, salads and quiches. Breakfast and lunch only. Budget.

BAINBRIDGE ISLAND SHOPPING

The Landing (190 Madison Avenue North; 206-780-1162) is a huge cooperative gallery with over 100 booths for artwork, crafts, antiques and gifts, as well as artists' demonstrations and special events.

BAINBRIDGE ISLAND BEACHES AND PARKS

Fay Bainbridge State Park (206-842-3931) is a small park (17 acres), but it curls itself around a long sandspit to present some 1400 feet of shoreline. The only campground on Bainbridge Island is located here. Facilities also include picnic and play areas, a boat ramp, horseshoe pits and volleyball courts; the water is chilly for swimmers and there's no lifeguard. You'll find the park at Sunrise Drive Northeast and Lafayette Road at the northeast tip of Bainbridge Island.

Located at the south end of Bainbridge Island, **Fort Ward State Park** offers 137 acres of paths, forest and picnic sites, as well as a mile-long beach, for day-use visitors.

Kitsap Peninsula

Only an hour from the heart of Seattle, the Kitsap Peninsula is framed on the east side by Puget Sound and the west by Hood Canal. Historic company towns, naval museums and remote parks make this area a fine retreat from the city.

An interesting loop trip west of Seattle begins in the Navy town of **Bremerton**. Take the ferry or drive to Bremerton and, from here, you can explore some of the region's history, as well as the more remote reaches of southern Puget Sound.

The **Puget Sound Naval Shipyard** (Burwell Street and Pacific Avenue, near the ferry dock) in Bremerton is where you'll find the **Bremerton Naval Museum** (a half-block north of the ferry dock on Washington Avenue; 360-479-7447), which looks back to the days of Jack Tar and square-riggers. The best way to get here is the Washington State Ferry (cars and walk-ons; one hour) or the foot-ferry (50 minutes) from Seattle's Coleman Dock (Pier 52) through Rich Passage to Bremerton.

Docked along the Bremerton waterfront by the Navy shipyard is the **USS Turner Joy** (206-792-2457), a former Navy destroyer where the bridge, engine room and berth areas can be explored on self-guided tours.

Offshore from Bremerton on Blake Island is **Tilicum Village**, a huge cedar longhouse styled after the dwellings of the Northwest Coast Native Americans situated on the edge of a 475-acre forest preserve. On weekend nights from May 1 through October 31, the village offers traditional salmon bakes and performances by the Tilicum Village Dancers who have appeared in several episodes of the television series "Northern Exposure." Transportation to and from Tilicum Village is arranged through **Kitsap Harbor Tours** (206-377-8924), which offers departures from the Bremerton waterfront by the USS *Turner Joy*.

From Bremerton, Route 3 runs up the eastern side of the Kitsap Peninsula. Turn down Route 305 past Liberty Bay and you'll come to

The main attraction at the Puget Sound Naval Shipyard is the famous WWII battle-ship USS Missouri, on which the peace treaty ending the war with Japan was signed.

the charming town of **Poulsbo**. There are some wonderful samples of historic architecture on a **walking tour** of town; the **Poulsbo Chamber of Commerce** (19131 8th Avenue Northeast; 360-779-4848) can provide a guide map. At the **Marine Science Center** (18743 Front Street Northeast, Poulsbo; 360-779-5549; admission), you check out the various forms of marine life that inhabit the waters of southern Puget Sound; they even have a touch tank of friendly sea creatures.

A good place to learn about the region's Native American heritage is the town of **Suquamish**, southeast of Poulsbo. Chief Seattle and the allied tribes he represented are showcased at the **Suquamish Museum** (Route 305, Suquamish; 360-598-3311 ext. 422). There's an outstanding collection of photographs and relics, along with mock-ups of a typical Native American dwelling and the interior of a longhouse. Several award-winning video presentations are shown in a small theater.

Chief Seattle's Grave, set under a canopy of dugout canoes in a hillside graveyard overlooking Seattle (his namesake), is just a few miles down Suquamish Way. Follow the road signs.

The **Thomas Kemper Brewery** (22381 Foss Road Northeast; 360-697-1446), one mile north of Poulsbo off the road to Kingston, offers informal, 30-minute tours of the facility, has a small pub and beer garden with live music and sponsors a grand Oktoberfest celebration every year.

One of the West's last company towns, **Port Gamble** is a favored visitor stop. Located at the northern terminus of Route 3 and situated on a bluff at the intersection of Admiralty Inlet and Gamble Bay, this century-old community is owned by the Pope and Talbot lumber firm.

The town is home to about 150 sawmill workers and their families, who rent homes from the company. Picturesque frame houses, towering elms and a church with Gothic windows and a needle spire give the community a New England look. Don't miss the mock-ups of Captain Talbot's cabin and A. J. Pope's office at the **Pope and Talbot Historical Museum** (Rainier Avenue; 360-297-3341; admission) or the **Sea and Shore Museum** (360-297-2426) on the second floor of the 1853 **Port Gamble Country Store** (Rainier Avenue; 360-297-2623). Other historic homes and buildings are occupied by current Pope and Talbot employees, but can be viewed from the outside; a walking-tour guide can be obtained at the Country Store.

South of Bremerton is the **Longbranch Peninsula**, a showcase of southern Puget Sound's outdoor treasures. Quiet coves and lonely forests, dairy farms, funky fishing villages with quiet cafés, shellfish beaches and oyster farmers, a salmon hatchery, fishing piers and wharves all await leisurely exploration. Take Route 16 to Route 302, proceeding west until you reach Key Center. The **Key Peninsula Highway**, running south from this community, is the main road bringing you to most attractions.

To visit the hamlet of **Lakebay** on Mayo Cove, turn east from Peninsula Highway three-and-a-half miles south of Home (the town, not your Home Sweet) onto Cornwall Road and follow it to Delano Road. On the south side of the cove is **Penrose Point State Park** (360-884-2514) with 152 acres of forest, two miles of beaches, hiking trails, fishing, picnicking and camping. At the end of the highway is another bayside village, **Longbranch**, on the shores of Filucy Bay, one of the prettiest anchorages in these waters.

Hartstene Island (northeast of Shelton via Route 3 and Pickering Road) is connected to the mainland by a bridge, providing auto access to a quintessential southern Puget Sound island experience. Many of the island's public beaches are poorly signed, but **Jarrell Cove State Park** (at the foot of Wingert Road, off North Island Drive; 360-426-9226) and a marina on the other side of the cove are easily found at the island's north tip. You'll see plenty of boats from both sides of the cove, and at the park you can stroll docks, fish for perch, walk bits of beach or explore forest trails. Main roads loop the island's north end, or head for the far southern tip at Brisco Point with views overlooking Peale Passage and Squaxin Island.

The eastern shore of **Hood Canal** is a mere mile or two from the western side of the channel, but in character it's worlds apart. Beach access is limited, but views across the canal to the Olympic Mountains are splendid, settlements few and quiet and back roads genuine byways—few tourists ever get here. This is also where the canal bends like a fishhook to the east, called the "Great Bend."

To see the east shore in its entirety, begin at Belfair, leaving Route 3 for Route 300. At three miles, watch for Belfair State Park on the left. The road now narrows and traffic thins on the way to the modest resort town of Tahuya; shortly beyond, the canal makes its great bend. The road dives into dense forest, bringing you in about 11 miles to a T-junction; bear left, then left again to the ghost town of Dewatto. Take Dewatto Bay Road eastward out of town, then turn north and follow signs 12 miles to a left turn into the little town of Holly, or continue north 15 miles more to **Seabeck**, founded in 1856 as a sawmill town and popular today with anglers, scuba divers and boaters.

KITSAP PENINSULA LODGING

If you can afford the high tariff, a stay at the **Manor Farm Inn** (26069 Big Valley Road Northeast, Poulsbo; 360-779-4628, fax 360-779-4876) is like stepping onto the set of *All Creatures Great and Small*, complete with a working farm. Plush rooms are country cozy, and the food can't be

"Velkommen til Poulsbo" is an oft-repeated phrase in "Washington's Little Norway."

beat, but the best thing about this place is the chance to stroll among the calves, kittens, chickens, pigs, sheep, rabbits, doves and horses in the farm's white-fenced pastures. Or better still, the opportunity to pull on a pair of rubber boots and head to the quiet trout pond to drop a line and wait for a nibble. Ultra-deluxe; book well in advance.

Rooms at the Poulsbo's **Cypress Inn** (19801 7th Avenue Northeast; 360-697-2119, 800-752-9991, fax 360-697-2707), part of a small chain in the Northwest, are modern and comfortably furnished with big beds, satellite television, individual air conditioning and other basic amenities; a few are equipped with kitchenette or jacuzzi. Moderate.

KITSAP PENINSULA RESTAURANTS

Locals swear by the sandwiches and clam chowder at **Judith's Tearoom and Rose Café** (18820 Front Street Northeast, Poulsbo; 360-697-3449), but we found the staff to be abrupt to the point of rudeness. Anyway, try something from the daily dessert tray where the selections often include fruit, nut or cream pies, bread pudding and cheesecake. They also have homemade soups. The Black Forest soup is a meal to contend with—including cabbage, potatoes, mushrooms and German sausage. Lunch and formal tea. Budget.

The New Day Seafood Eatery (325 Hostmark Street Northeast, Poulsbo; 360-697-3183) is actually the outlet for the fresh catch brought in every day by the vessel *New Day* and features fast and inexpensive fish and chips (or clams, shrimp, scallops, oysters or chicken and chips). Diners choose from booths inside or picnic tables on the large deck overlooking Liberty Bay and the wharf. Lunch and dinner. Budget.

For ice-cream treats, head to the soda fountain at the **Poulsbo Drug Store** (18911 Front Street Northeast, Poulsbo; 360-779-2737).

KITSAP PENINSULA SHOPPING

Looking like a lane in some far-away Scandinavian hamlet, the main street of Poulsbo is lined with wonderful galleries and boutiques. You'll find paintings, pottery, weavings, cards, rosemaling, baskets, even food products created by local artists at the **Verksted Cooperative Gallery** (18884 Front Street Northeast; 360-697-4470), while **Potlatch Gallery** (18830-B Front Street Northeast; 360-779-3377) carries a fine selection of prints, glasswork, pottery, jewelry and Native American art.

For merchandise from the five Scandinavian countries, in Poulsbo visit **Five Swans** (18846 Front Street Northeast; 360-697-2005) or

Loretta's Gifts (18924 Front Street Northeast; 360-779-7171). For sweets, head to **Boehm's Chocolates** (18864 Front Street Northeast; 360-697-3318) and **Sluys Bakery** (18924 Front Street Northeast; 360-779-2798) for pastries and cookies.

KITSAP PENINSULA BEACHES AND PARKS

Manchester State Park (360-871-4065) is a one-time military installation overlooking Rich Passage. The park includes abandoned torpedo warehouses and interpretive displays explaining its role in guarding Bremerton Navy Base at the turn of the century. The park is infamous for its poison oak—stay on the two miles of hiking trails, or try the 3400 feet of beach. There are campsites and picnic areas. The rocks off Middle Point attract divers. Located on East Hilldale Road off Beach Drive, east of Port Orchard.

Old Man House State Park was once the site of a longhouse used as a meeting place by Chief Seattle and the Suquamish Indians. Check out the interpretive and historical displays at this day-use only park. A small, sandy beach overlooks the heavy marine traffic that cruises through Agate Passage. Located just north of Agate Pass off Route 104.

A private resort with beach access, **Point No Point Beach Resort** (8708 Northeast Point No Point Road; 360-638-2233) sits on the northern tip of the Kitsap Peninsula overlooking Admiralty Inlet and mid-Puget Sound. The swimming is good here, although the water is very cold, and the fishing is outstanding. The waters off the point teem with salmon, attracting anglers from the world over. Other sites of interest include the Point No Point Lighthouse and the 35-acre Point No Point Nature Park with trails, viewpoints for watching eagles and a beach for clam digging. Facilities offered are restrooms, showers, laundromat and picnic tables, plus four tent sites and 38 RV hookup sites. You can find boat rentals, launch and groceries nearby in Hansville.

Near Hansville on the northern tip of the Kitsap Peninsula, picturesque **Buck Lake County Park** (360-895-3895) is a good spot for quiet, contemplative fishing or a relaxing summer swim. There are picnic tables and playground, a bath house and boat launch. To get to the park, take Route 104 from Kingston to Hansville Road and follow it north.

Salisbury Point (360-895-3895) is a tiny six-acre park with a small stretch of saltwater beach next to Hood Canal Floating Bridge, but it offers views of the Olympic Mountains across the canal. Though camping here is very limited (in the parking lot, in a self-contained vehicle), this is the closest you'll come to accommodations near historic Port Gamble, just seven miles west. It's a good place to fish or swim and you'll find picnic shelters, a boat launch and playground. Turn left on Wheeler Road and follow the signs.

Washington State fishers catch more than 1.3 billion pounds of fish and seafood annually, more than half the nation's total edible catch.

Four miles south of Hood Canal Floating Bridge, **Kitsap Memorial State Park** (360-779-3205) is a 58-acre park that has a quiet beach well-suited for fishing and collecting oysters and clams. Between the canal and beach and playground facilities, there's plenty to keep the troops entertained, making this a good choice for family camping. There are showers, shelter, tables and stoves, boat moorage, playground with horseshoe pits and baseball diamond; some facilities are wheelchair accessible. From Kingston, take Route 104 (which turns into Bond Road) to Route 3, then go north until you reach the park.

Illahee State Park (360-478-6460) offers wooded uplands and 1700 feet of saltwater shoreline separated by a 250-foot bluff. A steep hiking trail connects the two park units. On the beach is a fishing pier; at the south end are tide flats for wading. There are campsites (no hookups), picnic area, baseball field, play area, horseshoe pits and high-tide boat ramp. The park is located at the east foot of Sylvan Way (Route 306) two miles east of Route 303 northeast of Bremerton.

Twanoh State Park (360-275-2222) has many of the amenities of a city park, but its 182 acres also include the forests, trails and camping of a more remote site. A two-mile hiking trail takes you through a thick forest of second-growth conifers next to Twanoh Creek, as well as a half-mile of saltwater beach to explore. Facilities offered here include picnic areas, showers, boat launch and dock, tennis, horseshoe pits and concession stand. Located on Route 106, eight miles southwest of Belfair.

Two creeks flow through 63-acre **Belfair State Park** (360-275-0668), affording both fresh and saltwater shorelines. Along its 3700 feet of beach, the saltwater warms quickly across shallow tide flats, but occasionally pollution makes swimming here risky (although there is a lagoon with a bathhouse); shellfish are usually posted off-limits. There are campsites and picnic areas. Located on Route 300, three miles west of Belfair.

Well-named, **Scenic Beach State Park** (360-830-5079) offers glorious views across Hood Canal to the Olympics and north up Dabob Bay. Nearly 1500 feet of cobblestone beach invites strolls; scuba divers also push off from here. In May, native rhododendrons burst into bloom. There are 52 campsites for tents and RVs as well as picnic and play areas here. You'll also find a horseshoe pit, volleyball and community center. Fishing is good at the nearby artificial reef (a boat launch is next to the park). The park is on Miami Beach Road Northwest, just west of Seabeck.

With nearly two miles of saltwater shoreline, 152-acre **Penrose Point State Park** (360-884-2514) provides some of the most accessible public clamming in southern Puget Sound. Try the half-mile of sandspit in Mayo Cove exposed at low tide. You can also swim at the park's sandy, shallow-water beaches, hike along two miles of trail, launch a canoe or kayak, picnic and camp. Located off Delano Road at the foot of 158th Avenue near Lakebay on the Longbranch Peninsula west of Tacoma.

The Sporting Life

BOATING

A wide range of rentals including sea kayaks, sailboats, runabouts and sportfishing boats are available from **Rent a Boat and Charters** (8827 North Harbor View Drive, Gig Harbor; 206-858-7341). Kayak rentals and instruction are offered by **Olympic Outdoor Center** (18971 Front Street, Poulsbo; 206-697-6095).

SCUBA DIVING

A good spot to dive is the Hood Canal Floating Bridge on the Kitsap Peninsula. For equipment rentals in Tacoma, try **Underwater Sports Inc.** (9606 Southwest 40th Street; 206-588-6634), **Lighthouse Diving** (3630 South Cedar Street; 206-475-1316) or **Northwest Divers Inc.** (4815 North Pearl Street; 206-752-3973).

HORSEBACK RIDING

Saddle up at **Su Dara Riding** (Puyallup; 206-531-1569) and the popular **Forest View Stables** (12915 Marksman Road Southwest, Olympia; 360-943-0462), where you must reserve in advance. Also try **E-Z Time Outfitters** (18703 SR706, Elbe; 206-569-2449) or **The Horse Ranch** (8615 336th Street South, Roy; 206-458-7074).

BICYCLING

Cyclists find the moderately difficult **Poulsbo–Port Gamble Loop**, with its 20 hilly miles featuring outstanding views of Hood Canal, the Cascade Range and the Olympic Mountains, a worthwhile ride.

BIKE RENTALS   Try **Mt. Constance Mountain Shoppe** (1550 Northeast Riddell Street, Bremerton; 206-377-0668).

HIKING

TACOMA AND OLYMPIA AREA TRAILS   Nisqually National Wildlife Refuge, Green River Gorge and Point Defiance Park in Tacoma are

Shuttle service to the northern Kitsap Peninsula from Sea–Tac Airport is available through the **Kitsap Airporter** *(360-876-1737).*

a hiker's haven. A wonderful river-delta walk, **Brown Farm Trail** (5 miles) loops through Nisqually National Wildlife Refuge. You may see bald eagles, coyotes, deer, great blue heron, red-tail hawks and a variety of waterfowl such as wood, canvasback and great-scalp ducks, as well as mallards and pintails. Views stretch from Mt. Rainier to the Olympics. You'll also see many of the islands in the south, Steilacoom and the Tacoma Narrows Bridge.

KITSAP PENINSULA TRAILS   Located southwest of Bremerton, **Gold Mountain Hike** (4 miles) is a moderate-to-strenuous climb with a 1200-foot elevation gain. You will survey the twisting waterways of southern Puget Sound and Hood Canal from a 1761-foot point that also offers vistas from the Olympics to the Cascades and Edmonds to Olympia. The walk begins at a gate on Minard Road, about one-and-a-half miles from old Belfair Valley Road, five-and-a-half miles west of Route 3.

Transportation

BY CAR

Route 5 is the main north-south highway connecting Seattle, Tacoma and Olympia. **Route 16** leads north from Tacoma, across the Tacoma Narrows Bridge toward Gig Harbor and farther north toward Bremerton. On Bainbridge Island, the main thoroughfare is **Route 305** that runs northwest across the island and onto the Kitsap Peninsula to Poulsbo.

BY AIR

Ten miles north of Tacoma and 20 miles south of downtown Seattle is **Seattle–Tacoma International Airport**, also known as Sea–Tac. See the "Transportation" section of Chapter Four for detailed information.

BY BUS

In the Kitsap Peninsula area, **Kitsap Transit** (360-373-2877) provides routed service in Poulsbo, Bremerton, Kingston and Bainbridge Island; otherwise, you will have to depend on a car or taxis for transportation around the peninsula.

SIX

The Olympic Peninsula
and Washington Coast

One of the most spectacular sights for many Washington visitors is watching the sun set behind the stark profile of the Olympic Mountains while sitting by the dock of the bay (Seattle's Elliott Bay, that is).

The Olympic Peninsula is a vast promontory bounded on the east by Puget Sound, the west by the Pacific Ocean and the north by the Strait of Juan de Fuca. With no major city—the largest town is Port Angeles, a community of only 19,000 people—it retains a feeling of country living on the edge of wilderness, which indeed it is.

The Olympic National Park, which dominates the peninsula, is a primeval place where eternal glaciers drop suddenly off sheer rock faces into nearly impenetrable rainforest, where America's largest herd of Roosevelt elk roams unseen by all but the most intrepid human eyes, where an impossibly rocky coastline cradles primitive marine life forms as it has done for millions of years. No fewer than five Indian reservations speckle sections of a coast famed as much for its shipwrecks as for its salmon fishing.

South of the national park, the Washington coast extends down the Northwest's finest sand beaches and around two enormous river estuaries to the mouth of the Columbia River and the state of Oregon. In this region, two towns have become major resort centers—Ocean Shores and Long Beach.

The Washington coast is known for its heavy rainfall, and justifiably so. Though the Olympics are not high by many standards—its tallest peaks are under 8000 feet—they catch huge amounts of precipitation blowing in from the Pacific Ocean. So much snow falls that more than

The local Dungeness crab, named for an Olympic Peninsula town, is internationally famous as a delicacy.

60 glaciers survive at elevations as low as 4500 feet. Even greater amounts of precipitation fall on the windward slopes: 140 inches a year and more in the Forks area. Not only does this foster the rapid growth of mushrooms and slugs, but it has also led to the creation of North America's greatest rainforest in the soggy Hoh River valley. Yet a mere 40 miles away as the raven flies, Sequim—in the Olympic rain shadow—is a comparative desert with a mere 15 inches of rain per year.

The first residents of the peninsula and coast were tribes like the Makah, Ozette and Quileute, whose descendants still inhabit the area today. A seafaring people noted for their woodcarving, they lived in a series of longhouses facing the sea and are known to have inhabited this region for as long as 2500 years.

Their first contact with Europeans came in 1775, when they massacred a Spanish landing party. Three years later, the ubiquitous British captain James Cook sailed the coast and traded for sea otter furs with Vancouver Island natives; his report opened the gates to the maritime fur trade.

American entrepreneur John Jacob Astor established a fort at the mouth of the Columbia River in 1803, and two years later Meriwether Lewis and William Clark led a cross-country expedition that arrived at Cape Disappointment, on the Washington side of the Columbia, in late 1806. White settlement was slow at first, but by the mid-19th century, Port Townsend had established itself as Puget Sound's premier lumber-shipping port, and other communities sprang up soon after.

Olympic National Park was annexed to the national park system in 1938. But long before that, Washingtonians had discovered its natural wonders. A fledgling tourism industry grew, with lodges constructed at several strategic locations around the park, including lakes Crescent and Quinault, Sol Duc Hot Springs and Kalaloch, overlooking the Pacific. Coastal communities were also building a visitor infrastructure, and quiet beach resorts soon emerged.

Today, typical Olympic Peninsula visitors start their tour in Port Townsend, having arrived by ferry and car from Seattle or Whidbey Island, and use Route 101 as their artery of exploration. Port Townsend is considered the most authentic Victorian seacoast town in the United States north of San Francisco, and its plethora of well-preserved 19th-century buildings, many of them now bed and breakfasts, charms all visitors. Less than an hour's drive west, the seven-mile Dungeness Spit (a national wildlife refuge) is the largest natural sand hook in the United States and is famed for the delectable crabs that share its name. Port

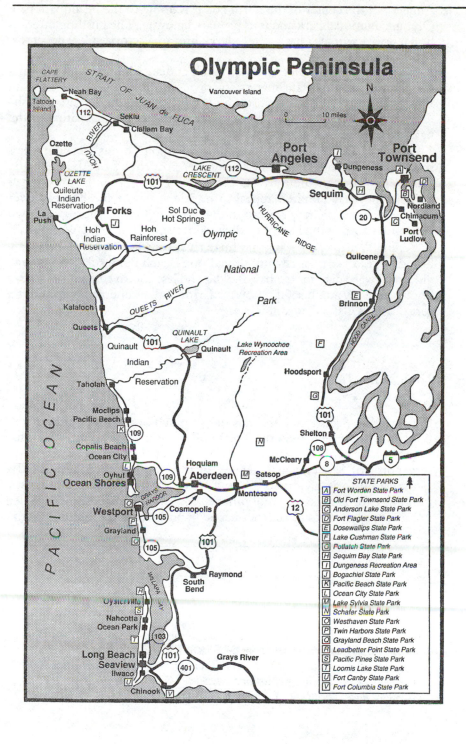

Olympic Peninsula

STRAIT OF JUAN de FUCA

CAPE FLATTERY
Vancouver Island

N

0   10 miles

Tatoosh Island
Neah Bay
112
Sekiu
Clallam Bay

Ozette

HOKO RIVER

OZETTE LAKE

Quileute Indian Reservation

La Push

LAKE CRESCENT
112
101

Forks
[J]

Sol Duc Hot Springs

Hoh Indian Reservation
Hoh Rainforest

Port Angeles
[I]
Dungeness

Sequim
[H]
20

Port Townsend
[A]
[D]
[B]
Nordland
[C] Chimacum
Port Ludlow

HURRICANE RIDGE

Olympic

National

QUEETS RIVER

Kalaloch

Queets

Quinault
101

QUINAULT LAKE

Quinault

Indian

Reservation

Taholah

Park

Lake Wynoochee Recreation Area

Quilcene

[E]
Brinnon

HOOD CANAL

[F]

Hoodsport

[G]
101

Moclips
Pacific Beach
[K] **109**

Copalis Beach
Ocean City
[L]

Oyhut
Ocean Shores
109

Hoquiam
Aberdeen
[M] Satsop

Montesano

[N]

McCleary
Shelton
108
8
5

GRAYS HARBOR

[O]
Westport
[P]
105
Cosmopolis

Grayland
[Q] **105**

101

12

WILLAPA BAY

[R]
Oysterville

Nahcotta
Ocean Park
[S]

[T]
103

Long Beach
Seaview
Ilwaco
[U]
101
401

South Bend
Raymond

Grays River

Chinook
[V]

STATE PARKS 🌲	
[A]	Fort Worden State Park
[B]	Old Fort Townsend State Park
[C]	Anderson Lake State Park
[D]	Fort Flagler State Park
[E]	Dosewallips State Park
[F]	Lake Cushman State Park
[G]	Potlatch State Park
[H]	Sequim Bay State Park
[I]	Dungeness Recreation Area
[J]	Bogachiel State Park
[K]	Pacific Beach State Park
[L]	Ocean City State Park
[M]	Lake Sylvia State Park
[N]	Schafer State Park
[O]	Westhaven State Park
[P]	Twin Harbors State Park
[Q]	Grayland Beach State Park
[R]	Leadbetter Point State Park
[S]	Pacific Pines State Park
[T]	Loomis Lake State Park
[U]	Fort Canby State Park
[V]	Fort Columbia State Park

PACIFIC OCEAN

Angeles, in the center of the north coast, is home to the headquarters of Olympic National Park and is its primary gateway. The bustling international port town also has a direct ferry link to Victoria, Canada, across the Strait of Juan de Fuca.

Neah Bay is the home of the Makah Indian Museum and Cultural Center and an important marina for deep-sea fishing charters. Clallam Bay, to the east, and La Push, south down the coast, are other sportfishing centers. The logging town of Forks is the portal for visitors to the national park's Hoh Rainforest.

Route 101 emerges from the damp Olympic forests to slightly less moist Grays Harbor, with its twin lumber port towns of Aberdeen and Hoquiam. Though these towns combined have a population of over 25,000, they have limited appeal to travelers, who typically head over the north shore of Grays Harbor to the hotels of Ocean Shores, or down the south shore of the harbor to the quaint fishing village of Westport.

Serene Willapa Bay is another huge river estuary south of Grays Harbor. The resort strip of 28-mile-long Long Beach Peninsula, which provides a seaward dike for the bay, is older and less contrived than the Ocean Shores area. Wildlife refuges, oyster farms and cranberry bogs lend it a sort of 1950s Cape Cod ambience.

Port Townsend Area

Before either Seattle or Tacoma were so much as a tug on a fisherman's line, Port Townsend was a thriving lumber port. Founded in 1851, it has retained its Victorian seacoast ambience better than any other community north of San Francisco. Much of the city has been designated a National Historic Landmark District, with nearly 70 Victorian houses, buildings, forts, parks and monuments. Many of the handsomely gabled homes are open for tours and/or offer bed-and-breakfast accommodations.

A FLOATING BRIDGE

Visitors driving to Port Townsend typically cross the one-and-a-half-mile **Hood Canal Floating Bridge** *on Route 104 from the Kitsap Peninsula. Located 30 miles southeast of Port Townsend, it is the world's only floating bridge erected over tidal waters and one of the longest of its kind anywhere. Constructed in 1961, the bridge was washed away during a fierce storm in February 1979, but was rebuilt in 1982.*

The Whitney Gardens in Brinnon, on Route 101, boast an extensive collection of rhododendrons, Washington's official state flower.

The best way to see Port Townsend is on foot. When you drive into town on Route 20, you'll first want to stop at the **Port Townsend Chamber of Commerce** visitors information center (2437 East Sims Way; 360-385-2722). Then continue east on Route 20 as it becomes Water Street. At the corner of Madison Street, you'll find the **Jefferson County Historical Society Museum** in City Hall (210 Madison Street; 360-385-1003), with Victorian antiques, artifacts and hundreds of photos of Port Townsend's early days. Guided historical walking tours leave from here at 10 a.m. and 2 p.m. daily, May through October. Some special tours can be arranged after October.

Heading west on Water Street by foot, note the elegant stone and wood-frame buildings on either side of the street, most of them dating from the 1880s and 1890s. Turn right on Adams Street; halfway up the block on the right is the **Enoch S. Fowler Building**, built in 1874, the oldest two-story stone structure in Washington. A former county courthouse, it now houses the weekly newspaper. Turn left at Washington Street and five blocks farther, on your right, you'll see the **James House** (1238 Washington Street; 360-385-1238), built in 1889. It has five chimneys and a commanding view of the harbor—and in 1973 became the Northwest's first bed and breakfast.

Turn right up Harrison Street, then right again at Franklin Street. Two blocks farther, at Franklin and Polk streets, the **Captain Enoch S. Fowler Home**, built in 1860, is the oldest surviving house in Port Townsend and is typical of New England–style homes. Two more blocks ahead, the **Rothschild House** (Franklin and Taylor streets; admission) was built in 1868 by an early Port Townsend merchant. Notable for its outstanding interior woodwork, it's maintained by the State Parks Commission for public tours.

A block north, at Jefferson and Clay streets, **Trinity Methodist Church** (1871) is the state's oldest standing Methodist church. Its small museum contains the Bible of the church's first minister. A block east, the 1889 **Ann Starrett Mansion** (744 Clay Street; 360-385-3205; admission), now a bed-and-breakfast inn, offers public tours from noon until three. At Clay and Monroe streets, the **Lucinda Hastings Home** was the most expensive house ever built in Port Townsend when it was erected in 1889 at a cost of $14,000. Turn right here, and return down Monroe to Water Street and your starting point at City Hall.

Get back in your car and drive north on Monroe Street. (This artery staggers a half-block right at Roosevelt Street onto Jackson Street, then turns right onto Walnut Street.) All roads flow into W Street, the south boundary of **Fort Worden State Park** (360–385–4730). If the fort looks familiar, it could be because it was used in the filming of the Richard Gere–Debra Winger movie, *An Officer and a Gentleman*. Authorized in 1896, it includes officers' row and a refurbished **Commanding Officer's House** (admission), the **248th Coast Artillery Museum** (admission), gun emplacements, a balloon hangar, marine interpretive center and **Point Wilson Light Station**. Fort Worden offers long stretches of beach that command impressive views of the Cascades and nearby islands.

On the dock at Fort Worden is the **Port Townsend Marine Science Center** (360–385–5582; admission). Of special interest are its four large touch tanks, representing different intertidal habitats, and a "wet lab" where creatures like starfish, anemones and sea cucumbers can be handled by curious visitors.

Traveling south from Port Townsend, Route 20 joins Route 101 at Discovery Bay. Twelve miles south of the junction is the town of **Quilcene** on the Hood Canal, a serpentine finger of Puget Sound. The town is especially noted for its oyster farming and processing and is the location of a state shellfish research laboratory (not open to the public). The **Mount Walker Observation Point**—five miles south on Route 101, then another five miles on a gravel road that starts at Walker Pass—offers a spectacular view of the Hood Canal and surrounding area.

PORT TOWNSEND AREA LODGING

The James House (1238 Washington Street, Port Townsend; 360–385–1238, 800–385–1238) claims to have been the Pacific Northwest's first bed and breakfast. Just a few steps from shops and restaurants at the foot of the bluff that stands behind lower downtown, it dates from 1889, though it's only been a bed and breakfast since 1973. The house is unmistakable for its five chimneys; inside, the floors are all parquet. Some, but not all, of the 12 rooms have private baths. There's also a library, and a full breakfast is served. Save a few moments to enjoy the English gardens with an impressive view of the water. Kids are welcome, but only if they're over 12 years old. Moderate to deluxe.

For those less than enthralled with bed and breakfasts, the **Palace Hotel** (1004 Water Street, Port Townsend; 360–385–0773) provides historic accommodation in a former seafarers' bordello. Though nicely renovated, this is a bit rustic. After checking in at the main lobby, you must climb a long flight of stairs (or two) to your room. There are 15 guest chambers, each with antiques recalling the red-light flavor of the past. The madam's former room even has a kitchenette. Moderate.

The renowned **Ann Starrett Mansion Victorian Bed and Breakfast Inn** (744 Clay Street, Port Townsend; 360–385–3205, 800–321–

*Some say the budget-priced **Shanghai Restaurant** (Point Hudson, Port Townsend; 360-385-4810) serves the best Chinese food this side of Vancouver's Chinatown.*

0644, fax 360-385-2976), a National Historic Landmark built in 1889, is a classic mansion in Victorian style. High on a bluff overlooking downtown Port Townsend and Puget Sound, it combines diverse architectural elements—frescoed ceilings, a free-hung spiral staircase, an eight-sided dome painted as a solar calendar, the requisite gables and dormer windows—into a charming whole. The 11 guest rooms are furnished with antiques, of course. The gourmet breakfast menu changes daily. All units have private baths; deluxe to ultra-deluxe.

With so many heritage choices, few visitors actually opt for a motel stay. If you're in that minority, check out **The Tides Inn** (1807 Water Street, Port Townsend; 360-385-0595, 800-822-8696), along the waterfront at the south end of town. Among the 21 units are five efficiencies and nine with hot tubs; most units have balconies overlooking the bay. Moderate to ultra-deluxe.

For students and budget travelers, there are two **youth hostels** in eastern Jefferson County—one at **Fort Worden State Park** (Port Townsend; 360-385-4730), open year-round except the Christmas holiday period, the other at **Fort Flagler State Park** (10621 Flagler Road, Nordland; 360-385-1288), open May to October.

South of town about 20 miles, **Port Ludlow Resort and Conference Center** (9483 Oak Bay Road, Port Ludlow; 360-437-2222, 800-732-1239, fax 360-437-2482) is one of Washington's premier family resorts. It boasts a championship golf course, tennis courts, swimming pools, a marina, hiking and bicycling trails and 1500 acres of land. There are 180 suites with fireplaces, kitchens and decks and a restaurant with marvelous views of water and mountains. Deluxe to ultra-deluxe.

PORT TOWNSEND AREA RESTAURANTS

For an evening of fine dining, it would be hard to top the **Manresa Castle** (7th and Sheridan streets, Port Townsend; 360-385-5750). Located in an 1892 hilltop inn that overlooks the town and bay like a German castle on the Rhine River, it combines an elegant restaurant and an Edwardian pub. The menu offers two different styles, depending on how much one wants to eat: an à la carte moderately priced "light supper" featuring everything from curry chicken and bouillabaisse to seafood fettuccine, and a deluxe full-dinner that offers the likes of grilled salmon, grilled polenta primavera, Dungeness crab cakes and beef tournedos and prawns.

Port Townsend shops feature the work of talented local painters, sculptors, weavers, potters, poets and writers.

With a great waterfront location offering spectacular views, the **Surf Seafood and Chowder House** (106 Taylor Street; 360-385-2992) complements its surroundings with pleasant blue-and-white contemporary decor and marine artwork. Fresh, simply prepared local seafood, particularly salmon, clams, mussels and oysters, is the specialty. Moderate.

Ask locals where to eat, and chances are they'll recommend the **Fountain Café** (920 Washington Street; 360-385-1364). You'll probably have to stand in line, but the wait is worth it. Occupying the ground floor of a historic building (is there anything else in downtown Port Townsend?), the Fountain serves outstanding seafood and pasta dishes, including oysters as you like 'em. Soups and desserts are homemade. The decor is in keeping with the eclectic penchant of many young local artists. Moderate.

Breakfasts draw full houses at the **Salal Café** (634 Water Street, Port Townsend; 360-385-6532). On Sunday, in fact, breakfast is served all day, perhaps to give customers time to peruse the newspaper. Huge omelettes and various seafood and vegetarian recipes get oohs and ahs. Lunch features gourmet homestyle cooking, along with pastas and sandwiches. Budget.

The Chimmacum Café (9253 Rhododendron Drive, Chimmacum; 360-732-4631), nine miles south of Port Townsend, is a local institution. This is food like grandma should have made—country-fried chicken dinners, baked ham and so forth, followed, of course, by homemade pies brimming with fresh fruit. Breakfast and lunch are also served. Budget.

PORT TOWNSEND AREA SHOPPING

Port Townsend offers the most interesting shopping on the peninsula with its array of galleries, antique and gift shops, bookstores, restaurants and cafés and all-purpose emporiums. Proprietors have paid particular attention to historical accuracy in restoring commercial buildings.

For antiques, try the **Port Townsend Antique Mall** (802 Washington Street; 360-385-2590) or any of the many other shops along the 600 through 1200 blocks of Water or Washington streets.

Among the many fine galleries for contemporary arts and crafts are **Northern Exposure** (764 Lawrence Street; 360-385-7078), where the work of 36 Northwest artists is showcased; **Ancestral Spirits Gallery** (921 Washington Street; 360-385-0078), which features Inuit and Northwest Coast tribal artwork and **Artisans on Taylor** (236 Taylor Street; 360-379-8098), which specializes in handwoven textiles and hand-formed glass beads.

PORT TOWNSEND AREA NIGHTLIFE

In Port Townsend, you'll find live rock music or rhythm-and-blues week-ends at the **Back Alley** (923 Washington Street; 360-385-2914). At **Lanza's** (1020 Lawrence Street; 360-385-6221) you can listen to jazz, opera or Celtic harp while you enjoy your dinner or later in the evening with a glass of wine. Both are rustic establishments, popular with locals.

PORT TOWNSEND AREA BEACHES AND PARKS

A 446-acre estate right in Port Townsend, **Fort Worden State Park** (360-385-4730) showcases a turn-of-the-century fort that includes re-stored Victorian officers' houses, barracks, theater, parade grounds and artillery bunkers. A beach and boat launch are on Admiralty Inlet, at the head of Puget Sound. Facilities here also include campsites and picnic areas. Camping reservations are strongly recommended year-round. The park entrance is on W Street at Cherry Street.

Kah Tai Lagoon Nature Park (360-385-2722) features 50 acres of wetlands and 35 acres of grasslands and woodlands, and is a great place for birdwatching: more than 50 species have been identified here. There are two-and-a-half miles of trails, places to picnic, a play area for kids and interpretive displays. Located on 12th Street near Sims Way in Port Townsend.

Old Fort Townsend State Park (360-385-3595) has 40 campsites, picnic areas, seven miles of trails and a beach on Port Townsend (the inlet). You can fish from the shore. The park is located three miles south of the town of Port Townsend off Route 20 on Old Fort Town-send Road.

The long-abandoned fort building, which dates from 1898, is a minor attraction at **Fort Flagler State Park** (360-385-1259): bigger is the saltwater beach on Admiralty Inlet, popular for clamming and beach-combing. Fishing is good for salmon, halibut, sole and shellfish. There are also picnic areas, hiking trails, a boat launch and campsites. The park is on the north tip of Marrowstone Island, eight miles northeast of Had-lock off Route 116 .

At the mouth of the Dosewallips River on the Hood Canal, a long, serpentine arm of Puget Sound, the 425-acre **Dosewallips State Park** (360-796-4415) is especially popular among clam diggers and oyster hunters during shellfish season. You can fish for winter steelhead in the river; salmon and bottomfish in Hood Canal. There are picnic areas, a mudflat beach and hiking trails. Camping is an option here. Located in Brinnon, 37 miles south of Port Townsend on Route 101.

Port Angeles Area

The northern gateway to Olympic National Park, as well as a major terminal for ferries to British Columbia, the Port Angeles area is one of northwest Washington's main crossroads. Sequim on Route 101, 31 miles west of Port Townsend, and nearby Port Angeles are two of the peninsula's more intriguing towns. On the Strait of Juan de Fuca at the foot of the Olympic Mountains, this region is often dry when it's pouring rain just a few miles south.

The town of **Sequim** (pronounced "Squim") is graced with a climate that's unusually mild for the Northwest: it sits in the Olympic rain shadow. A major attraction just north of town is the **Olympic Game Farm** (1423 Ward Road; 360-683-4295; admission), whose animals—lions, tigers, bears, buffalo and many others—are trained for film roles. Driving tours of the farm, including a studio barn, are available year-round; walking tours are offered during the summer.

In the Sequim–Dungeness Valley, the **Museum and Art Center** (175 West Cedar Street; 360-683-8110) preserves the native and pioneer farming heritage of Sequim and showcases the work of local artists. For visitor information, contact the **Sequim–Dungeness Valley Chamber of Commerce** (1192 East Washington Street, Sequim; 360-683-6197).

To the north off Route 101, the Dungeness Valley is dotted with strawberry and raspberry fields. Weathered barns left over from the area's dairy farming days are still visible. Visit the **Cedarbrook Herb Farm** (1345 Sequim Avenue South; 360-683-7733), where 300 different varieties of herbs and spices fill the air with a marvelous (but undefinable!) aroma and inspire many a gourmet chef to go on a culinary buying spree.

Seventeen miles west of Sequim on Route 101 is the fishing and logging port of **Port Angeles**, the Olympic Peninsula's largest town. A major attraction here is the **City Pier** (360-457-0411). Adjacent to the ferry terminal, it boasts an observation tower, promenade decks, a picnic area and the

---

THE DUNGENESS SPIT

*Opposite the mouth of the Dungeness River is one of the Olympic Peninsula's most remarkable natural features: the **Dungeness Spit**, almost seven miles long and the largest natural sand hook in the United States. A short trail within the adjacent **Dungeness Recreation Area** provides access to this national wildlife refuge. The spit and the surrounding bay and estuary are teeming with wildlife, including birds, seals, fish, crabs and clams.*

Arthur D. Feiro Marine Laboratory (360-452-9277; admission), where visitors can observe and even touch local marine life.

As the gateway to Olympic National Park, Port Angeles is home to the park's headquarters. At the **Olympic National Park Visitors Center** (3002 Mount Angeles Road, Port Angeles; 360-452-4501), you'll find an excellent slide show and exhibits on the natural and human history of the park.

The **Clallam County Museum** (223 East 4th Street; 360-417-2364) in the old county courthouse building has a variety of interesting regional historical displays. For tourist information, contact the **North Olympic Peninsula Visitor & Convention Bureau** (338 West 1st Street, Port Angeles; 360-452-8552).

PORT ANGELES AREA LODGING

You'll feel good right down to your cockles—as well as your steamer clams, butter clams and horse clams—after shellfishing on the saltwater beach outside the **Sequim Bay Resort** (2634 West Sequim Bay Road, Sequim; 360-681-3853). The eight fully equipped housekeeping cottages here are suitable for families and shoreline lovers. There are also guest laundry facilities and RV hookups. Budget.

Just a spit from the Spit—Dungeness, that is—is the **Groveland Cottage** (4861 Sequim-Dungeness Way; 360-683-3565, 800-879-8859, fax 360-683-5181), by the coast north of Sequim. The turn-of-the-century building has four rooms, two with private baths, above a country craft shop. There is also a private cottage with a queen-size bed and private bath. The rooms may be simple, but service is not: coffee and the morning paper are delivered to your room in anticipation of the four-course gourmet breakfast. Prices are moderate. They also rent 11 vacation cottages in the area.

Perhaps the nicest motel-style accommodation in these port communities is the **Red Lion Bayshore Inn** (221 North Lincoln Street, Port Angeles; 360-452-9215, fax 360-452-4734). A modern gray building that extends along the Strait of Juan de Fuca opposite the ferry dock, it offers rooms with private balconies overlooking the water. A private strand of beach and swimming pool beckon bathers. Moderate to deluxe.

Situated on the water with spectacular views of the San Juan Islands, the **Domaine Madeleine Bed and Breakfast** (146 Wildflower Lane, Port Angeles; 360-457-4174) excels in both comfort and hospitality. There are three rooms and a honeymoon cottage at this charming inn: the deluxe-priced Renoir Room with impressionist art and feather beds; the ultra-deluxe Monet Room with Monet prints and a jacuzzi; the ultra-deluxe Ming Room, with 19th-century antiques, a variety of French perfumes, a jacuzzi and private balcony; and the ultra-deluxe honeymoon cottage, with a solarium, kitchenette, reading room and bathroom jacuzzi. All rooms have fireplaces. Relax in front of the 14-foot-high basalt fireplace or try your hand at the handcrafted harpsichord. The full gourmet breakfast is elegantly presented—don't miss it. Gay-friendly.

Victoria, across the strait on Vancouver Island, is said to be "more British than the British"—but the same slogan could almost apply to **The Tudor Inn** (1108 South Oak Street, Port Angeles; 360-452-3138). Hosts Jane and Jerry Glass serve a traditional English breakfast and afternoon tea in the restored Tudor-style home. Most of their antique collection is Old English, and the well-stocked library will steer you to books on the United Kingdom. Two bedrooms have private baths; three others share two baths. Moderate.

PORT ANGELES AREA RESTAURANTS

One-and-a-half miles west of Sequim is **Casoni's Seafood and Pasta House** (105 Hooker Road, Sequim; 360-683-2415), the north coast's best Italian eatery. Mamma Casoni herself is queen bee of the kitchen, which dishes up generous portions of pasta, seafood, veal and chicken dishes, as well as some remarkable cheesecakes for dessert. Dinner only. Moderate.

If retired physicist Tom Wells and his Cambodian-born wife, Lay Yin, aren't off studying a solar eclipse somewhere around the globe, you'll find them at the **Eclipse Café** (139 West Alder Street, Sequim; 360-683-2760). Yin's culinary touch dominates: Southeast Asian taste temptations stand out. This one's for hungry adventurers. Breakfast and lunch only; budget.

The undisputed winner in the northern Olympic Peninsula fine-dining sweepstakes is **C'est Si Bon** (23 Cedar Park Drive, four miles east of Port Angeles; 360-452-8888). The decor is modern and dramatic, with handsome oil paintings and full picture windows allowing panoramas of the Olympic Range. The cuisine, on the other hand, is classical French: tournedos with crabmeat and a shallot sauce, coquilles St. Jacques, veal Normande with apples and calvados. There are French wines and desserts, too, of course. Dinner only. Deluxe.

You'll find bistro-style food, service and ambience at **The Greenery** (117-B East 1st Street, Port Angeles; 360-457-4112), including homemade soups and pasta. Fresh fish specials are served all day, and caesar salads are prepared tableside "the old way." Moderate.

Practically next door is the **First Street Haven** (107 East 1st Street, Port Angeles; 360-457-0352), one of the best places around for quick and tasty breakfasts and lunches. Have a homemade quiche and salad, along with the house coffee, and you'll be set for the day. No dinner. Budget.

PORT ANGELES AREA SHOPPING

There are good antique dealers in Sequim. Try **Country Cottage Antiques** (243 West Washington Street; 360-683-8983) or **Today's and Yesterday's** (131 East Washington Street; 360-683-5733), which is primarily a hair salon but also sells collectibles.

PORT ANGELES AREA NIGHTLIFE

You didn't come to this part of the state for its nightlife, and that's good. What little entertainment there is usually exists only on Friday and Saturday nights.

Your best bet in the Port Angeles area may be the lounge of the **Red Lion Bayshore Inn** (221 North Lincoln Street, Port Angeles; 360-452-9215) for contemporary soft-rock music.

PORT ANGELES AREA BEACHES AND PARKS

Surrounding Olympic National Park on its east, south and northwest sides, **Olympic National Forest** (360-956-2300) provides ample recreational opportunities. It includes five wilderness areas on the fringe of the park. There are campgrounds and picnic areas throughout the forest. Best bets for fishing are Lakes Cushman and Wynoochee and the Dosewallips, Dungeness and Soleduck rivers. Access is via a number of roads branching off Route 101, especially south of Sequim, and between Quilcene and Hoodsport.

Water sports and hiking, both along the shore and up the Jimmycomelately Creek (that's its name, honest), are the main attractions at **Sequim Bay State Park** (360-683-4235) on Sequim Bay, sheltered from rough seas by two spits at its mouth and from heavy rains by the Olympic rain shadow. There are picnic areas, campsites, a beach and boat launch. Located on Route 101, four miles east of Sequim.

SALT CREEK RECREATION AREA

*One of the finest tide pool sanctuaries on the Olympic Peninsula is the three-mile stretch of rocky beach set aside as the **Salt Creek Recreation Area** (ten miles west from Port Angeles on Route 112, then three miles north on Camp Hayden Road; 360-928-3441). Starfish, sea urchins, anemones, mussels, barnacles and other invertebrate life can be observed here in their natural habitat . . . but not removed.*

The Dungeness Spit is a national wildlife refuge, but a **Dungeness Recreation Area** (360-683-5847) trail provides access. Marine birds and seals are among the impressive wildlife to be seen. The recreation area also provides opportunities for camping and picnicking, and fishing is okay from the shore. Located five miles west of Sequim on Route 101, then four miles north on Kitchen–Dick Road.

Olympic National Park

The Olympic Peninsula's main attraction—in fact, the reason most tourists come here at all—is **Olympic National Park**. This spectacular national park, 900,000 acres (1400 square miles) in area and ranging in elevation from sea level to nearly 8000 feet, contains everything from permanent alpine glaciers to rainforest to rocky tidepools rich in marine life. Rugged, glaciated mountains dominate the park, with rushing rivers tumbling from their slopes. The rainier western slopes harbor an extraordinary rainforest, and a separate 57-mile-long coastal strip preserves remarkable tidepools and marvelous ocean scenery.

Wildlife in the park includes the rare Roosevelt elk, as well as deer, black bears, cougars, bobcats, a great many smaller mammals and scores of bird species. There are steelhead in the rivers and colorful birds everywhere. Three large lakes, Crescent (near Port Angeles), Ozette (on the coast) and Quinault (on the southwestern edge), are especially popular destinations.

There are no lack of facilities throughout the park: picnic areas, hotels, restaurants and groceries; information, 360-452-0330 (Port Angeles) or ranger stations in Forks (360-374-5450). Route 101 circles the park and the many access roads are well marked.

The most direct route into the park from Port Angeles is the Heart of the Hills/Hurricane Ridge Road. It climbs almost 5000 feet in just 17

LAKE QUINAULT LODGE

*If you're planning a stay in the corner of Olympic National Park that includes beautiful Lake Quinault, consider the **Lake Quinault Lodge** (South Shore Road, Quinault; 360-288-2571, fax 360-288-2901)—especially if you can get a lakefront room in the historic cedar-shingled lodge itself. Constructed in the 1920s, the huge building arcs around the shoreline, a totem-pole design on its massive chimney facing the water. Antiques and wicker furniture adorn the sun porch, dining room and bar. There are nice rooms in a newer wing, but they lack the lodge's historic ambience. You can rent boats or hike year-round, or relax in the pool, sauna or jacuzzi. Moderate to deluxe.*

America's lushest rainforest (the Hoh) can be found in Olympic National Park.

---

miles to the **Hurricane Ridge Lodge**, where there are breathtaking views of 7965-foot Mt. Olympus, the highest peak in the Olympic Range, and of other glacier-shrouded mountains. Visitors to Hurricane Ridge can dine in the day lodge, picnic, enjoy nature walks or take longer hikes. In winter, enjoy the small downhill ski area here and many cross-country trails.

Twenty miles west of Port Angeles on Route 101 is **Lake Crescent**, one of the three large lakes within park boundaries. Carved during the last ice age 10,000 years ago, it is nestled between steep forested hillsides. A unique subspecies of trout lures anglers to its deep waters. There are several resorts, restaurants, campgrounds and picnic areas around its shores. From National Park Service–administered Lake Crescent Lodge, on the southeast shore, a three-fourth-mile trail leads up Barnes Creek to beautiful **Marymere Falls**.

West of Lake Crescent, the Sol Duc River Road turns south to **Sol Duc Hot Springs**, 14 miles off Route 101. Long known to Native Americans, the therapeutic mineral waters were discovered by a pioneer in 1880 and like everything else the white settlers touched, soon boasted an opulent resort. But the original resort burned to the ground in 1916 and today's refurbished resort, nestled in a valley of old-growth Douglas fir, is more rustic than elegant. The springs remain an attraction. Sol Duc is a major trailhead for backpacking trips into the park; also here is a ranger station (360-327-3534).

On the west side of the national park are three more major points of entry. The **Hoh Rainforest** is 19 miles east of Route 101 via the Hoh River Road, 13 miles south of Forks. For national park information here, call the **Forks Ranger Station** (360-374-5450). There's a less well-known rainforest at the end of the **Queets River Road**, 14 miles off Route 101, 17 miles west of Quinault. Finally, **Quinault Lake**, on Route 101 at the southwestern corner of Olympic National Park, is the site of several resorts and campgrounds, including the venerable Lake Quinault Lodge. Watersports of all kinds are popular at this glacier-fed lake, surrounded by old-growth forest.

OLYMPIC NATIONAL PARK LODGING

The rustic **Log Cabin Resort** (3183 East Beach Road, 21 miles west of Port Angeles; 360-928-3245, fax 360-928-2280) is a historic landmark on the shores of gorgeous Lake Crescent along Route 101. Budget-watchers can stay in the main lodge; more upscale are lakeshore chalets and cabins. There's also an RV park with full hookups on Log Cabin

Creek. The handsome log lodge has a restaurant and a gift shop; all manner of boats are rented at the marina. The resort is open May to October. Moderate to deluxe.

The **Sol Duc Hot Springs Resort** (Sol Duc River Road, 40 miles west of Port Angeles; 360-327-3583, fax 360-327-3398) is another historic property, this one built in 1910 around a series of hot sulphur pools 14 miles south of Route 101. The 32 cabins (six with kitchens) have undergone occasional renovations since then, including indoor plumbing! The best plunge, however, after a day of hiking or fishing, remains the springs, kept at 98 to 104 degrees. Campsites and RV hookups are available. The resort is open May to October. Cabins are moderate.

OLYMPIC NATIONAL PARK RESTAURANTS

The best choice for dining in the park is the **Log Cabin Resort** (6540 East Beach Road, 21 miles west of Port Angeles; 360-928-3325). Enjoy the view of beautiful Lake Crescent, where anglers dip their lines for the unique crescenti trout, a subspecies of rainbow trout that may wind up on your platter in the restaurant. Northwest cuisine is a specialty. Open May to October. Moderate.

There's another dining room at the **Sol Duc Hot Springs Resort** (Sol Duc River Road, 44 miles west of Port Angeles; 360-327-3583), just behind the hot sulphur springs. As at Lake Crescent, the food is solid Northwest fare, including Dungeness crab from the north Olympic Coast. Open May to October. Moderate.

A mile high in the Olympic Range, 17 miles south of Port Angeles, the **Hurricane Ridge Lodge** (Hurricane Ridge Road; 360-928-3211) frames glaciers in the picture windows of its coffeeshop. Come for the view, but the standard American fare served here isn't half-bad either. Open daily mid-May through September, weekends mid-October to April. Moderate.

Olympic Coast

Largely undeveloped, the rough-and-tumble Olympic Coast is one of Washington's hidden gems. Home to America's finest Native American research centers, this region is also famous for its archaeological preserves, maritime sanctuaries and pristine beaches. It features some of the finest wilderness hiking in the region.

Fifty miles west of Port Angeles via Route 112, where the Strait of Juan de Fuca approaches the Pacific Ocean, are the sister communities of **Clallam Bay** and **Sekiu** (pronounced "C-Q"). These are prime sportfishing grounds for salmon and huge bottomfish, especially halibut. If you're spending time at a fishing resort in one of these towns, don't miss the wonderful tidepools northeast of Clallam Bay at **Slip Point**. Just west of Sekiu, at the mouth of the Hoko River, visitors can view the remains of a 2500-year-old Makah Indian fishing village at the **Hoko Archaeological Site**.

If you drive on Route 112 toward Sekiu, Lake Ozette Road branches south at the Hoko River. The road leads 20 miles to the northernmost of three tiny Indian reservations (the Ozette) surrounded by the coastal strip of Olympic National Park. **Ozette Lake** is the largest of the national park's three lakes; a strip of land just three miles wide separates it from the ocean. Two trails lead from here to the sea. The Indian Village Trail to **Cape Alava**, the westernmost point of the contiguous United States, leads to the **Ozette Dig**, a 500-year-old Indian village excavated by archaeologists in the 1970s.

Much of the Olympic coastline remains undeveloped. Hikers can wander along the high-water mark or on primitive trails, some wood-planked and raised above the forest floor. Offshore reefs have taken many lives over the centuries since European exploration began, and two memorials to shipwreck victims are good destinations for intrepid hikers. Nine miles south of Ozette, the **Norwegian Memorial** remembers seamen who died in an early 20th-century shipwreck. Six miles farther south, and about three miles north of Rialto Beach opposite La Push, the **Chilean Memorial** marks the grave of 20 South American sailors who died in a 1920 wreck.

Return to Sekiu to continue your drive south down the coast. Twenty-seven miles south of Clallam Bay on Route 101 is **Forks**, with 3000 people, the largest town between Port Angeles and Hoquiam. Steelhead fishing, river rafting and mushroom gathering are major activities here, but the one most evident to visitors is the timber industry. Some days, in fact, there seem to be more log trucks on the roads than passenger cars. The **Forks Timber Museum** (Route 101 North; 360-374-9663) is

---

HISTORIC NEAH BAY

*For more than 2500 years, **Neah Bay**, in the Makah Indian Reservation 18 miles west of Sekiu on Route 112, has been the home of the Makah tribe. The **Makah Cultural and Research Center** (Bay View Avenue, Neah Bay; 360-645-2711; admission) houses the prehistoric artifacts discovered at the Hoko and Ozette village digs, including baskets, whaling and sealing harpoons and canoes, along with a replica of a 15th-century longhouse. Visitors can enjoy excellent charter-fishing excursions from the harbor, which is also home to a commercial fishing fleet.*

filled with exhibits of old-time logging equipment and historical photos, as well as pioneer and Indian artifacts.

On the coast 14 miles west of Forks is the 800-year-old Indian fishing village of **La Push**, center of the **Quileute Indian Reservation** (360-374-6163). Sportfishing, camping and beachcombing are popular year-round. An abandoned Coast Guard station and lighthouse here are used as a school for resident children.

A national park road eight miles west of Forks branches off the La Push Road and follows the north shore of the Quileute River five miles to **Rialto Beach**, where spectacular piles of driftwood often accumulate. There are picnic areas and campgrounds here, and a trailhead for hikes north up the beach toward Cape Alava.

The **Hoh Indian Reservation** is 25 miles south of Forks, off Route 101. Of more interest to most visitors is the **Kalaloch Lodge** (360-962-2271), 35 miles south of Forks on Route 101. A major national park facility, it affords spectacular ocean views at the southernmost end of the park's coastal strip.

OLYMPIC COAST LODGING

The main population center on the Olympic Coast, and the nearest to the Hoh Rainforest, is the lumber town of Forks. Among several budget-priced bed and breakfasts here is the **River Inn on the Bogachiel** (2596 West Bogachiel Way; 360-374-6526), an A-frame chalet on the banks of the Bogachiel River two-and-a-half miles from town. Two bedrooms have private baths and share the sundecks. You can fish from the shore or relax in the hot tub while keeping your eyes open for elk, deer and river otter.

Much nearer to shops and restaurants is the **Miller Tree Inn** (5th and East Division streets, Forks; 360-374-6806). A quiet and comfortable farm homestead on three acres, it has six attractive rooms (two with half-baths) that practice an "open-house" policy not common among

---

FLATTERY WILL GET YOU NOWHERE, BUT THE VIEW'S TERRIFIC

*A winding, scenic coastal drive to the end of Route 112 climaxes at **Cape Flattery**, the northwesternmost corner of the contiguous United States. The road at times runs within feet of the water, providing spectacular blufftop views of the Strait of Juan de Fuca and Tatoosh Island—a great location for whalewatching between March and May. A short trail leads to the shore. Beach hikers can find some of the last wilderness coast in Washington south of here.*

Forks is Washington's rainiest town, with well over 100 inches a year.

bed and breakfasts: children, pets, even smokers are welcome! And visitors love the fresh farmhouse breakfasts. Moderate.

Forks also has a youth hostel: the **Rain Forest Hostel** (mile marker 169.3, Route 101 North, 23 miles south of Forks; 360-374-2270). As with other lodgings of its ilk, it offers dorm bunks and community bathrooms and kitchen. The common room is a bonus with its fireplace and library. There is also one room for a couple and one room for a family. Budget.

An alternative lodging on the lake is the **Rain Forest Resort Village** (516 South Shore Road, Quinault; 360-288-2535, 800-255-6936: reservations only), with 18 deluxe-priced cabins (five with kitchens, ten with fireplaces, five with whirlpool bathtubs), 16 moderately priced motel rooms and 31 RV spaces (budget). Here, you'll find most of the amenities of the lodge, including restaurant and lounge, boat rentals, general store and laundry, but you don't have to pay for the atmosphere. Moderate.

Sixteen miles west of Forks in the Quileute Indian Reservation, surrounded by the coastal strip of Olympic National Park, is the **La Push Ocean Park Resort** (700 Main Street, La Push; 360-374-5267, 800-487-1267). The driftwood-speckled beach is just beyond the lodgings, which fall into three categories: cabins with fully supplied kitchenettes and fireplaces; older townhouse units with balconies overlooking the beach; and rustic A-frames with wood stoves (haul your own fuel from the woodshed) and toilets (showers are in a communal washroom). Budget to moderate.

North of Forks 31 miles, the hamlet of Sekiu flanks Route 112 on the protected shore of Clallam Bay, on the Strait of Juan de Fuca. The lone waterfront hotel here is **Van Riper's Resort and Charters** (Front and Rice streets, Sekiu; 360-963-2334). Family owned and operated, it's a cozy getaway spot. More than half the 15 rooms have great views of the boats on the picturesque strait. Budget.

One of the few cabin resorts open year-round is **The Cape Motel and RV Park** (Bayview Avenue, Neah Bay; 360-645-2250). The property has ten motel rooms and four cottages; the latter all have kitchens, and one has a fireplace. Budget.

Back in Olympic National Park, one of the most picturesque spots on the Washington coastline is the **Kalaloch Lodge** (157151 Route 101, 35 miles south of Forks; 360-962-2271). Accommodations here include eight lodge units, ten motel units, 20 log cabins with kitchenettes (but no utensils provided) and a half-dozen duplexes atop the bluff. The lodge has a dining room and lounge overlooking the Pacific Ocean, as well as a general store, gas station and gift shop. It's open year-round. Prices are moderate to deluxe.

OLYMPIC COAST RESTAURANTS

Sunsets from the **Kalaloch Lodge** (157151 Route 101, 35 miles south of Forks; 360-962-2271), high on a bluff overlooking the ocean in the national park's coastal strip, can make even the most ordinary food taste good. Fortunately, the fresh salmon and oysters served here don't need the view for their rich flavor. A lounge adjoins the dining room. Moderate.

The restaurant at the park's **Lake Quinault Lodge** (South Shore Road, Quinault; 360-288-2571) faces another gorgeous lake surrounded by lush cedar forests. As you've come to expect along this coast, the seafood is excellent. Prices are moderate; the lodge is open year-round.

Other than the national park lodges, pickings are slim in the restaurant department along this stretch of highway. A mile north of Forks, the **Smoke House Restaurant** (Route 101 at La Push Road; 360-374-6258) serves a superb alder-smoked salmon. You can also get generous portions of other seafood and meats, plus a salad bar, for a moderate tab.

OLYMPIC COAST SHOPPING

For authentic Northwest Indian crafts, you won't do better than the gift shop at the **Makah Cultural and Research Center** (Bayview Avenue, Neah Bay; 360-645-2711) on the Makah Indian Reservation near Cape Flattery at the end of Route 112.

OLYMPIC COAST BEACHES AND PARKS

Bogachiel State Park (360-374-6356) is famous for its salmon and steelhead runs. Located on Route 101 six miles south of Forks not far from the Hoh Rainforest, this eternally damp park sits on the Bogachiel River. Hiking and hunting in the adjacent forest are popular activities. There are camping and picnic areas and fishing is excellent in the river during runs.

Ocean Shores–Pacific Beach

A six-mile-long, 6000-acre peninsula, Ocean Shores was a cattle ranch when a group of investors bought it for $1 million in 1960. A decade later, its assessed value had risen to $35 million. Today, it would be hard to put a dollar figure on this strip of condominium-style hotels and second homes, many of them on a series of canals. The main tourist beach destination on the Grays Harbor County coastline, it's located along Route 115 three miles south of its junction with Route 109.

Folks come to Ocean Shores for oceanside rest and recreation, not for sightseeing. One of the few "attractions" is the **Ocean Shores Environmental Interpretive Center** (Point Brown Avenue; 360-289-4617) four miles south of the town center near the Ocean Shores Marina. Open summers only, it has exhibits describing the peninsula's geological formation and human development.

The 22-mile strip of beach that parallels Routes 115 and 109 north to Moclips is an attraction in its own right. Beyond Moclips, however, the coastline gets more rugged. Eight miles past Moclips in the village of Taholah, the **Quinault Indian National Tribal Headquarters** (360-276-8215), on the Quinault Indian Reservation, offers guided fishing and rafting trips on reservation land and a variety of tribal gifts in a small shop.

OCEAN SHORES–PACIFIC BEACH LODGING

The nearest ocean beach area to the Seattle–Tacoma metropolitan region, Ocean Shores' condominiums and motels are frequently booked solid during the summer and on holiday weekends, even though prices can be high. Other times, it can be downright quiet . . . and inexpensive.

Like almost every other lodging on this stretch of shoreline, **The Polynesian Resort** (615 Ocean Shores Boulevard, Ocean Shores; 360-289-3361, 800-562-4836, fax 360-289-0294) is as close to the water as you can get—a good mile trek across the dunes to the high-tide mark. The three-story building has 70 rooms ranging from motel units to three-bedroom penthouse suites. It has an indoor pool and spa, an outdoor games area popular with families and a restaurant and lively lounge. Deluxe to ultra-deluxe.

Across the street from the Polynesian is Ocean Shores' largest property, with 83 units, and one of its least expensive: the **Gitche Gumee Motel** (648 Ocean Shores Boulevard Northwest; 360-289-3323, 800-448-2433). Basic sleeper units are small, but kitchen units (many with fireplaces) are good-sized. Rooms have televisions and phones; everyone can use the sauna and indoor and outdoor pools. Budget.

Neighboring units at **The Grey Gull** (647 Ocean Shores Boulevard, Ocean Shores; 360-289-3381, 800-562-9712, fax 360-289-3673) are fewer in number (36), but they're all studios or suites with fireplaces, microwave ovens, videocassette recorders and private decks or balconies. The Gull has an outdoor pool and jacuzzi guarded by a wind fence. Deluxe.

One of few accommodations away from "the strip" is the **Discovery Inn** (1031 Discovery Avenue Southeast; 360-289-3371, 800-882-8821), a condo motel close to the Ocean Shores Marina near the cape's southeast tip, five miles from downtown. Rooms are built around a central courtyard with a seasonal pool. A private dock on Ocean Shores' grand canal encourages boating and fishing. Moderate.

North up the coast from frenetic Ocean Shores are numerous quiet resort communities and accommodations. At Ocean City, four miles north, the **Pacific Sands Motel** (2687 Route 109; 360-289-3588) is one of the top choices on the coast. There are just nine units, but they're well-kept; seven have kitchens and three have fireplaces. The extensive grounds include a nice swimming pool, playground, picnic tables and direct beach access across a suspension bridge. Budget.

The **Iron Springs Resort** (3707 Route 109, Copalis Beach; 360-276-4230) has 29 units in 25 cottages built up a wooded hill and around a handsome cove at the mouth of Iron Springs Creek. The beach here is popular for razor clamming, crabbing and surf fishing; the cottages are equally popular for their spaciousness and panoramic views. All have kitchens and fireplaces. There's an indoor pool, playground and gift shop. Moderate.

Ocean Crest Resort (Sunset Beach, Route 109, Moclips; 360-276-4465, 800-684-8439) may be the most memorable accommodation on this entire stretch of beach. It's built atop a bluff, so getting to the beach involves a 132-step descent down a staircase through a wooden ravine. But the views from the rooms' private balconies are remarkable, and all but the smallest rooms have fireplaces and refrigerators. There are exercise facilities with a pool, jacuzzi and weight room open to all guests free of charge. Moderate to deluxe.

OCEAN SHORES–PACIFIC BEACH RESTAURANTS

Mariah's (615 Ocean Shores Boulevard; 360-289-3315) provides a spacious, relaxing cedar dining room with a domed ceiling and skylights. Dinner specialties include honey-baked salmon, prime rib and chicken baked with artichoke hearts. Moderate to deluxe.

The **Home Port Restaurant** (854 Point Brown Avenue opposite Shoal Street, Ocean Shores; 360-289-2600) is appointed like the private garden of a sea captain home from the waves. Moderately priced steaks, seafood and pasta dominate the menu, but travelers watching their pennies can come between 4:00 and 6:30 p.m. for ample "budget-stretcher" dinners.

Numerous Ocean Shores restaurants appeal to more casual budget diners. **Flipper's Fish Bar** (Chance a la Mer at Ocean Court; 360-289-4676) has excellent fish and chips. **Barnacle Bill's** (Holman Square, Point Brown Avenue; 360-289-0218) is the place for chowder. And the **Sand Castle Drive-in** (Point Brown Avenue north of Chance a la Mer; 360-289-2777) is the in-spot for hamburgers.

Yesterday's (Damon Road at Chickaminn Avenue, Oyhut; 360-289-8657), on the access road for those who plan to drive the beach at

You can drive on some sections of the beach at Ocean City State Park.

Ocean City State Park, is another local favorite. The restaurant serves traditional American favorites at budget prices, and its lounge—with a great sunset view—has live music performed several nights a week.

North up the coast, **The Lighthouse Restaurant** (1st and Main streets, Pacific Beach; 360-276-4190) has an extensive menu of steaks, seafoods and other American traditions, like the three-quarter-pound Lighthouse burger and liver and onions. Fish can be grilled, poached or fried; steaks are well trimmed. Dinners include a salad bar and a sunset view across a playground to the blue Pacific. Moderate.

For a gourmet Continental dinner in spectacular surroundings, check out the **Ocean Crest Resort** (Route 109, Moclips; 360-276-4465). Attentive service and superb meals (with a focus on seafood and Northwest regional cuisine), amid an atmosphere of Northwest Indian tribal art, only add to the enjoyment of the main reason to dine here: the view from a bluff, through a wooded ravine, to Sunset Beach. Priced in the moderate range.

OCEAN SHORES–PACIFIC BEACH SHOPPING

The most interesting galleries in Grays Harbor County are, not surprisingly, in the beach communities. For a wide range of works by regional artists, including oil paintings, watercolors, ceramics and textile crafts, seek out **The Cove Gallery** (Route 109, Iron Springs; 360-276-4360) and **Gallery Marjuli** (865 Point Brown Avenue, Ocean Shores; 360-289-2858).

OCEAN SHORES–PACIFIC BEACH NIGHTLIFE

In Ocean Shores, at the Polynesian hotel, **Mariah's** (615 Ocean Shores Boulevard; 360-289-3315) features live contemporary music on Friday and Saturday nights.

Located at the Ocean Shores Golf and Country Club, **Mulligan's Sports Bar** (Canal Road and Albatross Street; 360-289-0929) offers a big-screen television that broadcasts sports events via satellite. On weekend nights there is live rock and rhythm-and-blues.

OCEAN SHORES–PACIFIC BEACH BEACHES AND PARKS

Popular activities at **Pacific Beach State Park** (360-276-4297) include beachcombing, kite flying, jogging and (in season) surf fishing and razor clam digging. You'll also find picnic areas and campsites, but swimming is not recommended because of the undertow and riptide. The broad, flat, sandy North Beach extends for 22 miles from Moclips to the north jetty of Grays Harbor at Ocean Shores. The park is located on Pacific Beach just off Route 109. From November through February, the park is open on weekends and holidays only.

Ocean City State Park (360-289-3553) stretches for several miles along the Pacific coastline. This North Beach park offers a dozen access points. There are picnic areas, clamming and fishing (in season), horseback riding and surf kayaking in summer, kite flying when the wind blows, birdwatching especially during migratory periods and beachcombing year-round. Swimmers should beware of the riptides. The park is located off of Route 115 and Route 109 north of Ocean Shores; a campground is situated two miles north of Ocean Shores off Route 115.

Grays Harbor Area

Industrial towns are not often places of tourist interest. The twin cities of Aberdeen and Hoquiam, on the northeastern shore of the broad Grays Harbor estuary, are an exception. A historic seaport, a rich assortment of bird life and numerous handsome mansions built by old timber money make it worthwhile to pause in this corner of Washington.

Aberdeen has about 16,500 people, **Hoquiam** around 9000, and the metropolitan area includes some 30,000. Wood-products industries provide the economic base, and boat building and fisheries, both more important in past decades, remain key businesses. For information, check with the **Grays Harbor Chamber of Commerce** (Duffy Street at Route 101, Aberdeen; 360-532-1924).

If you're coming down Route 101 from the north, it's wise to follow the signs and make your first stop at **Hoquiam's Castle** (515 Chenault Avenue, Hoquiam; 360-533-2005; admission). A stately, 20-room hillside mansion built in 1897 by a millionaire lumber baron, it has been fully restored with elegant antiques like Tiffany lamps, grandfather clocks and a 600-piece, cut-crystal chandelier. With its round turret and bright-red color, the house is unmistakable.

Also in Hoquiam is the **Arnold Polson Museum** (1611 Riverside Avenue at Route 101; 360-533-5862; admission). Built in the early 1920s by a pioneer timber family, the 26-room home contains original furnishings. It is surrounded by native trees and the Burton Ross Memorial Rose Gardens.

The Grays Harbor National Wildlife Refuge is one of four major staging areas for migratory shorebirds in North America.

A couple miles west of Hoquiam on Route 109, at Bowerman Basin on Grays Harbor, is the **Grays Harbor National Wildlife Refuge** (360-532-1924). Although this basin represents just two percent of the intertidal habitat of the estuary, fully half the one million shorebirds that visit each spring make their stop here. It's the last place to be flooded at high tide and the first to have its mudflats exposed, giving the avians extra feeding time. April and early May are the best times to visit.

A major attraction in neighboring Aberdeen, just four miles east of Hoquiam on Route 101, is the **Grays Harbor Historical Seaport** (813 East Heron Street; 360-532-8611; admission). Craftspersons at this working 18th-century shipyard have constructed a replica of the *Lady Washington*, the brigantine in which Captain Robert Gray sailed when he discovered Grays Harbor and the Columbia River in 1783. There are informational and hands-on exhibits, and visitors can stay and watch the shipbuilders at work.

A few blocks west, the **Aberdeen Museum of History** (111 East 3rd Street; 360-533-1976) offers exhibits, dioramas and videos of regional history in a 1922 armory. Displays include several re-created turn-of-the-century buildings: a one-room school, a general store, a church, a blacksmith's shop and more.

Inland from Aberdeen, Route 12 aims directly east toward Olympia. Near Elma, 20 miles east, the **Satsop Nuclear Power Plant** (471 Lambert Road, Elma; 360-482-4428 ext. 5052) offers public tours at 10 a.m. Fridays or by appointment. Visitors can see the reactor and turbine buildings and observe the control room. The plant is operated by the Washington Public Power Supply System (WPPSS), known as "Whoops!" to many Washingtonians.

Route 105 follows the south shore of Grays Harbor west from Aberdeen to the atmospheric fishing village of **Westport**, at the estuary's south head. Perhaps the most interesting of several small museums here is the **Westport Maritime Museum** (2201 Westhaven Drive; 360-268-0078), housed in a Nantucket-style Coast Guard station commissioned in 1939 but decommissioned in the 1970s. Historic photos, artifacts and memorabilia help tell the story of a sailor's life. The museum also has exhibits of skeletons of marine mammals, including whales.

Other points of interest here in Westport are the **Westport Aquarium** (321 Harbor Street; 360-268-0471; admission), with tanks of fish and other ocean creatures; and **Shellflair** (102 South Forest Street; 360-268-9087; admission), featuring displays of seashells, crustacea and fossils.

GRAYS HARBOR AREA LODGING

Like any regional center, the twin cities of Aberdeen and Hoquiam have a strip of lookalike motels along Route 101. Though it's hard to choose one above another, the **Olympic Inn Motel** (616 West Heron Street, Aberdeen; 360-533-4200, fax 360-533-6223) is notable for its modern, spacious rooms. Decor in the 55 units is simple but pleasant. Moderate.

There's considerable character at the **Lytle House Bed & Breakfast** (509 Chenault Street, Hoquiam; 360-533-2320, 800-677-2320, fax 360-533-4025), a three-story Victorian hillside mansion. Each of the eight guest rooms has a different theme, such as nautical (Harbor View room) and equestrian (Esquire). Period antiques include clawfoot tubs in the shared bathrooms. Guests choose a full gourmet breakfast from a menu offered the previous night. The house hosts murder-mystery parties by guest appointment. Moderate.

Just southeast of Aberdeen, the **Cooney Mansion** (1705 5th Street, Cosmopolis; 360-533-0602) is located in a secluded wooded area on a golf course with an adjoining tennis court and park. A National Historic Landmark built in 1908 by a lumber baron, its interior was designed to show off local woods. Now a bed and breakfast, it has nine bedrooms, five with private baths, as well as a jacuzzi, sauna, sundeck and exercise room. Moderate to deluxe.

East of Grays Harbor in the county seat of Montesano is the **Abel House** (117 Fleet Street South; 360-249-6002, 800-235-2235). This stately 1908 home has five bedrooms, two with shared baths. There are also a gameroom and reading room and an exquisite English garden. A full breakfast and afternoon tea are included with the room. Moderate.

Farther east—halfway from Montesano to Olympia, in fact, but still in Grays Harbor County—**The Old McCleary Hotel** (42 Summit Road, McCleary; 360-495-3678) maintains antique-laden rooms that seem to be especially popular with touring bicyclists. Budget.

In Westport, at the mouth of Grays Harbor, the largest motel is the **Château Westport** (710 Hancock Avenue; 360-268-9101, 800-255-9101). Many of the 108 units have balconies and fireplaces, and a third are efficiency studios with kitchenettes. The upper floors of the four-story property, easily identified by its gray mansard roof, have excellent ocean views. Dip into the indoor pool and hot tub. Moderate.

More atmospheric is the **Glenacres Inn** (222 North Montesano Street; 360-268-9391), which will celebrate its 100th anniversary in 1998. Appointments are still turn-of-the-century in style, and all 12 units—five spacious bedrooms, three deck rooms and four cottages (each of which sleep 4 to 12)—have private baths. Outdoor recreation on nine acres centers around a huge deck with a gazebo-covered hot tub. Priced in the moderate range.

More trees are harvested in Grays Harbor County than in any other county in the United States.

GRAYS HARBOR AREA RESTAURANTS

It's a comfort to know that Grays Harbor has more memorable restaurants than memorable accommodations. The best of the best is **The Levee Street** (709 Levee Street, Hoquiam; 360-532-1959), which extends over the Hoquiam River on pilings. Though it's just a block off Route 101, it has a nondescript entrance that's easy to miss. Inside, though, it's a real charmer, with fresh seafood, steaks and an excellent wine list. Dinner only, Tuesday to Saturday. Moderate.

When Chef Pierre Gabelli moved to the Washington coast from his native Italy, it was only natural that he should open the **Parma Ristorante Italiano** (116 West Heron Street, Aberdeen; 360-532-3166). Gourmet pastas like gnocchi and tortelli d'Erbetta, as well as seafood fettuccines and a handful of outstanding meat dishes, are served. Best of all are the homemade desserts. Budget to moderate.

Bridges Restaurant (112 North G Street, Aberdeen; 360-532-6563) is a handsome, garden-style restaurant with one dining room that's actually a greenhouse. As the size of its parking lot attests, it's very popular locally, for its lounge as well as its cuisine. Local seafood, steaks, chicken and pasta highlight the menu. Moderate.

For historic flavor, you needn't look further than **Billy's Bar and Grill** (322 East Heron Street, Aberdeen; 360-533-7144). Named for an early 20th-century ne'er-do-well notorious for mugging loggers and shanghaiing sailors, Billy's boasts an ornate century-old ceiling, huge antique bar and wall murals that are colorful if not downright bawdy. This is the place to settle back with a burger and a beer and soak up the past. Budget.

Elsewhere in the Grays Harbor area, the **Hong Kong Restaurant** (1212 1st Street, Cosmopolis; 360-533-7594) is surprisingly authentic for a town so far removed from China! It has chop suey and egg foo yung, yes, but it also has egg flower soup, moo goo gai pan and other tastes from the old country. Budget.

Out in Westport, whose resemblance to a New England fishing village may be coincidental, is **Constantin's** (320 East Dock Street; 360-268-0550), whose similarity to Greek restaurants in the Aegean is no accident. The specialties revolve around seafood and seafood-meat combinations including lamb chops, filet mignon and crab and black tiger prawns. There is also an extensive wine list featuring local and imported wines. Moderate to deluxe.

Nearby Grayland has **The Dunes Restaurant** (783 Dunes Road; 360-267-1441), one-quarter mile off Route 105 in an eclectic beachcombers' hideaway surrounded by seagrass and sand dunes. (Look for the sign of the giant geoduck on the highway.) Come here for the seafood: fresh clam chowder, oysters, crab, salmon and much, much more. All meals come with fresh vegetables and homemade rolls. Moderate.

GRAYS HARBOR AREA SHOPPING

For a sampling of creations by regional artisans, visit the **Pacific Center of the Arts and Crafts** (1767 Route 105, Grayland; 360-267-1351), which features pottery, original art and locally made gift items.

GRAYS HARBOR AREA NIGHTLIFE

Folks in the Grays Harbor area show a predilection for **Sidney's Restaurant and Sports Bar** (512 West Heron Avenue, Aberdeen; 360-533-6635), where a deejay spins disks regularly; the Victorian bar at **Billy's Bar and Grill** 322 East Heron Avenue, Aberdeen; 360-533-7144); and the posh lounge at **Bridges Restaurant** (112 North G Street; 360-532-6563).

GRAYS HARBOR AREA BEACHES AND PARKS

At **Lake Sylvia State Park** (360-249-3621), visitors can circumambulate the narrow, forest-enshrouded lake on a two-mile hiking trail. Also here are picnic areas, campsites, a swimming beach, fishing and boat rentals. The park is two miles north of Montesano off Route 12, via North 3rd Street.

Schafer State Park (West 1365 Schafer Park Road, off Route 12, twelve miles north of Elma; 360-482-3852) was once a family park for employees of the Schafer Logging Company. Now this tranquil 119-acre site on the East Fork of the Satsop River is still popular with families. Located in a heavily forested area, it's ideal for picnics, hikes and fishing. There's a beach, but the water's cold. Campsites are available.

An Army Corps of Engineers water-supply and flood-control project created the four-and-a-half-mile-long lake at **Lake Wynoochee Recreation Area** (360-877-5254) in 1972 by a dam on the Wynoochee River. The visitors center has interpretive displays. A 12-mile trail winds around the lake, past a beach and designated swimming area. Trout fishing, waterskiing and wildlife watching are also popular. You can camp at nearby Coho campground in the national forest; information, 360-877-5254. The lake is located 37 miles north of Montesano on Forest Service Road 22, off Route 12.

The Washington coast's largest campground dominates Twin Harbors State Park.

Westhaven State Park, which occupies the southern headland at the mouth of Grays Harbor, is a great place for watching birds and wildlife, including harbor seals and whales during migratory periods. Surfing is excellent here and there are yearly competitions. Westhaven is adjacent to **Westport Light State Park**, which surrounds a historic lighthouse that's warned coastal ships of the entrance to Grays Harbor since 1897. There is a multi-use paved trail connecting the two parks that's open for hiking, bicycling, roller-skating and other nonmotorized forms of transportation. Surfing is good at the jetty, but swimming is not recommended because of riptides. Both parks are about one-half mile from downtown Westport; Westhaven is on East Yearout Drive and Westport Light is at the end of Ocean Avenue (information, 360-268-9565).

Twin Harbors State Park (360-268-9565, 360-268-9717) is a 168-acre park with picnic areas and plenty of campsites. It also includes the Shifting Sands Nature Trail with interpretive signs for dunes explorers. Beachcombing, kite flying and clamming are popular activities on the broad, sandy beach. You can fish in the surf or from a charter boat. Swimming is not recommended because of riptides. Located on Route 105, about four miles south of Westport and four miles north of Grayland.

Grayland Beach State Park (360-267-4301), like other coastal beaches, is broad and flat and ideal for clam digging, beachcombing, kite flying and other seaside diversions. An interpretive self-guided trail leads through the dunes of the 402-acre park, one of the larger of the coastal reserves. You can picnic and camp, or just fish in the surf, but riptides make it unsafe for swimmers. On Route 105, one mile south of Grayland.

Long Beach–Willapa Bay

The largest "unpopulated" estuary in the continental United States, this region's pristine condition makes it one of the world's best places for farming oysters. From Tokeland to Bay Center to Oysterville, tiny villages that derive their sole income from the shelled creatures display mountains of empty shells as evidence of their success. Begin your visit on Route 105 south from Westport, then head east along the northern shore of Willapa Bay.

Thirty-three miles from Westport, Route 105 rejoins Route 101 at **Raymond**. This town of 3000, and its smaller sister community of **South Bend** four miles south on Route 101, are lumber ports on the lower Willapa River.

You'll find murals—43 of them, to be exact—on walls from Ocean Shores to the Columbia River, Elma to Ilwaco. Chambers of commerce and other visitor information centers have guide pamphlets. But no mural is larger than the 85-foot-wide painting of an early logger on the **Dennis Company Building** (5th Street, Raymond). The company's outdoor display of old-time farm equipment is across the street.

Attractions in South Bend include the **Pacific County Museum** (1008 West Robert Bush Drive; 360-875-5224), with pioneer artifacts from the turn of the century and the 1911 **Pacific County Courthouse** (300 Memorial Drive off Route 101; 360-875-9300), noted for its art-glass dome and historic foyer wall paintings.

The **Long Beach Peninsula**, reached via Route 101 from South Bend (43 miles), has had a significant flow of vacationing Northwest urbanites for over a century. But its economy is more strongly founded in fish processing and cranberry growing. Information is available from the **Long Beach Peninsula Visitor Bureau** (Route 101 and Route 103, Seaview; 360-642-2400).

Route 103, which runs north-south up the 28-mile-long, two-mile-wide peninsula, is intersected by Route 101 at **Seaview**. The town of **Long Beach** is just a mile north of the junction. Its principal attraction is a 2300-foot wooden **boardwalk** (South 10th to Bolstad streets), elevated 40 feet above the dunes, enabling folks to make an easy trek to the high-tide mark. The beach, incidentally, is open to driving on the hard upper sand, and to surf fishing, clamming, beachcombing, kite flying and picnicking everywhere.

During the peak blooming season in May, the **Clarke Rhododendron Nursery** (Sandridge Road, Long Beach; 360-642-2241) is a dazzling place to view rhododendrons and azaleas in all their splendor.

Ten miles north of Long Beach is **Ocean Park**, the commercial hub of the central and northern Long Beach Peninsula. Developed as a Methodist camp in 1883, it evolved into a small resort town. Older yet is **Oysterville**, another three miles north via the Peninsula Highway. Founded in 1854, this National Historic District boasts the oldest continuously

---

GO FLY A KITE

Kite flying is a big thing on the Washington coast, so it's no accident that the **World Kite Museum and Hall of Fame** *(3rd Street Northwest at Route 103; 360-642-4020; admission) can be found in Long Beach. The museum has rotating exhibits of kites from around the world—Japanese, Chinese, Thai, and so on— with displays of stunt kites, military kites and more.*

operating post office in Washington (1858) and 17 other designated historic sites. Get a walking-tour pamphlet from the **Old Church** beside the Village Green on Territory Road.

South of Seaview just two miles on Route 103 is **Ilwaco**, spanning the isthmus between the Columbia River and the Pacific Ocean. Local history is featured at the impressive **Ilwaco Heritage Museum** (115 Southeast Lake Street; 360-642-3446; admission). A series of galleries depicts the development of southwestern Washington from early Indian culture to European voyages of discovery, from pioneer settlement to the 20th century.

About eight miles southeast, a short distance before Route 101 crosses the Columbia River to Astoria, Oregon, **Fort Columbia State Park** (Route 101, Chinook; 360-777-8221) is a highly recommended stop for history buffs. Two buildings at the site are museums: the **Fort Columbia Interpretive Center**, exhibiting artifacts of early 20th-century military life in a former coastal artillery post, and the **DAR House**, which the Daughters of the American Revolution have restored to depict the everyday lifestyle of a military officer of the time.

LONG BEACH–WILLAPA BAY LODGING

Possibly the most delightful accommodation anywhere on the Washington coast is **The Shelburne Country Inn** (4415 Pacific Way, Seaview; 360-642-2442, fax 360-642-8904). The oldest continually operating hotel in the state, it opened in 1896 and is still going strong. Fifteen guest rooms are furnished with Victorian antiques and fresh flowers. All have private baths and decks. A hearty country breakfast is served in the morning. Moderate to deluxe.

Another one-of-a-kinder, but for very different reasons, is **The Sou'wester Lodge Cabins and Tch! Tch!** (Beach Access Road, 38th Place, Seaview; 360-642-2542): It's a place much beloved by youth hostelers who, well, grew up. Proprietors Len and Miriam Atkins have intentionally kept the accommodation simple and weathered. They advertise it as a B&MYODB—"bed and make your own damn breakfast." Kitchen rights extend to the living room, including the fireplace and library. Sleeping options include rooms in the historic lodge, cedar-shingled housekeeping cabins, a dozen-or-so vintage mobile homes ("Trailer Classics Hodgepodge") and an area for RVs and tent campers. Budget to moderate prices.

Numerous beachfront cabin communities speckle the shoreline of the Long Beach Peninsula north from Ilwaco and Seaview. One of the best is the **Klipsan Beach Cottages** (22617 Pacific Highway, Ocean Park; 360-665-4888). Each of the ten cottages, in a lovely wooded setting eight miles north of the town of Long Beach, has a kitchen and fireplace or woodburning stove (with free firewood). Some two- and three-bedroom units are available. Moderate.

Shakti Cove (253rd Place and Park Street, Ocean Park; 360-665-4000) is located just five minutes from the water. Ten rustic cabins all are fully equipped with kitchens and sleep up to four guests. The units are furnished with queen-size beds, older couches and feature eclectic decor. Budget to moderate. Gay-friendly.

The Inn at Ilwaco (120 Williams Street Northeast, Ilwaco; 360-642-8686) blends its elements in a unique manner: Housed in what once was the Ilwaco Presbyterian Church, it's a bed and breakfast, theater and wedding chapel! The nine guest rooms (seven with private baths) occupy the old Sunday school wing; the sanctuary is a performing arts center. And yes, you can get married here. Moderate.

Willapa Bay oyster lovers frequent the beds near the north end of the Long Beach Peninsula, and this is where they'll find the **Moby Dick Hotel** (Sandridge and Bay avenues, Nahcotta; 360-665-4543, fax 360-665-6887). An 11-room bed-and-breakfast inn that first opened its doors in 1930, it maintains a country nautical atmosphere, with rambling grounds, its own vegetable garden and oyster farm. A fireplace and piano beckon on rainy days. Moderate.

The **Hostelling International—Fort Columbia** (Route 101, Chinook; 360-777-8755) occupies the former Coast Artillery Infirmary. There are two dorms—a 13-bunk room for men, a five-bunk room for women—and a single family room. Guests share kitchen, bathroom and living facilities. For fifty cents, guests can cook up an all-you-can-eat pancake breakfast. Budget.

LONG BEACH–WILLAPA BAY RESTAURANTS

For a unique dining experience, visit the **Blue Heron Inn** (Bay Center Road, Bay Center; 360-875-9990), on an off-the-beaten-track peninsula that juts into Willapa Bay 12 miles south of South Bend. Oysters, of course, are a specialty at this café-tavern. The fish market here also sells fresh crab and smoked salmon. Budget to moderate.

Expensive, but worth it. Everything is exquisite in **The Shoalwater Restaurant** (Shelburne Inn, 4415 Pacific Way, Seaview; 360-642-4142), one of Washington's most highly acclaimed country restaurants. From the seafood mousseline to the mussel chowder, the rabbit sirloin to the sautéed Willapa Bay oysters with a Thai-style wild mushroom sauce, and the creative preparations of the day's fresh catches, a deluxe meal here is one to savor. The turn-of-the-century ambience adds an element of comfort. Opposite the restaurant entrance is The Heron & Beaver Pub, with light meals produced by the same kitchen for moderate prices.

My Mom's Pie Kitchen (Route 103 at South 12th Street, Long Beach; 360-642-2342) has great pies—from wild blackberry to chocolate almond to sour-cream raisin—but that's not the only reason to dine in this charming double-wide trailer. Soups, chowders, salads and sandwiches are served for lunch, and the chicken-almond pot pie is a mouthwatering delight. Budget.

Kopa Wecoma (900 Pacific Avenue South, Long Beach; 360-642-4224) is decorated in original artwork and evokes a casual country atmosphere. Visitors may not be prepared for the generous portions offered at this serendipitous beachfront diner. Come for the famous fish and chips, the clam chowder, the seafood plates, the sandwiches. Open Friday to Monday only. Budget.

Mountains of oyster shells surround **The Ark Restaurant and Bakery** (270 3rd Street and Sandridge Road, Nahcotta; 360-665-4133), located near the north end of the Long Beach Peninsula on oyster-rich Willapa Bay. In fact, the restaurant has its own oyster beds—as well as an herb and edible-flower garden and a busy bakery. Nearby are cranberry bogs and forests of wild mushrooms. All these go into the preparation of creative dishes like pan-fried salmon with wild mushrooms, sundried tomatoes and balsamic crème sauce and filet mignon with pinenuts and caramelized garlic sauce. Lunch and dinner during summer; Thursday through Sunday dinner and Sunday brunch only in winter. Prices fall in the moderate-to-deluxe range.

Dining at **The Sanctuary** (Route 101 and Hazel Street, Chinook; 360-777-8380) is a sacred ritual to some folks. And well it should be: The restaurant occupies the premises of the historic Methodist Episcopal Church of Chinook (1906–1978). Few renovations have been made to the building, although wine is taken much more often than during communion, and sundaes can sometimes be sinful. The varied menu includes Swedish meatballs and fish cakes, steaks and fresh seafood. Dinner only. Moderate.

THE CRANBERRY HARVEST

In October and early November, the cranberry harvest takes precedence over all else on the Olympic Peninsula. Most fields are owned by the folks from Ocean Spray. The **Pacific Coast Cranberry Museum** *at Washington State University (Pioneer Road, Long Beach; 360-642-2031) provides a historic view of the west coast cranberry industry. Exhibits include hand tools, cranberry boxes, labels, pickers, sorters and separators. Free tours of the cranberry bogs are offered during harvest, and other times by appointment.*

LONG BEACH–WILLAPA BAY SHOPPING

On the Long Beach Peninsula, there's wonderful bric-a-brac at **Marsh's Free Museum** (409 Pacific Avenue South, Long Beach; 360-642-2188), from the world's largest frying pan (so they say) to antique music boxes. Noted watercolorist Eric Wiegardt displays his work at the **Wiegardt Studio Gallery** (Bay Avenue between Route 103 and Sandridge Road, Ocean Park; 360-665-5976).

Perhaps the souvenir most typical of beach recreation here would be a colorful kite. Look for them at **Ocean Kites** (511 Pacific Avenue South, Long Beach; 360-642-2229) and **Long Beach Kites** (104 Pacific Avenue North; 360-642-2202).

LONG BEACH–WILLAPA BAY NIGHTLIFE

The Lightship Restaurant (Nendel's Edgewater Inn, 409 Southwest 10th Street, Long Beach; 360-642-3252) has the Long Beach Peninsula's only ocean-view restaurant from its fourth-story loft; come for a sunset drink. Things may be a bit livelier at the **Bent Rudder Pub and Galley** (1700 Pacific Avenue South, Long Beach; 360-642-8330), which often features live rock bands. Quiet beers are best quaffed at **The Heron & Beaver Pub** (Shelburne Inn, 4415 Pacific Way, Seaview; 360-642-4142).

LONG BEACH–WILLAPA BAY BEACHES AND PARKS

Shifting dunes and mudflats, ponds and marshes, grasslands and forests make **Leadbetter Point State Park** (360-642-3078) at the northern tip of the Long Beach Peninsula an ideal place for those who like to observe

---

AT THE MOUTH OF THE COLUMBIA RIVER

*The point where the Columbia River meets the Pacific Ocean has been a crossroads of history for two centuries. The Lewis and Clark expedition arrived at this dramatic headland in 1805 after more than a year and a half on the trail. Two 19th-century lighthouses—at North Head on the Pacific and at Cape Disappointment on a Columbia sandbar—have limited the number of shipwrecks to a mere 200 or so. Located here, Fort Canby was occupied from the Civil War through World War II. Today, the 1800-acre **Fort Canby State Park** (Southwest of Ilwaco on Route 101; 360-642-3078) contains the Lewis and Clark Interpretive Center (with exhibits and a multimedia program), numerous forest, beach and cliff-top trails, boat launch, campsites and summer interpretive programs. Surf fishing is particularly good here.*

nature. As many as 100 species of migratory bird stop over here. There are picnic areas and numerous hiking trails. Swimming is not recommended due to riptides and undertows. Located three miles north of Oysterville on Stackpole Road, via Route 103 and Sandridge Road.

Pacific Pines State Park (360-642-3078) is a day-use park offering picnic areas and beach access for activities like beachcombing, kite flying, jogging, surf fishing and razor clam digging in season. You can drive on the uppermost sand, but be sure it's hard-packed; more than one car owner has needed a tow after getting bogged in the sand. Riptides make it too dangerous for swimming. The address is 274 Place off Park Avenue, one mile north of Ocean Park.

Loomis Lake State Park (360-642-3078) is situated on a narrow, three-mile-long freshwater lake south of Klipsan Beach. This day-use park has picnic areas and offers the swimming that's discouraged in the surf, as well as good fishing from shore. The park is located, appropriately enough, on Park Road, via 199 Place off Route 103, four miles south of Ocean Park.

Southwest Washington

Heading east from the coast via Route 401 and Route 4, you'll want to take the cutoff south to the circa 1905 **Grays River Covered Bridge**. Continue east another 17 miles to Skamokawa, a town that's hard to pronounce and easy to visit. The site of an Indian village that dates back to the time of Christ, this lumber town is on the Lewis and Clark Trail. Local Skamokawa Vista Park is a good spot to watch traffic on the Columbia River shipping channel. At **Redman Hall** (1394 West Route 4, Skamokawa; 360-795-3007), a turn-of-the-century schoolhouse has become a community museum. Step inside the three-story landmark to learn more about this 19th-century riverfront town now on the National Register of Historic Places.

To the east, you won't want to miss the **Julia Butler Hansen National Wildlife Refuge** (Route 4, Cathlamet; 360-795-3915). A sanctuary for the Columbian white-tailed deer, this waterfront refuge is also a place to spot elk and migratory birds.

The refuge is next door to Cathlamet, a historic logging town. Begin your visit at the **Wahkiakum County Museum** (65 River Street, Cathlamet; 360-795-3954; admission). The collection is strong on community artifacts, victrolas, dolls and railway equipment. A self-guided walking tour brochure available here will lead you to local landmarks like the Kimball Butler Hansen House at 35 Butler Street. At the Pioneer Cemetery, you'll find the grave of Chief Wahkiakum.

Before harvesting shellfish, call the Red Tide Hotline (800-562-5632) to find out if the waters are healthy.

The Sporting Life

FISHING

Lakes and rivers—and, of course, the sea—offer a plethora of opportunities to catch everything from rainbow trout to salmon and halibut.

The Strait of Juan de Fuca is one of the nation's great salmon grounds, with chinook, coho and other species running the waters through the summer months. Other fish include halibut (up to 240 pounds), ling cod, true cod, red snapper and black bass. Port Townsend, Port Angeles, Sekiu, Clallam Bay and Neah Bay are the main ports for charter vessels. Operators include **Sea Sport Charters** (P.O. Box 805, Port Townsend, WA 98362; 360-385-3575); **Thunderbird Boathouse** (P.O. Box 787, Port Angeles, WA 98362; 360-457-3595) and **Woodie's Charter Service** (Clallam Bay; 360-963-2421).

Farther down the coast, on the south side of Grays Harbor, the year-round fishing port of Westport matches deep-sea anglers with charter boats. Operators include **Deep Sea Charters** (Float 6; 360-268-9300) and **Neptune Charters** (2601 Westhaven Drive, across from Float 14; 360-268-0124).

At the mouth of the Columbia, Ilwaco is another deep-sea fishing center. Salmon and sturgeon are caught near the river mouth, while tuna, rockfish, cod and sole are in deeper waters. See **Seabreeze Charters** (185 Howerton Way Southeast, Ilwaco; 360-642-2300) or **Tidewind Charters** (151 Howerton Way Southeast, Ilwaco; 360-642-2111).

Inland, Olympic National Park and Olympic National Forest have marvelous trout fishing in their lakes and streams. The rivers flowing from the mountains are busy from December through April with steelhead. Licensed guide service is offered in most river communities. Check with **Quinault Indian Nation Fish and Game Department** (134 West Quinault, Taholah; 360-276-8211); **3-Rivers Resort & Guide Service** (Box 280, Forks, WA 98331; 360-374-5300) or **Fish-Hawk Guide Service** (P.O. Box 396, Forks, WA 98331; 360-374-5488).

Many folks prefer shellfishing—the pursuit of clams, oysters, mussels, scallops, clams and the like—to dropping a line into the briny. Dungeness Spit, north of Sequim, is the home of the renowned Dungeness crab. Willapa Bay is famous for its oysters. Littleneck, butter, horse and Manila hardshell clams can be dug from the beaches along with that

Northwest oddity, the geoduck (say "gooey-duck"), whose huge foot cannot fit within its shell.

RIVER RAFTING AND KAYAKING

Three of the rivers falling from the Olympics, the north-flowing Elwha and the west-flowing Hoh and Queets, attract whitewater rafters. **Olympic Raft and Guide Service** (239521 Route 101 West, Port Angeles; 360-452-1443) is the major outfitter in the area. Kayakers can run the Elwha, Sol Duc, Dosewallips or Wynoochee with the **Olympic Outdoor Center** (18971 Front Street, Poulsbo; 360-697-6095). Port Townsend is a sea-kayaking center; call **Sport Townsend** (1044 Water Street, Port Townsend; 360-379-9711).

Kayaks and More (P.O. Box 176, Carlsborg, WA 98324; 360-683-3805) provides guided sea kayak tours through the Discovery Bay and Port Williams area near Port Angeles. There are also tours to view the sand-bluff art of local artist Tim Quinn on the Miller Peninsula.

WHALE-WATCHING

Gray whales and humpbacks migrate up the Pacific Coast, from tropical to Alaskan waters, between March and May. Orcas, or killer whales, are frequently seen in the waters of the Strait of Juan de Fuca. Many fishing charter operators throughout the region convert to whale-watching cruises at this time. In Ocean Shores, the **Silver King Motel** (360-289-3386) arranges harbor/whale-watching tours aboard *El Matador* from October through May. From Westport, there's a number of specialty whale-cruise operators, including **Ocean Charters** (Float 6; 360-268-9144) and **Whales Ahoy** (Float 8; 360-268-9150).

SKIING

The snow-covered Olympics offer many opportunities for cross-country skiers, and one for downhillers. The Hurricane Ridge Ski Area, 17 miles south of Port Angeles via Hurricane Ridge Road, has several miles of cross-country trails starting from the Hurricane Ridge Lodge. Rentals of downhill, cross-country and snowshoeing equipment are also available (open December through March, weekends only). Contact **Olympic National Park** (3002 Mount Angeles Road, 360-452-0330). For road conditions, call 360-452-0329.

For biking, hiking, canoeing and country life, you can't beat Puget Island, a bucolic retreat just minutes from Cathlamet connecting Washington to Oregon via ferry.

HORSEBACK RIDING AND PACK TRIPS

For casual riding, one of your best bets is **Seahorse Ranch** (Mile 9, Route 109, east of Hoquiam; 360-532-6791). There are numerous trails around the 400-acre ranch and an indoor arena for rainy days. **Nan Sea Stables** (255 Route 115, Ocean Shores; 360-289-0194) offers guided trail rides and sunset beach rides.) Horseback rides and overnight pack trips in the Olympic Mountains are offered by **R.D.N. Ranch** (258053 Route 101, Port Angeles; 360-457-3923)

Llama lovers will be delighted to accompany an Andean pack animal into the Olympics, thanks to **Kit's Llamas** (5494 Southeast Burley-Olalla Road, Olalla; 360-857-5274), **Wooley Packer Llama Company** (Box 674, Forks, WA 98331; 360-374-9288) and **Olympak Llamas** (3175 Old Olympic Highway, Port Angeles; 360-452-4475).

GOLF

Full 18-hole courses in the region include the **Chevy Chase Golf Club** (7401 Cape George Road, Port Townsend; 360-385-0704); **Port Ludlow Golf Course** (9483 Oak Bay Road, Port Ludlow; 360-437-2222); **Dungeness Golf & Country Club** (1965 Woodcock Road, Sequim; 360-683-6344); **Sunland Golf and Country Club** (109 Hilltop Drive, Sequim; 360-683-6800); **Port Townsend Golf Club** (1840 Blaine Street; 360-385-0752; **Ocean Shores Golf Course** (Canal Road and Albatross Street, Ocean Shores; 360-289-3357); and **Oaksridge Golf Course** (1052 Monte–Elma Road, Elma; 360-482-3511).

BICYCLING

Except along the southwestern shore areas, bicycling this part of Washington requires strength and stamina. There's spectacular beauty here, but there's also rain—lots of it—and challenging terrain.

One of the gentlest biking opportunities is the 14-mile **Ocean Shores Loop** from North Beach Park. Other recommended road tours in this region include the 85-mile **Upper Peninsula Tour** from Sequim to Neah Bay; the 55-mile trip down Route 101 from **Port Angeles to Forks**; the 69-mile **Aberdeen–Raymond–Westport loop** on Routes 101 and 105; and the 42-mile **Seaview–Naselle** loop in Pacific County.

BIKE RENTALS   For rentals try **Port Townsend Cyclery** (100 Tyler Street, Port Townsend; 360-385-6470). In Forks, there's **Olympic Mountains Bike Shop** (88th Street; 360-374-9777).

HIKING

Olympic National Park and adjacent areas of Olympic National Forest are rich in backpacking opportunities. Most trails follow rivers into the high country, with its peaks and alpine lakes. Coastal areas of the Olympic Peninsula have hiking trails as well. Along the southwestern Washington coast there are few inland trails, but the long stretches of flat beach appeal to many walkers.

PORT TOWNSEND AREA TRAILS   Mt. Walker Trail (2 miles) ascends the Olympics' easternmost peak (2804 feet) through a rhododendron forest. The view from the summit, across **Hood Canal an**d the Kitsap Peninsula to Seattle and the Cascades, is unforgettable. The trailhead is one-fifth mile off Route 101 at Walker Pass, five miles south of Quilcene.

PORT ANGELES AREA TRAILS   **Dungeness Spit Trail** (5.5 miles) extends down the outside of the longest natural sandspit in the United States, and back the inside. The spit is a national wildlife refuge with a lighthouse at its seaward end. The trail begins and ends at the Dungeness Recreation Area.

OLYMPIC NATIONAL PARK TRAILS   **Elk Mountain Trail** (7.6 miles) leads from the Deer Park Campground to Obstruction Point, following a 6500-foot ridgeline.
An unnamed 28.5-mile trail starts at the Dosewallips Ranger Station on the park's eastern boundary, follows the Dosewallips River to its source in the Anderson Glacier, then goes down the East Fork of the Quinault to the Graves Creek Campground.
Seven Lakes Basin Loop (22.5 miles) has several trail options, starting and ending at Sol Duc Hot Springs.
Hoh River Trail (18 miles) wanders through North America's most famous rainforest from the Hoh Ranger Station, to Glacier Meadows, at the base of the Blue Glacier on 7965-foot Mt. Olympus, the park's highest point.
Cape Alava Loop (9 miles) crosses from the Ozette Ranger Station to Cape Alava, follows the shoreline south to Sand Point, from which there is beach access to shipwreck memorials farther south, and returns northeast to the ranger station. Prehistoric petroglyphs and an ancient Indian village can be seen en route.

The Ozette Loop Trail weaves past 56 petroglyphs that depict various aspects of historic Makah life.

SOUTHWEST COAST TRAILS   At Twin Harbors State Park south of Westport, **Shifting Sands Nature Trail** (.5 mile) teaches visitors about plant and animal life in the seaside dunes.

Leadbetter Point Loop Trail (2.5 miles) weaves through forests and dunes and past ponds, mudflats and marshes of the state park/wildlife sanctuary at the northern tip of the Long Beach Peninsula. Accessible from Oysterville, it's of special interest to birdwatchers.

Willapa Bay National Wildlife Refuge (3.2 miles) on Long Island has an interpretive trail through an important grove of old-growth red cedar, some as large as 11 feet wide and 150 feet tall.

Transportation

BY CAR

Route 101 is the main artery of the Olympic Peninsula and Washington coastal region, virtually encircling the entire land mass. Branching off Route 5 in Olympia, at the foot of Puget Sound, it runs north to Discovery Bay, where **Route 20** turns off to Port Townsend; west through Port Angeles to Sappho; then zigzags to Astoria, Oregon, and points south. Remarkably, when you reach Aberdeen, 292 miles after you start traveling on 101, you're just 36 miles from where you started!

Traveling from Seattle, most Olympic Peninsula visitors take either the Seattle-Winslow ferry (to Route 305) or the Edmonds-Kingston ferry (to Route 104), joining 101 just south of Discovery Bay. From Tacoma, the practical route is **Route 16** across the Narrows Bridge. From the north, the Keystone ferry to Port Townsend has its eastern terminus midway down lanky Whidbey Island, off **Route 20**. Northbound travelers can reach the area either through Astoria, on Route 101, or via several routes that branch off Route 5 north of Portland.

BY AIR

Fairchild International Airport, in Port Angeles, links the northern Olympic Peninsula with major cities throughout the United States and western Canada via Horizon Air Lines.

BY BUS

Port Angeles–Seattle Bus Lines (360-681-7705, 800-764-2287) is a small, privately owned bus company serving the Olympic peninsula and connecting with Greyhound in Seattle at the depot on 9th and Stewart streets. Connections are also made with Amtrak and the Coho Ferry in Seattle. Tickets can be purchased at Jackpot gas stations (Front and Ennis streets, Port Angeles, 360-547-4580; Red Ranch, off Route 101, Sequim, 360-683-7415).

BY FERRY

Washington State Ferries (206-464-6400) serves the Olympic Peninsula directly from Whidbey Island to Port Townsend and indirectly across Puget Sound (via the Kitsap Peninsula) from Seattle and Edmonds. The **Black Ball Ferry** (360-457-4491) offers direct daily service between Port Angeles and Victoria, B.C., and **Victoria Rapid Transit** (360-452-8088) provides foot-passenger service mid-May through October. Some smaller cruise lines may make stops in Port Angeles.

CAR RENTALS

In Port Angeles, **Budget Rent A Car** (800-527-0700) can be found at the airport or in town. Another agency is **Dan Wilder Volkswagen** (800-927-9372). In Aberdeen, you'll find **U-Save Auto Rental** (800-272-8728).

PUBLIC TRANSPORTATION

For local bus service in the northern Olympic Peninsula, including Port Angeles and Sequim, call **Clallam Transit System** (360-452-4511) in Port Angeles. Port Townsend, Sequim and eastern Jefferson County are served by **Jefferson Transit** (360-385-4777). The **Grays Harbor Transportation Authority** (360-532-2770) offers bus service to Aberdeen, Ocean Shores and the surrounding region.

Bus service between Raymond, Long Beach and Astoria, Oregon, is provided by the **Pacific Transit System** (206-642-9418).

SEVEN

Northern Puget Sound
and the San Juan Islands

"Every part of this land is sacred to my people. Every shining pine needle, every sandy shore, every mist in the dark woods, every clearing and humming insect is holy in the memory and experience of my people . . . . We are part of the earth and it is part of us. The perfumed flowers are our sisters; the deer, the horse, the great eagle, these are our brothers. The rocky crests, the juices in the meadows, the body heat of the pony and man—all belong to the same family." This was part of Chief Seattle's poignant reply when, in 1854, the "Great White Chief" in Washington pressed to purchase some of the land around Puget Sound then occupied by several Northwest Native American tribes. And those sentiments still ring true today as the natural beauty and appeal of northern Puget Sound and the San Juan Islands remain undiminished.

The Native Americans had good reason to hold this awe-inspiring land in such high regard. It supported them, providing for all their needs with verdant woods full of deer and berries and crystal waters full of salmon, letting them live in peaceful coexistence for hundreds of years. Even the weather was kind to them here in this "rain shadow," shielded by the Olympic and Vancouver mountain ranges.

Things slowly began to change for the Northwest tribes and the land with the arrival of Juan de Fuca in 1592, who came to explore the coastline for the Spanish. The flood gates of exploration and exploitation weren't fully opened, however, until Captain George Vancouver came in 1792 to chart the region for the British, naming major landmarks such as Mt. Baker, Mt. Rainier, Whidbey Island and Puget Sound after his compatriots.

The bulk of the world's seed crops are grown in the Skagit Valley.

Establishment of trade with the Native Americans and the seemingly inexhaustible quantity of animals to supply the lucrative fur trade drew many pioneers. Before long, industries such as logging, mining, shipping and fishing began to flourish, supporting the early settlers (and still supporting their descendants today).

The geographical layout of the 172 islands of the San Juan Archipelago made for watery back alleys and hidden coves perfect for piracy and smuggling, so the history of the area reflects an almost Barbary Coast-type of intrigue where a man could get a few drinks, a roll in the hay and be shanghaied all in one night. Chinese laborers were regularly brought in under cover of darkness to build up coastal cities and railroads in the late 1800s. This big money "commodity" was replaced first by opium and silk, and then booze during Prohibition.

Smuggling has since been curbed, and while things are changing as resources are diminished, logging and fishing are still major industries in the region. However, current booms in real estate and tourism are beginning to tilt the economic scale as more and more people discover the area's beauty.

The area referred to as northern Puget Sound begins just beyond the far northern outskirts of Seattle, where most visitors first arrive, and extends up the coast to the Canadian border. Communities along the coast such as Everett, Bellingham and Blaine tend to be commercial in nature, heavily flavored by the logging and fishing industries, while other small towns such as La Conner and Mt. Vernon are still very pastoral, dependent on an agriculturally based economy. Springtime along this stretch of land is particularly lovely, especially in the Skagit Valley when the fields are ablaze in daffodils, iris and tulips.

Of the 172 named islands of the San Juans, we concentrate on the five most popular. These also are very pastoral, with rich soil and salubrious conditions perfectly suited to raising livestock or growing fruit. The major islands are connected to the mainland by bridges or reached by limited ferry service, an inhibiting factor that helps preserve the pristine nature here.

Although it's not considered part of the San Juans, Whidbey is the largest island in Puget Sound. Situated at Whidbey's northern tip is Fidalgo Island, home of Anacortes and the ferry terminal gateway to the San Juans. Lopez is by far the friendliest and most rural of the islands, followed closely by San Juan, the largest and busiest. Shaw Island is one of the smaller islands, and lovely Orcas Island is the tallest, capped by 2400-foot Mt. Constitution.

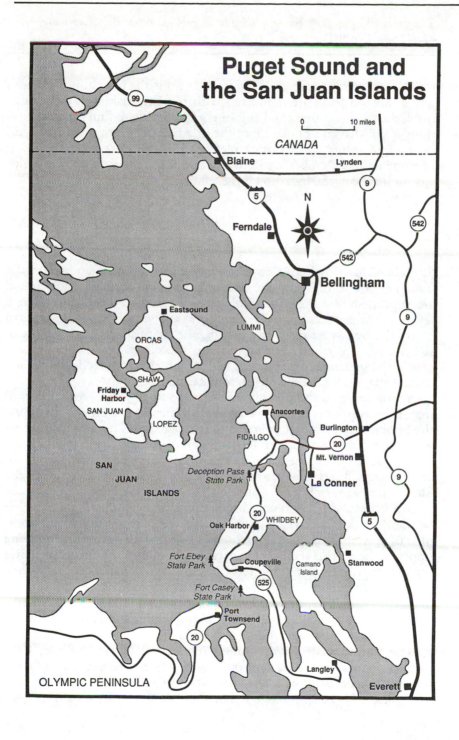

Puget Sound and the San Juan Islands

The world's biggest single grower of tulip bulbs—Washington Bulb Company—is based in the Skagit Valley.

The ferry system is severely overtaxed during the busy summer season when the San Juans are inundated with tourists, making it difficult to reach the islands at times and absolutely impossible to find accommodations if you haven't booked months in advance. The crowds drop off dramatically after Labor Day, a pleasant surprise since the weather in September and October is still lovely and the change of seasonal color against this beautiful backdrop is incredible.

Northern Puget Sound

Stretched along the fertile coastline between the Canadian border and the outer reaches of Seattle, the communities along northern Puget Sound are dependent on agriculture, fishing and logging, so the distinct pastoral feel of the area is no surprise. Verdant parks and vista spots where you can enjoy the beauty of the many islands not far offshore head the list of sightseeing musts here. But islands and shorelines are just part of the scenic and geographic mix in this region, which also includes rivers and delta wetlands, forests and picturesque farmlands.

As you drive north from Seattle along Route 5, you'll cross a series of major rivers issuing from the Cascade Mountains. In order, you'll pass the Snohomish River (at Everett), the Stillaguamish (not far from Stanwood), the Skagit (at Mt. Vernon/Burlington) and the Nooksack (Bellingham). The lower reaches of these streams offer wetlands and wildlife to see, fishing villages to poke around in, a vital agricultural heritage in the Skagit and Nooksack valleys, and small towns by the handful.

In **Everett**, you'll find your best harbor vantage point from the dock behind Marina Village (1728 West Marine View Drive), a sparkling complex of upscale shops and restaurants. The boxy little temporary building opposite the marina serves as an interpretive site and information center for the popular summertime Jetty Island Days, when a free ferry ride takes you to picturesque **Jetty Island** for guided nature walks, birdwatching, campfires, a hands-on "Squirmy, Squiggly and Squishy" program to teach children about small marine animals and the only warm saltwater beach on the Sound.

The **Snohomish River Queen** (docked at Marina Village, 1712 West Marine View Drive, Everett; 206-259-2743) operates daily in summer. This handsome replica of a 19th-century riverboat (capacity, 150) schedules daily cruises through the Snohomish River delta. Choose from lunch, dinner and moonlight cruises, as well as historic river trips and wildlife watching outings.

The **Firefighter's Museum** (13th Street Dock, Everett) offers a storefront display of turn-of-the-century firefighting equipment. The collection is set up for 24-hour, through-the-window viewing. The Everett/Snohomish County Convention and Visitor Bureau (1710 West Marine View Drive; 206-252-5181) can provide more information.

On the hillside above the marina, ornate mansions of the lumber barons who once ruled the Northwest economy line Grand and Rucker streets from 16th Street north. None are open to tour, but a slow drive up and down these avenues will give you a feel for the history of the city.

On the south side of town, you'll find a free industrial tour at **Boeing** (Tour Center, State Road 526, Everett; 206-342-4801), a massive facility (the largest in the world by volume) where they construct those gigantic commercial airplanes that carry over one million passengers every day. The 90-minute tours include films on the history of flight and growth at Boeing followed by a narrated walk viewing the production lines where they build the 747 and 767 models. Reservations for these popular tours are available for groups of ten or more; otherwise, the best way to obtain tickets is to be in line at the tour center by 8 a.m. during the busy summer months. Call for directions and tour times; no children under ten admitted.

Another fascinating tour is available at the **Millstone Coffee Plant** (729 100th Street South East, Everett; 206-347-3848), where you'll learn firsthand how they sample, select, roast, flavor and package some of the Northwest's favorite specialty coffees. The retail shop at the front of the warehouse sells the freshest beans around. Call the plant manager about schedules for the ten-minute tour.

If you plan to catch the Mukilteo ferry to Clinton on Whidbey Island, be sure to allow enough time to visit the historic **Mukilteo Light-**

SCENIC SKAGIT VALLEY

The Skagit Valley has become a year-round retreat for city visitors, as nourishing to the soul in winter as it is inspiring to the adventurous spirit in summer. Indeed, artists and writers have been gathering in the Skagit for decades, including members of the famed "Northwest School" beginning in the 1930s—Mark Tobey, Morris Graves, Kenneth Callahan, Clayton James, Guy Anderson and many others. They were drawn by the Skagit's enchanting blend of meandering river levees and farm fields, bayous and bays, nearby islands and distant misty mountains, along with the extraordinary quality of the valley's ever-changing light.

With topsoil up to several feet deep, the Skagit Valley is the world's third-most fertile river delta, according to Skagitonians to Preserve Farmland.

---

house (206-353-2923; summer weekends only, 12 to 4 p.m.) built in 1905. There are picnic tables above a small rocky beach cluttered with driftwood and a big grassy field for kite flying adjacent to the lighthouse in little Mukilteo State Park.

Just west of Route 5, in the delta of the Stillaguamish River, the small farming town of **Stanwood** hides its main street away, signing it 271st Street. Many tourists never discover its shops and pubs, ethnic restaurants and bakery specializing in "lefse," popular among the descendants of pioneer Scandinavian farmers.

A few miles west, across a bridge on Route 532, lies **Camano Island**, not one of the famous San Juans, but boasting three bed-and-breakfast inns (at last count) and blessed with one magnificent public park, 134-acre **Camano Island State Park**. Located midway down the island's west shore, the park offers splendid forest and beach trails and sweeping views across Saratoga Passage to Whidbey Island. Also on the island is a wonderful art gallery. Called **"History of the World—Part IV"** (331 South East Camano Drive, Camano Island, 360-387-5225), the name suggests the owner's whimsical way with art. Jack Gunter is fast earning a reputation as a painter and folk artist, but prefers to describe himself as a creator of "pseudo naive surrealistic narrative art." You'll find plenty to chuckle over here—wry paintings, entertaining sculpture, playful art glass.

Someday, the Skagit Valley may become as famous as the well-known tourist attractions that surround it. But for now, out-of-state visitors tend to speed through this 25-mile-wide floodplain, missing its beauty as they hurry to or from the San Juan Islands, the Olympic Peninsula, Whidbey Island, North Cascades National Park, or Vancouver and Victoria, B.C.

Alas, they're missing something special. **The Skagit**, about halfway between Seattle and Vancouver (and an hour's drive or so from either city via Route 5) is very likely the most glorious union of countryside and seashore in the Northwest. It's centered on the largest, most pristine river delta on Puget Sound, whose sweeping estuary—an important stop on the Pacific Flyway—nurtures an extraordinary diversity of marine life and waterfowl.

Big-city folk from both sides of the border also flock to the Skagit to explore the valley's country roads and small towns, especially historic La Conner (see below). They come to pedal a bike or stroll a beguiling stretch of coast, to boat and fish for salmon in season. To watch in winter for the delta's treasure of hawks and eagles, snow geese and trumpeter swans. To marvel at blooming tulips that paint the valley in vivid colors every April and herald the return of spring.

Other visitors from Seattle and Vancouver, seeking respite from urban life, come to unwind in the Skagit's numerous delightful country inns and bed-and-breakfast homes. Here, you can sprawl before a roaring fire with a good book in hand. Or idle away a Sunday morning over a splendid country breakfast. Or just stare in silent reverie from a farmhouse veranda across open fields to the sea.

Today, the Skagit is gateway both to Whidbey Island and the San Juans (westward on Route 20 from Route 5), and to the North Cascades (Route 20, eastbound). The valley is a travelers' crossroads, with adventures enough for a month of sightseeing. You won't find a better place to begin than picturesque La Conner.

La Conner, built on pilings over the banks of Swinomish Channel, got its start in the 1880s as a market center for farmers in the Skagit Flats. Located on saltwater, La Conner emerged as a vital water link with markets in Seattle and elsewhere around Puget Sound in the days when steamships supplied most of the transportation. Later, the town developed a fishing fleet, remnants of which can still be seen. In all, La Conner remains a fine example of American life at the turn of the century, with many well-preserved homes and buildings from the late 1800s. You can obtain maps and a visitors guide from the **La Conner Chamber of Commerce** (104 East Commercial, La Conner; 360-466-4778).

La Conner today is also most definitely a town intent upon luring tourists. Its picturesque setting and many beguiling shops and waterside eateries are hard to resist. Most of the historic structures along the waterfront now house craft boutiques, galleries and restaurants. But the most prominent historic building is the **Gaches Mansion** (703 South 2nd Street; 360-466-4446; admission). This grand Victorian is filled with

---

A BLOOMING VALLEY

*Each spring, the fields between La Conner and neighboring Mt. Vernon are alive with color as the daffodils, tulips and, later, the iris begin to appear. The best time for a visit is usually mid-April during the two-week-long Skagit Valley Tulip Festival. The **Skagit Valley Tulip Festival Office** (220 East College Way, Suite 174, Mt. Vernon; 360-428-8547) can provide an events calendar and tour map of the valley's nurseries and display gardens. Along the backroads of Fir Island or west of Mt. Vernon, you can admire the innumerable farm gardens that bring blooms to the valley from March into October.*

When heading east from Mt. Vernon, for every mile traveled toward the Cascade Mountains, the average annual rainfall increases by one inch.

period furnishings. The **Museum of Northwest Art** (121 South 1st Street, 360-466-4446; admission), the only art museum between Seattle and Bellingham, houses a fine collection from the "Northwest School."

To learn more about the history of the area, take a walk through the collection of automobiles, farm and fishing equipment, vintage clothing, household furnishings and photographs at the **Skagit County Historical Museum** (501 South 4th Street; 360-466-3365; admission).

Mt. Vernon, a neighbor of La Conner situated on the broad banks of the Skagit River, has done little to capitalize on its superior riverside location. But it does claim the liveliest "main street" in the valley. The true main street is signed as First Street here; it is lined with a variety of vintage architecture in both brick and wood dating to the turn of the century. Preservation or recycling of old buildings is in full swing. Don't miss **The Granary** (1st and Division streets), which includes Scott's Bookstore and the adjoining Longfellow Café. Here, too, is the valley's land trust, **Skagitonians to Preserve Farmland** (360-336-3974), where you can learn how concerned citizens are working to save farmlands and the valley's agricultural heritage.

Across railroad tracks just to the west is the old **Condensary Building**, now remodeled into offices and the lively Bridgeside Bakery and Deli.

South of Division Street, but still on First Street, is the Uptowne Centre. It houses the **Skagit Valley Food Co-op**, where you can find organically grown produce from the valley, pottery and other local crafts. The Deli Next Door continues the organic theme with appetizing vegetarian fare.

Stroll south on First and you'll find more old buildings housing vintage books and records, handcrafts from around the valley, jewelry, art and outdoor gear, and the 1926 **Lincoln Theater** (now an art film house). Several more eateries and coffee bars also compete for your patronage.

Burlington, the next city north of Mt. Vernon, is famous for a different sort of shopping. Bargain-hunters from Seattle and Vancouver come to seek out the discount designer merchandise at Pacific Edge Outlet Center. Neighboring Cascade Mall offers a more classic array of mall shops.

If you want to explore more, a local guide service, **Easy Going Outings** (1460 Augusta Lane, Burlington; 360-757-3062) can plan day trips—hiking, biking, van touring, boating, art tours—throughout every corner of the Skagit Valley and beyond.

For the perfect counterpoint to the sort of creeping suburbanism encountered in Burlington, drop in on **Bay View**, **Edison** and **Bow**. This trio of country hamlets (located in the northern valley across Route 20) are treasures of the old way of life and are rarely discovered by the average tourist. Here, you'll see century-old farmhouses rising behind white picket fences, boatworks (some still active) that once turned out fishing boats, country taverns alive with the rustic merriment of farmers, loggers, truck drivers and dairymen. Here, too, are a smattering of art galleries, antique shops, country cafés and upscale eateries.

Located just north of Bay View, **Padilla Bay National Estuarine Research Reserve** (1043 Bay View–Edison Road, Bay View; 360-428-1558) is a good place to find bald eagles, great blue herons and dozens of other species of waterfowl and raptors. The interpretive center offers exhibits on the region's natural and maritime history.

For a view-rich and slow-paced alternate to Route 5 that will take you north to Bellingham, opt for **Chuckanut Drive** (Route 11), a signed exit from the freeway just north of Burlington. The "drive" takes you north through gorgeous farmlands, in and out of the village of Bow in a twinkling, and then along the rocky and precipitous shoulder of the Chuckanut Mountains overlooking the San Juan Islands (you can stop and savor the scene from numerous pullouts). The drive continues all the way to the funky 1880s brick town of **Fairhaven**, now a suburb of Bellingham. This slightly counterculture community is a treasure of refurbished brick Victorians housing shops, galleries, artists' studios and bohemian eateries. Most are concentrated around 11th Street and Harris Avenue.

But Fairhaven also boasts the new **Bellingham Cruise Terminal**, southern terminus for ferries of the Alaska Marine Highway (foot of Harris Avenue). The terminal presents dynamite views over the harbor, a seafood restaurant (Barnacles; 360-647-5072) and a variety of shops. Here, too, the sightseeing vessel *Victoria Star* (360-738-8099) is moored for daily departures in summer through the San Juan Islands to Victoria, B.C.

Another boating operator also serves the San Juans. **Island Shuttle Express** (360-671-1137) departs daily in summer from Squalicum Harbor Marina in Bellingham for sightseeing cruises to Orcas Island and Friday Harbor on San Juan Island.

Early growth in **Bellingham** centered around the industries of mining and logging. To this day, the city retains an industrial nature with thriving ports that are home to a large fishing fleet and, more recently, the Alaska Marine Highway Ferry System terminal, tempered by a firm agricultural base. Perhaps it is because of this outward appearance that visitors are often amazed at the array of cultural arts and international dining experiences to be enjoyed here.

Bellingham has two noteworthy museums. The **Children's Museum Northwest** (227 Prospect Street; 360-733-8769; admission) has several hands-on, career-oriented theme centers to delight the kids (ages 2–12), along with the current dinosaur exhibit. Just down the street, the red

The Darigold plant in Lynden produces some 340,000 pounds of non-fat dry milk a day and is the largest powdered milk factory in the U.S.

brick Victorian architecture of the **Whatcom Museum** (121 Prospect Street; 360–676–6981; admission) is as interesting as the fine collections of Northwest art, regional history and rotating contemporary art shows featured inside. It's also a good point to start a walking tour of the many outdoor sculptures scattered around downtown. A Sculpture Walk route guide is available from the **Bellingham/Whatcom County Visitor and Convention Bureau** (904 Potter Street; 360–671–3990).

At the **Maritime Heritage Center** (1600 C Street; 360–676–6806), you can tour the hatchery, watch fish make their way up the ladder, learn about the life cycle of salmon, or just toss a line into the abutting creek for steelhead, cutthroat trout or salmon.

No visit to Bellingham is complete without a trip to the **Big Rock Garden** (2900 Sylvan Street; 360–671–1069), a fantastic, open-air gallery of northwestern and Japanese art set in a serene Japanese garden. There are patio and deck areas where visitors can sit and take it all in.

Don't miss the opportunity to stroll through the grounds of **Western Washington University** (South College Drive, Bellingham; 360–650–3963) on the Western Sculpture Tour to enjoy the fountains, sculptures and tremendous variety of architecture on this rich green campus. An excellent sculpture walk (now numbering more than a score of works) is mapped out for visitors. Immediately adjacent to the campus in the Sehome Hill neighborhood, the **Sehome Hill Arboretum** (25th Street; 360–676–6985) has 165 acres laced with seven miles of hiking trails and fern-lined footpaths under a cool green canopy of moss-covered trees; only the hum of traffic and the view from the observation tower remind you that you are in the city rather than some forest primeval.

The **Nooksack River Valley** east of Bellingham is a treasure of rolling green dairy pastures, berry fields, Christmas tree farms and charming small towns, like Lynden. Settled by Dutch dairymen more than a century ago, **Lynden** and its main street (Front Street) offer a colorful collection of storefronts looking as if they were plucked right out of Amsterdam, including a windmill hotel. A beguiling array of import shops proffers wooden shoes, Delft tiles, kitchenwares and other goods from Holland. Several eateries also specialize in Dutch fare. Festivals such as Sinterklaas (Santa Claus) in December and Holland Days in May also reflect the Dutch heritage.

The **Lynden Pioneer Museum** (217 West Front Street, Lynden; 360–354–3675; admission) tells the story of early Dutch and Northern European settlers. Don't miss the Fred K. Polinder buggy collection.

Just outside of town begin several superb bike routes that follow winding and picturesque country roads, one of which brings you to a first-rate winery, **Mt. Baker Vineyards** (4298 Mt. Baker Highway, Deming; 360-592-2300), famous for its excellent German-style white wines.

Hovander Homestead Park (5299 Neilsen Road, Ferndale; 360-384-3444; admission) features a 19th-century farmhouse and handsome Victorian residence. Laced by the Nooksak River, the 720-acre park also includes Tenant Lake, where you'll find a boardwalk leading out over the lake and a fragrance garden with braille signs. There's also an interpretive center.

Another Ferndale stop is **Pioneer Park** (1st Avenue at Cherry Street; 360-384-6461). Here is the largest collection of original log homes in the state. Each of the 12 buildings is a mini-museum. You'll see a post office, stagecoach inn, granary, veteran's museum, schoolhouse and a residence. Don't miss the little log church. Open May to September.

Another site in the northern Puget Sound area worth visiting is **Peace Arch State Park** (Follow the signs off Route 5; 360-332-8221). The large, white arch, flanked by American and Canadian flags, is surrounded by bountiful formal gardens and symbolizes the ongoing friendship between the two countries. The park is meticulously groomed, and spills across the international boundary.

NORTHERN PUGET SOUND LODGING

In addition to its outstanding waterfront location, the friendly 28-room **Marina Village Inn** (1728 West Marine View Drive, Everett; 206-259-4040, 800-281-7037) is loaded with special touches. The spacious harborside rooms have sunken sitting areas with custom sleeper sofas, cushioned seats built into large bay windows and personal telescopes for viewing Whidbey, Hat and Jetty islands. One room with a view of the village fits into the moderate range, while those with harbor views are deluxe to ultra-deluxe; reservations are required.

Only a few years ago, Camano Island didn't have a single bed and breakfast; today there are three. **Log Cabin Lodge Bed and Breakfast** (360-387-2346) chooses not to list an address and is open only six months a year. But this wonderful log house, recently built, sits atop a high bluff with views westward toward the Olympics, and is well worth searching out. All four rooms are moderate in price.

Salal Hill Bed and Breakfast (850 North West Camano Drive; 360-387-3763) is tucked in the woods on 13 acres, which include a duck pond (trout and bass fishing) and nature trail. Three rooms in the recently remodeled home are furnished with antiques and collectibles. There's a game room, hot tub and fireplace. Sterling silver and crystalware make breakfast by candlelight a real occasion. Moderate.

Willcox House Bed and Breakfast (1462 Larkspur Lane; 360-629-4746) overlooks Skagit Bay and winter waterfowl from a bluff-top on Camano. The wraparound porch captures views northward to Mt. Baker and east across farmlands to the main line of the Cascades. Although the home is new, all four rooms are filled with antiques and local arts and crafts (all for sale). Moderate.

La Conner and the Skagit Valley now boast several new bed and breakfasts and two new first-class inns. One of them is the **La Conner Channel Lodge** (205 North 1st Street, La Conner; 360-466-1500, fax 360-466-1525), a handsome luxury inn, the only hostelry in town on the Swinomish Channel. Each of its 41 rooms (deluxe to ultra-deluxe) looks out to the channel and the ceaseless parade of fishing boats and pleasure craft.

The **Wild Iris** (121 Maple Avenue, La Conner; 360-466-1400) is the newest inn hereabouts, on the edge of town overlooking farm fields and mountains. Each of its 20 rooms is decorated individually in bold and fearless strokes. Breakfast fare is generous and varied, a hallmark of this inn's overall attention to quality. Room prices fall in the moderate-to-deluxe range.

Next door to the Wild Iris, the **Heron** (117 Maple Avenue, La Conner; 360-466-4626) offers the same views in smaller, cozier style, with 12 rooms at moderate prices.

The **Hotel Planter** (715 1st Street; 360-466-4710, 800-488-5409, fax 360-466-1320), originally built in 1907, is right in the thick of things when it comes to shopping and dining in downtown La Conner. This 12-room hotel has been renovated; sunlights, lighter paint and carpeting, floral chintz comforters and pine furnishings in the tight bedrooms brighten and update its look. There's also a jacuzzi under the gazebo on the garden terrace. Moderate to deluxe.

Opening in 1977, **La Conner Country Inn** (107 South 2nd Street, La Conner; 360-466-3101) was the first inn in these parts. It's still a favorite with long-time visitors, partly because several of its 28 rooms are so affordable (moderate to deluxe). It's also close to shops and restaurants.

Katy's Inn (503 South 3rd Street, La Conner; 360-466-3366, 800-914-7767) is one of the oldest homes in town, built by a sea captain in 1876, and appeals strongly to history-minded folk. Its four rooms are moderately priced.

In a home loaded with a lifetime's collection of art, **Art's Place** (511 Talbot Street, La Conner; 360-466-3033) offers a one-room addition with balcony bedroom, jacuzzi bath; moderate.

Wilma's Guest House (328 Washington Street, La Conner; 360-466-4289) with two moderately priced rooms, has a private garden and entrance that make this quiet residence off main streets a bit of a secret to many visitors.

The T. G. Richards & Co. building (1308 E Street) in Bellingham is the oldest brick building still standing in the state, dating from 1858. Its bricks came around Cape Horn from Philadelphia.

About a mile east of town, the **Rainbow Inn** (1075 Chilberg Road, La Conner; 360-466-4578, fax 360-466-5700) is surrounded by farm fields. This classic Victorian built in 1907 offers eight guest rooms and oodles of old-fashioned charm. Moderate.

A Dutch Colonial farmhouse with five guest rooms, the **Ridgeway Bed and Breakfast** (1292 McLean Road, about four miles northeast of La Conner; 360-428-8068, 800-428-8068) is situated very close to the daffodil and tulip fields, just right for spring visits. Moderate.

Six miles from La Conner, **White Swan Guest House** (1388 Moore Road, Mt. Vernon; 360-445-6805) offers moderate-to-deluxe accommodations in a country setting. The rooms are country casual and there's a superb collection of samplers spread across the house. The English country garden features a big orchard where you're welcome to pick your own apples and plums, as well as strawberries. A separate cottage offers kitchen facilities. And the owner's wit and charm add immeasurably to your overall visit. Country continental breakfast and homemade chocolate chip cookies are included.

Built in 1914, the **Benson Farmstead Bed and Breakfast** (1009 Avon-Allen Road, Bow; 360-757-0578) is a four-room charmer in the heart of "north valley" farms. Some guests come for the homemade desserts, big farm breakfasts and cozy rooms full of country antiques. Others come for the chance to stay on a working farm that's been in operation for more than eight decades. Still others stay for the proximity to some of the state's best country bicycling. Moderate.

South Fork Moorage (2187 Mann Road, Fir Island; 360-445-4803) is one of those true hideaways (dare we say, "unique") that travelers yearn to discover. The "moorage" is comprised of two houseboats floating in the usually placid waters of the South Fork of the Skagit River adjacent to a wildlife reserve. Bring your canoe, kayak or raft, and the owner will shuttle you up to Burlington for a lazy float back to the moorage. Or paddle across the river to an island full of wildlife. Or just sprawl like Huck Finn on the docks for a picnic as you watch the peaceful river unspool before you. No river shacks these—both houseboats boast leaded, stained-glass windows, fireplaces and champagne waiting in the cooler. Both are outfitted as housekeeping cabins, and each can accommodate up to four persons. And yet the prices are only moderate!

As you might guess from the name, **Schnauzer Crossing** (4421 Lakeway Drive, Bellingham; 360-733-0055, 800-562-2808) is presided over by a delightful pair of schnauzers. Choose from a spacious master suite with fireplace, library room, jacuzzi tub and double shower, a smaller lakeview room done in an iris motif or a recently completed cottage, perfect for families or couples seeking romantic seclusion. Well-thought-out amenities in each room include thick terry robes for the trip to the hot tub in the Japanese garden; gourmet breakfast included. Deluxe.

If you're looking for an escape from the everyday bustle or a cozy home base for skiing Mt. Baker, book a room at the **Anderson Creek Lodge** (5602 Mission Road, Bellingham; 360-966-2126, 800-441-5585), a tranquil retreat 15 minutes northeast of downtown Bellingham. Each of the six rooms in the inviting wooden lodge has a personality of its own; some feature family heirlooms, others have floral chintz or a distinctly Asian decor. There are even nature trails on the 65-acre spread. Moderate.

Tucked into the rose garden near the north end of picturesque Chuckanut Drive is the **Hostelling International—Bellingham** (107 Chuckanut Drive, Bellingham; 360-671-1750). You'll find this your typical hostel-environment: men's and women's dorms, showers and laundry facilities. All the action of the Fairhaven district is within walking distance. Budget.

Dutch Village Inn Hotel (655 Front Street, Lynden; 360-354-4440) is a local landmark. Besides several conventional motel-style rooms, it also offers six rooms in the colorful windmill tower (ask for the "windmill rooms"). All rooms boast Dutch decor and artifacts, and some present views across the Nooksack River Valley. A big Dutch breakfast is included in the moderate room rates.

Built in 1888 as the town hotel, the **Century House Bed and Breakfast** (401 South B.C. Avenue, Lynden; 360-354-2439) is a restored three-room guesthouse decorated with antiques from its previous incarnation. The third-floor suite commands sweeping views of the Nooksack Valley and the Cascades. Moderate.

Slater Heritage House Bed and Breakfast (1371 West Axton Road, Ferndale; 360-384-4273, 800-815-4273) is a handsomely restored 1904 Victorian surrounded by lovely well-tended gardens bursting with Northwest ornamentals. There are four guest rooms that range from budget to moderate in price.

Housed in the old Blaine Air Force Base a few miles from the Canadian border, the **Hostelling International—Birch Bay** (4639 Alderson Road, Building 630, Blaine; 360-371-2180) provides 50 beds in bare, shared rooms. Pluses here include a sauna, cable television and the hostel's proximity to Birch Bay State Park. Budget.

There is something for everyone at the sumptuous **Inn at Semiahmoo** (9565 Semiahmoo Parkway, Blaine; 360-371-2000, 800-770-7992, fax 360-371-5490), located on the tip of the sandy spit stretched between Semiahmoo Bay and Drayton Harbor. History buffs will enjoy

In 1903, 110 shingle mills operated in Whatcom County, a testament to the one-time productivity of the region's forests.

browsing through the inn's collection of early photography, romantics will delight in a walk on the beach or a leisurely sunset meal in one of the restaurants or lounges, and sports fanatics will flip over the array of activities. The 198 guest rooms are spacious and nicely appointed; some rooms have decks or patios, and others have fireplaces. Ultra–deluxe.

Loganita—A Villa By The Sea (2825 West Shore Drive, Lummi Island; 360–758–2651) is a charming bed and breakfast situated on a lawn that swoops down to a long sandy beach. It offers unobstructed views of Georgia Strait, two huge stone fireplaces and a hot tub. Two suites, two rooms and a detached carriage house—built between 1898 and the 1920s—range in price from moderate to deluxe.

The **Willows Bed and Breakfast** (2579 West Shore Drive, Lummi Island; 360–758–2620) was built in 1910 by the grandparents of the current owners. Today, it offers four guest rooms in the main lodge, plus a honeymoon cottage amid flower gardens and a two-bedroom guest house (moderate to ultra–deluxe). Cottage and guest house, complete with fireplaces, kitchens, and jacuzzis, are self-catered during the week. Views here are outstanding—west and northwest across other San Juan Islands to Vancouver, British Columbia.

NORTHERN PUGET SOUND RESTAURANTS

Anthony's Homeport (1726 West Marine View Drive; 206-252-3333) is the spot for seafood when it comes to waterfront dining in Everett. Prime picks on the menu include six varieties of fresh oysters, steamed Discovery Bay clams or Whidbey Island mussels, grilled steak and prawns, Dungeness crab cakes and pan-fried scallops sprinkled with gremolata. Their four-course Sunset Dinner (served from 4:30 to 6 p.m.) is a bargain and includes everything from appetizer to dessert. You can dine al fresco on the deck or pick a spot in the considerably less breezy dining room or lounge. Moderate.

The history of **Charles at Smugglers Cove** (8340 53rd Avenue West, Mukilteo; 206–347–2700) is as good as the food, making it doubly worth the drive to Mukilteo. This red-brick mansion-turned-restaurant was purportedly owned at one time by Mafia kingpin Al Capone. Today, the owners traffic in fresh seafood and steaks with French flair; their bouillabaisse, châteaubriand, rack of lamb, prawns in tarragon butter and baked Alaska are outstanding, and the setting in the elegant dining rooms or on the sheltered deck is splendid. Deluxe.

The same people own and operate the **Lighthouse Inn** (512 South 1st Street; 360-466-3149) in nearby La Conner, so you can expect extra-large servings here, as well, though the fare of this waterfront location is primarily seafood and pasta. Favorites include lobster, clam strips and prime rib, with fish and chips and burgers thrown in to please the little ones. The simple nautical decor leaves something to be desired, but the fresh flowers and dim lamps on the tables lend a slight air of romance. Moderate rates.

Best bet for breakfast or lunch in La Conner is the **Calico Cupboard** (720 South 1st Street; 360-466-4451) at the south end of the main drag, where they serve hearty and wholesome baked goods, soups, salads, sandwiches and vegetarian fare as good for the heart as for the taste buds. Don't be surprised if there is a line to get in to this modest café. Priced in the moderate range.

Palmer's of La Conner (205 East Washington Street; 360-466-4261) is not on the waterfront, but may just be the best restaurant in town nevertheless. One of the owners is from France, and all dishes on the wide-ranging Continental menu (seafood, pasta, chicken, beef) are served with distinctive French flair. All ingredients are fresh and, when possible, local, such as the locally reared beef. Deluxe.

Few tourists ever discover the **Marina Café** (611 North 2nd Street, La Conner; 360-466-4242), located off the beaten shopping track in the marina just north of town. But local anglers and working folk know it well. The lack of tourist attention means you get good café food at budget prices. The café opens for breakfast at 6 a.m. (for fishermen and boat builders), and also serves lunch; all-you-can-eat buffet dinners are served Thursday to Sunday. Specialties include Tex-Mex omelettes and chili, hearty homemade soups and chowder, fresh salads and good burgers. Budget.

The Norwegian proprietors of the **Farmhouse Inn** (1376 La Conner–Whitney Road, Mt. Vernon; 360-466-4411), a large restaurant with country decor dominated by heavy oak tables and chairs, believe in serving up solid, old country–style portions of meat and potato classics—fried chicken and french fries, roast turkey with mashed potatoes and gravy, rib eyes and baked potatoes—along with a hearty selection of daily baked goods thrown in for good measure. The lunch buffet is a real bargain. Budget.

The **Archer Ale House** (1212 10th Street, Fairhaven; 360-647-7002), tucked in the basement of one of Fairhaven's historic Victorians, is a smoke-free English-style pub. The main fare is upscale pub grub (check out the pizza) and an array of microbrewery and imported beers. Priced in the budget range.

Colophone Café (1108 12th Street, Fairhaven; 360-647-0092) shares a building—and an intellectual/bohemian ambience—with a neighboring bookstore. The café is known for its homemade soups (including a wonderfully spicy African peanut soup) and its sinfully rich desserts. Budget.

In addition to coffees and teas, the coffee shop in **Tony's Coffees & Teas** (1101 South Harris Avenue, Bellingham; 360-733-6319) serves up fresh daily soups, salads, sandwiches and pastries to an eclectic crowd of regulars. It's almost *too* bohemian, but the bagels with cream cheese and sprouts, Greek salad and cocoa mocha make it worth the trip. Budget.

Paper lanterns and fans add a dash of color to liven up the bare-bones decor of the new **Tokyo House** (1222 North Garden Street, Bellingham; 360-733-6784) with its industrial-style tables and chairs. Patrons don't come here for the atmosphere, but rather for tasty Japanese standards with interesting additions to the menu such as kim chee and sweet and sour pork. Service is prompt, and this budget eatery is as neat as a pin.

Warm reds and yellows in the dining room give **Il Fiasco** (1309 Commercial Street; 360-676-9136) an inviting and relaxed atmosphere. The walls are decorated with banners and paintings by local artists. The seasonal menu features salads, antipasto, pastas and *piatti forti* (usually fish, veal or duck) highlighted by whatever special the imaginative chef creates each day. Regulars come back often for the roast duckling or the herbed chicken breast. Ask any resident and they'll invariably tell you that this is *the* place for fine dining in Bellingham. Deluxe.

The tables at **Café Toulouse** (Crown Plaza Building, 114 West Magnolia Street, Suite 102, Bellingham; 360-733-8996) are always full, although the restaurant is now much bigger after recent relocation—a testament to the quality breakfast, lunch and dessert selections served here. Favorites include fresh fruit pancakes, curried chicken salad, roast pork loin with mint jelly or smoked turkey with cranberry-apple cream cheese sandwiches and anything from the fresh daily dessert board accompanied by piping espresso or latte. Budget.

Dutch Mother's Restaurant (405 Front Street; Lynden; 360-354-2174) is "the" place in Lynden for traditional (that's to say, hearty) Dutch cuisine. Waitresses sport Dutch dress, and often can be overheard speaking Dutch with locals. Budget.

For budget-to-moderate Mexican dining, try **Chihuahua's** (5694 3rd Avenue, Ferndale; 360-384-5820). Decorated with Mexican art, the dining room offers booth and table seating. There's also patio dining outside in the summer. Popular specialties are fajitas, carne asada, sopas and a wide variety of combination plates.

Since it is always so busy, locals would probably prefer not to share the **Vista Pizza, Rib and Steak House** (442 Peace Portal Drive, Blaine; 360-332-5155). Rumor has it that the amazingly low-priced one-pound steak dinner brings in enough business to this smoke-filled little diner to generate $1.4 million a year. Though it's not made clear on the menu, the generously portioned luncheon special of lasagna, spaghetti or pizza and a trip to the salad bar is still available in the evenings, making it possible to get a substantial meal for under $8 per person, tip included. Budget.

Just north of the ferry dock and across the street from the Beach Store and Café is the only public access beach on Lummi Island.

For romantic waterfront dining, it's hard to beat the Inn at Semiah-moo's elegant dining room, **Stars** (9565 Semiahmoo Parkway, Blaine; 360-371-2000). Soft piano music fills the room as diners feast on parch-ment-wrapped salmon, roasted antelope, venison, scallops, prime rib, Dungeness crab cannelloni and other rich entrées. For lighter fare, try the livelier **Packers Oyster Bar** just down the corridor for fresh steamer clams, baked brie, Fisherman's stew or homestyle burgers. Stars is de-luxe. Packers is budget.

Places to eat on Lummi Island are almost non-existent, so **The Wil-lows Bed and Breakfast** (2579 West Shore Drive; 360-758-2620) pre-pares marvelous evening meals of regional cuisine (seafood, poultry, lamb) served Friday and Saturday for guests (and island visitors by advance reservation); prices including wine are moderate to deluxe.

Near the ferry landing and offering gorgeous water views, the **Beach Store and Café** (2200 South Nugent Road; 360-758-7406) is the only place on Lummi Island where visitors can find deli quality picnic sup-plies and lunches to go. But it's also a terrific little restaurant where everything is homemade, where herbs, lettuce and other produce is grown in its own garden or elsewhere on the island. Seafood, a specialty, is also local—crab, salmon, halibut. The café is open from April through Octo-ber, serving breakfast, lunch and dinner, and Sunday brunch during the busy tourist season (budget to moderate).

NORTHERN PUGET SOUND SHOPPING

Snohomish, located seven miles east of Everett, is home to **Star Center Antique Mall** (829 2nd Street; 360-568-2131), a five-level mall with over 165 dealers, and dozens of other antique shops to browse through.

In Everett, the **Everett Public Market** (2804 Grand Avenue; 206-252-1089) is the prime browsing spot for antiques as well as Northwest arts and crafts.

Shopping is a draw of little La Conner, with most of the boutiques and galleries concentrated along First and Morris streets. Focus on **Earthen-works** (713 1st Street; 360-466-4422) and **The Scott Collection** (Pier 7 Building, 128 South 1st Street; 360-466-3691) for fine art, **Bunnies By The Bay** (617 East Morris Street; 360-466-5040) for collectibles and unique gifts and **Chez La Zoom** (112 Morris Street; 360-466-4546) and **The Town Clothier** (721 South 1st Street; 360-466-3086) for fashion-able attire. **The Wood Merchant** (709 South 1st Street; 206-466-4741) features handcrafted gifts and custom furniture by Northwest woodworkers. Ethnic folk art as well as fine art and crafts by regional artists are sold at **Janet Huston Gallery** (413 Morris Street; 206-466-5001).

If gardening, greenery or dried flowers are your thing, you'll enjoy the **Bonsai Grove** (6th and Morris streets; 360-466-2955) and the historic **Tillinghast Seed Company** (623 East Morris Street; 360-466-3329). At **Go Outside** (111 Morris Street; 360-466-4836), the owners' remarkable taste is reflected in an appealing collection of garden tools, clothing and art selected with great care.

. Don't miss **Cascade Candy** (605 South 1st Street; 360-466-2971) next to Tillinghast Seeds—it produces first-class truffles and other chocolate concoctions at about half the price of similar candy-makers in Seattle or Vancouver, B.C.

The best shops and galleries in Bellingham are generally located in the Fairhaven District. In the renovated **Marketplace Building** (12th Street and Harris Avenue), you'll find an eclectic collection of goods including steins, beerabilia and 200 varieties of beer, as well as food and cocktails, at **Bullie's Restaurant and Oyster Bar** (360-734-2855).

Other boutiques of interest nearby include **The Crystal Dolphin** (1209 11th Street; 360-671-5034) selling New Age crystals, jewelry, books, music and artwork; **Artwood** (1000 Harris Avenue; 360-647-1628), a co-op gallery of fine woodworking by Northwest artists; and **Inside Passage** (355 Harris Avenue, Suite 103; 360-734-1790) for gifts of the Pacific Northwest.

Dutch Village Mall (655 Front Street; Lynden; 360-354-4440) is a collection of 18 shops specializing in imported Dutch lace, foodstuffs, wooden shoes and the like. The "mall" is built around a 150-foot-long canal to re-create a typical Dutch street scene.

NORTHERN PUGET SOUND NIGHTLIFE

Everett's **Club Broadway Entertainment Center** (1611 Everett Avenue; 206-259-3551) offers several after-hours options under one roof, including a sports bar, dance club, jazz club and country-and-western

---

AN APPLE A DAY

*Between Bay View and Edison lies **Merritt's Apples** (896 Bay View–Edison Road; 360-766-6224), an orchard proving that western Washington apples (Gravensteins and Jonagolds) are serious and tasty rivals to the more famous Red Delicious of Yakima and Wenatchee. A shop open in summer and autumn offers samples of apples and cider, and sells jam and country crafts.*

Antique hounds will want to make the quick 15-minute trip east of Everett to Snohomish, antique capital of the Northwest.

bar. An Everett coffeehouse that features live jazz entertainment on Wednesday, Thursday and Friday evenings is **Tropic of Cancer** (1911 Hewitt Avenue; 206-252-1835).

Things are jumping at **Anthony's Homeport** (1726 West Marine View Drive, Everett; 206-252-3333), with great happy-hour prices and a nice sheltered deck overlooking the marina. For country music and dancing, visit **Gerry Andal's Ranch Restaurant** (620 South East Everett Mall Way; 206-355-7999).

Two Everett nightspots drawing a gay and lesbian crowd are **Buddies Beef and Brew** (1212 California Avenue; 206-259-1477), featuring deejay dancing and **Stage Stop** (3021 Rucker Street; 206-258-2399), which has a dancefloor and a CD jukebox.

The **La Conner Tavern** (702 South 1st Street; 360-466-9932), housed in a waterfront structure that was at one time Brewster's Cigar Store, is the primary watering hole in La Conner and does a booming business through the wee hours of the morning. Jazz and blues bands entertain and inspire some gleeful dancing on Wednesday and Sunday.

There are a half-dozen other country taverns scattered across the Skagit Valley, well-known to locals but nearly unknown to tourists, which also serve up terrific burgers, microbrewery ales and bitters, and weekend jazz and dancing. The **Conway Tavern and Eatery** (1667 Spruce, Conway; 360-445-4733) is best for burgers. The **Pit Stop Bar and Grill** (706 Old Highway 99 North, Burlington; 360-757-6446) has live country music on Friday and Saturday. The **Old Edison Inn** (583 Cains Court, Edison; 360-766-6266) is also very popular.

You'll find great happy-hour specials and the best sunset views in the little bar of **Le Chat Noir** (The Marketplace, 12th Street and Harris Avenue, Suite 301, Fairhaven; 360-733-6136). With an interior reminiscent of an old speakeasy, **Speedy O'Tubb's Rhythmic Underground** (1305 11th Street, Fairhaven; 360-734-1539) features a range of live music (rock, blues, reggae, jazz, etc.) and attracts a younger crowd from nearby Western Washington University.

NORTHERN PUGET SOUND BEACHES AND PARKS

Mukilteo State Park (360-353-2923), a swath of beach adjacent to the Whidbey Island–Mukilteo Ferry facilities on Puget Sound, is a day-use-only facility known primarily as a prime fishing spot with public boat launch. Noble little Elliott Point Lighthouse (also known as Mukilteo Lighthouse) on the tip will keep shutterbugs happy; it's also a fine place for beachcombing or picnicking while waiting to catch the ferry to Whidbey Island.

There are a handful of tiny beachfront pocket parks and boat ramps scattered around Camano Island (best is English Boom at the foot of Moore Road at the island's northeast corner). But there's just one true park, **Camano Island State Park** (360–387–2575), and it's a real stunner, boasting the finest stretch of shoreline in this part of Puget Sound. Here is well over a mile of enchanting beach to wander, in view of the Olympic Mountains rising to the west. You can find camping facilities and places to picnic; forest and beach hiking and nature trails; and plenty of opportunities for swimming, but cold water. To reach the park from Stanwood, drive west on Route 532 for five miles, then follow signs to West Camano Drive and the park.

Bay View State Park (360–757–0227), offering picnic tables and camping, is a tiny park overlooking the Padilla Bay National Marine Research Reserve, an ecological pocket of 11,600 acres of marsh and tidelands tucked between the north Skagit Valley at Bay View and March Point. To reach Bay View State Park, take Exit 230 off Route 5 in Burlington, follow Route 20 west to Bay View–Edison Road. Turn right, then follow the signs to the park.

Larrabee State Park (360–676–2093) on Samish Bay offers nine miles of hiking trails, including two steep trails to small mountain lakes (Fragrance and Lost lakes), and a stretch of beach with numerous tidepools for views of the local marine life. Facilities include campsites, picnic tables and shelters, fireplaces, kitchens, a playground, amphitheater and boat launch. There's good freshwater fishing in either of the mountain lakes and saltwater fishing in Chuckanut, Pleasant and Samish bays. Located seven miles south of Bellingham on Chuckanut Drive (Route 11).

Teddy Bear Cove was once a hidden haunt for nudists, but this secluded, narrow stretch of sand bordered by thick trees just south of the Bellingham city limits is now a public beach, with a well-signed parking lot along Chuckanut Drive, Route 11. The beach area curves out around

---

BREAZEALE PADILLA BAY INTERPRETIVE CENTER

*The **Breazeale Padilla Bay Interpretive Center** (360-428-1558), half a mile north of Bay View State Park on Bay View–Edison Road, is a good place to get better acquainted with the many forms of wildlife that inhabit the area. An upland nature trail winds through parts of the wildlife habitat area east of the center. Padilla Shore Trail, a few miles south of the center on Bay View–Edison Road, follows a dike-top away from traffic next to the estuary.*

the shallow cove, like a thumb jutting out toward Chuckanut Bay. There are no facilities here and swimming is very cold.

Whatcom Falls Park (360-676-6985) sprawls across 241 acres along the tumbling waters of Whatcom Creek. It's just the place to discover cooling breezes on a hot summer day as you stroll next to the woodland-bordered stream. There are hiking trails, waterfalls, fishing ponds and a hatchery, picnic shelters and barbecue pits. This popular park is near downtown at 1401 Electric Avenue, five miles east of the Maritime Heritage Center.

The highlight of 192-acre **Birch Bay State Park** (360-371-2800) is the warm, shallow bay, suitable for wading up to half a mile out in spots, bordered by a mile-long stretch of driftwood- and shell-strewn beach edged by grassland. The camping area is located inland in a stand of old-growth cedar and Douglas fir; nestled in the lush greenery, it's hard to tell that the park sits in the shadow of Arco's Cherry Point Refinery. Birdwatchers frequent the park to visit the marshy estuary at the south border that attracts over 100 varieties of birds. There's camping here, as well as picnic tables and shelters, trails and an underwater park. Fishing is good and swimming is excellent. Some facilities are accessible to the disabled. The park is eight miles south of Blaine off Birch Bay Drive.

Semiahmoo Park (360-371-5513) is a long, slender spit dividing Semiahmoo Bay and Drayton Harbor. The park is a favorite among beach lovers, who can comb sandy, narrow beaches on both sides of the spit, and of birdwatchers who come here to observe bald eagles, loons, heron and other species supported by this protected, nutrient-rich habitat. The spit was at one time home to the Semiahmoo Indians (thus its name) and later the site of a fish cannery; the history of both are reviewed in the park's museum. Facilities include picnic tables, fire pits and a bike path. You'll also find outstanding clamming on both sides of the spit. Located near Blaine; take the Birch Bay–Lynden Road exit west off Route 5, turn north onto Harbor View Road then west onto Lincoln Road, which becomes Semiahmoo Parkway and leads into the park.

Whidbey Island

Whidbey Island, stretching north to south along the mainland, is covered in a rolling patchwork of pasturelands, sprawling state parks, loganberry farms, hidden heritage sites and historic small towns. The artistic hamlet of Langley near Whidbey's southern tip is a current hot spot for weekend escapes from Seattle.

Most of the sights in **Langley** are concentrated along 1st and 2nd streets, where falsefront shops house small galleries, boutiques and restaurants. There's a lovely stretch of public beach flanked by a concrete wall adorned in Northwest Indian motifs just below **Seawall Park** (look for the totem pole on 1st Street), and a wonderful bronze statue by local artist Georgia Gerber above a second stairwell leading down to the beach.

In the spring months, you'll find a colorful tulip display at **Holland Gardens** (500 Avenue West and 30th Street Northwest, Oak Harbor). During the balance of the year, come to see the beautiful floral displays that make this small garden a local favorite.

With 2000 native and hybrid species spread across 53 acres, **Meerkerk Rhododendron Gardens** (Meerkerk Lane, off Resort Road, Greenbank; 360–678–1912) is a must. Magnolia, maple and cherry trees add to the beauty of this spot, which is also a test garden.

At **Whidbey's Greenbank Farm** (Wonn Road, Greenbank; 360–678–7700), they produce Whidbey's Port, Washington's only liqueur. A self-guided tour of their small facility followed by a visit to their gift shop and tasting room makes a great afternoon outing.

The **Ebey's Landing National Historical Reserve**, the first such reserve in the country, lies midway up Whidbey Island. The reserve takes in 17,400 acres that include Fort Ebey and Fort Casey state parks and the historic town of Coupeville, where 19th-century falsefront buildings line Front Street above the wharf. Here you'll find **Alexander Blockhouse** (Alexander and Front streets) and **Davis Blockhouse** (Sunnyside Cemetery Road), built by early settlers for protection against possible Indian attacks. There's a good collection of Native American and pioneer artifacts in the **Island County Historical Museum** (908 Northwest Alexander Street, Coupeville; 360–678–3310). Contact the Ebey's Landing National Historical Reserve (P.O. Box 774, Coupeville, WA 98239; 360–678–6084) for more information on maps and driving tours of the reserve.

Built in 1901, **Admiralty Head Lighthouse** at Fort Casey State Park (1280 South Fort Casey Road, Coupeville; 360–678–4519) features an interpretive center offering history on the region's military past. You'll also enjoy excellent views of Puget Sound.

WHIDBEY ISLAND LODGING

There are some 17 hotels on the island, mostly motel-style and clustered around Oak Harbor. But the big draw on Whidbey has always been bed–and–breakfast inns, around 50 of them at last count. Your choices run the gamut, from log cabins on the beach to posh retreats tucked into the forest. Many Whidbey Island bed and breakfasts offer only a single room, and come and go with regularity. Others have been in business for decades. For a comprehensive list, contact **The Greater Oak Harbor Chamber of Commerce** (P.O. Box 883, 5506 Route 20, Oak Harbor, WA 98277; 360–675–3535).

Serpentine Whidbey Island, with its thick southern tip reaching toward Seattle, is the longest island in the United States outside Alaska.

The beautiful **Inn at Langley** (400 1st Street, Langley; 360-221-3033) has perfected the fine art of hospitality at a polished property worthy of its magnificent waterfront setting. With a decorator's color palette taken directly from the beach, rooms in shades of gray, cream, tan and brown accented by lots of natural wood are elegant, presenting a delicate balance of modern art and furnishings, and are decked out with every possible amenity (fireplace, jacuzzi, Krups coffee set and large deck to take advantage of the view). An oriental garden set in front of the grand dining room is an added touch. If you can afford the ultra-deluxe tariff, this is the most luxurious selection available on the island.

Whidbey Inn (106 1st Street, Langley; 360-221-7115) overlooks Saratoga Passage and boasts six rooms with a view (deluxe). On the main shopping street, this long-established bed and breakfast also is close to shopping and other attractions. Although the rooms are not huge, they feel more cozy than cramped, and large antique-decorated suites with fireplaces also are available.

Garden Path Bed and Breakfast (111 1st Street, Langley; 360-221-5121), one of the older establishments in town, presents two luxurious and private suites decorated by the designer-owner with original art from the Northwest and around the world. Moderate to deluxe.

Twickenham House Inn (5023 Langley Road, Langley; 360-221-2334, 800-874-5009) is a typical country house built by the owner—from Twickenham, England—on ten acres of woods and pasture. The large inn includes six guest rooms, all decorated with European pine furnishings and each with an open fireplace. Guests can relax in an English pub, reading room, or music room. Moderate to deluxe.

Country Cottage of Langley (215 6th Street, Langley; 360-221-8709) sits on two acres of handsomely landscaped garden with an English country feel and oodles of lawn for endless games of croquet. Despite the country feel, this bed and breakfast is still within easy walking distance of downtown Langley. Choose from a central farm house built in the 1920s, a refurbished bungalow with a wraparound porch to capture water views, and a third cottage (formerly a creamery), also circa 1920. Antiques from various periods and materials decorate all the rooms. Prices remain surprisingly moderate.

Blue House Inn (513 Anthes Street, Langley; 360-221-8392) is distinguished by country French decor and English perennial gardens. Set atop a high vantage point, it also rewards guests with sweeping views of the Sound and Cascade Mountains. The two rooms are moderately priced, and Langley attractions are close.

Homemade truffles are the house specialty at **Cristy's Country Inn** (2891 East Meinhold Road, Langley; 360-321-1815). Situated on ten acres overlooking the Olympic Mountains, the property is mostly open pasture land, with creeks feeding a large duck pond stocked with trout. The inn is actually the top floor of the owner's Northwest contemporary home, some 1600 square feet that includes two beds and baths, a rambling deck, and full housekeeping kitchen if needed (deluxe). A recently built cottage (ultra-deluxe) on the property is even more private.

Gallery Suite (302 1st Street, Langley; 360-221-2978) overlooks Saratoga Passage, and includes a bedroom, parlor, kitchen and great views from a private deck. Furnished with contemporary pieces and an antique Japanese chest, this gay-friendly inn is convenient to good shopping and restaurants in turn-of-the-century Langley. Moderate to deluxe.

Though it's only a few miles north of downtown Langley, the **Log Castle Bed and Breakfast** (3273 East Saratoga Road; 360-221-5483) somehow feels like a retreat hidden away on a gorgeous, sandy beach far from everything. This colossal log home crowned by an eight-sided turret was built bit by bit over the years. The four rooms are warm and inviting, with private baths and comfortable furnishings; a couple even have private decks with grand views. Moderate to deluxe.

From a hot tub on the deck of **Eagles Nest Inn** (3236 East Saratoga Road, Langley; 360-221-5331), you can gaze east across Saratoga Passage and Camano Island to Mt. Baker and the Cascades. Guests come to enjoy the very rural setting, soak up the pampering country hospitality, and take long strolls on a nearby cobbled beach. Four traditional rooms; deluxe.

Kittleson Cove Bed and Breakfast (4891 East Bay Ridge Drive, Clinton; 360-341-2734) sits right on the beach near the Clinton ferry landing. Few visitors can resist the temptation of long, contemplative walks along the shore where the views stretch across the Sound to the Cascades. Privacy is the hallmark (you'll even do your own cooking), and couples or families seeking a true retreat will find it here. Children are welcome. Choose from a cottage or in-home suite; deluxe.

Home By The Sea Bed and Breakfast (2388 East Sunlight Beach Road; 360-321-2964) is really a splendid collection of cottages by the sea, on a lake, in the woods, and on a farm—all within five miles of each other. Variety is the hallmark, but all properties share romantic and private settings with grand views. The two cottages, one bed-and-breakfast room, and apartment suites (all deluxe) offer jacuzzis and hot tubs, beach and lakeshore walks, fishing and the like. Though the address is Clinton, Home by the Sea is actually closer to Freeland.

Cliff House (5440 Windmill Road, Freeland; 360-331-1566) is an architecturally stunning two-story structure of wood and sweeping panes of glass set on a wooded bluff overlooking Admiralty Inlet. Guests have the run of the entire two-bedroom house, with its open central atrium, wonderful gourmet kitchen, sunken sitting area and wraparound cedar deck with large jacuzzi. Ultra-deluxe.

Steeped in history, **Colonel Crockett Farm Bed and Breakfast Inn** (1012 South Fort Casey Road, Coupeville; 360-678-3711) is a five-room inn perched on a 40-acre rise above Crockett Lake, a 200-acre haven for waterfowl and wildlife watchers just a mile from the ferry to Port Townsend. This is a historic Puget Sound crossroads, and the inn (built between 1852 and 1855 by Colonel Walter Crockett) is reputedly the oldest home on island. The colonel's political life stretched back to President Andrew Jackson. Three acres of grounds and gardens feature antique trees and shrubbery more than a century old. Inside, you'll find faux-marble fireplaces, an enclosed sunporch, Victorian antiques throughout, including three large bed-sitting rooms, and a library with 2000 volumes—but no radios or televisions. Moderate.

The Captain Whidbey Inn (2072 West Captain Whidbey Inn Road, Coupeville; 360-678-4097, 800-366-4097), a well-preserved and maintained log inn on Penn Cove, is a fine example of the type of Northwest retreat all the rage 50 years ago and now coming back into fashion. This walk into the past offers several cozy, antique-furnished rooms that share two baths and waterfront views; more-recent additions to the property include two rows of spacious, pine-paneled rooms with baths and a few private cottages with fireplaces. A full breakfast is served in the dining room where the massive stone fireplace chases away the chill. This is one of only a handful of waterside accommodations in the region; to enjoy the water fully, arrange for an afternoon sail with Captain John Colby Stone, the third-generation innkeeper. Moderate.

The **Victorian Bed and Breakfast** (602 North Main Street, Coupeville; 360-678-5305) dates to 1889, with two rooms in the house, plus a cottage of similar vintage out back that once housed a pioneer dentist's office. Children welcome; moderate.

Within walking distance of shops and restaurants, the **Inn at Penn Cove** (702 North Main Street, Coupeville; 360-678-8000, 800-688-2683) is actually a pair of elegant century-old Victorian homes converted to bed and breakfasts. Together, they offer six spacious rooms, some fitted with gas fireplaces, one suite with double jacuzzi; most have views over Penn Cove. Each house boasts plenty of antiques. Prices are moderate to deluxe.

The **Coupeville Inn** (200 Northwest Coveland Street, Coupeville; 360-678-6668, 800-247-6162) has a French mansard–style roof that adds a touch of class to this otherwise straightforward two-story motel. Breakfast featuring homemade muffins is included in the budget to moderate room rates. Of the two dozen rooms, most have balconies, about half have water views. Possibly the best motel value on the island, given the free breakfast and excellent location.

From the flowering window boxes on the European-style exterior to the immaculately clean, antique-filled rooms, the **Auld Holland Inn** (5861 Route 20, Oak Harbor; 360-675-2288, 800-228-0148, fax 360-675-2817) is a moderately priced roadside motel with flair. Some rooms even have fireplaces and princess canopied beds topped with windmill quilts. For those seeking budget prices, there are 24 mobile home units with two or three bedrooms tucked behind the full-sized windmill housing the motel's office. If you're looking for more luxurious surroundings, there are six deluxe-priced units furnished with jacuzzis and fireplaces.

WHIDBEY ISLAND RESTAURANTS

Since 1989, **Café Langley** (113 1st Street, Langley; 360-221-3090) has served Greek favorites like spanikopita, moussaka and lamb shish kabobs along with fresh seafood (Penn Cove mussels, grilled salmon and halibut), pastas and steaks. The atmosphere here is airy Mediterranean, with stucco-like walls, exposed beams and an assortment of exotic fish etched on a glass partition. There are often people waiting in the park across the street for a table in this popular café. Moderate.

The **Star Bistro Café and Bar** (201½ 1st Street, Langley; 360-221-2627), a trendy café with art deco decor, is a popular meeting spot for lunch, dinner and drinks. Their pastas, salads and espressos are particularly good, and the grilled pesto King salmon on a french roll is inventive and tasty. On a calm day you can dine al fresco on the second-floor deck and enjoy a great view of the Saratoga Passage. Moderate.

The **Doghouse Tavern** (230 1st Street, Langley; 360-321-9996) is the place to go for great ribs, burgers, fish and chips and chowder. A totem on the side of this waterfront building points the way to their separate family dining room in case you've got the kids along. Budget.

The chef provides a floor show as well as fine cuisine at the **Inn at Langley** (400 1st Street, Langley; 206-221-3033). The dining area is a huge country kitchen where gleaming copper pots and pans hang from the ceiling and each table has a view of the culinary action. Served on weekend nights only, the dinners consist of five courses emphasizing regional flavors such as duck breast with loganberries or baked salmon with apples, leaks and chanterelles. Ultra-deluxe.

The **Raven Café** (197 2nd Street, Langley; 206-221-3211) provides a homey atmosphere with its hardwood floors, cinnamon-colored walls and collection of 1930s serving trays and coffee cans on display. The mostly vegetarian fare is simply and tasty, with an emphasis on hearty soups and scones in flavors ranging from raspberry-almond to spinach and feta cheese. Budget.

Award-winning **Rosi's Garden** (606 North Main Street, Coupeville; 360-678-3989) serves a blend of Northwest and European cuisine highlighting the many fresh products of Whidbey Island. On the menu, you'll find Penn Cove mussels, prime rib with crab béarnaise, halibut florentine and poached salmon in hollandaise; save room for the decadent desserts. Seating in the peach-and-mauve front room of this tiny seaside cottage is very limited, so reservations for dinner, the only meal they serve, are highly recommended. Moderate.

Christopher's (23 Front Street, Coupeville; 360-678-5480) specializes in "creative contemporary cuisine" with a menu that changes seasonally. The emphasis is on fresh, local fare, and runs the gamut from superb Penn Cove mussels, to beef and chicken, vegetarian dishes, and pasta; regional wines and microbrews are also available. Moderate.

Splendid views across Penn Cove are the chief attraction at **Captain's Galley** (10 Front Street, Coupeville; 360-678-0241), a new seafood and prime rib house. Prices are moderate and live music (blues and contemporary jazz) is featured on Saturday nights along with the hearty fare. There's karaoke on Wednesday night.

Toby's Tavern (8 Northwest Front Street, Coupeville; 360-678-4222) serves up a cheeseburger that was rated tops by actress Kathleen Turner, who starred in the film *War of the Roses*, which was filmed partly in and around Coupeville in 1989. Good fish-and-chips, Penn Cove steamed mussels and an upscale atmosphere add a touch of class to this waterfront watering hole. Moderate.

At **Kasteel Franssen** (5861 Route 20, Oak Harbor; 360-675-0724) lace table dressings, antiques, tapestries and fine art reproductions of Rembrandt and other masters set a romantic European tone well-suited to dishes such as *hollandaise biefstuk* (beef steak in hollandaise), Ellensburg rack of lamb and specials that feature venison, pheasant and other wild game. Dinner only; moderate.

WHIDBEY ISLAND SHOPPING

There's plenty to keep shoppers and browsers busy on Whidbey Island, especially in artsy Langley and historic Coupeville. The best art galleries are concentrated in Langley: **Museo Piccolo** (215 1st Street, Langley; 206-221-7737) specializes in art glass made by the owner and other regional artists; the **Childers/Proctor Gallery** (302 1st Street; 360-221-2978) showcases bronzes, paintings, sculpture and pottery; **Soleil** (308 1st Street; 360-221-0383) carries Nambe ware, double-sided aluminum pieces by Arthur Court and jewelry by local craftspeople; and the **Hellebore Glass Studio** (308 1st Street; 360-221-2067) has fine hand-blown glassworks and a studio where you can watch glassblowers work.

Other noteworthy shops in town include **The Star Store** (201 1st Street; 360-221-5223), a modern mercantile selling fun clothing and housewares; and the two shops of **Whidbey Island Antiques** (2nd Street and Anthes Avenue; 360-221-2393). Located a mile outside Langley, **Blackfish Studio** (5075 Langley Road; 206-221-1274) offers women's clothing with hand-painted designs on raw silk. Check out the adjoining gallery for Northwest photography.

In the revitalized waterfront district of Coupeville, you'll find wonderful antiques and collectibles at **Elk Horn Antiques** (15 Front Street; 360-678-2250); fine imported clothing and jewelry from Scotland and Ireland at **Tartans and Tweeds** (4 Front Street; 360-678-6244); and nautical gifts, artifacts and sportswear at **Nautical 'N' Nice** (22 Front Street; 360-678-3565).

Just three miles south of Coupeville is **Salmangundi Farms** (185 South State Route 20; 360-678-5888). It's listed in the National Historic Register and filled with antiques and old farm equipment.

WHIDBEY ISLAND NIGHTLIFE

If you're looking for a little dance action, head to **Hong Kong Gardens** (4643 East Route 525, Clinton; 360-221-2828) where, on the weekends, they clear the dinner tables off the dancefloor and hit the switch for the disco lights as the band plays popular rock tunes.

For local color in a friendly tavern, try the cozy pub in **The Captain Whidbey Inn** (2072 West Captain Whidbey Inn Road, Coupeville; 360-678-4097), where the walls are adorned with university pennants and business cards, or **Toby's Tavern** (8 Northwest Front Street, Coupeville; 360-678-4222), where they filmed the bar scene from the movie *War of the Roses.*

WHEN CONTINENTS COLLIDE

Geologists who have studied the record say that a now long-disappeared continent moving eastward out of the Pacific Ocean eons ago collided with, or "docked" against, the Puget Sound mainland, laying the foundation for the multiplicity of land forms—islands, estuaries, mountains, coastlines—that characterize the northern Puget Sound region today.

WHIDBEY ISLAND BEACHES AND PARKS

There are 340 acres with 4500 feet of rocky and sandy shoreline to explore in the lovely **South Whidbey State Park** (360-331-4559). Hikers will enjoy the one-and-a-half-mile loop trail through an old-growth stand of fir and cedar. Black-tailed deer, bald eagles and osprey are among the many creatures found here. There are picnic tables and a shelter; campsites on the wooded bluff above the beach are very secluded. To get there, take Route 525 nine miles north of Clinton to Bush Point Road, which after six miles becomes Smuggler's Cove Road.

History buffs and children will enjoy exploring the military fortification of 137-acre **Fort Casey State Park** (360-678-4519). While most of the big guns are gone, you'll still find panoramic views of the Olympic Mountains across the Straight of Juan de Fuca from the top of the concrete bunkers built into the escarpment. Wild roses and other flowers line the paths to the museum housed in pretty Admiralty Head Lighthouse and the beachside campground that overlooks the Keystone Harbor ferry terminal. Scuba enthusiasts swarm to the underwater trail through the park's marine wildlife sanctuary off Keystone Harbor. There are campsites and picnic tables. To get to the park, turn south off Route 20 at Coupeville onto Engle Road and follow the Keystone Ferry signs.

The massive guns are long gone from this coastal World War II fortification, but there are still bunker tunnels and pillboxes to be explored at **Fort Ebey State Park** (360-678-4636). The picturesque beach at Partridge Point is the hands-down favorite of the islanders; at low tide it's possible to walk the five-mile beach stretch to Fort Casey. Facilities include picnic tables and nature trails. There's good bass fishing on Lake Pondilla. Secluded campsites under a canopy of Douglas fir are much nicer than the crowded sites at nearby Fort Casey. From Route 20, turn west onto Libbey Road then south onto Hill Valley Drive and follow the signs.

Joseph Whidbey State Park (360-678-4636) has remained a secluded treasure, known only to locals, until recently signed on Route 20. Famous for its mile or so of sandy beach, this small park is just right for sunset strolls or picnics with views westward across Admiralty Inlet to the Olympic Mountains. There's no overnight camping. The park is three miles west of Oak Harbor on Swantown Road.

A full-scale windmill is the centerpiece of **Oak Harbor City Beach Park** (360-679-5551) on Oak Harbor Bay next to the sewage processing plant (not a deterrent, believe it or not). A sandy beach slopes down from the lighted walking path bordering expansive green fields suitable for flying kites or playing frisbee. There's a wading pool and protected swimming area. Facilities include picnic tables, ball fields, tennis courts and a playground. The park is located in downtown Oak Harbor off Pioneer Parkway, east of Route 20; watch for the windmill.

Deception Pass State Park (360-675-2417) is the most popular state park in Washington. It encompasses over 4800 acres laced with eight-and-a-half miles of hiking trails through forested hills and wetland areas and along rocky headlands. There are several delightful sandy stretches for picnics or beachcombing. Breathtaking views from the 976-foot steel bridge spanning the pass attract photographers from around the world. Camping is available and there's fly-fishing for trout on Pass Lake and swimming on Cranberry Lake in the summer. There are lots of facilities here, including a bathhouse, picnic tables, kitchens, shelters, fireplaces, concession stand, boat launches (salt and freshwater), environmental learning center and underwater park. Take the Mukilteo ferry to Whidbey Island and follow Route 525 and Route 20 to the park on the northern tip of the island.

Fidalgo Island

Anacortes—a two-hour drive northwest of Seattle on Fidalgo Island—is a good place to enjoy folk art, ride a charming excursion train and see impressive murals. Quiet inns and waterfront restaurants make this town a pleasant retreat.

But Anacortes is only the beginning of adventures on this charming island. Often called the first of the San Juans, Fidalgo is actually linked to the mainland by the Route 20 bridge over Swinomish Channel in the Skagit Valley, and to Whidbey Island by another bridge. Access is easy. Nevertheless, you can still find quiet beaches and parks to explore. Lonely trails wind through an enormous forest reserve to superb viewpoints. A mini "Lake District" clusters more than half-a-dozen splendid lakes. And a marvelous resort complex—Scimitar Ridge Ranch—combines a working Northwest horse ranch and a deluxe campground that includes covered wagons outfitted for camping.

But let's start with Anacortes. Because of its ferry terminal, **Anacortes** is known as "the gateway to the San Juans," but don't just zip on through because there's plenty to see and do here. One of the best ways to get acquainted with the city and its history is to make a walking tour of downtown to view the 40 life-sized murals attached to many of the historical buildings. As part of the **Anacortes Mural Project**, these murals are reproductions of turn-of-the-century photographs depicting everyday scenes and early pioneers of the town. A tour map is available from the **Anacortes Chamber of Commerce** (819 Commercial Avenue, Avenue G; 360-293-3832).

Other reminders of earlier days are the **W. T. Preston** (7th Street and R Avenue), a drydocked sternwheeler that once plied the waters of the Sound breaking up log jams, and, next door, the refurbished **Bur-**

lington Northern Railroad Depot (6th Street and R Avenue), now a community arts center. This is the spot to catch the **Anacortes Railway**, an elaborate miniature steam locomotive with three passenger cars built by a local resident. The train is operated on summer weekends.

At the **Anacortes Museum** (1305 8th Street; 360-293-1915), you'll find an entertaining collection of Fidalgo and Guemas islands memorabilia. In front of the building, there's a highly amusing drinking fountain with varying levels suited for dogs, cats, horses and humans, which was donated to the city by the Women's Temperance Union.

Even if you don't plan to stay at the **Majestic Hotel** (419 Commercial Avenue, Anacortes; 360-293-3355), stop by for a 360-degree view of Fidalgo and surrounding islands from the fantastic cupola above fourth-floor suites and ogle the amazing skylight and collection of art and antiques.

If you have an interest in totems, drive by **2102 9th Street** to see the display in front of the home of former State Senator Paul Luvera, Sr., who carved thousands of totems during his retirement before passing away several years ago.

The **Anacortes Community Forest Lands** (locally known as Mt. Erie Park) is a 2500-acre treasure of fishing and swimming lakes, wildlife wetlands, and tall conifers climbing the slopes of 1270-foot Mt. Erie, about five miles south of downtown Anacortes. Some 20 miles of foot trails offer days of wandering. For maps, stop at the Anacortes Visitor Information Office (819 Commercial Avenue; 360-293-3832). But you can also simply drive to the top of Mt. Erie and enjoy a series of vista points carved into its rocky summit that look out in all directions of the compass from the Cascades to the Olympics, across the San Juans, over Skagit Bay to Whidbey and all the way to Mt. Rainier.

Within the park and all around it are a handful of lakes—Heart, Erie, Campbell, Whistle, Cranberry, Pass. You can swing past Campbell Lake

---

DECEPTION PASS BRIDGE

*On Route 20, **Deception Pass Bridge** links Whidbey with Fidalgo Island. It also spans what one tour guide terms "The Grand Canyon of Puget Sound." Most tourists just drive slowly by, soaking up the sights. For more excitement, park and stroll out onto the bridge for vertigo-inducing views straight down into the swift, churning currents of Deception Pass. Watch as small boats, skippers unaware, hurl themselves at the tidal current, then fall back to re-think. You can also walk down to the shore on the footpaths of Pass Island to watch the streaming waters up close, or spread a picnic for a long and lazy look at the constant boat parade.*

and Pass Lake (good fishing) on Route 20 between Anacortes and Deception Pass. And you can visit Heart and Erie (picnicking, fishing) from Mt. Erie Road leading into the park. Whistle and Cranberry (good fishing) are reached by foot trail.

FIDALGO ISLAND LODGING

A lot of care and expense went into the painstaking renovation of the historic 1889 McNaught building, now the new **Majestic Hotel** (419 Commercial Avenue, Anacortes; 360-293-3355, fax 360-293-5214), which specializes in European elegance, from the plush feather bedding and antique furnishings to the warm and inviting mahogany-paneled library and grand English garden. Guests are treated to croissants and coffee each morning. The highly individual guest rooms vary in price from moderate to ultra-deluxe. Don't miss the stupendous 360-degree views from the cupola above the fourth floor.

At the **Nantucket Inn** (3402 Commercial Avenue, Anacortes; 360-293-6007), the proprietress was welcoming weary travelers into her home long before bed and breakfasts came into fashion. Each of the comfortable guest rooms is furnished in lovingly polished family antiques and cozy quilts; two of the rooms share a bath and a third has a bath across the hall. Moderate.

FIDALGO ISLAND RESTAURANTS

Since 1935, the **Bridgeway Café** (1541 Route 20, Anacortes; 360-293-9250) has served up fresh, handbreaded oysters and prawns, grilled burgers and mouthwatering pies. Look for this unpretentious roadside establishment on the hill four miles north of Deception Pass. Budget.

While it's not particularly well decorated or romantic, **La Petite** (3401 Commercial Avenue, Anacortes; 360-293-4644) is the only dinner spot in town fancy enough to have tablecloths. The fare here is solid Dutch gourmet, with often-repeated favorites such as *gemarinder de lam* (marinated lamb in herbs and red wine) and *kippige knoflock* (chicken breast over parmesan pasta). The traditional Dutch breakfast of egg cup, thinly sliced ham and cheese and piping hot loaves of bread draws a crowd. Deluxe.

Potted plants, taped classical music and tablecloths soften the rough edges of **Charlie's** (5407 Ferry Terminal Road, Anacortes; 360-293-7377), a roadside hash house overlooking the ferry terminal and water. Captive diners, here during the long wait for the ferry, choose from soups, salads, sandwiches and seafood at lunch and pasta, steak and seafood for dinner. Moderate.

FIDALGO ISLAND SHOPPING

Most of the great shops on Fidalgo Island are scattered along Anacortes' Commercial Avenue. **Left Bank Antiques** (1904 Commercial Avenue; 360-293-3022), housed in a renovated church, absolutely bulges with American and European antiques and gift items. The historic **Marine Supply and Hardware** (202 Commercial Avenue; 360-293-3014) is packed to the rafters with nautical antiques and memorabilia.

At **Sylvia's Garden** (1005 7th Street, Anacortes; 206-293-8359), you'll find an intriguing collection of wares from local artisans and farmers, including handwoven baskets, jewelry, fresh and dried flowers, herb-flavored vinegars and oils, gardening items and more. At fascinating and fun **Bunnies By The Bay** (2403 R Avenue, Anacortes; 360-293-8037), they create designer stuffed animals to complement any decor scheme.

Resist the temptation to buy smoked salmon to take home for friends and family until you visit **Specialty Seafoods** (605 30th Street, Anacortes; 360-293-4661) for alderwood smoked oysters, King, North Pacific or Sockeye salmon. Discount prices are terrific at the difficult-to-locate **warehouse** (605 30th Street). Take 22nd Street east toward the Anacortes Marina, turn right onto T Avenue and you'll find the warehouse in an industrial complex a block down on the right.

FIDALGO ISLAND NIGHTLIFE

If a quiet conversation over drinks in refined surroundings is your style, visit the **Rose and Crown Pub** (The Majestic Hotel, 419 Commercial Avenue, Anacortes; 360-293-3355).

SCIMITAR RIDGE RANCH

*Located about five miles east of Anacortes, **Scimitar Ridge Ranch** (527 Miller Road, just off Route 20; 360-293-5355, 800-798-5355) is a 400-acre dude ranch and resort stretched across a shoulder of Mount Erie adjoining a 2500-acre public park.*

Top attraction for many is the Northwest horse ranch. An entertainment pavilion hosts barbecues and cowboy storytelling staged around a roaring fire. The dude ranch features wagon rides and guided trail rides through forests and fern grottoes. There's a dance stage for hoe-downs and an outdoor amphitheater for top-notch country-and-western bands on summer weekends. All this is located next to deluxe RV campsites in a splendid forest and replicas of pioneer covered wagons outfitted for camping.

Lopez Island

The history of Lopez Island is well mapped out at the **Lopez Historical Museum** (Lopez Village; 360-468-2049) with its exhibit of pioneer farming and fishing implements. While you're here, pick up a historical landmark tour guide to the many fine examples of Early American architecture scattered around the island. Open during the summer only.

Stroll out to **Agate Beach Park** (MacKaye Harbor Road) to watch the sunset. Another good sunset view spot is **Shark Reef Park** (Shark Reef Road) where you might see some harbor seals, heron and, if you're lucky, a whale or two.

If you like horses, pull off the road at the bend on Center Road between Cross and Hummel Lake roads to admire the large herd of Shetlands frolicking in rolling pastures.

LOPEZ ISLAND LODGING

The **Islander Lopez** (Fisherman Bay Road, Lopez Village; 360-468-2233, 800-736-3434, fax 360-468-3382), once a dog-eared motel, is turning upscale with new owners and a major-league improvement program. All of the 28 rooms have been refurbished and several suites have been added (moderate to deluxe). The marina has been upgraded (new floats and piers, a seaplane dock) and rental runabouts made available for the protected waters of Fisherman Bay. An ambitious outings program for guests includes opportunities to bike, boat and fish.

Best bet here is the **Inn At Swifts Bay** (Port Stanley Road; 360-468-3636), a delightful bed and breakfast in an elegant Tudor home. "Posh" best describes the interior, with a comfortable mix of modern, Williams Sonoma–style furnishings and antique reproductions adorned in crocheted antimacassars and needlepoint pillows. Two rooms sharing one bath fall into the moderate category, and three suites with private entrances, gas fireplaces and baths are deluxe in price. The leisurely gourmet breakfast is without a doubt the most delicious morning repast available in the islands. Gay-friendly.

Edenwild (Lopez Village; 360-468-3238), a two-story Victorian, is another of the few lodging possibilities on the island. The eight guest rooms are pretty, with blond-wood floors, clawfoot tubs and antique furnishings; three rooms have romantic fireplaces, one is handicap accessible and those on the west side of the structure have views of Fisherman's Bay and San Juan Channel. Included in the deluxe-to-ultra-deluxe price is breakfast, served in the sunny dining nook or on the delightful garden terrace where they also serve afternoon tea and apéritifs.

There are a few budget-priced rooms to be found on the island. The **Lopez Lodge** (360-468-2500) above Island Family Video in the village has one room with private bath and two no–frills, motel–like rooms with a shared bath across the hall. The **Island Farm House** (Route 2, Box 3114, Hummel Lake Road; 206-468-2864) offers a more cozy and comfortable room with bath overlooking a pasture and pond. A separate private cabin also has its own bath and refrigerator.

LOPEZ ISLAND RESTAURANTS

The **Bay Café** (Lopez North; 360-468-3700) has an imaginative menu of ethnic cuisine featuring fresh Northwest products. There are always daily specials to choose from, with often-repeated favorites like scallops in Thai curry, marinated lamb kabobs in mint yogurt sauce, beef satay with peanut sauce and wok-seared beef with pinenuts, wild mushrooms and jasmine rice. Reservations are essential, especially during summer. Deluxe.

Set off to one side in the **Lopez Island Pharmacy** (Lopez Village; 360-468-2644) is an old-fashioned, pink-and-gray soda fountain, the best spot in town for lunch on Lopez. Grab a stool at the bar and order a sandwich, bowl of soup or chili or slice of pie to go with your phosphate, malt, float or other fountain treat. Budget.

Located next to the Lopez Village Market in a handsome Cape Cod–style building with weathered shingles and a terrace overlooking the water, **Gail's** (206-468-2150) uses fresh ingredients, including herbs and vegetables from the chef's garden, to create dishes bearing both Northwest and Pacific Rim influences. Among the menu highlights are steamed halibut wrapped in bok choy with black bean sauce, Thai curried prawns and salmon barbecued over alderwood. Moderate to deluxe.

The **Islander Lopez Restaurant** (Fisherman Bay Road, Lopez Village; 360-468-2234) is a true waterfront restaurant, looking west across

---

SHAW ISLAND

Shaw is one of only four of the San Juan Islands reached by ferry, but most visitors to the San Juans miss it. You need to stay on the ferry from Anacortes and get off at Shaw Island, one stop beyond Lopez Island. Those who do make the trip are in for a treat. Stop by the general store near the ferry landing (both operated by Franciscan nuns) for picnic supplies before heading out to **South Beach County Park** *(Squaw Bay Road) two miles to the south. Afterward, continue east along Squaw Bay Road, turn north on Hoffman Cove Road and make your way to the picturesque little red schoolhouse. Park by the school and cross the street to see the* **Shaw Island Historical Museum** *(Schoolhouse Corner; 360-468-4068), a tiny log cabin housing a hodgepodge of pioneer memorabilia.*

Life on pastoral Lopez Island is slow and friendly; residents wave to everyone and are truly disappointed if you don't take the time to wave back.

Fisherman Bay to spectacular evening sunsets. In summer, ask for a table on the outdoor dining patio. Specialties of the house include an award-winning clam chowder, barbecued baby-back ribs, wonderful salads (try the blackened scallop salad!) and a daily fresh sheet of local seafood—salmon, halibut, shark, mahimahi. Moderate.

LOPEZ ISLAND SHOPPING

For the most part, shopping here is limited to those establishments located in sleepy little Lopez Village. **Archipelago** (360-468-3222) sells natural-fiber clothing and a line of tourist T-shirts; **Panda Books** (360-468-2132) stocks an admirable selection of new and used books and regional music. For fine art, visit **Chimera Gallery** (360-468-3265), the cooperative showcase for prints, paintings, weaving, pottery, hand-blown glass and jewelry produced by local artists.

LOPEZ ISLAND BEACHES AND PARKS

Located on the eastern shore of the island, **Spencer Spit State Park** (360-468-2251) is a long stretch of silky sand that encloses a saltwater lagoon. The mile-long beach invites clamming, wading and swimming during warm summer months. There's excellent crabbing, shrimping and bottom fishing from offshore (if you have a boat), as well as camping facilities, beach bonfire pits and picnic shelters.

San Juan Island

San Juan Island, the namesake of the archipelago, is a popular resort destination centered around the town of Friday Harbor. This 20-mile-long island has a colorful past stemming from a boundary dispute between the United States and Great Britain. The tension over who was entitled to the islands was embodied in American and British farmers whose warring over, get this, a *pig*, nearly sent the two countries to the battlefield. When an American farmer shot a British homesteader's pig caught rooting in his garden, ill feelings quickly escalated. Fortunately, cooler heads prevailed so that what is now referred to as the "Pig War" of 1859 only resulted in one casualty: the pig. The history of this little-

The Whale Museum at Friday Harbor operates a 24-hour hotline (800-562-8832 in Washington only) to report whale sightings.

known war is chronicled through interpretive centers in the **San Juan Island National Historical Park** (360-378-2240), which is divided into **English Camp** (West Valley Road) on the north end of the island, with barracks, a formal garden, cemetery, guardhouse, hospital and commissary left intact, and **American Camp** (Cattle Point Road) on the south end of the island, where the officers and laundress's quarters, a cemetery and the Hudson Bay Company Farm Site remain.

San Juan Historical Museum (405 Price Street, Friday Harbor; 360-378-3949) is a charming turn-of-the-century frame building with a good collection of Native American baskets and stone implements, antique diving suits, period furniture and clothing. A place to learn about the region's maritime history, the museum also features an excellent collection highlighting this region's proud past.

Whalewatching is a big part of a visit to the San Juan Islands, so be sure not to miss the **Whale Museum** (62 North 1st Street, Friday Harbor; 360-378-4710; admission), where you can learn more about whales and other marine life found in the area. A photo collection with names and pod numbers will help you identify all of the islands' 90 or so resident orca whales by their distinctive grayish saddle patches and the nicks, scars or tears in their dorsal fins and tails. Displays and videos explain whale behavior, and there are all sorts of whale-related education materials, art and souvenirs available in the museum's gift shop.

Afterglow Vista (Roche Harbor Resort) is the mausoleum of one of the region's wealthy families. The structure itself is fascinating; an open, Grecian-style columned complex surrounds six inscribed chairs, each containing the ashes of a family member, set before a round table of limestone. A seventh chair and column have obviously been removed, some say as part of Masonic ritual, others believe because a member of the family was disinherited.

Oyster lovers and birdwatchers should make the trip down the dusty road to **Westcott Bay Sea Farms** (4071 Westcott Drive, Friday Harbor; 360-378-2489), where there are saltwater bins of live oysters and clams, and an array of birds attracted to the oyster beds that stretch out into the bay.

SAN JUAN ISLAND LODGING

Named for its view, **Olympic Lights** (4531-A Cattle Point Road, Friday Harbor; 360-378-3186, fax 360-378-2097) is a remodeled 1895 farmhouse set on five grassy, breeze-tossed acres overlooking the Olympic Peninsula across the Strait of Juan de Fuca. Guests kick off their shoes before heading up to the cream-carpeted second floor with four comfortably appointed, pastel-shaded rooms sharing two baths; a fifth room on the ground floor has a private bath. You'll find no frilly, Victoriana clutter here, just a peaceful night snuggled under down comforters topped off by a farm-fresh breakfast. Moderate to deluxe.

If you've dreamed of life on the water, you'll appreciate the **Wharfside Bed and Breakfast** (Port of Friday Harbor; 360-378-5661), a 60-foot, two-masted sailboat with two guest rooms. The forward stateroom with double bed and two bunks feels a bit cramped, while the aft stateroom with queen bed seems roomier. The moderate price includes a three-course breakfast. Children and pets welcome.

Friday's (35 1st Street; 360-378-5848, 800-352-2631, fax 360-378-2881) is a renovated bed and breakfast with nine individually decorated rooms in varying themes. You can stay in the Rose Room and watch

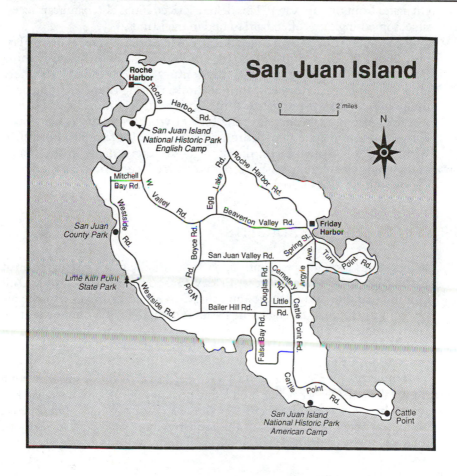

On a sunny afternoon, it's hard to beat a stroll through the fragrant herb gardens at Giannangelo Farms (5500 Limestone Point Road, Friday Harbor; 360-378-4218).

the sunset or the Orca Room and soak in the private jacuzzi. And all this romance is conveniently located in the heart of Friday harbor. Moderate to deluxe.

Set in the rolling West Valley near English Camp and surrounded by a working ranch, **States Inn** (2039 West Valley Road, Friday Harbor; 360-378-6240, fax 360-378-6241) is a bit of Sleepy Hollow in San Juan. Each of the nine rooms has a decor that hints at its namesake state—tiny Rhode Island comes closest, with shells and brass dolphins on the fireplace mantle, various renditions of ships on the walls and copies of the New England publication *Yankee* to peruse. The friendly and informative innkeeper and the multi-course country breakfasts make up for the slight sulphur odor that emanates from the tap water. This deluxe-priced inn is also handicap accessible, something that's often hard to find in the islands.

Roche Harbor Resort (4950 Tarte Memorial Drive, Roche Harbor; 360-378-2155, 800-451-8910, fax 360-378-6809) has something for everyone. You can check in to the century-old Hotel de Haro where gingerbread trim, parlor beds, antiques and a roaring fireplace bring back the good old days at budget to deluxe prices. In addition to this three-story, 20-room establishment, nine former workers' cottages have been converted into deluxe two-bedroom units, ideal for families. Furnished with Salvation Army pieces, the cottages are convenient to the swimming pool. For deluxe-to-ultra-deluxe-priced contemporary lodging, choose one of the condominiums.

SAN JUAN ISLAND RESTAURANTS

When locals look for a romantic spot, they usually make a reservation at **Café Bisset** (170 West Street, Friday Harbor; 360-378-3109). Dim lighting, candles and fresh bouquets of flowers add romance to the already intimate surroundings. The basics remain the same on the menu—lamb, duck, beef and three kinds of seafood—but the method of preparation changes daily, utilizing fresh local produce. Dinner only by reservation; deluxe.

Roberto's (205 A Street, Friday Harbor; 360-378-6333) sits on the hill overlooking the ferry landing. You'll find no fancy decor, but the Italian fare served here is a culinary escape. Try the "pasta tour of Italy" (with pesto, bolognese and alfredo sauces) or the Sicilian salmon in capers and onions, followed up by homemade cheesecake and fresh fruit tarts. Moderate.

Another welcome addition to Friday Harbor's dining scene is **The Blue Dolphin** (185 1st Street; 360-378-6116), an unpretentious diner serving hearty portions of homecooked breakfast and lunch favorites like biscuits and gravy, blueberry pancakes, chicken-fried steak and burgers. Prices are budget.

SAN JUAN ISLAND SHOPPING

Most shops are within blocks of Friday Harbor, giving you plenty to do while waiting for the ferry. Cannery Landing, next to the ferry terminal on Front Street, houses **Dolphin Arts** (360-378-3531), selling original screenprint art on cotton sportswear.

Art lovers visiting Friday Harbor will want to stop by **El Picaflor** (1 Front Street; 360-378-3051) for their collection of Latin American handicrafts; **Garuda & I** (60 1st Street; 360-378-3733) for an amazing selection of ethnic arts, crafts, beads, musical instruments and jewelry from India and Asia; and the **Sunshine Gallery** (85 Nichols Street; 360-378-5819) to view the locally produced basketry, sculptures, watercolors, ceramics and jewelry.

SAN JUAN ISLAND NIGHTLIFE

Friday Harbor Saloon (80 1st Street, Friday Harbor; 360-378-9106) is the local sidle-up-to-the-bar joint with the only pool tables in town. You'll find live music and dancing each weekend at **Ford's Bar and Grille** (175 Spring Street, Friday Harbor; 360-378-4747) and the **Roche Harbor Resort Lounge** (4950 Tarte Memorial Drive, Roche Harbor; 360-378-2155).

SAN JUAN ISLAND PARKS

If you really want to get away from the crowds, many of the smaller islands are preserved as state parks, including Doe, Jones, Clark, Sucia, Stuart, Posey, Blind, James, Matia, Patos and Turn. They are accessible by boat only and, in most cases, have a few primitive campsites, nature trails, a dock or mooring buoys off secluded beaches, but no water or facilities.

SAN JUAN ISLAND BEACHES AND PARKS

San Juan County Park (360-378-2992) is a good place to watch for the orca whales who frequently pass by the rocky shoreline of this 12-acre park set on the western edge of San Juan Island. Because of its location on Smallpox Bay, the park is a haven for kayakers and scuba divers who enjoy the easy waters in the shallow bay or the more challenging shelf that drops steeply off about 80 feet out. Facilities include picnic tables and campsites.

Lime Kiln Point State Park (360-378-2044) is situated on a rocky bluff overlooking Haro Straight, making this the prime whalewatching spot on the island. A footpath takes you to picturesque Lime Kiln Lighthouse, listed on the National Register of Historic Places. The site is named for an early lime kiln operation, with remnants of old structures still visible to the north of the lighthouse. There are picnic tables and interpretive displays. The park is just off Westside Road on the western shore of San Juan Island.

Though it takes a precarious scramble down a rocky ledge to reach it and picnic tables on the bluff above at **Cattle Point Picnic Area** lend little privacy, this gravelly half-moon is arguably the prettiest public beach on San Juan Island. Besides picnic tables, you'll find interpretive signs and a nature trail. To get there, follow Cattle Point Road through American Camp and on to the southern tip of the island.

Fourth of July Beach (360-378-2240) is a secluded, sandy crescent that the locals head to when they're looking for privacy. There are often bald eagles nesting in the trees, a poignant sign of this aptly named stretch. The shallow bay extends out a long way and is suitable for wading on hot days. Facilities include picnic tables and a fenced grassy area off the parking lot that's a good spot to toss a frisbee. Located on the northeastern edge of American Camp.

Orcas Island

Trendy, artsy-crafty and lovely to look at, Orcas Island is a place that caters to everyone from backpackers to the well-to-do. A nature sanctuary pocketed with charming towns, the island also boasts more sun than some of its neighbors.

One of Orcas Island's leading landmarks is Rosario Resort. Even if you're not planning to stay here during your trip, make sure to visit **Moran Mansion** (1 Rosario Way; 360-376-2222) for a fantastic evening show that includes music performed on a 1910 Steinway grand piano and an amazing pipe organ, along with entertaining narration and slides of life on the island in the early 1900s.

Lime Kiln Point is one of the best shoreline viewing spots for whalewatching.

Of the many small historical museums in the San Juans, the **Orcas Island Historical Museum** (North Beach Road, Eastsound; 360-376-4849; admission) is our favorite. A fine assemblage of relics and antiques stored in six interconnected log cabins of prominent early settlers maps the history and growth of industry on the island. Open summer afternoons.

Madrona Point, a pretty madrona tree–dotted waterside park saved from condo development by the Lummi Indian tribe, is a fine spot for a picnic. It's at the end of the unmarked road just past Christina's Restaurant in Eastsound.

ORCAS ISLAND LODGING

A stay at **Turtleback Farm Inn** (Crow Valley Road, Eastsound; 360-376-4914) is like stepping into the much-loved story *Wind in the Willows*, surrounded as it is by acres of forest and farm tracts full of animals as far as the eye can see. Rooms in this lovely, 100-year-old farmhouse vary in size and setup, but all seven guest rooms have a charming mix of contemporary and Early American furniture, cozy quilts and antique fixtures in private baths. Moderate to ultra-deluxe.

It's not unusual to find semi-tame deer roaming around the ample grounds of **Rosario Resort** (1 Rosario Way, Eastsound; 360-376-2222, 800-562-8820, fax 360-376-3680) tucked away on Cascade Bay on the east side of the horseshoe of Orcas Island. The motel-style rooms scattered along the waterfront or perched on the hillside overlooking the bay are clean and comfortable, but could use a decorating overhaul. Deluxe.

Accommodations at the funky **Doe Bay Village Resort** (Star Route 86, Olga; 360-376-2291) range from bunk houses to rustic cabins to tents with 22 units total. There are shared central bathrooms, a community kitchen and a small café on the grounds of this large retreat along with a splendid three-tiered sauna and three mineral baths perched on a covered deck. Budget.

ORCAS ISLAND RESTAURANTS

La Famiglia (A Street, Eastsound; 360-376-2335), an inviting, wood-paneled restaurant decorated with distinct Northwest accents, has been the preferred choice of islanders since opening in 1976. The lunch and dinner menus feature Italian classics with island flair—pasta primavera with salmon, seafood linguine, steamer clams in garlic and wine. There are even pizza and sandwiches to please the younger set. Moderate.

Orcas Island was named after Spanish explorer Don Juan Vincente de Guemes Pacheco y Padilla Orcasitees y Aguayo Conde de Revilla Gigedo (whew!) rather than orca whales.

Bilbo's Festivo (North Beach Road, Eastsound; 360-376-4728) specializes in Tex-Mex fare. A margarita or cerveza on the tiled garden patio surrounded by adobe walls rounds out the experience. Bilbo's serves dinner only, but opens **La Taqueria**, a lunch outlet in the courtyard, during summer months. Moderate.

The **Deer Harbor Inn** (Deer Harbor Road, Deer Harbor; 360-376-4110), tucked away in an expanse of orchard grove peering out over Deer Harbor and the Olympic Range, is where locals come for that special night out. The daily menu is chalked on the board; rock cod, coho salmon and choice steaks are prime picks. For diners on the deck, this is a great spot to watch the sunset. Dinner only; reservations recommended. Moderate.

ORCAS ISLAND SHOPPING

You'll find several interesting shops congregated in Eastsound. **Darvill's Rare Print Shop** (360-376-2351) carries antique maps, etchings and fine prints and has a connected bookstore that will please avid readers. For casual wear, try **Orcas North West** (360-376-2386), and for souvenirs, charts, maps and handicrafts of the island, visit **Gulls & Buoys Gifts** (360-376-2199). Another good place to browse in Eastsound is **Clarion** (Prune Alley; 206-376-6040). This gallery, housed in a charming small cottage, features paintings, pottery and sculpture by local artists.

Don't spend all your time and money in Eastsound because you won't want to miss **Orcas Island Pottery** (off West Beach Road; 360-376-2813), the oldest existing craft studio on Orcas. You can even watch potters at work through the windows of the studio. **The Right Place** (off West Beach Road; 360-376-4023) has more pottery strewn about the garden and in the showroom. A spinning and weaving shop, **The Naked Lamb** (360-376-4606), is also on the grounds.

At a bend in Horseshoe Highway as you reach the town of Olga is **Orcas Island Artworks** (360-376-4408), the cooperative art gallery showcasing stained glass, woodworking, jewelry, leatherwork and furniture all produced by local hands. Tucked away in the attic is the **Temenos Bookstore** (360-376-5645) with metaphysical books, crystals and incense.

ORCAS ISLAND NIGHTLIFE

Vista Lounge (Rosario Resort, 1 Rosario Way, Eastsound; 360-376-2222) is the place to go for live entertainment and great sunset views, with an occasional comedy night and special theme dance weekends thrown in for good measure.

ORCAS ISLAND BEACHES AND PARKS

Located near Eastsound, and accessible by state ferry from Anacortes, **Moran State Park** (360-376-2326)—Washington's fifth-largest park—consists of over 5000 verdant acres flanked by 1800 feet of saltwater shoreline and crowned by sweeping Mt. Constitution. The view from the stone tower at the peak takes in the San Juans, Mt. Baker and Vancouver, B.C. There are miles of forest trails connecting the four mountain lakes, numerous waterfalls and five campgrounds. There is fresh water fishing on lakes (boat rentals available). Swimming is good. Amenities include showers, kitchen shelters and picnic tables; some facilities are wheelchair accessible.

   Obstruction Pass State Park (360-755-9231) is a primitive, heavily forested locale on the southeastern tip of Orcas Island that's tricky to get to, so the crowds are kept to a minimum, a reward for those who care to search it out. The area is laced with hiking trails, has several free campsites and a beach where the fishing and swimming are both good. Here's how to get there: From the town of Olga, follow Doe Bay Road east, turn right on Obstruction Pass Road and keep right until you hit the parking area. From there, it's a half-mile hike to the campground.

The Sporting Life

BOATING

Spending time on the water is a part of daily life here, and certainly something that visitors should not miss. In fact, many of the 100-plus islands of the San Juans are accessible only by boat. Rental options are numerous; on the mainland, contact **Fairhaven Boatworks** (501 Harris, Bellingham; 360-647-2469).

   In the islands, try **North Isle Sailing** (2550 North Swantown Road, Oak Harbor; 360-675-8360); **Penmare Marine Co.** (2011 Skyline Way, Anacortes; 360-293-4839); or **Deer Harbor Charters** (P.O. Box 303, Deer Harbor, WA 98243; 360-376-5989, 800-544-5758).

   Kayaking is also immensely popular. Turn to **Northwest Sea Ventures** (926 29th Street, Anacortes; 360-293-3692); **Shearwater Sea**

Kayak Tours (P.O. Box 787, Eastsound, WA 98245; 360-376-4699) or **Island Kayak Guides** (Doe Bay Resort, Olga, Orcas Island; 360-376-4755) for lessons and tours. **Osprey Tours** (Eastsound, Orcas Island; 206-376-3677) offers both kayak rentals and guided tours around Orcas Island in traditional Aleut-style kayaks.

If you'd rather have someone else do all the work on a leisurely sunset cruise between Everett and Friday Harbor on San Juan Island, call **Mosquito Fleet Enterprises** (1724-F West Marine View Drive, Everett; 206-252-6800). Sailboat charters are offered by **Kismet Charters** (P.O. Box 111, Lopez Island, WA 98261; 206-468-2435). Or, for a thrilling jetboat ride from La Conner through the channel, try **Viking Cruises** (109 North 1st Street, La Conner; 360-466-2639).

SCUBA DIVING

The protected inland sea waters of Puget Sound hold treasures untold for the diver, where the craggy rock walls, ledges and caves of this sunken mountain range and enormous forests of bull kelp provide homes for a multitude of marine life. It is also the site of some of the most tremendous tidal changes in the world; the strong currents and riptides can be treacherous, so plan to use local dive charters or talk in detail with another diver experienced in the area.

There are hundreds of great dive spots to choose from, some little known and others crowded with divers. Favored dive sites in the San Juans are just off Henry, Stewart and Waldron islands. There are also several easily accessible protected underwater marine reserves in Fort Casey State Park, Deception Pass State Park and Birch Bay State Park.

Underwater Sports Inc. (205 East Casino Road, Everett; 360-355-3338), the **Whidbey Island Dive Center** (9050 900th Avenue West, Oak Harbor; 360-675-1112) and **Emerald Seas Aquatics** (2-A Spring Street, Friday Harbor; 360-378-2772) provide air fills, rentals and lessons, as well as dive charters.

SPORTFISHING

With thousands of miles of tidal coastline, Puget Sound and the San Juan Islands once boasted some of the best sportfishing opportunities in North America. These days, the fish—especially salmon—are in great peril from various abuses. For the present, there are still five varieties of Pacific salmon (chinook, coho, chum, pink and sockeye), and anglers can also try for cod, flounder, halibut, ling, rockfish, sea perch, squid and sturgeon. Scuba divers often concentrate their efforts on harvesting abalone, crab, octopus, shrimp and squid, while shellfishers are rewarded with

You can often see whales from shore during June, July and August, when they come closest to the islands to feed on migrating salmon.

butter and razor clams. Clamming and fishing licenses are required and are available in sporting goods stores.

Experienced charter operators in the northern Puget Sound region include **All Star Charters** (1724 West Marine Drive, Everett; 206-252-4188); **Sea Hawk Charters** (1620 South 15th Street, Mt. Vernon; 206-424-1350) and **Jim's Salmon Charter** (4434 Boblett Road, Blaine, WA 98230; 360-332-6724).

In the islands, try **Orcas Island Eclipse Charters** (Russell's Landing, Orcas Island; 206-376-4663); **Buffalo Works Fishing Charters** (P.O. Box 478, Friday Harbor, WA 98250; 360-378-4612) and **Trophy Charters** (P.O. Box 2444, Friday Harbor, WA 98250; 206-378-2110).

HORSEBACK RIDING

Because of soaring insurance costs, many horseback riding outfits have had to drop out of the business. However, **Lang's Pony and Horse Rides** (4565 Little Mountain Road, Mt. Vernon; 360-424-7630) and **Madrona Ridge Ranch** (2107 Madrona Way, Coupeville; 360-678-4124) have managed to hang in there. But the best of the bunch is undoubtedly **Scimitar Ridge Ranch** on Fidalgo Island (527 Miller Road, Anacortes; 360-293-5355, 800-798-5355), which combines marvelous forest and meadow trails with superb island and mountain views across 350 acres on the shoulder of Mt. Erie near Deception Pass. Reservations for riding should be made at least 24 hours in advance; proper riding attire required (pants, boots, etc.).

On Orcas Island, **Walking Horse Country Farm** (206-376-5306) offers trail rides, riding lessons and horse-drawn carriage rides.

GOLF

Golf enthusiasts will be pleased with the abundance of beautiful golf courses in the region, many offering unparalleled views of the Sound. With an average annual rainfall of 50 inches, courses in this temperate climate zone are lush and green.

Good choices along northern Puget Sound include **Walter E. Hall Memorial Golf Course** (1226 West Casino Road, Everett; 206-353-4653); **Kayak Point Golf Course** (15711 Marine Drive, Stanwood; 360-652-9676); **Overlook Golf Course** (1785 Route 9, Mt. Vernon; 360-422-6444); **Lake Padden Municipal Golf Course** (4882 Samish

Way, Bellingham; 360-676-6989); and the **Sudden Valley Golf and Country Club** (2145 Lake Whatcom Boulevard, Bellingham; 360-734-6435). Perhaps the most famous course is the **Semiahmoo Golf and Country Club** (8720 Semiahmoo Parkway, Blaine; 360-371-7005), designed by the legendary Arnold Palmer. The **Avalon Golf Club** (1717 Kelleher Road, Burlington; 360-757-1900) has the hottest new links around the Sound.

On Whidbey Island, visit **Lams Links** (585 Ducken Road, Oak Harbor; 360-675-3412) or **Island Greens Golf** (3890 East French Road, Clinton; 360-321-6042). Fidalgo Island offers **Similk Beach Golf Course** (1250 Christiansen Road, Anacortes; 360-293-3444). On other islands, try **Lopez Island Golf Course** (Airport Road, Lopez Island; 360-468-2679); **San Juan Golf and Country Club** (2261 Golf Course Road, Friday Harbor; 360-378-2254); and **Orcas Island Golf Club** (Horseshoe Highway, Eastsound; 360-376-4400).

TENNIS

No need to leave your racket at home with so many public courts to take advantage of. In Everett, you'll find courts at **Clark Park** (240 Lombard). In Bellingham, your best bets are the courts at **Lake Padden Park** (4882 Samish Way; 360-676-6989) or **Fairhaven Park** (107 Chuckanut Drive; 360-676-6985) downtown.

On Whidbey Island, you can use the lighted courts at **Coupeville High School** (South Main Street) or those at **Oak Harbor City Park** (70th Street West). On Fidalgo Island, try the **Anacortes High School facility** (20th Street and J Avenue). **Lopez High School** (Center Road) is your only option on Lopez Island. On San Juan, try the courts at the Friday Harbor High School (Guard Street) or head out to the **Roche Harbor Resort** (Roche Harbor Road).

WHALE-WATCHING EXCURSIONS

Island Mariner Cruises (5 Harbor Esplanade, Bellingham; 360-734-8866) offers day-long nature and whale-watching expeditions with commentary on the history, flora and fauna of the San Juans as you cruise through the islands. *Western Prince Cruises* (Friday Harbor; 360-378-5315, 800-757-6722) has similar naturalist-accompanied wildlife tours on a half-day basis. You can also try the *San Juan Boat Rentals and Tours* (Friday Harbor; 360-378-3499) for a three-hour whale-watching excursion.

The Skagit Valley's farmlands, estuaries and tide flats attract several species of hawks and is one of the best places in all of North America to go "hawkwatching."

BICYCLING

The **Waterfront Loop** in Everett takes you past the majestic old homes of early lumber barons and through the Everett Marina Village. There are no designated bike lanes along the dusty rural roads of Mt. Vernon, but you'll see rich fields and quiet lanes for miles. Bellingham offers several bike routes, some arduous, some easy, all highlighting the scenery and history of the area. One such trail is the moderate **Chuckanut Trail** (6 miles), which begins at the Fairhaven Parkway and ends at Larrabee State Park. The best of the bunch is the fairly easy, 45-minute Lake Padden Loop. For a map of bike routes, contact the **Bellingham Visitors Bureau** (904 Potter Street, Bellingham; 360-671-3990).

Those looking for a long-distance ride will enjoy the 50-mile **Island County Tour**, which begins at Columbia Beach on Whidbey Island and continues on to Deception Pass at the northern tip of the island. This trip is moderately strenuous, with high traffic on a good portion of the ride, but the spectacular views of the Strait of Juan de Fuca and the Saratoga Passage are reward enough.

Some of the best country bike routes in the state can be found in the **Skagit and Nooksack valleys**. Use the backroads east, northeast and southeast of La Conner to fashion loop tours from a few miles to over 20. Or, head for the north Skagit Valley and create a route using backroads starting in Bow on Chuckanut Drive, and heading west to Edison, south to Bay View, west over Bay View Ridge to Chuckanut Drive, then north back to Bow. Do the same in the slightly hillier Nooksack Valley, beginning in Lynden and circuiting Sumas, Everson and Nooksack, before returning to Lynden.

In the San Juans, there are several routes to choose from. The easiest and most popular is the **Lopez Island Perimeter Loop**, 32 miles of gently rolling hills and narrow, paved roads passing by Fisherman's Bay, Shark Reef Park, MacKaye Harbor and Agate Beach on the west side of the island and Mud Bay, Lopez Sound and Shoal Bay on the east side. Slightly more difficult is the 20-mile **San Juan Island Loop** along hilly, winding roads through Friday Harbor, Roche Harbor, San Juan Island National Historical Park and along the San Juan Channel. The Horseshoe Route on Orcas Island is by far the most difficult, with 16 miles of steep, twisting roads beginning at the ferry landing in Orcas, continuing through Eastsound, then on to Olga. An alternative route for the very hardy starts in Olga, passes through Moran State Park and ends in Doe

Bay, with a possible challenging 305-mile side trip up and back down Mt. Constitution.

Contact the **Washington State Department of Transportation** (Box 47329, Olympia, WA 98504; 360-705-7000) for a state trails directory and map. The *Sport Etc./NW Cyclist* (P.O. Box 9272, Seattle, WA 98109; 206-286-8566) is a helpful periodical with detailed information.

BIKE RENTALS   For bike rentals in the northern Puget Sound region, contact **The Bicycle Center** (4718 Evergreen Way, Everett; 206-252-1441); **Fairhaven Bicycle and Ski** (1103 11th Street, Bellingham; 360-733-4433); or the **Semiahmoo Marina** (9540 Semiahmoo Parkway, Blaine; 360-371-5700).

You'll find more options in the islands: **The Pedaler** (5603½ South Bay View Road, Langley; 360-321-5040); **Dean's Sports Plus** (8118 80th Northwest, Oak Harbor; 360-679-6145); the **Ship Harbor Inn** (5316 Ferry Terminal Road, Anacortes; 206-293-5177); **Lopez Bicycle Works** (Fisherman's Bay Road, Lopez Island; 360-468-2847); **The Bike Shop on Lopez** (School Road, Lopez Island; 206-468-3497); **Island Bicycles** (380 Argyle, Friday Harbor; 360-378-4941); **Dolphin Bay Bicycles** (Orcas Ferry Landing; 360-376-3093) and **Wildlife Cycles** (Eastsound; 360-376-4708).

HIKING

NORTHERN PUGET SOUND TRAILS   On the **Langus Riverfront Park Nature Trail** (3.2 miles) in Everett, hikers are likely to spot a red-tailed hawk or gray heron as they make their way through towering spruce, red cedar and dogwood trees along the banks of the Snohomish River, past Union Slough and on toward Spencer Island, a protected haven for nesting ducks.

EASY GOING OUTINGS

*A variety of intriguing guided hiking, biking and van tours of the Skagit Valley, Cascade Mountains, San Juans and Whidbey Island are available from **Easy Going Outings** (1460 Augusta Lane, Burlington; 360-757-3062). The owner is a master at creating bike routes that combine first-class scenery with easy terrain on lesser-traveled back roads. For hiking tours, the trails are typically short, scenic and easy enough for anyone in sound health to enjoy. Deluxe day tours by luxury van may include visiting artists in their home studios, organic farmers and other grass-roots entrepreneurs, all sorts of wildlife, or simply touring back roads and little-known corners of the region.*

There's great bike riding on often-overlooked Lummi Island.

The Padilla Bay National Estuarine Sanctuary (206-428-1558) close to the town of Bay View offers the best hikes in the area. Stringent rules on noise guide hikers on the **Padilla Bay Shore Trail** (2.2 miles) so that they do not disturb the migratory waterfowl that nest in the estuary, mudflat, sloughs and tidal marsh viewed along this path.

There are several good choices for hikes in Bellingham. The **Interurban Trail** (6 miles) begins near the entrance to Larrabee State Park, hugs the crest above Chuckanut Drive overlooking the bay and the San Juan Islands, then passes the rose gardens of Fairhaven Park into the revitalized Fairhaven District of the city.

There are three-and-a-half miles of rolling trails through the lush **Sehome Hill Arboretum**, crowned by incredible views of Mt. Baker and the San Juans from the observation tower at the summit. Since no motorized boats are allowed on Lake Padden, the path (1.5 miles) around the glistening lake and through some of the park's 1008 acres is both peaceful and rejuvenating.

In Birch Bay State Park in Blaine, the gently sloping **Terrell Marsh Trail** (.5 mile) winds through a thickly wooded area of birch, maple, red cedar, hemlock and fir, home to pileated woodpeckers, bald eagles, ruffed grouse, muskrats and squirrels, and on to Terrell Marsh Swamp, the halfway point on the loop, before passing back through the forest to the trailhead. Pick up a flora and fauna guide to the interpretive trail at the contact station just inside the park gate.

WHIDBEY ISLAND TRAILS   A number of picturesque hikes are found in and around Fort Ebey State Park. The **Ebey's Landing Loop Trail** (3.5 miles) has some steep sections on the bluff above the beach, but carry your camera anyway to capture the views of pastoral Ebey's Prairie in one direction and Mt. Rainier and the Olympics framed by wind-sculpted pines and fir in the other. Trimmed in wild roses, the trail swings around Perego's Lagoon and back along the driftwood-strewn beach.

The **Partridge Point Trail** (2 miles) connecting Fort Ebey State Park and the Department of Natural Resources' Partridge Point campsite climbs through a mix of coastal wildflowers on a windswept bluff 150 feet above the water with wide views of Port Townsend, Admiralty Inlet, Protection Island and Discovery Bay. A fenced path at the southern end drops down the headland to the cobbly beach below.

There are numerous trails to choose from in Deception Pass State Park. Locals prefer **Rosario Head Trail** (.3 mile) on the Fidalgo Island side, stretching over the very steep promontory between Rosario Bay and Bowman Bay with sweeping views of the San Juans, Rosario Strait and the Strait of Juan de Fuca, and continuing on the **Lighthouse Point Trail** (1.5 miles), which extends farther along the rocky bluff, past the lighthouse and into a dense stand of fir and cedar. On the Whidbey Island side of the bridge, climb the steep switchback on **Goose Rock Perimeter Trail** (1.2 miles) and you might see great blue heron on Coronet Bay, then follow the path down under the bridge next to the swirling waters of the pass and on to quiet North Beach to see the totem pole, located at West Point where North and West beaches converge. Heartier hikers might want to tackle the **Goose Rock Summit Trail** (1.2 miles), with an altitude gain of some 450 feet for an unparalleled view of Deception Pass and the Cascades.

FIDALGO ISLAND TRAILS   In Anacortes, your best bet is to head for the **Washington Park Loop Road** (2.3 miles), located on Fidalgo Head at the end of Sunset Avenue four miles west of downtown. Rewarding views on this easy, paved path with a few moderate slopes include incredible glimpses of the San Juans, Burrows Pass and Burrows Island. You'll also find quiet, cool stretches through dense woods and access to beaches and romantic, hidden outcroppings suitable for a glass of champagne to toast the breathtaking sunsets.

LOPEZ ISLAND TRAILS   Ideal hiking choices include the **Shark Reef Park Loop Trail** (.5 mile), a mossy path that meanders through a fragrant forest area and along a rock promontory that looks out over tidal pools, a large kelp bed, a gathering spot for seals and across the channel to San Juan Island. Spencer Spit State Park's **Beach Trail** (1 mile) travels down the spit and around the salt marsh lagoon alive with migratory birds; at the end of the spit is a reproduction of a historic log cabin built by early settlers.

SAN JUAN ISLAND TRAILS   Two of the best hiking alternatives on San Juan are the established hiking trails of the San Juan Island National Historical Park. The **Lagoon Trail** (1 mile) in American Camp is actually two trails intertwined, starting from a parking area above Old Town (referred to on maps as First) Lagoon and passing through a dense stand of Douglas fir connecting the lovely, protected cove beaches of Jakle's Lagoon and Third Lagoon. The highlight of the short but steep **Mt. Young Trail** (.75 mile) in English Camp are the plates identifying the many islands dotting the waters as far as the eye can see. If you want a closer view of the water, you can take the flat, easy **Bell Point Trail** (1 mile), also in English Camp, which runs along the edge of the coast.

ORCAS ISLAND TRAILS   Unless you plan to spend an extended period of time here, there's little chance of covering the many hiking trails that twist through Moran State Park on Orcas Island connecting view spots, mountain lakes, waterfalls and campgrounds. The **Moun-**

The greatest concentration of wintering bald eagles can be found at the Skagit River Bald Eagle Natural Area.

---

tain Lake Trail (3.6 miles) takes you from the summit of Mt. Constitution along a rocky ledge to Twin Lakes and the Mountain Lake Campground, with occasional views glimpsed through the thick trees. The **Around-the-Lake Trail** (3.6 miles) is fairly easy and takes in sights such as drooping log cabins and a dam and footbridge at the south end of Mountain Lake; for a little more challenge, try the **Twin Lakes Trail** (2.1 miles) that heads up the valley at the north end of Mountain Lake. If you're a waterfall lover, take the **Cascade Creek Trail** (2.7 miles) from the south end of Mountain Lake past Cascade and Rustic falls and on to Cascade Lake.

Transportation

BY CAR

Route 5 parallels the northern Puget Sound coastline all the way up to the Canadian border. **Route 20** from Burlington takes you into Anacortes, the main jumping-off point for ferry service to the San Juan Islands. **Route 16** leads from Tacoma across The Narrows and onto the Kitsap Peninsula, where it connects to **Route 3** skirting the Sinclair Inlet and continuing north to Port Gamble.

BY AIR

Visitors flying into the northern Puget Sound area usually arrive at either Bellingham International Airport or the much larger and busier **Seattle–Tacoma (Sea–Tac) International Airport** (see Chapter Four for detailed information on Sea–Tac). Carriers serving the **Bellingham International Airport** include Horizon Air and United Express.

The **Bellingham/Sea–Tac Airporter** (360-733-3600) provides express shuttle service between Bellingham, Mt. Vernon, La Conner, Anacortes, Oak Harbor and Sea–Tac Airport.

Both charter and regularly scheduled commuter flights are available into the tiny **Friday Harbor Airport** through Harbor Airlines and West Isle Air. Small commuter airports with limited scheduled service include **Anacortes Airport**, **Eastsound Airport** and **Lopez Airport**; all are served by Harbor Airlines and West Isle Air.

BY FERRY

Washington State Ferries (206-464-6400), which are part of the state highway system, provide transportation to the main islands of the San Juans—Lopez, Orcas, Shaw and San Juan—departing from the **Anacortes Ferry Terminal** (Ferry Terminal Road; 360-293-8166). Schedules change several times per year, with added service in the summer to take care of the heavy influx of tourists. The system is burdened during peak summer months, so arrive at the terminal early and be prepared to wait patiently (sometimes three hours or more) in very long lines if you plan to take your car along; walk-on passengers seldom have a long wait.

Hydrofoil ferry service among the Gulf islands from Roche Harbor is available through **Fairweather Water Taxi and Tours** (P.O. Box 1273, Friday Harbor, WA 98250; 360-378-2826) as are nature tours and shuttling to state and marine parks. **Island Shuttle Express** (119 North Commercial Street, Bellingham; 360-671-1137) runs between Bellingham and the San Juan Islands.

BY BUS

Greyhound Bus Lines provides regular service into Bellingham (1329 North State Street; 360-733-5251), Everett (1503 Pacific Avenue; 206-252-2144) and Mt. Vernon (1101 South 2nd Street; 360-336-5111).

BY TRAIN

Amtrak (2900 Bond Street, Everett; 800-872-7245) offers service into Everett on the Puget Sound shoreline via the "Empire Builder," which originates in Chicago and makes its final stop in Seattle before retracing its route. West Coast connections through Seattle on the "Coast Starlight" are also available. There's direct service from Portland, Oregon, the Columbia Gorge, Idaho, Denver and Chicago to Seattle via the "Pioneer."

CAR RENTALS

At Bellingham International Airport, you'll find **Avis Rent A Car** (800-331-1212), **Budget Rent A Car** (800-527-0700), **Hertz Rent A Car** (800-654-3131) and **National Interrent** (800-328-4567). **U-Save Auto Rental** (800-272-8728), located downtown, offers free airport pickup.

Less-expensive local rental agencies include **A#1 Rent A Car** (206-259-5058) in Everett; **The Inn at Friday Harbor Rentals** (360-378-4351) and **U-Save Auto Rental** (800-272-8728), in Anacortes.

*Close to five million vehicles a year cross the U.S./Canada border at Blaine,
Washington, making this the West Coast's busiest northern border station.*

PUBLIC TRANSPORTATION

Skagit Transit (206-757-4433) services La Conner, Anacortes, Mt.
Vernon and Burlington and is free. **Whatcom County Transportation Authority** (360-676-7433) provides public transit in Lynden,
Bellingham and Ferndale. In Everett you can get just about anywhere
for 50 cents via **Everett Transit** (360-353-7433). **Island Transit** (360-
678-7771) covers Whidbey Island, with scheduled stops at Deception
Pass, Oak Harbor, Coupeville, the Keystone Ferry, Greenbank, Freeland, Langley and the Clinton Ferry. In smaller towns on most of the
islands there are no public transportation systems set up; check the yellow pages for taxi service.

TAXIS

Cab companies serving the Bellingham International Airport incude
Superior Cabs (360-734-3478). For service from the Friday Harbor
Airport, contact **Primo Taxi Service** (360-378-3550). **Patsy's Taxi**
(360-293-3979) provides service at the Anacortes Airport.

EIGHT

The Cascades
and Central Washington

The Cascade Range contains some of the most beautiful mountain scenery in the United States, much of it preserved by two national parks, several national recreation areas and numerous wilderness areas that make this a major sports haven. There are glaciers galore; 318 are in the North Cascades National Park alone. Thousands of miles of trails and logging roads lace the Cascades, leading to mountaintop lookout towers, old gold mines, lakes, streams and other enticing sights.

The hand of man has done little to alter the Cascades. Not until 1952 did a highway cross the state north of Route 2. And when the North Cascades Highway (Route 20) was completed, it was with the understanding that it would be closed during the heavy snows, usually from October until May. Thus, most of the Cascades are wild and remote, seen and experienced by humans, but not transformed by them.

The most dominant features of the Cascades are its 15 volcanoes. Washington lays claim to five, with Mt. Rainier the grandaddy at 14,411 feet. Most peaks, however, are under 10,000 feet, and Harts Pass, the highest pass in the state, is only 6197 feet.

Although the range is not a comparatively high one, it served as an effective barrier to exploration and development until well into the 20th century. The pioneers who came over the Oregon Trail avoided it, choosing instead to go down the Columbia River to the Cowlitz River, travel up to present-day Toledo, then move overland to Puget Sound at Tumwater and Olympia.

Mining has always been part of the Cascades story. Although no major gold strikes have been found, several smaller ones have kept interest

The Cascade Range, about 700 miles long, begins at the Fraser River in southern British Columbia and extends southward through Washington and Oregon and into California just beyond Lassen Peak.

alive, and there's probably never been a day since the mid-1870s when someone wasn't panning or sluicing in the mountains.

Although most of the range is under the stewardship of the Forest Service, which by law has to practice multiple-use policies, most people think of the Cascades as their very own. It is used by mushroom gatherers, hikers, runners, birdwatchers, anglers, hunters, photographers, painters, skiers, horseback riders, loggers and miners. Whichever of these apply to you, enjoy.

North Cascades

Extending all the way from the Canadian border south into the Mt. Baker–Snoqualmie National Forest, the North Cascades region has more than 300 glaciers, valleys famous for their spring tulip fields and some of the best skiing in the Pacific Northwest. Backroads wind through old logging towns past mountain lakes to unspoiled wilderness areas. The North Cascades National Park forms the core of this realm that includes Rainy and Washington passes, two of the Cascades' grandest viewpoints.

Beginning at the northernmost approach, **Route 542** enters the Cascades from Bellingham, a pleasant, two-lane, blacktop highway that is shared by loggers, skiers, anglers and hikers. Much of the route runs through dense forest beside fast streams and with only rare glimpses of the surrounding mountains. The road deadends just beyond the Mt. Baker day-use lodge for skiers. In clear weather you will see 9127-foot **Mt. Shuksan**, one of the most beautiful peaks in the Cascades. It can't be seen from any other part of the range, but it probably appears on more calendars and postcards than its neighbor Mt. Baker or even Mt. Rainier.

The **Mt. Baker** ski slopes usually open in November and run all the way into June, making it the longest ski season of any area in Washington. During the summer the mountain is popular with day hikers and backpackers, who often hike over Austin Pass between Mt. Shuksan and Mt. Baker.

Route 20, one of America's premier scenic routes, meanders through North Cascades National Park. Along the way, the route provides access to hiking trails, roadside parks, boat launches and one of the more unusual tours in the Cascades, the **Seattle City Light Skagit Tours** (206-684-3030). This four-hour tour tells how Seattle built three dams on the

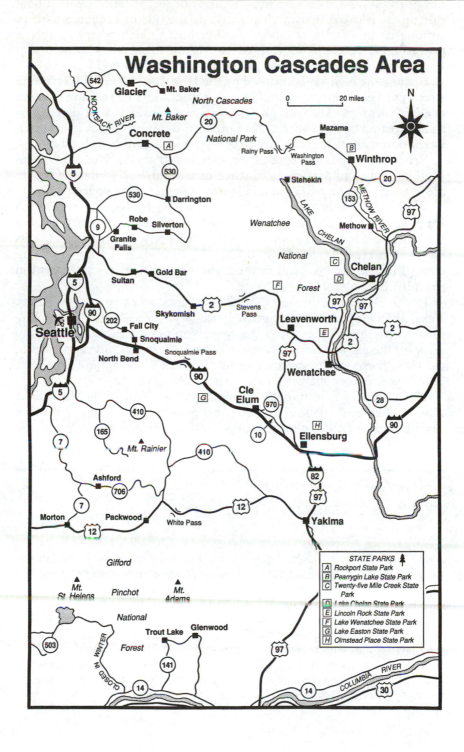

Washington Cascades Area

N

0   20 miles

STATE PARKS 🌲
- [A] Rockport State Park
- [B] Pearrygin Lake State Park
- [C] Twenty-five Mile Creek State Park
- [D] Lake Chelan State Park
- [E] Lincoln Rock State Park
- [F] Lake Wenatchee State Park
- [G] Lake Easton State Park
- [H] Olmstead Place State Park

Skagit to produce its electricity. The tour begins at Diablo with a boat ride up the lake to the dam, then a ride up the side of a mountain on an antique Incline Stairway Lift to another boat, which takes you to the powerhouse. After the tour, guests are taken to the cookhouse for an all-you-can-eat chicken dinner. Reservations are required.

Because the highway is enclosed by the Ross Lake National Recreation Area, new development is virtually nonexistent; the small company towns of Newhalem and Diablo look frozen in pre–World War II days. **Ross Lake**, created by the hydroelectric project, is a fjord-like lake between steep mountains that eventually crosses over into British Columbia.

When driving Route 20, be forewarned: No gas is available between Marblemount and Mazama, a distance of more than 70 miles, and there are few places to buy groceries. Fill your tank and bring your lunch.

Ross Lake on the Skagit River was formed by Ross Dam. Diablo Dam was built a short distance downstream, creating the much-smaller Diablo Lake. Ross Lake is an international body of water because its backwaters cross the border into Canada, and when timber was being cleared before the lake was formed, the work was done via a road in from British Columbia.

Route 20 plunges into the Cascades and goes over two passes—**Rainy Pass**, 4855 feet, and **Washington Pass**, 5477 feet—before descending into the Methow Valley. Stop at any viewpoint or turnout for stunning views of the region. One viewpoint above Ross Lake showcases miles of the long, narrow lake, and another just beyond Washington Pass gives a grandstand view of the jagged mountains behind the pass.

The only way to visit the resort town of **Stehekin**, at the tip of Lake Chelan, is by boat, plane or hiking. Most visitors take the trip up the lake on the **Lady of the Lake**, the tour-mail-supply boat for Stehekin and

---

THE SCENIC MOUNTAIN LOOP HIGHWAY

*An alternate way to reach Route 20 is over what is locally known as the **Mountain Loop Highway**, a favorite weekend drive before Route 20 was completed across the mountains. The Mountain Loop begins in Granite Falls with Route 92, which goes along the South Fork of the Stillaguamish River past the one-store towns of Robe, Verlot and Silverton. The road is crooked and slow driving because it follows the river route closely. It's always closed in the winter and sometimes landslides close it for much of the summer. Near the old mining town of Monte Cristo, the road turns north along the Sauk River and emerges in the logging town of Darrington. From here you can drive due north to catch Route 20 at Rockport or turn west on Route 530 and return to Route 5.*

Only Route 20 goes through North Cascades National Park, and it is closed in winter, generally from mid-November to April.

---

points between. The schedule allows you one-and-a-half hours in Stehekin, and you can buy lunch either on the boat or at the Stehekin landing.

NORTH CASCADES LODGING

The nearest lodging to Mt. Baker is the **Snowline Inn** (10433 Mt. Baker Highway, Glacier; 360-599-2788, 800-228-0119), a condominium complex with 45 units, about half with sleeping lofts. This two-story pseudo-chalet is set back in the trees away from the busy highway. The units with sleeping lofts can sleep up to four and have two double beds and a half-bath upstairs and a full bath with fold-out couch and bunk beds just inside the front door. The smaller units are also designed for up to four persons. All have completely equipped kitchens, and the loft units have microwaves. Moderate.

The **Glacier Creek Motel** (10036 Mt. Baker Highway, Glacier; 360-599-2991) earns its description of rustic. It is a motel with nine units and 12 blue-and-white cabins. The large lobby is a combination gift shop and espresso bar with a few café tables. The cabins are one or two bedrooms, with bath, a kitchen, double bed and tired furniture. The motel units are so small there's no room for a table. Budget to moderate.

One of the larger lakeside resorts is **Baker Lake Resort** (P.O. Box 100, Concrete, WA 98237; 360-853-8325), 20 miles north of Concrete on Baker Lake Road. It is a mixture of RV sites and 12 rustic cabins on the lake. Seven of the cabins have bathrooms and showers, a refrigerator, dishes and cooking utensils. Guests at all cabins must bring their own linen and towels. Boating and fishing are popular on the lake; boat rentals are available. Open summers only; moderate.

Rustic reigns in remote Stehekin. The most outdoorsy is the **Stehekin Valley Ranch** (P.O. Box 36, Stehekin, WA 98852; 509-682-4677), owned and operated by the Courtneys, the major family in the valley. The ranch is nine miles from town, up the Stehekin River Valley. The accommodations are tent cabins with plywood walls and canvas roofs. Showers and toilets are in the main building. Guests are encouraged to bring their own sleeping bags and towels to save $5 per person. All meals are included and served in the dining room, which has split logs for tables and seats. Horseback rides, river float trips, scenic flights and day hikes are among the activities offered. Budget.

The fanciest Stehekin lodging is **Silver Bay Inn** (P.O. Box 43, Stehekin, WA 98852; 509-682-2212), at the head of the Stehekin River a

Keep in mind that there are no public restaurants in Stehekin. The only dining facilities are in the lodging places, and those are exclusively for guests.

short distance from the village. It has a large suite in the owners' home that includes a private bath and soaking tub, two decks and a breakfast that features Devonshire cream for your fresh fruit and scrambled eggs with cashews. Outside are two cabins that will sleep six and are complete with kitchens and dishwashers. Moderate to deluxe.

NORTH CASCADES RESTAURANTS

A popular place along the Mt. Baker Highway is **Milano's Market and Deli** (9990 Mt. Baker Highway, Glacier; 360-599-2863), a combination small restaurant and deli. With its café tables and black-and-white tile floor, it offers a hearty supply of soups, salads and homemade desserts. It's a good place to have a picnic lunch made up. If the weather is right, the deck is open for outside dining. Budget to moderate.

A mile east of Glacier, near the Snowline Inn, is a much larger restaurant with more of a rural flavor. **The Chandelier** (10458 Mt. Baker Highway; 360-599-2233) is built in a chalet style and divided into two sections with a large fireplace in the entrance hall. To the left is a large bar with the obligatory big-screen television set and wooden chairs and tables. The restaurant serves straightforward American food, large burgers, steaks, seafood, barbecued chicken, fresh strawberry pie and homemade cheesecake. You can also have them make up box lunches for day trips. Budget to moderate.

On the western edge of Concrete, **North Cascades Inn** (4284 Route 20; 360-853-8771) has established a local reputation for good, plain American food (steaks, chops, seafood) and delicious pie (made by a local woman especially for the restaurant). The exterior is decorated with farm and logging equipment, but the interior decor is softened a bit with antique furnishings and clothing. There's also a full service bar. Budget to moderate.

NORTH CASCADES SHOPPING

If you're in Concrete on Saturday during the summer months, hit the **Saturday Market** in the **North Cascades Visitors Center** (Route 20) for arts and crafts and baked goods.

NORTH CASCADES NIGHTLIFE

The Cascades isn't the place to go for nightlife. After a day traipsing around in the mountains, most people return to town tired and only want to eat and go to bed. Consequently, only the busiest areas have live music.

Near Mt. Baker, the **Chandelier** (10458 Mt. Baker Highway; 360-599-2233) has live country and soft-rock music on weekends.

NORTH CASCADES PARKS

The 1.3 million-acre **Mt. Baker–Snoqualmie National Forest** (206-775-9702) begins at the Canadian border and goes south along the western slopes of the Cascades to Mt. Rainier National Park. Four east-west highways cross the national forest: Routes 90, 20, 2 and 410. The forest is dominated on the north by the inactive volcano, 10,778-foot Mt. Baker. Another inactive volcano, 10,568-foot Glacier Peak, lies in the middle of the forest. The Forest Service controls the land for the ski areas at Crystal Mountain, Mt. Baker and Snoqualmie Pass. Its best-known wilderness area is Alpine Lakes Wilderness, but it also includes the Glacier Peak and Mt. Baker Wilderness areas. Fishing is excellent for lake and rainbow trout in Baker Lake; other streams and lakes are equally good. Camping is permitted along the highways, trails and the Pacific Crest Trail, as well as at established campsites. RV sites with hookups are available for $6 to $10 a night.

Rockport State Park (360-853-8461) is essentially a large campground in a grove of old-growth Douglas fir. Most of the camping areas are shielded from one another by thick undergrowth. It is within easy walking distance of the Skagit River, which makes it a favorite with steelheaders. There are also picnic areas, restrooms, showers and five miles of footpaths; restaurants and groceries are a mile away on Route 20 in Rockport.

Howard Miller Steelhead County Park (Route 20, Rockport; 360-853-8808) is a popular park on the Skagit River for anglers and travelers alike. It covers 93 acres and has extensive museum exhibits,

MT. BAKER

Mt. Baker was named by George Vancouver on April 30, 1792, in honor of James Baker, a lieutenant on his ship. It was first climbed on August 17, 1868, by a party of four led by an experienced alpinist named Edmund T. Coleman. Although it is listed as an active volcano and occasionally steam is seen rising from it, Mt. Baker hasn't erupted for nearly 10,000 years.

including a historic cabin, an old river ferry and a dugout canoe. The clubhouse is a hangout for local anglers. Facilities include picnic areas, boat launch, playground, restrooms and showers. There are 75 year-round campsites.

Covering 505,000 acres in the north-central part of the state, **North Cascades National Park** is divided into two units. The northern unit runs from the Canadian border to **Ross Lake National Recreation Area**. The southern unit continues on to the **Lake Chelan National Recreation Area**. Much of its eastern boundary is the summit of the Cascade Range, and the western boundary is the Mt. Baker–Snoqualmie National Forest. It's the most rugged and remote of the national parks in Washington and has the fewest roads. All visitor facilities and roads in the northern portion are inside the Ross Lake National Recreation Area. On the southern end, the Lake Chelan National Recreation Area covers the heavy-use area on the north end of the lake, including the city of Stehekin. You'll find picnic areas and restrooms, but no restaurants or groceries. Rangers sometimes lead nature walks from the visitors center in Newhalem (206-386-4495) or Colonial Creek and Newhalem campgrounds; information, 360-856-5700. There's excellent fishing for rainbow trout in Ross Lake, steelhead in the Skagit River downstream from Newhalem, and rainbow and eastern brook trout in high lakes. There is camping year-round at Goodell Creek, Lone Fir and Early Winters, except when there's too much snow; $7 to $10 a night.

Methow Valley

The scenery changes quickly and dramatically once you've crossed Washington Pass into the Methow Valley. Located along Route 20 between Mazama and Pateros, this region includes the tourist center of Chelan, gateway to one of the state's most popular lake-resort areas.

As you descend the east slope of the Cascades, the thick, fir forest gives way to smaller pine with almost no underbrush. The mountains become bare, and you can see for miles. And by the time you arrive in **Winthrop**, you will wonder if you are in Colorado or Wyoming because the small town is all falsefronts, saloon doors, hitching rails and wooden porches.

The **Shafer Museum** (285 Castle Road; 509-996-2712) is in the cabin built by Winthrop's town founder Guy Waring in 1897 and has exhibits from the valley's early days, including a stagecoach and antique automobiles. Open weekends.

There are several areas around Winthrop worth driving to, including 6197-foot **Harts Pass** a short distance from town. This is the highest point to which you can drive in Washington. The views from the summit are spectacular and well worth an hour's drive on a gravel Forest Service road.

Not long after driving south on Route 153, the last of the timbered mountains are left behind, and the Methow Valley flattens into a series of irrigated ranches with broad hayfields. The valley is gaining popularity with people from Puget Sound looking for more space, so houses are beginning to line the low hills on both sides.

When you reach the **Columbia River** at Pateros, the landscape is one of basaltic cliffs on both sides of the river. Instead of a fast-flowing river there is a chain of lakes behind dams all the way past Wenatchee. Route 97 hugs the west side of the Columbia, then swings away from the river to go through the resort town of Chelan, which sits at the end of **Lake Chelan**.

The lake is a remnant of the ice ages. Scoured out of the mountains by glaciers, it is one of the deepest lakes in the region, more than 1500 feet deep in at least one place, which places its bed at 400 feet below sea level. It is 55 miles long but quite narrow, and the mountains rising from its shores make it look like a Norwegian fjord.

Chelan is a small town that has been given over almost entirely to tourism. Woodin Avenue is the main drag and the lakefront is lined with resorts, but the small-town atmosphere is retained so that a farmer can come to town and still buy a two-by-four or a cotter pin.

The **Lake Chelan Museum** (Woodin Avenue and Emerson Street; 509-682-5644) displays some Native American artifacts, early farming and orchard equipment. One room depicts a miner's cabin, and another shows a typical country kitchen. Open May to September.

METHOW VALLEY LODGING

The most elaborate place in the Methow Valley, and one of the best resorts in the Northwest, is **Sun Mountain Lodge** (Patterson Lake Road, Winthrop; 509-996-2211, 800-572-0493, fax 509-996-3133). Built at the 3000-foot level atop a small mountain, this lowrise, stone-

ORCHARDS, ORCHARDS EVERYWHERE

*Chelan has some of the best orchards along the eastern slopes of the Cascades. If you take a drive northwest of town on Route 150 to Manson, you will see thousands of acres of apple orchards climbing up the sun-baked hills from the lake. Every Wednesday, the largest shipper in the area, **Blue Chelan** (100 Route 150; 509-682-4541), offers tours through its facility. Open March through early August.*

and-timber resort gives a 360-degree view of the Cascades, Pasayten Wilderness, Okanogan Highlands and Methow Valley. The 87 units are spread over two buildings atop the mountain and down the road in nine rustic, cozy cabins. The resort has just about everything: several miles of hiking trails that become cross-country ski trails in the winter, pool, two hot tubs, exercise room, the largest string of saddle-and-pack horses in the state, mountain-bike rentals, canoe and sailing on the lake, heli-skiing and tennis. It also has a great restaurant. Rooms feature bentwood furniture, a fireplace (only the suites have real wood-burning fireplaces), coffee, the thickest and softest towels you can hope for and no television. Deluxe to ultra-deluxe.

Right in the heart of western-themed Winthrop, you'll find the **Trails End Motel** (156 Riverside Street; 509-996-2303) with its tall falsefront and wooden porch. The 12 units, which have VCRs, are simply furnished, and big windows look down onto Main Street. In season, the area's oldest irrigation canal runs behind the motel. A bookstore anchors one end of the building, while the video store and café anchor the other end. Budget to moderate.

On the south edge of Winthrop is the **Virginian Resort** (808 North Cascades Highway; 509-996-2535, 800-854-2834). Located on the high bank of the Methow River, the riverfront rooms in this 39-unit motel have balconies. Cedar was used extensively, and most units retain the pleasant aroma. The seven cabins are a bit more expensive, but several have fireplaces and room enough for six. Kitchens are large and well equipped. Moderate.

On a hilltop facing Lake Chelan, the **Proctor House Inn** (495 Lloyd Road, Manson; 509-681-6361, 800-421-1233, fax 509-687-6106) is a contemporary inn surrounded by apple orchards. Six individually decorated rooms include the elegant Lake Chelan Suite which has a black marble fireplace with an ornate Victorian oak mantle, deep burgundy walls and iron artwork by local artist Theo Ramey. Guests have access to a top-floor lounge that offers a library and a wooden deck with 360-degree views of the lake and mountains. The moderate to deluxe rates include a continental breakfast.

The oldest and most reliable resort in Chelan is **Campbell's Resort** (104 West Woodin Avenue; 509-682-2561, fax 509-682-2177), which has been in business since 1901. With 148 rooms, it is still growing along the lakeshore in the heart of town. It has two heated pools, indoor and outdoor jacuzzis, good beach and boat moorage. The rooms range from standard with queen-size beds to larger rooms with kitchenettes and two queen beds, decorated in softer pastels. Deluxe to ultra-deluxe.

One of the most complete resorts inside the Chelan city limits is **Darnell's Resort Motel** (901 Spader Bay Road; 509-682-2015, 800-967-8149), a few blocks southwest of the city center on Route 150. It

Winthrop adopted a Wild-West theme several years ago, and it has revitalized the sawmill town and surrounding area into one of the state's most popular destinations.

has a heated pool and hot tub, sauna and exercise room, putting greens, lighted tennis courts, swimming beach, boat and bicycle rentals, water-skiing, volleyball, badminton and conference rooms. The resort is divided into two three-story buildings. All rooms come with balconies and a view of the lake. All units are called suites because they have separate bedrooms; some have two bedrooms, and the larger units have sleeping lofts. The penthouse suites have two fireplaces and private jacuzzi. Deluxe to ultra-deluxe.

Mary Kay's Romantic Whaley Mansion (415 3rd Street, Chelan; 509-682-5735) is actually a bed and breakfast. This white Edwardian house trimmed in pink has six rooms decorated with antiques from the family collection. A footstool has antlers for legs; ribbons and garlands of artificial flowers are everywhere. The guest rooms, on the second and third floors, are decorated with flowered wallpaper and have old-fashioned beds and private baths. In addition to a gourmet breakfast that includes hand-dipped chocolates, Mary Kay will sing with the player piano accompanying her. Gay-friendly. Deluxe.

On the eastern edge of Chelan is the clean and comfortable **Apple Inn Motel** (1002 East Woodin Avenue; 509-682-4044) with white stucco walls and black wood trim. The 41 rooms are decorated in knotty pine and are small; some have kitchenettes. The outdoor pool is heated, and a hot tub is open year-round. Budget to moderate.

METHOW VALLEY RESTAURANTS

One of the newest restaurants to get statewide attention is the **Sun Mountain Lodge Dining Room** (Patterson Lake Road, Winthrop; 509-996-2211). The room is cantilevered with views of the Methow Valley and Winthrop 3000 feet below. All tables come with a view, and the cuisine is noteworthy. The Southwest-flavored specialties include unusual items like cactus-pear salad. Other dishes include Northwest game sausage and smoked scallops with Thai red curry sauce, steaks and seafood. Deluxe to ultra-deluxe.

One of Winthrop's trendy restaurants is the oddly named **Duck Brand Cantina** (248 Riverside Avenue; 509-996-2192) in the hotel of the same name. The menu reflects an effort to please several palates, including Mexican, American, Continental and vegetarian. The restaurant is divided into two areas: a dining room with several old oak tables and hanging greenery, and a deck overlooking Winthrop's sole street. Moderate.

Another moderate-priced establishment is **Virginian Restaurant** (Virginian Resort, 816 North Cascades Highway; 509-996-2536), decorated in Old World–style with cedar walls and wooden tables and chairs, potted plants and baskets. The menu is strictly American: steak, prawns, chicken and pork. Off the entrance is the Bicycle Bar with a gas-powered fireplace and casual seating.

Although **Campbell's Resort** (104 West Woodin Avenue, Chelan; 509-682-2561) is so large that it overwhelms some people, it is hard to find a better place in the area for a good meal. The restaurant seats about 130 and is pleasantly decorated in Early American furnishings and maroon walls with an eclectic collection of prints, documents and paintings. The menu is also large: prime rib, medallions of pork, broiled leg of lamb, chicken stir-fry, prawns provençal and pastas. Prices range from moderate to deluxe.

A few doors down from Campbell's Resort on the lakefront is **Grayday's by the River** (114 East Woodin Avenue; 509-682-3648). It has two floors—a sunroom on the top floor and an enclosed patio on the lower—and specializes in lunches of sandwiches (some are purely vegetarian), soups and salads. Dinner offerings include a series of specials throughout the week—seafood, prime rib and chicken among them. Budget to moderate.

METHOW VALLEY SHOPPING

Art is a big deal and often very good in Winthrop, especially at **Hildabob's Gallery** (231 Riverside Avenue; 509-996-3279), where you will find paintings, sculpture and handknit apparel. Other artworks, some by nationally known artists such as Richard Beyer, are usually on exhibit in the public rooms at **Sun Mountain Lodge** (Patterson Lake Road; 509-996-2211). For photographs by the area's best-known photographer, call **Bob Spiwak** (509-996-2777).

Art is also a growth industry in the Chelan area. Beyer and Rod Weagant exhibit at the **Weagant Studio** (Washington and Ford streets, Manson; 509-687-3959). It is open weekends during the summer and by appointment. The **Wapato Studio** (108 East Woodin Avenue, Chelan; 509-682-2423) featuring watercolors, oils and sculpture by local artists. For antiques and collectibles, try **The Antique Goose** (208 East Woodin Avenue, Chelan; 509-682-4058), a 12-dealer antique mall.

Art may be big, but apple is king in Chelan, and the **Harvest Tree** (109 East Woodin Avenue; 509-682-3618) is a mail-order store for packaged apples and other food items. Their competition is **Ellen's Happy Apples** (2621 2nd Street, Entiat; 509-784-1815), just down the road a piece from Chelan. Ellen's ships apples in a variety of wooden boxes.

METHOW VALLEY NIGHTLIFE

In Winthrop, the **Winthrop Palace** (149 Riverside Avenue; 509-996-2245) offers live rock and blues on weekends during the summer.

Chelan has a few more choices, nearly all featuring live disco, rock and country music and dancing during the summer months. **Chelan's House** (502 East Woodin Avenue; 509-682-2013) has live disco music on weekends.

METHOW VALLEY PARKS

Pearrygin Lake State Park (509-996-2370) is a popular park for travelers in RVs because it is close to Winthrop and has a sandy beach on a small lake surrounded by mountains. It is also a hotspot for boaters and anglers during the summer and snowmobilers during the winter, although the park is closed from November until April. There are campsites, picnic areas, restrooms and showers. Swimming is permitted here, but there's no lifeguard. It's located five miles north of Winthrop on Route 20.

Located nine miles west of Chelan on Route 971, **Lake Chelan State Park** (509-687-3710) is a favorite for Puget Sound youths yearning for sunshine. In July and August, the beach looks more like California than Washington with its broad, sandy beach, lifeguards and play area. Because it has docks and launching areas for skiers, it is equally popular with power boaters and waterskiers. There's also fishing in the lake away from watersports; camping is available.

Twenty-Five Mile Creek State Park (509-687-3610) is more remote than Lake Chelan State Park, a draw for those more interested in mountain scenery than body watching. It's a quiet place, with the Chelan Mountains behind and the jagged peaks of the Sawtooth Wilderness across the lake. The small beach is mostly for wading. There are campsites, picnic areas, restrooms, showers and a playground; the concession offers snacks, groceries and fishing supplies. Located 18 miles west of Chelan on 25-Mile Creek Road.

Lincoln Rock State Park (509-884-8702), named for a rock outcropping that resembles Abraham Lincoln's profile, is a heavily used state park located in the Columbia River canyon six miles north of Wenatchee on Route 2. In addition to swimming and boating, park users may also take tours of the Rocky Reach Dam a mile away. Several species of wildlife reside in the park, including rabbits, deer, beaver, groundhogs, nighthawks and swallows. Facilities include campsites, picnic shelters, restrooms, showers, horseshoe pits, volleyball courts, and a playfield and play equipment for children.

Wenatchee Area

Famous for its apple orchards, the sunny Wenatchee Area is located in the heart of Washington. Well-known to rafters and gold panners, this region is also home to one of the state's most picturesque gardens.

You have a choice of two highways when leaving Chelan: You can continue along Route 97, which cuts through the Cascade foothills back to the Columbia River and south to Wenatchee, or cross the Columbia at Chelan Falls, hardly more than a junction, and follow the lesser-used Route 151 south through the orchard town of Orondo to East Wenatchee. Stop at **Rocky Reach Dam** (509-663-7522), 28 miles south of Chelan, to visit the Fish Viewing Room where migratory salmon and steelhead swim past the windows. The dam also has two small museums, one showing the natural and human history of the Columbia River, complete with a handcarved Native American canoe, parts of steamboats and orchard equipment. The Gallery of Electricity also has hands-on exhibits that let you create electricity.

Wenatchee is the largest town in this region and directed more toward orchards than tourists, although you will certainly feel welcome. On the northern edge of town, overlooking the Columbia River, Wenatchee and Rocky Reach Dam, the **Ohme Gardens** (3327 Ohme Road; 509-662-5785; admission) has nine acres of alpine gardens built by an orchardist on the steep, rocky outcroppings at the edge of his property.

Located downtown, the **North Central Washington Museum** (127 South Mission Street; 509-664-5989) has several permanent exhibits including a 1919 Wurlitzer theater pipe organ and an apple-packing shed featuring an apple wiper, sizing machine and a 1924 orchard truck. On the western edge of town is the **Washington Apple Commission Visitors Center** (2900 Euclid Avenue; 509-663-9600), which has another museum exhibit, but this one offers apple tasting; samples of different varieties of apples are given.

Ten miles west via Routes 2 and 97, **Cashmere**, so-named because it reminded a pioneer of Kashmir, India, has an Early American theme to its downtown buildings. The **Chelan County Historical Museum and Pioneer Village** (600 Cottage Avenue; 509-782-3230) has more than two dozen original buildings from Chelan and Douglas counties assembled to re-create a pioneer village, including a blacksmith shop, school, gold mine and hotel.

From Cashmere, Routes 2 and 97 follow the swift Wenatchee River into the Cascades. Shortly before reaching Leavenworth, Route 97 turns south toward the Route 90 Corridor towns of Cle Elum and Ellensburg by going over 4102-foot **Swauk Pass**. An alternative route, in the summer only, is to follow the **Old Blewett Pass Highway**, which has been preserved by the Wenatchee National Forest. The old highway is a series

Liberty Orchards (117–123 Mission Street, Cashmere; 509-782-2191) offers tours of its candy factory with samples of its nationally known products—Aplets and Cotlets.

of switchbacks with sweeping views of the Cascades. No services are available until Cle Elum and Ellensburg, other than a small grocery store at **Liberty**, a gold-mining town just off the highway that is making a comeback as people move into the modest cabins lining its single street.

WENATCHEE AREA LODGING

Most hotels in Wenatchee are spotted along North Wenatchee Avenue. The newest and tallest is the **West Coast Wenatchee Center** (201 North Wenatchee Avenue; 509-662-1234, 800-426-0670, fax 509-662-0782), at nine stories one of the tallest buildings along the eastern edge of the Cascades. The 148 rooms are larger than at most other hotels in town and suites have double sofas and potted plants. The ample lobby has a baby grand piano. The hotel has a restaurant, an indoor-outdoor pool and a fitness center. Moderate.

For a budget-priced place, try the **Orchard Inn** (1401 North Miller Street; 509-662-3443, 800-368-4571, fax 509-663-1665). It has 103 rooms on three floors decorated with subtly flowered bedspreads, unobtrusive furniture and wallhangings. A heated pool and spa, and conference room round out the package.

If you want to be close to Routes 2 and 97, the best place is across the Columbia River in the **Rivers Inn** (580 Valley Mall Parkway, East Wenatchee; 509-884-1474, 800-922-3199, fax 509-884-9179). With 55 units on two floors that surround the heated pool, it is unpretentious but has basic, comfortable rooms with cable television, and there's always coffee in the office (after 7 a.m. free rolls are available). Moderate.

The **Cashmere Country Inn** (5801 Pioneer Avenue; 509-782-4212) is putting the town of Cashmere on the map. Owners Dale and Patti Swanson are unofficial ambassadors for this town, having remodeled an old farmhouse into a five-room inn that follows an early French country style. All rooms have private baths. An area also has been set aside for guests' lounging. Breakfasts are imaginative with fruit, crêpes and other lighter-than-air fare. Moderate.

Somewhat less personal is the **Village Inn Motel** (229 Cottage Avenue, Cashmere; 509-782-3522, 800-793-3522, fax 509-782-2619) in the heart of town. The white-and-green motel has 21 units, six with refrigerators. Clean, quiet and reasonably priced. Budget to moderate.

WENATCHEE AREA RESTAURANTS

Want Italian? Try **Viscounti's Italian Restaurant** (1737 North Wenatchee Avenue; 509-662-5013). Both Southern and Northern Italian dishes are offered in a family-friendly atmosphere. Moderate.

A top-notch steakhouse is **The Windmill** (1501 North Wenatchee Avenue; 509-663-3478). You'll find it down to earth, with waitresses who have been there for years. A blackboard keeps a running total of the number of steaks sold there since 1982, when the present owners took over. Seafood and pork chops also are offered, and fresh-baked pies add the final touch. Moderate to deluxe.

As a reflection of Central Washington's growing Latino population, **Tequila's** (800 North Wenatchee Avenue; 509-662-7239) is owned by former residents of Mexico. The refried beans are homemade, and the salsa is as tangy as you'd get in Guadalajara. Budget to moderate.

One of Wenatchee's apple-pioneer homes has become a popular restaurant. The owners of the **John Horan House** (2 Horan Road; 509-663-0018) have turned three upstairs bedrooms into rooms for private parties, and the downstairs dining room has a fireplace that is welcome on chilly evenings. The menu boasts a large selection of seafood, steak and lamb dishes. Save room for the homemade desserts. Moderate to deluxe.

Located in an old stone warehouse with cathedral ceilings and a magnificent antique cherry-wood bar, **Goochi's** (29 North Columbia Avenue, Wenatchee; 509-664-3200) serves grilled steaks, prime rib, seafood and a variety of pasta dishes. Over 30 imported and domestic beers are offered on tap, including many from microbreweries in the region. Moderate.

WENATCHEE AREA SHOPPING

In Wenatchee, **Victorian Village** (611 South Mission Street) is a small mall constructed in the best of the Victorian Carpenter Gothic style—round towers, falsefronts and steeples. You will find fabrics, antiques and, oddly juxtaposed with a Victorian theme, a Mexican restaurant. And if you need a fix for an urban-size mall, the **Wenatchee Valley Mall** (511 Valley Mall Parkway, East Wenatchee) has 47 stores, making it the largest shopping center you'll encounter in the shadow of the Cascades.

WENATCHEE AREA NIGHTLIFE

Although Wenatchee is the largest town along the Cascades, it doesn't offer any wider choice for nightlife than its smaller neighbors. The Chieftain's **Pow Wow Room** (1005 North Wenatchee Avenue; 509-663-8141) features live rock and country dance music every Tuesday through Saturday.

At 2.1 million acres, Wenatchee National Forest is one of the largest national forests in the United States.

On weekend nights, **Goochi's** (29 North Columbia Avenue; 509-664-3200) offers jazz and acoustical entertainment in the bar area and a basement danceclub with a deejay.

WENATCHEE AREA PARKS

Wenatchee National Forest (509-662-4335) encompasses seven wilderness areas, hundreds of lakes, downhill-ski areas and 2500 miles of trails for hiking, riding and biking (including the Pacific Crest National Scenic Trail). It also joins two of the state's three national parks, North Cascades and Mt. Rainier. There are more than 140 campgrounds. Salmon, steelhead, cutthroat trout, bull trout, bass, crappie, walleye and sturgeon are among the fish found in the forest's streams and lakes. The forest is crossed by Routes 20, 2 and 90.

Leavenworth Area

Think Bavarian! That is the order of the day when visiting **Leavenworth**, one of the major tourist spots in the Cascades. Almost everything here—architecture, hotels, restaurants, annual events—is centered around that theme. Mountains are on three sides, and a river rushes through town. During most of the summer, free concerts and dancing exhibitions are given in the City Park, and outdoor art exhibits are held on weekends.

Just west of Leavenworth, Route 2 enters **Tumwater Canyon**, which follows the Wenatchee River some 20 miles. It's marked by sheer canyon walls, plunging river rapids and deciduous trees along the riverbank that turn into brilliant colors each autumn.

Route 2 continues over **Stevens Pass**, a popular ski area and where the **Pacific Crest National Scenic Trail** (see "Hiking" at the end of the chapter) crosses the highway. Soon after crossing the summit and passing Skykomish, the **Skykomish River** parallels the highway. This is one of Washington's favorite whitewater rivers. Most trips originate in the small alpine village of **Index**, a short distance off the highway. The sheer-faced, 5979-foot **Mt. Index** looms behind the town. From there, the river rumbles down past the small towns of **Gold Bar** and **Sultan**, then flattens out onto the Puget Sound lowlands.

If you like cuckoo clocks, fancy woodwork, beer steins and alpenhorns, you'll love staying in Leavenworth.

LEAVENWORTH AREA LODGING

One of the most pleasant spots in Leavenworth is the **Pension Anna** (926 Commercial Street; 509-548-6273). It has 15 rooms with furniture and decor imported from Austria and has been decorated in the theme of a farmhouse. Heavy, wooden bed frames and cupboards are used throughout. Three suites come with fireplace and jacuzzi, and all rooms have private baths. Breakfast is included. Moderate to ultra-deluxe.

A Bavarian wood carver was imported to fashion the rails and ceiling beams of the **Enzian Motor Inn** (590 Route 2; 509-548-5269), and the entire 104-room motel with its turret and chalet-styled roofs shows similar touches. The seven suites have king-size beds, spas and fireplaces. It has indoor and outdoor pools and a year-round hot tub. During the winter, free cross-country ski equipment is available to guests. The complimentary buffet breakfast is served in the big solarium on the fourth floor. Moderate to ultra-deluxe.

More and more bed and breakfasts and inns are opening outside town. One is **Run of the River** (9308 East Leavenworth Road; 509-548-7171, 800-288-6491, fax 509-548-7547), a mile out on the Icicle River. The building is made of logs and has cathedral ceilings with pine walls and handmade log furniture. The six rooms have private baths and cable television. Three of the rooms have woodstoves and three have jacuzzis. Stay here, kick back and just contemplate the beautiful setting. Breakfasts are country-style. (For the health-conscious, this inn is for non-smokers only). Deluxe to ultra-deluxe.

Located in a wooded setting on the banks of the Wenatchee River, the **All Seasons River Inn** (8751 Icicle Road, Leavenworth; 509-548-1425, 800-254-0555) offers spacious rooms, all with private decks overlooking the river and some with fireplaces and jacuzzis. The inn provides full breakfasts and bicycles for touring the nearby Icicle Loop. Moderate to deluxe.

Skykomish is the closest town to Stevens Pass and where some skiers spend the night. One of the few inexpensive hotels in the tiny downtown area is the **Cascadia Hotel and Café** (210 Railroad Avenue; 360-677-2356). Located directly across the street from the old depot, it is a reminder of when passenger trains stopped there. The rooms are bare-bones in amenities but clean. All 16 rooms share baths. (A few permanent residents live there.) Prices are budget.

Farther down the mountain you'll find the **Dutch Cup Motel** (918 Main Street, Sultan; 360–793–2215, 800–844–0488, fax 360–793–2216), which is popular with skiers. The two-story motel has 22 units with queen-size beds and cable television. Prices are tabbed in the budget-to-moderate range.

LEAVENWORTH AREA RESTAURANTS

Reiner's Gasthaus (829 Front Street; 509–548–5111) is one of the best restaurants in Leavenworth for such delights as potato pancakes, home-made egg dumplings, pan-fried veal and beef goulash along with a variety of steaks and pork tenderloin. Moderate.

Edel Haus Inn (320 9th Street, Leavenworth; 509–548–4412, 800–487–3335) offers an outdoor patio overlooking the Wenatchee River and an intimate dining room with candlelit tables, ceiling fans and Victorian furnishings. Unusual for the area, the menu offers an eclectic assortment of international dishes, ranging from Japanese soba noodles with vegetables to Cajun-style blackened seafood items. Moderate to deluxe.

Gingerbread Factory (828 Commercial Street, Leavenworth; 509–548–6592) is a delight for children and parents alike with all the cookies and gingerbread houses. It's a café and sells pastries, salads and all sorts of gifts related to gingerbread.

The first place to eat after coming down off Stevens Pass is the **Sky Chalet** (Route 2, Skykomish; 360–677–2223), a large restaurant with a choice of buffet line or menu service. It has large booths with high backs and open tables and serves country breakfasts all day. Lunch specials might be Swedish meatballs or chicken-fried steak. The dinner menu is unembellished—steaks, pork chops, chicken and salmon in season. Budget to moderate.

In Index, the best place to eat is in the **Bush House Country Inn** (300 5th Street; 206–793–2312). Here, in the century-old hotel dining room, you will find a big, stone fireplace and gourmet country cuisine that uses very fresh meat, seafood, fish, fruits and vegetables. The Sunday brunches include omelettes, homemade pastries and fresh fruit. Prices fall in the moderate range.

The Dutch Cup Restaurant (927 Main Street, Sultan; 360–793–1864) is one of the most popular restaurants on the Stevens Pass route. It opens at 5 a.m. to catch the ski crowd as they head up the highway, and stays open until 12:30 a.m. to get them on the way home. The menu includes country breakfasts, burgers, soups and sandwiches for lunch, steaks and chicken and weekend specials for dinner. Moderate.

LEAVENWORTH AREA SHOPPING

Leavenworth has the best selection of specialty shops in the Cascades; about 100 are crammed into a two-block area. **A Different Drummer** (725 Front Street; 509-548-5320) sells international greeting cards, other paper supplies and children's books. **The Cuckoo Clock** (725 Front Street; 509-548-4857) has a large collection of antique and contemporary timepieces. It is a resonant place on the hour, quarter and half hour when the cuckoos perform a veritable symphony.

Train buffs will love the **Train Shop at Leavenworth** (217 9th Street, Leavenworth; 509-548-6839) for its railroad memorabilia, which includes pen-and-ink drawings, pins and artwork. **Village Book and Music** (215 9th Street; 509-548-5911) has a good selection of Northwest books and artwork and a wide selection of European tapes—handbell music and that sort of thing. Located in the Motteler Building is another one-of-a-kind store, the **Hammock Shop** (9th and Front streets, Leavenworth; 509-548-4880), which sells Brazilian hammocks, handcrafted chairs and other unusual home items. **Cabin Fever Rustics** (923 Commercial Street, Leavenworth; 509-548-4238) offers a quality assortment of antiques, collectibles and Northwest gifts.

LEAVENWORTH AREA NIGHTLIFE

Leavenworth has almost no nighttime entertainment; its movie theater collapsed beneath a heavy snowfall several years ago and hasn't been replaced, and only one or two places offer live music after dark. One such establishment is the **Leavenworth Brewery** (636 Front Street; 509-548-4545). They regularly have music, usually in the Tyrolean Ritz Hotel. And just across the street is **The Adler** (633 Front Street; 509-548-7733), a beer garden and rathskeller. Bavarian music plays on weekends.

LEAVENWORTH AREA PARKS

Lake Wenatchee State Park (509-763-3101) is tucked away near Stevens Pass and is popular in summer for canoeing, kayaking, sailing, swimming and fishing, and in the winter for cross-country skiing and snowmobiling. The secluded, wooded campsites are great. There are also picnic areas, restrooms, showers and horseback riding, as well as rental boats just outside the park boundary. The park is located on Route 207, about 16 miles north of Leavenworth and four miles off Route 2.

Route 90 Corridor

From pristine snow-capped peaks to dramatic waterfalls, the Route 90 corridor is one of Washington's scenic treasures. It extends from Snoqualmie across the Cascades to Ellensburg and the Kittitas Valley. Fasten your seat belts for a breathtaking ride past volcanic peaks, fir forests and rivers where anglers are likely to land tonight's dinner.

The Cascades begin rising only a half-hour's drive east of Seattle. The town of **Snoqualmie** has an ornate, old railroad depot that is home to the **Puget Sound Railway** (109 King Street, Snoqualmie; 206-888-3030), which makes a seven-mile trip through the Snoqualmie Valley on weekends (April–October) and runs a special Christmas train. Nearby is **Snoqualmie Falls**, a thundering cataract with a small park, observation platform and trails leading to the river below the 268-foot falls.

The town of **North Bend** has adopted an alpine theme for its downtown buildings, but it hasn't caught on with the same vigor of Winthrop and Leavenworth. Fans of the television show "Twin Peaks" will recognize Mt. Si, which looms behind town, from the show's opening credits.

The summit of **Snoqualmie Pass** has four major ski areas, for both downhill and cross-country, and a Forest Service combination museum and information center where you can pick up brochures and outdoor-recreation information. The small collection of artifacts relate to pioneers of the pass and antique ski equipment.

In **Cle Elum**, a Native American name meaning "swift water," you will find the unusual **Cle Elum Historical Telephone Museum** (221 East 1st Street; 509-674-5958) where old telephones, switchboards and other equipment from the area are displayed. At the foot of Fourth Street in South Cle Elum is the access point for the 25-mile-long **Iron Horse State Park**, a section of the former railroad right of way with the rails and ties removed and the roadbed smoothed over for walking, jogging and cross-country skiing. It is part of the **John Wayne Pioneer Trail** that will eventually run the width of the state.

Three miles away is the tiny town of **Roslyn**, which is being used as the set for television's "Northern Exposure." It was formerly a coal-mining town with a large population of Italians, Croats, Slavs and Austrian immigrants who worked in the mines. There are separate cemeteries—23 in fact—for these nationalities.

As you drive through the Kittitas Valley to Ellensburg, notice that the prevailing wind off the Cascades gives trees a permanent lean toward the east. When you reach Ellensburg, you are out of the Cascades and entering the arid climate that characterizes most of the eastern side of Washington. **Ellensburg** is perhaps best known for its rodeo each Labor Day weekend, and in keeping with the western legacy, the Western Art Association has its headquarters there and holds an annual show and sale each fall. The **Clymer Museum Gallery** (416 North Pearl Street; 509-962-6416; admission) displays work by the famous Western artist who lived in Ellensburg. The **Kittitas County Museum** (114 East 3rd Avenue; 509-925-3778) displays Native American artifacts and pioneer tools and crafts. Four miles east of town is the **Olmstead Place State Park** (921 North Ferguson Road; 509-925-1943), a "living historical farm" that uses pioneer horse-drawn equipment. The 217-acre farm and all its buildings were deeded to the state.

ROUTE 90 CORRIDOR LODGING

An affordable place to stay is the **Edgewick Inn** (14600 468th Avenue Southeast, North Bend; 206-888-9000, fax 206-888-9400). It is a straightforward motel with 44 clean and quiet units three miles east of town. Moderate.

About the only place to stay at Snoqualmie Summit is the **Summit Inn** (Route 906, Snoqualmie Pass; 206-434-6300, fax 206-434-6396). Outfitted for skiers, the inn has a complimentary ski-storage area, as well as coin-operated laundry facilities. Its 81 rooms come with king- or queen-size beds. The large lobby is stocked with comfortable sofas and wing-back chairs set around the native-stone fireplace. Moderate.

A former railroad boarding house, **The Moore House** (526 Marie Street, South Cle Elum; 509-674-5939) has been converted into one of the state's best inns. The 12 rooms, half with shared baths, are named for former roomers. All are decorated in turn-of-the-century antiques—with an emphasis, not surprisingly, on railroad trinkets and tools. There's even a remodeled caboose sporting a queen-size bed, refrigerator and sundeck with hot tub. The Moore House is adjacent to the Iron Horse State Park, where cross-country skiing, bicycling and walking are popular. Moderate to deluxe.

SALISH LODGE

*"Twin Peaks" aficionados will recognize the **Salish Lodge at Snoqualmie Falls** (37807 Southeast Fall City–Snoqualmie Road; 206-888-2556, 800-826-6124, fax 206-888-2420). But it deserves better than the way it was shown in the spooky opening credits. The Salish perches on the cliff overlooking the spectacular falls, one of the more dramatic settings for a hotel and restaurant in the Northwest. The 91 rooms are decorated in an upscale-country motif with down comforters, wicker furniture and wood-burning fireplaces. Only a few rooms have views of the falls, but the interiors are so well done that most visitors are content to watch the falls from the lounge. Ultra-deluxe.*

Although this is supposedly the state's oldest dude ranch, it is one of those places that keeps being "discovered." **Hidden Valley Guest Ranch** (3942 Hidden Valley Road; 509-857-2322, fax 509-857-2130) is 11 miles from Cle Elum nestled at the edge of a broad valley and at the base of low mountains. In addition to the main building, where guests gather for trail rides, hikes and the community meals, the ranch has 14 cabins that haven't had all the rustic removed, so don't expect sound- or cold-proofing. However, the fireplaces are great for taking off the chill, as are the heated swimming pool and communal hot tub. All meals, and they are very large meals, are eaten in the buffet-style dining room. Two-night minimum stay on high-season weekends; moderate to deluxe.

On the western edge of town, the **TimberLodge Motel** (301 West 1st Street, Cle Elum; 509-674-5966, fax 509-674-2737) has 29 bright, clean rooms far enough off the street to deaden the noise of the busy main drag. Amenities include an exercise room. Budget.

Murphy's Country Bed and Breakfast (2830 Thorp Highway South; 509-925-7986) four miles west of Ellensburg has two rooms in a ranch home built in 1915. It has a broad porch made of local stone with views across the valley. The large guest rooms have antique furnishings. The rooms share one-and-a-half baths, and a full country breakfast is served. Moderate.

ROUTE 90 CORRIDOR RESTAURANTS

The **Salish Lodge at Snoqualmie Falls** (37807 Southeast Fall City–Snoqualmie Road; 206-888-2556), offers spectacular views over the falls and canyon below, and the food is first rate. The menu leans toward what has become known as Northwest cuisine: lots of seafood, fresh fruits and vegetables, game, a lengthy wine list and dessert list almost as long. Deluxe to ultra-deluxe.

Nearby in Fall City is **The Herbfarm** (32804 Issaquah–Fall City Road, Fall City; 206-784-2222). What began as a roadside stand selling herbs has grown into one of the region's most unusual and successful restaurants. Be warned: It may take months to get a dinner reservation. The menu changes constantly because it is built around seasonal herbs. Each meal takes at least three to four hours because they begin with a tour of the herb gardens, then during the meal the owners go from table to table discussing herbs with the patrons and explaining how they were used in the dishes. Ultra-deluxe.

Cle Elum is better known for its inns and small hotels, but it does have at least one good restaurant, **Mama Vallone's Steak House and Inn** (302 West 1st Street; 509-674-5174). Tables are placed in most of the downstairs rooms, and you never have to wait for someone to re-plenish your water or bring more bread. A specialty is *bagna cauda*, a fondue-style mixture of olive oil, anchovy and garlic served with dipping strips of steak or seafood. Moderate to deluxe.

You can order patty melts (if you must) in one of three or four truck stops at the Ellensburg cloverleaf, but for lighter fare that won't add so many calories, try **Giovanni's on Pearl Italian Restaurant** (402 North Pearl Street; 509-962-2260). Owner John Herbert, from the Isle of Jersey, has a menu of lamb, fish, chicken and other light entrées. A nice touch is the candlelight and flowers on each table. Moderate to deluxe.

A short walk away is **The Valley Café** (105 West 3rd Street; 509-925-3050). Food is American with a dash of Mexico. Fish (frequently salmon) and chicken dominate the dinner menu. Moderate.

ROUTE 90 CORRIDOR SHOPPING

In North Bend, 25 miles east of Seattle, the **Factory Stores of America** is a mall with 40 stores selling well-known brands—Van Heusen, Big Dog, Bass, Hanes—at discount prices.

Very few wineries have opened thus far in the Cascades, so when one does exist, it is an event. **Snoqualmie Winery** (1000 Winery Road, Snoqualmie; 206-888-4000) produces ten varieties of wine, from riesling to merlot, and is open for tours and tasting daily.

Antique hunters will enjoy **Ellensburg**, which has at least half a dozen antique stores in a three-block area, including a mall. **Anchor in Time** (310 North Main Street; 509-925-7067) has antiques, rare books and western artifacts, and espresso. The **Showplace Antique Mall** (103 East 3rd Street; 509-962-9331) is a restored art deco theater with up to 40 antique dealers displaying at a time.

ROUTE 90 CORRIDOR NIGHTLIFE

Cle Elum has almost nothing in nightlife other than taverns with jukeboxes, although occasionally **Moore House** guests will bring their own instruments for a sing-along. In Ellensburg, there is little entertainment between the rodeos, but **Adeline's** (315 North Main Street; 509-962-2888) has a deejay or canned rock music on the weekend.

ROUTE 90 CORRIDOR PARKS

Lake Easton State Park (Route 5, one mile west of Easton; 509-656-2230) located near Snoqualmie Pass, is used as a base for skiers and snowmobilers in winter. This lakeside park with picnic areas and forested trails also serves as a lunch stop for travelers. Hiking, swimming and fishing are popular in the summer. The lake is stocked with trout. You can also camp here.

Mt. Rainier Area

It is always a dramatic moment when Mt. Rainier suddenly appears ahead of you (in the Northwest it is often just called "The Mountain"). You could spend weeks in this area and only sample a small portion of its recreational possibilities. Whether you approach from the east or the west, the forest gets thicker and thicker and the roadside rivers get swifter and swifter. The national park is almost surrounded with national forest wilderness areas as buffer zones against clear-cut logging. Located southeast of Seattle, this peak is adjacent to the aptly named town of Paradise.

The most heavily used national park in Washington, **Mt. Rainier National Park** (360-569-2211) is everybody's favorite because the mountain can be approached from so many directions and the area around it is glorious no matter the time of year. Entrances to the park are on Route 165 on the northwest, Route 410 on the northeast, Route 706 on the southwest and Route 123 on the southeast. The mountain is climbed by groups under the leadership of Rainier Mountaineering, a concessionaire. The lower elevations are notable for the vast meadows that are covered with wildflowers from late June until August and feature dramatic fall colors in September and October. Numerous trails lead day hikers to viewpoints, and backpackers can explore the lower elevations on a permit system. Much of the park is open year-round with special areas set aside for wintersports at Paradise. The park offers four information centers and museums, and self-guided nature trails. There are five car campgrounds, a few walk-in sites and overnight hike-in backcountry areas on a first-come, first-served basis. Fishing is permitted without a state license. Check with a ranger for regulations.

If you arrive via Route 706 you will have to go through Elbe, which has the **Mt. Rainier Scenic Railroad** (54124 Mountain Highway East; 360-569-2588), a steam-powered train that makes a 14-mile trip through the forest and across high bridges to Mineral Lake. It runs daily in summer, on Saturday and Sunday in September and special holidays the rest of the year. A four-hour dinner train is offered April to November.

Once inside the park you may be almost overwhelmed by the scenery. The mountain is so monstrous (14,411 feet) that it makes everything around it seem trivial. Mt. Rainier has numerous visitors centers and interpretive exhibits along winding roads.

In **Paradise**, head to the **Henry M. Jackson Visitors Center**, which has several exhibits and audiovisual shows. Paradise is one of the most beautiful places in the park, and the visitors center one of the busiest. It has a snack bar and gift shop. The **Longmire Museum** emphasizes the natural history of the park with rock, flora and fauna exhibits. It is also an information center for hikers, and you can rent cross-country skis. The **Ohanapecosh Visitors Center** down in the southeast corner near a

---

Mt. Rainier is the tallest mountain in the Northwest and has more glaciers—26—than any other mountain in the contiguous 48 states.

---

grove of giant, ancient cedar trees, has history and nature exhibits. The **Sunrise Visitors Center** has geological displays and, at 6400 feet, is the closest you can drive to the peak. Several trails fan out from the center for day hikes. For reservation information, call Mt. Rainier Guest Services (360-569-2275).

Nearby, at the intersection of Routes 410 and 12 east of the mountain, you can watch elk and bighorn sheep being fed by game officials during the winter at the **Oak Creek Wildlife Recreation Area**.

MT. RAINIER AREA LODGING

Two inns are inside Mt. Rainier National Park, and several other places to stay are around the park in Ashford, Packwood, Elbe, Crystal Mountain, Morton and the White Pass area.

The most popular is **Paradise Inn** (Route 706, Ashford; 360-569-2275, fax 360-569-2770). In the middle of the park, this inn has 125 rooms and a lobby that boasts exposed beams, peeled-log posts, wooden furniture, Indian-made rugs and two huge fireplaces. The views are grand, but the rooms are ordinary, and most of the bathrooms are museum pieces. Open May to October. Nonsmoking; moderate.

The other in-park hotel is the **National Park Inn** (Route 706, Ashford; 360-569-2275, fax 360-569-2770) six miles from the Nisqually entrance. Offering much of the rustic charm of the Paradise Inn, it is much smaller with only 25 rooms, two-thirds of which have private baths. Some rooms have views of the mountain. In keeping with the rustic theme, there are no telephones or televisions. The lobby has an enormous stone fireplace. Moderate.

Equally popular with lovers of old inns is **Alexander's Country Inn** (37515 Route 706 East, Ashford; 360-569-2300, 800-654-7615). This inn was built in 1912 as a small hotel designed to look like a manor with turret rooms and grand entrance hall. It retains an Old World look while adding modern conveniences such as a hot tub. Breakfast included. Moderate to deluxe.

In Packwood on the southern flank of the national park is the **Cowlitz River Lodge** (13069 Route 12; 360-494-4444, fax 360-494-2075). It is notable for clean, brightly decorated rooms and views of the mountains, although not "The Mountain." It is set back from the busy Route 12 far enough for the logging trucks to be a distant hum rather than an immediate roar. Moderate.

On the northeast boundary of the park is **Crystal Mountain Resort** (1 Crystal Mountain Boulevard, Crystal Mountain; 360-663-2558, fax 360-663-0145), a year-round resort that is best known for its skiing. Visitors can choose from a number of places to stay, ranging from condominiums to inexpensive motels. Don't expect much charm because skiing, not hotel amenities, is the focus here. Typical is **Silver Skis Chalet Condominiums**, which has a cluster of one- and two-bedroom units, some with fireplaces and views. All have kitchens and cable television. They are decorated in the traditional rental-condo manner of plastic furniture and durable fabrics and can sleep up to four persons. Deluxe to ultra-deluxe.

A bit farther east toward Yakima is the White Pass ski area with **The Village Inn Condominiums** (Route 12; 509-672-3131). The complex has 52 rental units designed for large groups, up to eight in many units, and they have a bit of variation in decor since all are privately owned. Some have fireplaces and sleeping lofts. Moderate.

MT. RAINIER AREA RESTAURANTS

Good restaurants are hard to find around Mt. Rainier. Two of the best are in Ashford:

Wild Berry Restaurant (37720 Route 706 East; 360-569-2628) is a mile outside the park, and lunch items on the menu will be packed to go on request. As the name suggests, it tends toward ferns and granola (the owners call it "mountain yuppie") but the food is imaginative—quiche, wild blackberry pie—and budget-priced.

Nearby is the more traditional **Alexander's Country Inn** (37515 Route 706 East; 360-569-2300) serving breakfast, lunch and dinner. The dining room has windows looking out across the forest. Trout is a favorite, along with seafood, and all the breads and desserts are homemade. They also make box lunches. Moderate. Open weekends only in the winter.

One of the most popular restaurants between Mt. Rainier and Mt. St. Helens is **Peters Inn** (13051 Route 12, Packwood; 360-494-4000), a large, old-fashioned place where they serve burgers, steaks, veal and some seafood and have a large salad bar. Pies and cinnamon rolls are made locally. Budget.

MT. RAINIER AREA NIGHTLIFE

Nightlife is meager. Try **Crystal Mountain Resort** (Crystal Mountain; 206-663-2558), which has an occasional small group in spite of skiers' notorious reputation for going to bed early. Live bands play on weekends and holidays.

Mt. St. Helens Area

At the southern end of the Washington Cascades an hour north of Portland, Mt. St. Helens might best be described as a cross between a geology lesson and a bombing range. East of this landmark is Gifford Pinchot National Forest and Mt. Adams Wilderness, the heart of a popular recreation area ideal for rafting and fishing.

On May 18, 1980, Mt. St. Helens, dormant for 123 years, blew some 1300 feet off its top and killed 59 persons, causing one of the largest natural disasters in recorded North American history. Today, access to this composite volcano remains limited because the blast and resulting mudslides and floods erased the roads that formerly entered the area.

A major sightseeing destination, **Mt. St. Helens National Volcanic Monument Visitors Center** (360-274-2100), is on Route 504 at Silver Lake, five miles east of Route 5. The center is elaborate and includes a walk-in model of the inside of the volcano. A 22-minute film on the eruption plays almost continuously, and an equally dramatic nine-minute slide show runs every 30 minutes. There is also the new **Coldwater Ridge Visitors Center** (360-274-2131), 38 miles farther east on Route 504. It is located in the area where the volcano erupted and offers guided walks from June to October.

Windy Ridge is the closest you can get to the volcano, and it is reached by driving south from Randle on a series of Forest Service roads. Hourly talks are given by rangers in the amphitheater there in summer. **Meta Lake Walk** is on the way to Windy Ridge, and rangers tell how people survived the blast. A 30-minute talk is given in **Ape Cave** on the southern end of the monument. It includes a walk into the 1900-year-old lava tube that got its name from a reputed confrontation between some miners and what they believed were the legendary, ape-like creatures known as Sasquatches by Northwest Native Americans.

East of Mt. St. Helens, continue south through **Gifford Pinchot National Forest** on paved logging roads that are better maintained than many state or county roads. First, buy a copy of the national forest map at the visitors center or from a ranger station. You can drive to the edge of **Indian Heaven Wilderness Area** and hike through peaceful meadows and acres of huckleberry bushes, or continue east to the edge of **Mt. Adams Wilderness** (509-395-2501) with views of that mountain reflected in lakes. Day and overnight permits are required to enter Mt. Adams Wilderness and are available free at all trailheads in the area. This whole area is known for wild huckleberries, and there are two seasons for them; in the lower elevations they ripen in July and into August, then a week or two later the higher-elevation berries are ready for picking.

The logging roads will eventually take you to **Trout Lake**, a small town close to a naturally disintegrating lake of the same name that re-

There are few certitudes in travel writing, but here's one: Don't miss Mt. St. Helens.

flects Mt. Adams in clear weather. Here you'll find all services and a Forest Service Ranger Station. Just west of town is a vast lava flow called the Big Lava Bed and a lava tube called Ice Cave, which is chilly all through the summer. Both are reached on Forest Service roads.

From Trout Lake, drive east 19 miles to the small cowboy town of **Glenwood**. There's not much more than a country tavern and post office to the town, but in the Shade Tree Inn restaurant you can get directions to some of the more unusual sights in the area, such as a group of quartz crystals more than 200 feet in diameter and what is locally called "volcano pits," a series of small craters left behind by cinder cones.

From Glenwood, take the Glenwood–Goldendale Road to the junction with Route 142 and drive back southwest to Klickitat and the Columbia Gorge at Lyle. This takes you through the deep, winding **Klickitat River Canyon** with views of the river, a steelheaders' favorite. Mt. Adams often frames the scene.

MT. ST. HELENS AREA LODGING

The **Seasons Motel** (200 Westlake Avenue, Morton; 360–496–6835, fax 360–496–5127), about halfway between Mt. Rainier and Mt. St. Helens, has 50 rooms in a slate-blue, two-story frame building at the intersection of Routes 12 and 7. All beds in this moderately priced establishment are queen-sized, and the rooms have flowered drapes and bedspreads.

Located 16 miles west of Morton in the tiny town of Salkum, **The Shepherd's Inn** (168 Autumn Heights Drive; 360–985–2434, 800–985–2434) is about an hour and a half away from both Mt. Rainier and Mt. St. Helens. Set on 40-plus acres of wooded land, guests can enjoy the region's natural beauty on any of the numerous walking trails that web through the property. The inn's five rooms offer Victorian furnishings and brass beds. If you have the urge to tickle the ivories, you may do so on the grand piano upstairs. There's also a jacuzzi. Breakfast includes wild huckleberry crêpes. Moderate.

Mio Amore Pensione (53 Little Mountain Road, Trout Lake; 509–395–2264) is in a renovated 1904 farmhouse on the southern edge of Trout Lake, the closest town to Mt. Adams. Each of the three rooms in the main building has a theme—wine, gardening and Venus (love)—so the latter is used for the honeymoon suite and has its own bathroom and views of Mt. Adams. There is a fourth room in a converted ice house. Moderate to ultra-deluxe.

Also on the southern edge of Mt. Adams is the outdoor-oriented **Flying L Ranch** (25 Flying L Lane, Glenwood; 509-364-3488). Originally a working ranch, the Flying L has been a guest ranch without horses since 1960. Hiking is popular here as are photography and fishing in the nearby Klickitat River. Bikes are available free of charge to get around the mostly flat roads in the area. In the winter, cross-country skiing and snowshoeing trail access is nearby. The main lodge has six rooms, half with shared bath; a two-story guest house has five rooms with private baths, and two separate cabins sleep up to five. Breakfast is provided and served in the cookhouse. The main lodge also has a large common kitchen where guests can prepare their own lunch and dinner. Moderate.

MT. ST. HELENS AREA RESTAURANTS

On the south edge of Trout Lake is **Mio Amore Pensione** (53 Little Mountain Road, Trout Lake; 509-395-2264), one of the more remote first-rate restaurants in the Cascades. Owners Tom and Jill Westbrook have simplified the eatery's operation by offering only one entrée—the first person to call for a reservation establishes the choice for the evening. The husband half of the team is an accomplished chef who learned his craft in Italy; dishes range from seafood to steak to wild game. Most dinners begin in the living room with drinks and often end there with Jill Westbrook's specialties: She makes the desserts and is an accomplished guitarist and songwriter. Deluxe.

MT. ST. HELENS AREA PARKS

Mt. St. Helens National Volcanic Monument (360-247-5473) covers 110,000 acres and was created in 1982 to preserve and study the area that was devastated by the eruption. Interpretive centers and overlooks show the much-altered Spirit Lake, vast mud flows and the forests that were flattened by the blast. Access to the monument is limited to a few Forest

---

BARDINI'S

*A former logger's tavern, **Bardini's** (40011 Northeast 221st Avenue, Amboy; 360-247-5352) has been upgraded into a favorite dinner house, attracting clientele from miles around. You'll enjoy specialties like pasta celeste, spaghetti, pizza, cannelloni, ravioli, steaks and seafood. Dimly lit, with both booth and table seating, the carpeted restaurant 25 miles southwest of Mt. St. Helens is worth the trip from Vancouver on Route 503. Moderate.*

Service and county roads, most of which are closed in the winter. You will find excellent fishing for bass and trout in Silver Lake, while fishing is good for trout in lakes behind dams on Lewis River, south of the monument. To get to the monument from the north, Forest Service roads branch off Route 12 at Randle. From the west, Route 504 from Route 5 leads five miles to the Mt. St. Helens National Volcanic Monument Visitors Center on the shores of Silver Lake, and Route 503 leads up the Lewis River to the monument headquarters at Amboy and the southern flank of the monument.

The 1.4 million-acre **Gifford Pinchot National Forest** (360–750–5000) covers most of the southern Cascades to the Columbia River, marked by the Mt. St. Helens National Monument on the west and Mt. Adams on the east. Enclosing seven wilderness areas, most of its forest roads have been paved by the logging companies that are now restricted from much of the area. Of particular interest are the **Big Lava Beds**, 14 miles west of Trout Lake, where unusual formations of basalt are found, and the **Ice Cave**, six miles southwest of Trout Lake, a lava tube where ice remains until late summer. There are picnic areas and restrooms, and over 50 campgrounds to choose from. Fishing is excellent in lakes, which are stocked frequently, and in all rivers flowing out of the forest. This is the most remote of the national forests and is traversed only by Route 12.

The Sporting Life

SPORTFISHING

Winter steelhead, Dolly Varden, rainbow trout, eastern brook trout, walleye, catfish, bass, perch and crappie all can be caught in the interior and along the flanks of the Cascade Range. Fishing is typically done from the banks or on private boats, but most resorts on lakes and rivers have boats and fishing tackle for rent.

The rivers that drain into Puget Sound—particularly the Nooksack, Skagit, Skykomish and Snohomish—have steelhead and sea-run cutthroat trout. A few professional guides work on the Skagit where winter steelheading is very popular. Two are **Fred Hunger** (360–826–3646) and **John Bates** (360–856–5817).

The other Cascade rivers, such as the Methow, Wenatchee, Yakima, Snake and Klickitat, drain into the Columbia River. All have good trout, walleye and steelhead fishing. The Klickitat River has summer steelhead runs as does the Columbia. Fewer and fewer salmon can be caught upstream from Bonneville Dam, the first of 14 dams on the river, as their numbers continue to dwindle. In the Lake Chelan area, which is noted for lake trout, landlocked salmon and steelhead, outfitters include **Rush's**

During the salmon runs, Native Americans still fish with their traditional dip nets from the Fisher Hill Bridge near Klickitat.

Fishing Guide Service (P.O. Box 1481, Lake Chelan, WA 98852; 509-682-2802) and **Graybill's Guide Service** (509-682-4294). You'll need a Washington State Fishing License to fish in most places, although not in all national parks. You can buy one at most bait shops.

RIVER RAFTING

On the Skagit, **Downstream River Runners** (12112 Northeast 195th Street, Bothell; 206-483-0335) runs whitewater trips as well as tours to watch bald eagles and osprey. **All Rivers** (Cashmere; 509-782-2254) runs a variety of rivers and leads scenic and natural history tours. **Alpine Whitewater** (Clocktower Building, Route 2, Leavenworth; 509-548-4159) leads trips on the Wenatchee, Methow, Tieton, Skykomish and Skagit rivers. Located on the farthest reaches of Lake Chelan, accessible only by boat or floatplane, **Stehekin Valley Ranch** (P.O. Box 36, Stehekin, WA 98852; 509-682-4677) offers river rafting on the Stehekin River. **Orion Expeditions** (1516 11th Avenue, Seattle; 206-547-6715) offers trips on most of the rivers in Washington.

SKIING

It's all downhill from here: Yes, friends, we are going to take you skiing. Whether you are into slopes or cross-country, the best ski areas in Washington are stretched along the Cascades from Mt. Baker to Mt. Rainier.

Beginning at the northernmost ski area and working south toward the Columbia River, **Mt. Baker** (Route 542; 360-734-6771) is 56 miles east of Bellingham and has an elevation range from 3500 to 5040 feet. The state's only helicopter skiing is **North Cascade Heli-Skiing** (509-996-3272), which operates out of Mazama.

Some skiers prefer **Stevens Pass** (206-353-4400), located on Route 2 about 80 miles east of Everett, because at times it has more powdery snow than spots at the summit of Snoqualmie Pass. One of the smaller ski areas is **Echo Valley** (509-687-3167), which sits ten miles northwest of Chelan on a dirt road off Route 150 and has elevations of 3000 to 3500 feet. Another small one is **Leavenworth Ski Hill** (509-548-6486) a mile north of Leavenworth with a 400-foot vertical drop and a network of cross-country trails.

Probably the best powder snow at a large ski area is at **Mission Ridge** (Mission Ridge Road; 509-663-7631), 13 miles southwest of Wenatchee.

But the largest operation of all is at Snoqualmie Pass 47 miles east of Seattle. Four major ski areas are to be found in a space of two miles: **Alpental, Ski Acres, Snoqualmie** and **Hyak**. The average summit elevation is 5400 feet and base is 3000 feet. For information on these mountains, call 206-434-7669; for snow conditions, call 206-236-1600.

Way up in the sky is **Crystal Mountain** (360-663-2265). Forty miles east of Enumclaw just off Route 410 and in the shadow of Mt. Rainier, the summit has an elevation of 7000 feet. Crystal has 55 major runs and 1000 acres of backcountry for cross-country skiing. In the same general area, **White Pass** (509-453-8731) is 20 miles east of Packwood on Route 12 southeast of Mt. Rainier.

Cross-country skiing is particularly popular on the eastern slopes of the mountains. Some of the best is in the Methow Valley where 110 miles of trails are marked, the majority of which are groomed. The **Methow Valley Sport Trail Association** (P.O. Box 147, Winthrop, WA 98862; 509-996-3287) has a hotline for ski-touring information (800-682-5787) and a brochure showing the major trails.

Echo Valley (509-682-4002), a ski center near Chelan on Cooper Mountain Road, has cross-country and downhill skiing. A good Nordic ski center, Bear Mountain, was devoured by the July 1994 fire that swept through these hills. The Leavenworth Area maintains several ski trails, including the **Icicle River Trail** (7 miles) and **Ski Hill** (3 miles).

GOLF

Nearly every community in the foothills has a golf course. Around Mt. Baker you'll find the **Peaceful Valley Country Club** (8225 Kendall Road, Maple Falls; 360-599-2416).

Along the eastern slopes of the North Cascades in the Methow Valley you can play at the **Bear Creek Golf Course** (8 Golf Course Road; 509-996-2284) or **Lake Chelan Golf Course** (1501 Golf Course Road, Chelan; 509-682-5421). Wenatchee has two courses nearby: the **Three Lakes Golf Course** (2695 Golf Drive; 509-663-5448) and **Wenatchee Golf and Country Club** (1600 Country Club Drive; 509-884-7105).

In Leavenworth, tee off at the **Kahler Glen Golf Course and Condominiums** (20890 Kahler Drive; 509-763-4025) or **Leavenworth Golf Club** (9101 Icicle Road; 509-548-7267).

Among the Route 90 Corridor links are the **Mt. Si Golf Course** (Meadowbrook North Bend Road Southeast; 206-888-1541), **Cascade Golf Club** (Cedar Falls Road, North Bend; 206-888-0227); **Sun Country Golf Course** (Golf Course Road, Cle Elum; 509-674-2226); and **Ellensburg Golf Club** (3231 Thorp Highway South, Ellensburg; 509-962-2984).

HORSEBACK RIDING AND PACK TRIPS

Cascade Corrals (P.O. Box 67, Stehekin, WA 98852; 509-682-4677) operates in Glacier Peak Wilderness, Lake Chelan Sawtooth Wilderness and North Cascades National Park. **Sun Mountain Lodge** (Patterson Lake Road; 509-996-2211) has the largest stable of riding horses in the Cascades, available for hourly rides, day trips, dinner and breakfast trips or overnight pack trips. **Icicle Outfitters and Guides** (P.O. Box 322, Leavenworth, WA 98826; 509-763-3647) has hourly guided rides, day trips and summer pack trips. **Eagle Creek Ranch** (7951 Eagle Creek Road; 509-548-7798) runs trips into the Alpine Lakes, Glacier Lakes and Henry M. Jackson Wilderness areas. **Longhorn Cattle Co.** (2151 Brick Mill Road; 509-925-5811) offers four cattle drives a year lasting from four to six days. Horseback riding in the Stehekin Valley wilderness area on Lake Chelan is offered by **Stehekin Valley Ranch** (P.O. Box 36, Stehekin, WA 98852; 509-682-4677). Stehekin is accessible by boat or floatplane only.

BICYCLING

The popularity of bicycling is growing in the Cascades, and one of the most popular trips is from Route 5 over Route 20 across the North Cascades. Although the highway has only two lanes, the shoulders are wide enough for biking in safety.

Several loop routes have been established along the eastern slopes of the Cascades. The **Leavenworth–Lake Wenatchee loop** is 50 miles long and goes from Leavenworth along Route 209 north to Route 207 at Lake Wenatchee State Park and south to Route 2 and back to Leavenworth.

The **Wenatchee–Chelan loop** is 90 miles along the Columbia River and Lake Entiat. It goes north on Route 2 from East Wenatchee, then north on Route 151 to Chelan Station, across the Columbia River, then south on Route 97 to Wenatchee again.

WHAT'S YOUR ZONE?

The Cascade Range supports an incredibly wide variety of plants and wildlife because it has so many climatic zones. Naturalists have given names to eight distinct ones: Western Hemlock Forest Zone, Silver Fir Zone, Mountain Hemlock Forest Zone, Subalpine Zone, Alpine Zone, Eastside Meadow Zone, Douglas Fir Zone and Ponderosa Pine Zone. Each zone has its own unique mix of plants, animals and birds.

BIKE RENTALS   The options are limited because the area is so remote, so it's best to bring along your own bicycles. If you want to try for rentals, check out resorts and any bike shops in towns along the way.

HIKING

The Cascades are a backpacker's paradise laced with thousands of miles of maintained trails.

NORTH CASCADES TRAILS   The **Pacific Crest National Scenic Trail** (510 miles) has its northern terminus in Washington. It is a hard hike in many places but can be broken into easier chunks, such as from Stevens Pass to Snoqualmie Pass. Contact the **Forest Service Information Center** (915 2nd Avenue, Suite 442, Seattle, WA 98174; 206-220-7450) for further details.

Coleman Glacier (6 miles round trip) is a popular hike that is accessed on Road 39 at Heliotrope Ridge. Contact the visitors center (206-599-2714) for more information.

Perhaps the most historic route in the North Cascades is **Cascade Pass Trail** (9 miles), the Native Americans' route across the mountains for centuries. It is also a lengthier route from Marblemount to Stehekin, if you want to really make a trip of it.

All along **Route 20** are signs denoting trailheads, and all are worth exploring. They tell the destination of the trail and the distance.

For a long trip—allow three or four days—**Image Lake** (32 miles) is considered one of the most beautiful in the central Cascades. The lake mirrors Glacier Peak, the most remote and inaccessible of the Washington volcanoes.

LEAVENWORTH AREA TRAILS   **Icicle Creek** (1 mile) is an interpretive loop trail a short distance west of Leavenworth.

Enchantment Lakes (18 miles) is Washington's most beloved backpacking trip because the lakes are otherworldly. They are approached from Icicle Creek near Leavenworth. The hike is a hard one, and permits must be obtained through the Wenatchee National Forest. Call the Leavenworth Ranger Station for information (509-782-1413).

ROUTE 90 CORRIDOR TRAIL   **Iron Horse State Park** (113 miles) is a former railroad right-of-way that is used by hikers, horse riders, cross-country skiers and bicyclists. No motorized vehicles are allowed on the trail, which goes from North Bend over Snoqualmie Pass to Vantage.

MT. RAINIER AREA TRAILS   **Naches Wagon Trail** (10 miles), east of Yakima, is a historical hike because this was a route pioneers used on their way to Puget Sound. They left behind blazed trees and other evidence of crude road building.

Guided tours of Mt. St. Helens are provided by several operators departing from Seattle, Olympia and Vancouver, while scenic flights are available out of area airports.

Wonderland Trail (94 miles) goes entirely around Mt. Rainier and can be made in stages ranging from the 6.5-mile section between Longmire and Paradise to the 39-mile section from Carbon River to Longmire.

Northern Loop Trail (17 miles) runs through the wilderness with frequent views of the mountain between Carbon River and Sunrise.

MT. ST. HELENS AREA TRAILS   **Klickitat Trail** (16 miles one-way) takes you through a remote part of the Gifford Pinchot National Forest and is believed to be part of an old Native American trail network.

Conboy Wildlife Refuge Trail (3 miles) wends through the refuge just south of Glenwood with interpretive signs showing you nesting sites, migratory patterns and discussions on the ecology of the lava and desert area.

People return again and again to **Indian Heaven** (10 miles) a beautiful section of the **Pacific Crest National Scenic Trail**. It is near Trout Lake and goes past numerous lakes reflecting the surrounding mountains.

Transportation

BY CAR

Route 542 travels east from Bellingham through Glacier to deadend at Mt. Baker Lodge. **Route 20**, also known as the North Cascades Highway, goes east from Route 5 at Burlington to the Methow Valley. **Route 2**, one of the last intercontinental, two-lane, blacktop highways, runs from Everett to Maine and is called the Stevens Pass Highway in Washington. From Seattle, **Route 90** goes over Snoqualmie Pass to Cle Elum and Ellensburg.

BY AIR

Only one airport, **Pangborn Field** located in Wenatchee, serves this area and only one airline, Horizon Airways, offers regular service to it. Planes fly in eight times daily from Seattle. The roadless Lake Chelan area is served by Chelan Airways, which makes scheduled and charter flights between Chelan and Stehekin.

BY BUS

Greyhound Bus Lines offers service to Leavenworth and Wenatchee (301 1st Street; 509-662-2183), with a stop in Cashmere. **Link Transit** (509-662-1155) serves Cashmere, Chelan, Dryden, East Wenatchee, Entiat, Leavenworth, Malaga, Manson, Monitor, Peshastin and Wenatchee. **Empire Lines** (509-624-4116) goes to Chelan, Entiat, Pateros, Wenatchee and Ellensburg.

BY TRAIN

Amtrak (800-872-7245) travels from Seattle and Spokane to Wenatchee via the "Empire Builder."

BY FERRY

The 350-person passenger ferry **Lady of the Lake** (Box 186, Chelan, WA 98816; 509-682-2224) provides daily transportation in the summer to Chelan, Manson, Fields Point, Prince Creek, Lucerne, Moore and Stehekin. You can also catch the smaller **Lady Express**, which has fewer stops but faster service. The Lady Express also runs in the winter on Monday, Wednesday, Friday, Saturday and Sunday.

CAR RENTALS

Car rental agencies at the Wenatchee airport include **Budget Rent A Car** (800-527-0700), **Hertz Rent A Car** (800-654-3131) and **U-Save Auto Rental** (800-272-8728). Ellensburg has **Budget Rent A Car** (800-527-0700).

NINE

East of the Cascades

If state boundaries were determined by similar geography, customs and attitude, Washington and Oregon as we know them would simply not exist. Instead, they'd be split into two more states using the crest of the Cascades as the dividing line or would run vertically from California on the south to Canada on the north with one state taking either side of the mountain range.

Well, who ever said life was perfect? So what we have is a state whose eastern and western halves bear almost no resemblance to each other. From the Cascades west, the land is damp, the forests thick and the climate temperate. The eastern side of the range is almost exactly the opposite: Very little rain falls and most crops are irrigated by water from the Columbia Basin Project created by Grand Coulee Dam, or by water from deep wells. Here, the winters are cold and the summers are hot.

If urban amenities such as hotels, finer restaurants, theater and shopping centers are what you're after, head to eastern Washington's larger cities—Spokane, Walla Walla, the Tri-Cities and Yakima. Elsewhere, you'll find RV parks and inexpensive but clean motels. On the lakes and streams are rustic resorts, some with log cabins.

Away from the cities, hunting and fishing abound. Many streams and lakes are stocked regularly with trout, and a few sturgeon are still caught in the Snake and Columbia rivers. Deer, elk and an occasional black bear are popular quarry, as are waterfowl, pheasant, grouse and quail. Don't be startled while driving along a mountain road during hunting season if you spot someone in camouflage clothing carrying a rifle emerging from the forest.

Some of the most interesting geology in North America is found in this part of Washington due to its tortured creation by volcanoes, lava flows

The northeastern corner of Washington is an area of pine forests, sparkling lakes, sprawling wheat farms and urban pleasures in a rural setting.

through vast fissures and floods gigantic beyond imagining. Throughout this region you will find vivid reminders of this creation process, like the dramatic Coulee Country along the Columbia River and the beautiful Palouse Country with its steep, rolling hills. One stretch of landscape of unusual origin is the Channeled Scablands south and west of Spokane, which was created by floods from a lake formed at the end of the last ice age in the valley around Missoula, Montana.

The forests are mainly pine with little underbrush. Along some parts of the eastern slope of the Cascades, you will find larch, the only species of coniferous trees that are deciduous. They are brilliantly colored in the fall and stand out as vividly as sumac and maples in the dark-green forest.

East of the mountains is another treasure: peace and quiet. There are lonesome roads undulating off into the distance, small rivers stocked with trout, open pine forests, vast lakes made by man, and mornings so tranquil you can hear a door slam a mile away.

As is the case across much of America, the general rule here is that the smaller the town, the friendlier the people. Don't be surprised if folks stop to talk about anything or nothing in particular. Another plus is that you'll find nearly everything is less expensive than along the coast.

Traveling these remote areas you will have a continual sense of discovery as you visit places barely large enough to get themselves onto state maps. And you will find small towns that don't bother opening tourist bureaus but have a clean motel, a good café, friendly people to talk to and a small city park for your picnic.

A few remnants of the pioneer years still remain standing in eastern Washington. Here and there you'll see the remains of a cabin with perhaps the tall tripod of a windmill where a homesteader tried but failed to "prove up" the land given him by the Homestead Act. You'll also see remains of ghost towns (although some have been rediscovered and are peopled again). Most of these towns were built at or near mines and abandoned when the mines began coughing up only rocks and sand.

To help you explore this fascinating eastern strip of Washington, which extends from the Canadian border on the north to the Columbia Gorge that separates Washington from Oregon on the south, we've divided this chapter into the following sections:

The Okanogan Highlands, often called the Okanogan Country or simply the Okanogan, has boundaries that are fairly easy to determine: Route 97 to the west, the Canadian border to the north, the Columbia River on the east and the Colville Indian Reservation on the south.

Grand Coulee area includes all the Columbia River system from where it swings west at the southern end of the Colville Indian Reservation and follows past Grand Coulee Dam south to the Vantage–Wanapum Dam area, where the Columbia enters the Hanford Nuclear Reservation.

The Spokane area covers the only true metropolitan center east of the Cascades.

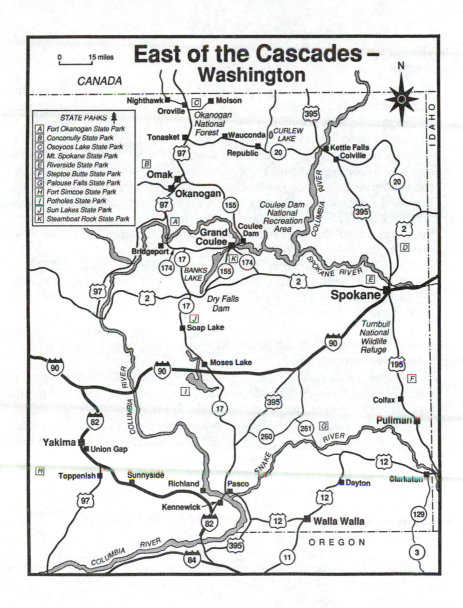

East of the Cascades – Washington

Palouse Country is considered the best wheat-growing land in the world.

Southeastern Washington encompasses the famed Palouse Hills between Spokane and Pullman; the Snake River town of Clarkston; Walla Walla; the Tri-Cities of Pasco, Kennewick and Richland; and Yakima and the agricultural and wine-producing valley of the same name.

Okanogan Highlands

One of the pleasures of touring the Okanogan Highlands in the northeast corner of Washington is simply driving down country roads to see where they lead. A number of ghost towns, some no more than a decaying log cabin today, dot the map.

Most visitors enter the Okanogan Country from Route 97, the north-south corridor that runs up the Columbia River valley to Brewster and then follows the Okanogan River valley north toward Canada. This is desert-like country, with irrigated orchards on either side of the highway and open range climbing back up the mountains. To begin your visit, contact the **Omak Visitor Information Center** (401 Omak Avenue, Omak; 509-826-1880) for brochures and maps.

The **Okanogan County Historical Museum** (509-422-4272), also headquarters for the county historical society, is on Okanogan's Main Street and has a collection of Indian artifacts, pioneer farm and ranch implements and historical photos. This is also a good place to start all your travels because members of the volunteer staff have lived in the region for many years and know where everything is, including skeletons in the county's closets.

Antiques of all ages are the biggest thing going in **Oroville**, north of Okanogan on Route 97. In keeping with the theme, some of the town's storefronts have been decorated with falsefronts.

A popular drive is to **Nighthawk**, just west of Oroville, which was a ghost town until recently. The paved county road, which heads west from Route 97 near the Canadian border, curves along the Similkameen River valley, then swings south into a valley between the mountains of the Pasayten Wilderness of the North Cascades National Park and a series of steep ridges to the east. This area is dotted with old mines, some still worked from time to time, but most of the land along the valley floor and stretching up the hillsides a few hundred feet has been turned into orchards and vineyards. Nighthawk is far from being a ghost town now, as is **Loomis**, the other mining town farther south on this loop drive. The highway passes Palmer Lake and Spectacle Lake, both of which have public beaches, before rejoining Route 97.

In Colville, several buildings comprise the **Keller Historical Park** (700 North Wynne Street; 509-684-5968), set at the junction of Route 20 and Route 395. Sponsored by the Stevens County Historical Society, the complex has a museum, a fire lookout tower, Colville's first schoolhouse, a trapper's cabin and the home of the pioneer Keller family.

Another historical site is **St. Paul's Mission**, 12 miles north of Colville in Kettle Falls where Route 395 crosses the Columbia River. It was built as a chapel for Native Americans in 1845 and operated until the 1870s. A modest museum is also here.

Follow Route 20 east and you'll come to the town of **Republic**. Created by a gold rush in the late 1890s, a gold mine still operates a short distance outside town. The **Stonerose Interpretive Center** (509-775-2295) lets visitors dig for fossils on a hillside on the edge of town. The site is named for an extinct rose fossil found there. The center is closed November through April.

OKANOGAN HIGHLANDS LODGING

The most modern motel in Okanogan is the **Cedars Inn** (Route 97 and Route 20; 509-422-6431, fax 509-422-4214), with 78 moderately priced rooms, an unpretentious dining room and heated pool. A budget-priced Okanogan motel is the **Ponderosa Motor Lodge** (1034 South 2nd Avenue; 509-422-0400, fax 509-422-4206), an older but clean two-story motel of basic design with a pool.

The **U and I Motel** (838 2nd Avenue; 509-422-2920) has nine small "cabinettes" with rustic paneling; one unit has a kitchen. They come equipped with deck chairs, so you can sit and look across a lawn and flower garden to the Okanogan River. Budget.

THE THREE MOLSONS

One interesting drive is to **Molson**, a ghost town 12 miles northeast of Tonasket off Route 97 near the Canadian border; follow the highway signs in downtown Tonasket. Molson was founded when a nearby mine attracted hundreds of prospectors and workers. Due to a land-claim mix-up, a farmer took over the whole town, so a new one had to be built and it was named **New Molson**. The two towns, less than a mile apart, fought over everything except education for their children. They built a school halfway between the towns, and it became **Center Molson**. Today, Old Molson is an outdoor museum, and the Center Molson school building is also a museum.

One of the few bed and breakfasts in these parts is the **Hidden Hills Guest Ranch** (144 Fish Lake Road, Tonasket; 509–486–1890, 800–168–1890), a Victorian-style inn surrounded by fields of wildflowers and pine trees. The ten guest rooms, most of which offer mountain views, have a turn-of-the-century feel with flocked wallpaper, pedestal sinks, brass beds and gleaming woodwork. Moderate rates.

In Omak, you'll find several small, budget-priced generic motels including the **Thrift Lodge** (122 North Main Street; 509–826–0400, fax 509–826–5635) and **Leisure Village Motel** (630 Okoma Drive; 509–826–4442).

Several small resorts are scattered along lakes in the area. Among them are **Bonaparte Lake Resort** (695 Bonaparte Lake Road, Tonasket; 509–486–2828), 26 miles from both Republic and Tonasket. There are ten airy and clean log cabins along the lakeshore. Only one—called, of all things, the Penthouse—has a bathroom, bedding, towels and kitchen supplies. There's a public shower and bathroom. Budget.

A mile east of Kettle Falls on Route 395 is **My Parent's Estate Bed and Breakfast** (719 Route 395; 509–738–6220), one of the first bed and breakfasts in this part of the state. It was formerly a Catholic mission with a convent added later, then a boys' school. It offers three rooms with baths, queen-size beds and central air conditioning. Each room is named for its period decor and furnishings: Queen Anne Lace, English Cottage room and French Country room. Included on the 47 acres are a gazebo, gymnasium, pond and a trail to the Colville River. Moderate.

OKANOGAN HIGHLANDS RESTAURANTS

Standard fare is pretty much the order of the day here. For starters, there is the **Cedars Inn Restaurant and Lounge** (Route 97 and Route 20, Okanogan; 509–422–6431), which serves straightforward lunches and dinners and farmer-size breakfasts. Moderate.

For some local color and reasonable prices, try the **Double J Café** (Okanogan Livestock Market, 529 Van Dyne Road; 509–422–3660).

IT'S ALL RECENT HISTORY

Compared with the rest of the country, Washington's history is both recent and benign. The Northwest is so newly settled that East Coast visitors look askance when they find that the major cities weren't founded until the latter part of the last century. Very little recorded history goes back before 1800; the Lewis and Clark Expedition of 1804–1806 was the first overland crossing between the original 13 states and the Pacific Coast, and they were the first to describe the lower Snake River.

Osoyoos Lake is a prime nesting area for Canadian geese.

This is a place where you can have an old-fashioned breakfast and lunch—complete with homemade soups, stews and pies—while listening to the auctioneer selling horses and cattle. Wednesday through Friday only; budget.

The choices are fewer in Omak, but one café that rates high is the **Breadline Café** (102 South Ash Street; 509-826-5836), where the lunch menu features big sandwiches on whole-grain breads and the dinner menu includes shrimp creole, jambalaya, mushroom marinara over pasta and pork loin medallion. It may be the only place in the twin towns where you can ask for bean sprouts and get them. And there's antique decor to boot. Moderate.

Oroville has a few places to grab a bite to eat, including the **Whistle Stop Restaurant** (1918 North Main Street; 509-476-2515). It is decorated with railroad memorabilia in keeping with the town's emphasis on antique stores. Moderate.

In Tonasket you can dine, dance and gamble in the **Villa Fare** (21 West 6th Street; 509-486-4127). Breakfasts—big ones—are served all day. The drinking and gambling are done in the Bullpen Lounge. Moderate.

One of the more interesting places to stop for a snack or down-home American meal is **Wauconda** (Route 20, Wauconda; 509-486-4010), the one-store town on Route 20 east of Tonasket. A lunch counter to the left of the door is crammed between the cash register and a small dining room with a few booths overlooking a valley and low mountains beyond. The food is uncomplicated and hearty, and the portions are generous, especially the prime rib that is the house special on Friday and Saturday. Budget to moderate.

OKANOGAN HIGHLANDS SHOPPING

One of the area's largest antique and arts-and-crafts stores is the **Country Harvest General Store** (509-476-3118), in the center of Oroville on Route 97. In addition to antiques, it stocks pottery, paintings, crafts and toys made locally.

In Chesaw, a town of some 30 souls a few miles east of Molson that is making a comeback from ghost-town status, the **Country Gift Shop** specializes in the work of "artisans of rural Washington."

OKANOGAN HIGHLANDS NIGHTLIFE

Most nightlife in this cowboy and fruit-picking area is limited to taverns, a few of which have live bands on weekends and during the Omak Stampede, the rodeo held each August.

OKANOGAN HIGHLANDS PARKS

Northwest of Omak on Conconully–Okanogan Highway, you'll find **Conconully State Park** (509-826-7408) strung along the edge of the town of the same name. This site is popular with boaters, swimmers, campers, families and anglers. For hikers, there is a nature trail. Other facilities include picnic areas and a wading pool.

Primarily an interpretive park, **Fort Okanogan** (509-689-2798, 509-923-2473) is set above the junction of the Okanogan and Columbia rivers and features a visitors center on the bluff overlooking the fort's original site, now under the waters of Wells Dam backwaters. The center tells the history of Fort Okanogan, which played an important role in the nation's fur trade. There are picnic sites and restrooms. The park is located at the junction of Routes 97 and 17 between Brewster and Bridgeport.

Osoyoos State Park (509-476-3321) is the most popular state park in the area. Located one mile north of Oroville, the park stretches along the southern end of Osoyoos Lake and offers some of the few trees in the area for shade while picnicking and camping. It is heavily used by Canadians and Americans alike since it is almost on the Canadian border. You can fish year-round for trout and spiny-ray.

On 128 acres, **Curlew Lake State Park** (509-775-3592) lies in a pine forest on the southeastern shore of a lake that is dotted with several islands. Remnants of homesteaders' cabins can be seen near the park, and a large variety of animals, including chipmunks, squirrels and deer, live in the area. Several species of birds also make the park their home. The park is surrounded by Colville National Forest. There are picnic areas, restrooms, campsites, swimming area and boat launch; the fishing is good. Located ten miles north of Republic on Route 21.

SCENIC ROUTE 20

*One of Washington's best highways for leisurely rural driving is **Route 20**, especially east of Route 97 as it traverses the Okanogan Country on its way to the Idaho border. It comes in from the Cascades to Omak–Okanogan, joins Route 97 north to Tonasket, swings east across the heart of the highlands through Wauconda and Republic, crosses the Columbia River at Kettle Falls and continues on to Tiger, where it traces the Pend Oreille River south to the Idaho border at Newport. There it disappears. The highway follows the path of least resistance along valleys and beside streams where ranches stretch off across the rolling hills that eventually turn into pine forests.*

Grand Coulee Dam was built in the 1930s and memorialized by the songs of Woody Guthrie.

Grand Coulee Area

The centerpiece of the Grand Coulee Area, not surprisingly, is Grand Coulee Dam. The sheer mass of the dam is almost overwhelming and for decades it was the largest concrete structure in the world.

Also of interest are the many lakes created by the dam, which have become some of Washington's most popular recreation areas. The backwaters of the dam itself, named in honor of President Franklin D. Roosevelt, reach far north nearly to the Canadian border and east into the Spokane River system. A chain of lakes and some smaller dams were built as part of an irrigation project to hold water for distribution south and east of the dam. These include Banks Lake and the Potholes Reservoir, known as the Winchester Wasteway. Don't be put off by the name because wasteway refers to the water that has been used for irrigation and has seeped along bedrock to emerge again ready for reuse. These lakes continue on south to the Crab Creek Valley before re-entering the Columbia River below Vantage.

Grand Coulee Dam (509-633-9265) was the largest concrete pour in the world for many decades after its completion at the beginning of World War II. It stands 550 feet above bedrock, as tall as a 46-story building, and at 5223 feet, it's nearly a mile long. While its 12 million cubic yards of concrete may be difficult to imagine, the Bureau of Reclamation points out that this is enough to build a standard six-foot-wide sidewalk around the world at the Equator.

In addition to the 151-mile-long Roosevelt Lake used to power the hydroelectric system, the dam serves the additional purpose of irrigating more than 500,000 acres. Water is pumped 280 feet up the canyon wall to fill Banks Lake's reservoir, from which the water is moved through canals and pipes to the area's farmland.

Visitors are welcome at the dam and can go on self-guided tours. One of the most popular events is the nightly **laser show**, a free, 40-minute demonstration that uses the spillway of the dam for its screen. It is shown from Memorial Day through September.

In Coulee Dam, the **Colville Tribal Museum and Gift Shop** (516 Birch Street; 509-633-0751) displays authentic village and fishing scenes, coins and metals dating from the 1800s.

The best way to appreciate the stark beauty of the Grand Coulee area is to drive south from the dam on Route 155 along **Banks Lake**. The artificial lake is used for all watersports, and its color and character change dramatically with the time of day and weather.

At Coulee City you come to the **Dry Falls Dam**, which holds Banks Lake water and sends it on south into a system of canals. Pinto Ridge Road heads due south from Coulee City and passes **Summer Lake**, a favorite picnic spot. The falls are created by the irrigation water from Banks Lake.

The main route out of Coulee City is across Dry Falls Dam, then south on Route 17 past Dry Falls and Sun Lakes State Park, along a series of smaller lakes in the coulees—Park Lake, Blue Lake, Lake Lenore (where you can see the form of a small rhinoceros that was trapped in a prehistoric lava flow) and finally to Soap Lake.

South of Soap Lake, the coulees flatten out and the landscape away from the Columbia River becomes Washington's gently rolling wheat-growing region. **Moses Lake** is the last town of any size connected with the Columbia Basin and is better known as a hub for farmers of the basin than as a tourist destination. The lake for which the town is named joins the Potholes Reservoir to the south.

GRAND COULEE AREA LODGING

If you want a room with a view, there are two good places near the dam. One is **Ponderosa Motel** (10 Lincoln Street, Coulee Dam; 509-633-2100, 800-633-6421, fax 509-633-2633), right across the street from Grand Coulee Dam. Each room has a view of the spillway and the nightly laser light shows in the summer. The 20-year-old motel has 34 rooms on two floors. Two rooms have jacuzzis, and you pay for it. Moderate.

The other is **Coulee House Motel** (110 Roosevelt Way, Coulee Dam; 509-633-1101, 800-715-7767, fax 509-633-1416), which is up a steep hill and provides a top-notch view. It has clean, unremarkable rooms. Moderate.

Also in the moderate-price range, **Four Winds Guest House** (301 Lincoln Street, Coulee Dam; 509-633-3146, 800-786-3146) is a large, wood-frame Cape Cod bed and breakfast across the street from City

---

COULEE CAN BE CONFUSING

This area is frequently baffling to visitors because of the similarity of place names. The towns of Coulee Dam and Grand Coulee are at the site of Grand Coulee Dam itself, while Coulee City is 30 miles away at the southern end of Banks Lake. In the same area are still two more small towns with names that often get confused: Elmer City and Electric City.

During the summer months, Grand Coulee Dam hosts spectacular laser light shows.

Hall. It was originally used as a rooming house while the dam was being built in the 1930s. All rooms have furniture from that period, and all have wash basins. Two rooms have a shared bath; otherwise, the bathrooms are at the end of the hall.

Several budget-priced motels and resorts are along the shores of Banks and Roosevelt lakes. One of the cleanest and least expensive is the **Lakeview II Motel & Spa** (9811 Fordair Road Northeast, Coulee City; 509-632-5792) at the south end of Banks Lake a half-mile off Route 2 at the intersection with Route 155. The motel has picnic tables, a whirlpool and a sauna. Some rooms have kitchens; all have refrigerators.

In Soap Lake, **Notaris Lodge** (242 Main Street; 509-246-0462) is the best known and most modern motel in town. It also boasts an unusual decor in its rooms with names like the "Bonnie Guitar" room (the entertainer grew up in the area). Another room is called the "Ben Snipes" in honor of a pioneer cattleman and has cowboy gear for decoration. The accommodations are spacious and equipped with microwave ovens, refrigerators and breakfast nooks. Massages, whirlpool and mineral baths in Soap Lake water are available. Moderate.

Moses Lake is one of the most popular RV destinations in the central part of the state because several lakes are in the immediate vicinity, and hot, sunny weather is almost guaranteed. Several motels are also located along the Route 90 corridor and the lake, including the **Best Western Hallmark Inn** (3000 Marina Drive; 509-765-9211, 800-235-4255, fax 509-766-0493), which has 160 units right on Moses Lake. In addition to boating and waterskiing, right off the dock, the motel has tennis courts, a heated pool and sauna. Moderate.

The **Lakeshore Motel** (3206 West Lakeshore Drive; 509-765-9201, fax 509-765-1800) is also on the lake and has a marina with waterskiing available, as well as a heated pool. There are also nine housekeeping cabins. Budget to moderate in price.

GRAND COULEE AREA RESTAURANTS

The best-known eatery in this region is the **Wildlife Restaurant** (113 Midway Avenue, Grand Coulee; 509-633-1160). It has a bar with oak decor, big dining room with Spanish motif and a large menu with an emphasis on beef and seafood. Moderate.

In Grand Coulee, try the **Sage Inn** (413 Midway Avenue; 509-633-0550) for diner-style food: soups, sandwiches and pie. Budget.

If you're craving Italian, stop in at **That Italian Place** (515 Grand Coulee Boulevard, Grand Coulee; 509-633-1818), a popular family-style eatery. This restaurant serves up pizza, pasta, calzone and hoagie sandwiches at budget prices.

Also in Grand Coulee, if you want Oriental food, **Siam Palace** (213 Main Street; 509-633-2921) will have it. Thai, Chinese and American dishes are served. Budget.

GRAND COULEE AREA SHOPPING

In Coulee Dam, the **Colville Tribal Museum and Gift Shop** (516 Birch Street; 509-633-0751) sells local beadwork and other artwork by tribal members.

GRAND COULEE AREA NIGHTLIFE

Moses Lake (Route 17 out of Coulee City; 509-765-7888) has a series of free concerts, all beginning at 8 p.m. from May to September, in its 3000-seat outdoor amphitheater on the lakeshore. Nationally known musicians perform.

GRAND COULEE AREA PARKS

Coulee Dam National Recreation Area (Route 155, north of Coulee City; 509-633-9441) stretches 151 miles along the entire length of Roosevelt Lake, including parts of the Spokane and Kettle rivers. Due to the arid climate, the lake has miles and miles of sandy beaches and outcroppings of dramatic rocks. Only when you get close to the Spokane River do trees begin appearing along the shoreline. It is a particular favorite for waterskiers. Sailing and windsurfing are also popular. There are numerous campgrounds and picnic areas. You can fish for more than 30 species, including walleye, rainbow trout, sturgeon, yellow perch and kokanee, the land-locked salmon.

SOAP LAKE

Soap Lake was so named because the water forms foam, or "soap suds," along the shore when the wind blows. The water is rich in minerals—sodium, chloride, carbonate, sulphate, bicarbonate and others—so it has attracted a number of motels that pump water for use in the rooms. Spas are also located here and people come to soak in the mineral-rich water, seeking relief from a variety of skin, muscle and bone afflictions.

More than 200 species of fossilized trees have been identified in Ginkgo Petrified Forest State Park.

Steamboat Rock State Park (Route 155, south of Grand Coulee; 509-633-1304) requires camping-space reservations because of its popularity. The park is on the shores of Banks Lake at the foot of the butte by the same name. The ship-shaped butte rises 700 feet above the lake and has a good trail to the 640-acre flat top. There are picnic tables, playground equipment, a bathhouse and snack bar. Swimming and fishing are both good here.

Sun Lakes State Park (Route 17, seven miles southwest of Coulee City; 509-632-5583) is located on the floor of the coulee that was scoured out when the Columbia River's normal course was blocked by ice and debris at the end of the last ice age. The river, three miles wide, flowed over nearby 400-foot-high Dry Falls, which was the original name of the state park but was changed because of the lakes and recreation. It is now home to boating, riding, hiking and golfing. Included in the park is Camp Delaney, an environmental learning center with air-conditioned cabins; information, 360-586-6022. Note: A private concessionaire (Sun Lakes Park Resort, HCR 1 Box 141, Coulee City, WA 98115; 509-632-5291) operates many of the services within the park, including cabin rentals, a trailer park and hookups, a general store, the restaurant and soda-fountain, service station, heated swimming pool, boat rentals, riding stables, laundry and a nine-hole golf course.

The Potholes Reservoir was created when water from the Columbia Basin Project seeped in to fill depressions around the coarse sand dunes in the area. Now the sand dunes stand above the water level and are used for campsites, bird blinds and picnic areas at **Potholes State Park** (6762 Route 262 East, 12 miles south of Moses Lake; 509-346-2759). The area supports a large population of waterfowl and other birds, including blue herons, white pelicans, sand-hill cranes, hawks and eagles. A lawn and shade trees, tables and stoves are beside the lake. There are boat ramps and fishing for rainbow trout, bass, perch, crappie, bluegill and walleye.

An area of barren hillsides and lava flows, **Ginkgo Petrified Forest State Park** boasts one of the largest fossil forests in the world. The park has an interpretive center overlooking the Columbia River with a wide selection of petrified wood. No camping, fishing or swimming is permitted at Ginkgo, but you can head four-and-a-half miles south on the Columbia River to the **Wanapum Recreation Area**. It also has hiking trails, and there is a one-mile interpretive trail at Ginkgo, as well. There are picnic areas and restrooms; information, 509-856-2700. The park is located on the edge of Vantage, a tiny town at the spot where Route 90 crosses the Columbia River.

Spokane Area

Spokane is where the Midas-rich miners from Idaho came to live in the late 19th century, so the city has an abundance of historic homes, museums, bed and breakfasts and inns, and one of the most beautiful city park systems in the West.

The best way to become acquainted with Spokane is to take the self-guided "City Drive Tour" outlined in a brochure from the city that is available in all hotels and at the **Spokane Convention and Visitors Bureau** (926 West Sprague Avenue; 509-624-1341). Another useful brochure is the self-guided tour of historic architecture in downtown Spokane. The "City Drive Tour" takes you along Cliff Drive where many of the finest old homes stand and through **Manito Park** (Stevens Street and 5th Avenue), one of the city's largest parks. In Manito Park, you'll find the **Duncan Formal Gardens**, whose lush scenery looks like something out of a movie set in 18th-century Europe.

The tour continues past **St. Stephen's Episcopal Church** (57th Avenue and Hatch Road) and **Comstock Park** (High Drive Parkway and 29th Avenue), which has a large public swimming pool and picnic area. It continues on to the **Cheney Cowles Memorial Museum** (2316 West 1st Avenue; 509-456-3931; admission) with its major collection of regional history and fine art. Next is **Finch Arboretum** on Sunset Boulevard, which features an extensive collection of trees from all over the world. From here, the tour leads you back to the downtown area.

The city is most proud of **Riverfront Park** (507 North Howard Street; 509-625-6600), located downtown and known for the natural beauty of its waterfall and island. It has the restored 1909 Looff Carrousel, a gondola skyride over Spokane Falls, various other rides, food concessions and a 70mm IMAX Theater. It also has footpaths, natural amphitheaters, lawns and hills, and always the roar of the waterfall for a backdrop.

Commemorating Spokane's most famous native son, Gonzaga University's **Bing Crosby Memorabilia Room** (502 East Boone Avenue;

CHÂTEAU COURTHOUSE

*In Spokane, a must-see is the **Spokane County Courthouse** (across the river from downtown on Broadway just off Monroe Avenue; 509-456-2211). It resembles the 16th-century Château de Chambord and Château d'Azay Le Rideau. Oddly enough, the courthouse was designed in the 1890s by a young man whose only formal training in architecture came from a correspondence course. It is a magnificent conglomeration of towers and turrets, sculpture, iron and brickwork in a French Renaissance style.*

There's a Japanese garden in Manito Park created by Spokane's sister city in Japan.

509-328-4220) is home to the crooner's Oscar, gold records, photographs and other items. More memorabilia is on display at the **Gonzaga Alumni Association** (East 508 Sharp Street), Crosby's boyhood home.

Spokane has several wineries with sales and tasting rooms. **Worden Winery** (7217 West 45th Avenue; 509-455-7835) is one of the largest in the area with a capacity of 50,000 gallons. **Arbor Crest Wine Cellars** (4705 North Fruithill Road; 509-927-9894) is in a building designated a National Historic Site and perched on a bluff overlooking the Spokane River. **Latah Creek Wine Cellars** (13030 East Indiana Avenue; 509-926-0164) has a Spanish-style building with a large courtyard and a tasting room decorated with oak. **Knipprath Cellars** (163 South Lincoln Street; 509-624-9132) is in the downtown area and offers a tasting room decorated with Victorian furnishings.

SPOKANE AREA LODGING

Spokane has some pleasant hotels that don't carry big-city rates like those in Seattle and Portland. You won't find deluxe or luxury accommodations here, but the down-home hospitality of the hotel staffs more than makes up for it.

Two of the largest offer perhaps the best rooms and service. The **West Coast Ridpath** (515 West Sprague Avenue; 509-838-6122, 800-426-0670, fax 509-459-1034) is an old establishment downtown, divided into two buildings across the street from each other with a second-story skywalk connecting them. The second building has the larger rooms, and all look inside to the courtyard and swimming pool. The lobby is small, but the staff is cheerful. There are two restaurants. Moderate.

The **Sheraton Spokane Hotel** (322 North Spokane Falls Court; 509-455-9600, 800-848-9600, fax 509-455-6285) was built for Spokane's 1974 World's Fair and has the best location, right along the Spokane River and on the Riverfront Park. The lobby is impressive, and most rooms have good views of the river, park and downtown. It also has a covered pool. Moderate to deluxe.

The **Friendship Inn** (4301 West Sunset Boulevard; 509-838-1471) is a favorite of many who visit Spokane frequently. Built on a hill west of town, it is roughly halfway between the airport and downtown, is quiet and affords good views of the city's growing skyline. Budget.

A newer downtown establishment is **Cavanaugh's Inn at the Park** (303 West North River Drive; 509-326-8000, 800-843-4667, fax 509-335-7329). It has 400 rooms and is across North River Drive from the

Riverfront Park. Unfortunately, it is just far enough away from the river to lose some of the waterfront charm. The inn is walking distance from downtown, and some of the rooms have private decks. Moderate to deluxe.

SPOKANE AREA RESTAURANTS

Spokane's most popular Asian cuisine comes from the two **Mustard Seed Oriental Cafés** (245 West Spokane Falls Boulevard, 509-747-2689; and East 9806 Sprague Avenue; 509-924-3194). The menu offers specialties from several provinces in China, as well as Japanese and American dishes. The downtown location is open and airy, and the service brisk and friendly. Moderate.

The most striking restaurant in Spokane is **Patsy Clark's** (2208 West 2nd Avenue; 509-838-8300). Located in a mansion designed for a millionaire miner, it has marble from Italy, wood carvings from England and an enormous, stained-glass window from Tiffany. Meals are served in several rooms, and during good weather drinks are served on the second-story veranda. The restaurant maintains a high standard for steaks, seafood, duckling, lamb and veal. Deluxe to ultra-deluxe.

Fort Spokane Brewery (401 West Spokane Falls Boulevard; 509-838-3809) is Spokane's only microbrewery, and pub food is served daily. Moderate.

SPOKANE AREA SHOPPING

The Skywalk in the downtown core, a series of weatherproof bridges that connect 15 blocks on the second level, makes downtown shopping pleasant year-round. It leads to the major downtown department stores such as **Nordstrom** (Post Street and Main Avenue; 509-455-6111) and **Bon Marche** (Main Avenue and Wall Street; 509-747-5111), several specialty shops, restaurants and art galleries.

Spokane has had a surge of discount stores, from national chain stores to the West Coast warehouse stores. Shopping centers have sprung up

---

BED-AND-BREAKFAST BEST

Fotheringham House (2128 West 2nd Avenue; 509-838-1891, fax 509-838-1807) is Spokane's best bed and breakfast, and, for that matter, one of the best in the state. Fotheringham House is in the Brown's Addition, Spokane's equivalent of San Francisco's Nob Hill, the part of town where many of the mining barons built their homes. There are three guest rooms with Victorian furnishings in keeping with the architecture. A pleasant bonus is their prices, which are moderate.

Canadians will drive over a hundred miles to do their shopping in Spokane, where nearly all goods are less expensive.

on the north and northeast edges of town. Covered shopping areas include **Northtown Mall** (Division Street and Wellesley Avenue), **Franklin Park Mall** (Division Street and Rowan Avenue) and **University City** (Sprague Avenue and University Street).

The **Flour Mill** (West 621 Mallon Street) is one of the more charming places to shop. It was built as a flour mill, but was turned into a specialty shopping center in 1974 with more than 20 shops, including bookstores, clothing and gift stores, cafés and restaurants.

Fresh vegetables, fruit and berries are one of the area's best buys. The **Green Bluff Growers** (East Bay Road, Mead; 509-238-4709), a marketing cooperative, publishes a map each year with directions to its member orchards, vegetable farms and Christmas-tree farms.

SPOKANE AREA NIGHTLIFE

You'll find live jazz and Top-40 music and dancing at **Ankeny's** on the top floor of the Ridpath Hotel (515 West Sprague Avenue; 509-838-2711) Monday through Saturday.

JJ's Lounge (Sheraton Hotel, 322 North Spokane Falls Court; 509-455-9600) has Top-40 music Tuesday through Saturday. Cover.

For a lively spot, try **Papagayo's Cantina** (4111 North Division Street; 509-483-8346), where locals gather for televised sporting events.

Dempsey's Brass Rail (West 901 1st Street; 509-747-5362) is a popular gay and lesbian nightspot with dancefloor and piano bar.

The **Spokane Jazz Orchestra** (P.O. Box 40137, Spokane, WA 99202; 509-458-0366) performs big band–style concerts throughout the year at various venues around town.

The **Spokane Symphony Orchestra** (601 West Riverside Drive; 509-624-1200) performs a number of times throughout the year, including outdoor concerts in Comstock Park in the summer.

The **Spokane Civic Theater** (1020 North Howard Street; 509-325-1413) presents musicals, dramas and comedies year-round.

SPOKANE AREA PARKS

On the northwest edge of Spokane at the junction of Route 291 and Aubrey L. White Parkway, 7655-acre **Riverside State Park** (509-456-3964) includes nearly eight miles of Spokane River shoreline. There are odd basaltic formations in the river and Indian paintings on rocks. The park is wheelchair accessible and houses the Spokane House interpretive center, which tells the history of Spokane. You can fish for rainbow trout in the river. You'll also find horse trails and places to picnic.

Mount Spokane State Park (509-456-4169) is used as much or more in the winter as summer, but warm-weather visitors will find the views from the 5881-foot mountain spectacular: Idaho, Montana, Canada and much of Washington can be seen from the summit. It is especially pretty during the spring when its slopes are blanketed with flowers and in the fall when the fields are brown and the leaves have turned. For those into winter sports, there are downhill and cross-country skiing, snowmobiling and sledding. During warm weather, the park has some of the best mountain biking in Washington. The park is located at the end of Route 206, 30 miles northeast of Spokane.

Turnbull National Wildlife Refuge (509-235-4723) is one of the most popular natural places for day trips in the Spokane area. The refuge was established primarily for waterfowl in 1937. It has several lakes and undisturbed wooded areas and a marked, self-guided auto-tour route. You'll also find hiking and cross-country skiing trails. On Badger Lake Road, five miles south of Cheney.

Southeastern Washington

The drive from Spokane south to Oregon is one of unusual beauty, especially early or late in the day, or in the spring or fall. The entire region between the wooded hills around Spokane to the Blue Mountains is known as the Palouse Country. Here, the barren hills are low but steep, and wheat is grown on nearly every acre.

Proceeding south from Spokane along Route 195, you'll find that the two best places to view the Palouse Hills are **Steptoe Butte State Park** (see "Southeastern Washington Beaches and Parks" below) and Kamiak Butte in **Kamiak Butte County Park**, which stands 3650 feet high and offers bird's-eye views of the Palouse Hills. The park has picnic areas, camping, a hiking trail and, unlike Steptoe Butte, a fringe of trees

---

WASHINGTON'S WINERIES

Yakima County is the state's wine center. Some 40 wineries have been built between Walla Walla and Yakima, and they have helped create a tourist industry that has encouraged the growth of country inns and bed and breakfasts. Brochures listing the wineries and locations are available in visitors centers and many convenience stores, and once you're off Route 82, signs mark routes to the wineries.

The cemetery at Fort Walla Walla contains victims from both sides of the first conflicts with the Indians.

on its crest and more than 100 kinds of vegetation, including the Douglas fir more common to the damp, coastal climate. Kamiak Butte is 18 miles east of Colfax and 15 miles north of Pullman off Route 27.

The town of Pullman is almost entirely a product of Washington State University, although a few agricultural businesses operate on the edge of town. Continuing south from this campus town, Route 195 gains elevation through the small farming communities of Colton and Uniontown, then crosses over into the edge of Idaho just in time to disappear into Route 95 and then take a dizzying plunge down the steep Lewiston Hill, where you drop 2000 feet in a very short time over a twisting highway. The old highway with its hair-pin turns is still passable and is exciting driving if your brakes and nerves are in good condition.

Clarkston, Washington, and Lewiston, Idaho, are separated by the Snake River, which flows almost due north through Hell's Canyon before taking a sudden westward turn where Idaho's Clearwater River enters in Lewiston. Most of the Snake River boat operators are head-quartered in these two towns. For more information, contact the **Clarkston Chamber of Commerce** (502 Bridge Street; 509-758-7712).

The population has followed the Snake on its way west to join with the Columbia, but it is a tamed river now, a series of slackwater pools in deep canyons behind a series of dams: Lower Granite, Little Goose, Lower Monumental and Ice Harbor. The main highway doesn't follow the Snake River because of the deep canyon it carved, so from Clarkston you follow Route 12 west through the farming communities of Pomeroy and Dayton to Walla Walla, then on to the Tri-Cities area around Richland, where the Snake enters the Columbia River. Along the way is Dayton, an agricultural town with a large asparagus cannery. The town raised funds to preserve the beautiful **Dayton Depot** (Main Street; 509-382-4825), a classic Victorian building that had an upper floor for the station master's quarters.

Walla Walla looks much like a New England town that was packed up and moved to the rolling hills of eastern Washington, weeping willows, oak and maple trees included. Best known for its colleges, Whitman and Walla Walla, the town has many ivy-covered buildings, quiet streets lined with old frame houses, enormous shade trees and, rather incongruously amid this Norman Rockwellian beauty, the state penitentiary.

You can learn about the heritage of southeast Washington at the **Fort Walla Walla Museum Complex** (755 Myra Road, Walla Walla; 509-525-7703; admission). A pioneer village composed of 16 early frontier buildings and replicas and five large exhibit buildings make this museum an excellent place to begin your visit to the Walla Walla area. A pioneer cabin built in 1877 and furnished with period artifacts, an old country rail depot, a completely outfitted one-room school and a doctor's office are among the highlights. Above the pioneer village, you'll find wide-ranging displays featuring family heirlooms, agriculture and World War II's impact on the region.

You'll enjoy seeing the stately old trees centered around Pioneer Park and the Whitman College campus. With 360 acres of parks, Walla Walla is a pleasure to explore. Be sure to visit the town's splendid late 19th-century **Kirkman House** (Colville and Sumach streets). To see more of the city by foot, stop by the **Chamber of Commerce** (29 East Sumach Street; 509-525-0850) to pick up the *Walking Guide to the Big Trees of Walla Walla.*

At **Whitman Mission National Historic Site** (509-529-2761; admission), one of the Northwest's worst tragedies occurred because of a basic misunderstanding of Native American values by an American missionary, Marcus Whitman and his wife, Narcissa, who founded a mission among the Cayuse tribe in 1836 in an attempt to convert them to Christianity. As traffic increased on the Oregon Trail, the mission became an important stop for travelers. Eleven years later, the Cayuse felt betrayed by Whitman because his religion hadn't protected them from a measles epidemic that killed half the tribe. On November 29, 1847, the Cayuse killed the Whitmans and nine others and ransomed 50 others to the Hudson's Bay Company. The site is seven miles west of Walla Walla on Route 12 and is administered by the National Park Service. There's a visitors center, memorial monument, millpond and walking paths to sites where various buildings once stood. None of the original buildings remain.

The Columbia River runs free for about 60 miles through the Hanford Reservation, but when it swings through the Tri-Cities (Richland, Pasco and Kennewick) it becomes Lake Wallula, thanks to McNary Dam. Several city parks with picnic and boating facilities are along the river, such as **Columbia Park** in Kennewick.

A SCENIC DRIVE DOWN A CROOKED HIGHWAY

Only in the late 1980s was the highway completely paved between the Snake River Canyon and the Wallowas in Oregon. But now you can take one of the prettiest mountain drives in the Northwest by following Route 129 south from Clarkston in the southeastern corner of Washington through Anatone, then down into the Grande Ronde River valley over probably the most crooked highway in the Northwest. Be sure your brakes (and fortitude) are in good condition.

Fort Simcoe is arguably the best-preserved frontier army post in the West.

The Tri-Cities are best known for the nuclear-power plant and research center in nearby Hanford. It was here that the components for the first atomic bombs were assembled. Two nuclear-related visitors centers tell the nuclear story. **Hanford Museum of Science and History** (Federal Building, on Jadwin Avenue near Lee Boulevard, Richland; 509-376-6374) is operated by Westinghouse for the Department of Energy and tells of the various sources of energy. Another nuclear facility for visitors is the **Washington Public Power Supply System Plant 2 Visitors Center** (12 miles north of Richland off Stevens Drive; 509-377-4558), which offers a tour of the state's first commercial nuclear-power plant.

From the Tri-Cities, the population follows the Yakima River. The **Yakima Valley** is one of the state's richest in terms of agriculture: Yakima County ranks first nationally in the number of fruit trees, first in the production of apples, mint and hops, and fifth in the value of all fruits grown.

Fort Simcoe State Park (end of Fort Simcoe Road, about 35 miles south of Yakima; 509-874-2372) is home to one of the few forts where no shots were fired in anger. It was used in the late 1850s during the conflict with the Native Americans. It has a museum and interpretive center. Four of the original buildings are still standing, including the commanding officer's home.

If you are a rail buff, you can ride the rails on **Yakima Interurban Lines** (509-575-1700), which runs from 3rd Avenue and Pine Street in downtown Yakima five miles to Selah on weekends and holidays.

Three important museums are in the Yakima Valley. One is the **Yakama Nation Cultural Center** (Route 97, Fort Road, Toppenish; 509-865-2800; admission). Here, the history of the tribe is told in dioramas and writings by and about the tribe preserved in a large library. The center also has a theater for films and concerts.

The Central Washington Agricultural Museum (4508 Main Street, Union Gap; 509-457-8735) has a good-size collection of early farm machinery, including a working windmill, a blacksmith shop and a tool collection.

The **Yakima Valley Museum** (2105 Tieton Drive, Yakima; 509-248-0747; admission) has the most comprehensive collection of horse-drawn vehicles west of the Mississippi, an extensive collection of furniture and other belongings of the late Supreme Court Justice William O. Douglas and a fine pioneer photo collection.

Another museum that recalls the early days of the region is the **Sunnyside Historical Museum** (704 South 4th Street, Sunnyside; 509-837-6010). The elegant white building houses displays of Native American artifacts and a pioneer kitchen and dining room. Across the street is the **Ben Snipes Cabin**, dating from 1859.

An alternate route from Yakima down to the Columbia River is the **Mabton–Bickleton Road**, which heads south from the small town of Mabton through the even smaller Bickleton. An unincorporated town with a scattering of Victorian houses and falsefront store buildings, Bickleton's claim to fame is hundreds of houses for (are you ready for this?) bluebirds. Maintained by residents, the houses are on fence posts along the highway and country lanes and literally all over town. The one in front of the community church is a miniature copy of the church itself.

Twelve miles outside of Bickleton sits the funky **Whoop N Holler Museum** (1 Whitmore Road at East Road; 509-896-2344; admission). The owners showcase a vast array of turn-of-the-century pioneer memorabilia, much of which was handed down through their families. Highlights are the large classic auto collection and various horse-drawn vehicles, including an antique hearse on sled runners.

SOUTHEASTERN WASHINGTON LODGING

It's difficult to find anything other than your basic, cookie-cutter motel in southeast Washington, although Yakima shows some imagination.

Pullman has about half a dozen motels, none particularly distinguished, and all budget or moderate in price. The best view is offered by the **Hilltop Motor Inn** (Davis Way; 509-334-2555, fax 509-332-3120). The **Quality Inn** (1050 Bishop Boulevard; 509-332-0500, 800-669-3212, fax 509-334-4271) is near both the campus and the airport.

Walla Walla has about ten motels, most of them in the moderate range. One is **Nandell's Whitman Motor Inn** (107 North 2nd Street; 509-525-2200, 800-237-4436, fax 509-522-1428), which also has some deluxe-priced rooms. A block away is the **Tapadera Budget Inn** (211 North 2nd Street; 509-529-2580, 800-722-8277, fax 509-522-1380), which offers a continental breakfast. Budget.

The Tri-Cities area offers several fair-sized motels, many with meeting rooms since the Hanford Nuclear Center is nearby. One of the largest is the **Ramada Inn on Clover Island** (435 Clover Island; 509-586-0541, 800-628-7458, fax 509-586-6956), built on an island in the Columbia River. Every room has a view of the river, and the restaurant is open 24 hours a day. It has a pool, hot tub and sauna. Moderate.

Yakima does a lively convention business, and one of the best places to stay is next door to the convention center. **Cavanaugh's** (607 East Yakima Avenue; 509-248-5900, 800-843-4667, fax 509-575-8975) has 152 large, comfortable rooms with colorful furnishings and spacious bathrooms, two heated pools, dining room and coffee shop. Moderate.

SOUTHEASTERN WASHINGTON RESTAURANTS

In Pullman, *the* place to eat is **The Seasons** (205 Southeast Paradise Street; 509-334-1410), on the hill near Washington State University. It is an elegant setting in a renovated house and has a menu that changes frequently. Moderate.

The **Hilltop Steakhouse** (Davis Way; 509-334-2555) shares the steep hill with the Hilltop Motor Inn. It caters to the local trade with thick steaks, Sunday brunches and afternoon dinners. Moderate.

If you're good at what you do, so goes the saying, the world will beat a path to your door. This could be the slogan for **Patit Creek Restaurant** (725 East Dayton Avenue, Dayton; 509-382-2625). It has been in business since 1978 and has built a national reputation for excellent dishes in what is most accurately described as French country cuisine. Meat is the specialty—beef and lamb. Most of the food is grown locally, some by the staff, and since some of the luxurious plants inside and around the outside are herbs, they may one day season your food. Moderate.

If you're feeling nostalgic for New York delis, **Merchant's Ltd.** (21 East Main Street, Walla Walla; 509-525-0900) will help. It has a wide choice of foods and a sidewalk café ideal for Walla Walla's mostly sunny weather. Budget.

The **Cedars** (7 Clover Island, Kennewick; 509-582-2143) is one of the Tri-Cities' most striking restaurants. It is cantilevered over the Columbia River with boat-docking facilities. The specialties are steaks, seafood and prime rib. Moderate to deluxe.

Emerald of Siam (1314 Jadwin Avenue, Richland; 509-946-9328) serves authentic Thai food in a former drug store that has a combination of French, Thai and American decor and menu. A buffet lunch is served on weekdays, or you may order from the menu. Budget.

Located in Yakima's North Front Street Historical District, **Deli de Pasta** (7 North Front Street; 509-453-0571) is a charming, small Italian restaurant located in a turn-of-the-century storefront that was once the

---

DINE AT BIRCHFIELD MANOR

*Over the years, **Birchfield Manor** (2018 Birchfield Road, Yakima; 509-452-1960) has won more magazine awards than any other Washington restaurant outside the Puget Sound region. The owners restored an old farmhouse and filled it with antiques, then opened the restaurant with a menu including fresh salmon in puff pastry, filet mignon, rack of lamb and chicken breast scaloppine. Local fruit and vegetables are used, and the deluxe price includes appetizer, salad and a homemade chocolate treat.*

Commercial Saloon. House-made ravioli and other pastas are the specialty. Moderate.

SOUTHEASTERN WASHINGTON SHOPPING

Yakima offers several intriguing shopping areas. One is the **North Front Street Historical District**, where the city's oldest buildings, some of them made of rough-hewn local rock, still stand, now housing an assortment of boutiques, restaurants and brew pubs. Located in the old Opera House is **Windy Hollow Kitchen Shoppe** (25 North Front Street; 509-248-0615) with hard-to-find kitchen items. The former train depot is now the site of the **Paper Station** (Front and Yakima avenues; 509-575-1633), where you can shop for books, cards and custom stationery. Calling the original City Hall home, **Thurston Wolfe Winery and Tasting Room** (27 North Front Street; 509-452-0335) is a family-owned winery that has won awards for its dessert wines.

Another shopping area in Yakima with a history theme is **Track 29** (1 West Yakima Avenue; 509-453-7272), where stores are built into restored train cars. Among them is **Stefan's** (1 West Yakima Avenue; 509-457-8855), a gift shop with a large selection of cuckoo clocks. **Yesterday's Village** (15 West Yakima Avenue; 509-457-4981) is a collection of shops in the former Fruit Exchange Building. Most of the interior has been left intact so you can see how fruit was cooled and processed, but the old building houses some 110 shops that sell antiques, glassware, jewelry and various kinds of food.

The **Residential Fruit Stand** (South 3rd Street at Nob Hill, Yakima) is an institution where many locals go for their fruit, vegetables, berries and even Christmas trees.

SOUTHEASTERN WASHINGTON NIGHTLIFE

Walla Walla has several restaurants with dancefloors; a few have live entertainment. The **Red Apple Restaurant and Lounge** (57 East Main Street; 509-525-5113) has entertainment and dancing on weekends.

One of the widest selections of nightlife in southeastern Washington is in Yakima, ranging from cultural events to country-and-western taverns. **Grant's Brewery Pub** (32 North Front Street; 509-575-2922) serves British pub food and frequently offers live music on weekends. **Jack-son's Sports Bar** (432 South 48th Avenue; 509-966-4340) offers big screen TV, pool tables and a variety of games.

The **Golden Kayland Chinese Restaurant** (Summitview Street and 40th Avenue; 509-966-7696) has live music on weekends. In addition, it has frequent concerts sponsored by the Ladies' Musical Club and the **Yakima Symphony Orchestra** (509-248-1414).

In the vocabulary of geologists, the word "steptoe" has come to mean any remnant of an older geological feature standing out from a newer feature.

Square dancing is very popular in the Yakima Valley, and numerous clubs welcome travelers to their dances. For information, the Friday *Yakima Herald-Republic* publishes a square dance column listing all the club news.

SOUTHEASTERN WASHINGTON PARKS

Steptoe Butte State Park consists of the butte and a picnic area at the base, but has no amenities at all. The reason for the park's existence is the butte itself, which rises to an elevation of 3612 feet out of the rolling Palouse Hills with panoramic views that are popular with photographers. The butte is actually the top of a granite mountain that stands above the lava flows that covered all the other peaks. Located 33 miles south of Spokane just off Route 195.

On the eastern slope of the Blue Mountains, **Fields Spring State Park** (509-256-3332) is set in forested land. It's just below Puffer Butte, a 4450-foot mountain that overlooks the Grand Ronde River Canyon. For hikers, there's a one-mile trail to the summit of Puffer Butte. Winter-sports enthusiasts will find cross-country skiing, snowshoeing and tubing. You can also camp here. On Route 129, south of Anatone.

Fort Walla Walla Park (509-527-3770; admission) is set on the site of a 208-acre former Army fort and cemetery. It also has 16 buildings, (some authentic and others replicas) of pioneer homes, schools and public buildings. One of the largest collections of horse-drawn farm equipment in the Northwest is also owned by the museum. There are nature and bicycle trails, campsites, picnic areas, play equipment and volleyball courts. In Walla Walla on Myra Road between Dalles Military Road and Rose Street.

Out in the rugged Channeled Scablands, **Palouse Falls/Lyons Ferry State Park** (509-646-3252) is a remote, two-part park. One part consists of a pleasant, grassy area with boat ramps at the confluence of the Snake and Palouse rivers. About two miles up the Palouse River is the other part, a dramatic picnic area and viewpoint overlooking the thundering Palouse Falls. Camping is permitted at both parts of the park. Located southeast of Washtucna on Route 261.

McNary National Wildlife Refuge (509-547-4942) is one of the major resting areas in the Pacific Flyway for migratory waterfowl, especially Canada geese, American widgeon, mallards, pintails and white pelicans. The population peaks in December, and the few summer mi-

---

From the crest of Puffer Butte, you can see parts of three states: Washington, Oregon and Idaho.

---

gratory birds, such as the pelicans and long-billed curlews, arrive in the spring and summer. The refuge covers 3600 acres along the Snake River just before it enters the Columbia River at Pasco. There's a self-guided wildlife trail through the marsh and croplands, and fishing for large-mouth black bass, catfish and crappie. Located southeast of Pasco just off Route 395 on the Snake River.

The Sporting Life

FISHING

For information on fishing in Banks and Roosevelt lakes in the Grand Coulee area, contact **Coulee Playland** (P.O. Box 457, Electric City, WA 99123; 509-633-2671).

Fishing excursions on the Snake River between the Idaho/Washington border are offered by **Beamer's Hells Canyon Tours** (1450 Bridge Street, Clarkston; 509-758-4800) and **Snake River Adventures** (227 Snake River Avenue, Lewiston, ID; 208-746-6276).

RIVER RAFTING

Near Yakima, the Tieton River is good for rafting. Contact **Blue Sky Outfitters** (P.O. Box 124, Pacific, WA 98047; 206-931-0637), **Chinook Expeditions** (P.O. Box 324, Index, WA 98256; 206-793-3451) or **Rivers, Inc.** (P.O. Box 2092, Kirkland, WA 98083; 206-822-5296).

Another popular location for rafting is the Snake River between the Washington and Idaho border. Outfitters to contact are **O.A.R.S. Dories** (P.O. Box 216, Altaville, CA 95221; 209-736-0811) and **Northwest Voyagers** (P.O. Box 373, Lucile, ID 83542; 208-628-3021).

SKIING

Downhill and cross-country skiing are both popular in this region, particularly the latter because there is so much open country and powdery snow. Cross-country trails are maintained at most downhill areas, but any country road, most golf courses and parks may be used by skiers.

Loup Loup (509-826-2720) between Okanogan and Twisp on Route 20 has a 1250-foot drop for downhill and a groomed area for cross-country skiers. **Sitzmark** (509-485-3323), 12 miles northeast of Tonasket, is more modest with only a 650-foot drop. **Ski Bluewood** (509-382-4725), 22 miles southeast of Dayton at the end of a Forest Service road, has 1125 vertical feet of downhill skiing and a ski school. **49 Degrees North** (509-935-6649), ten miles east of Chewelah, has four chairlifts on 1900 feet.

GOLF

Golfers have a number of options, with greens fees running considerably lower than in urban areas. Try the **Okanogan Valley Golf Club** (Golf Club Road; off the Okanogan-Conconully Route between Omak and Okanogan; 509-826-9902) or **Oroville Golf Club** (Nighthawk Road, two miles west of Oroville; 509-476-2390), which has nine holes.

In the Grand Coulee Area is **Banks Lake Golf Course** (two-and-a-half miles south of Grand Coulee on Route 155; 509-633-0163), with nine holes.

If you've seen San Francisco's Lincoln Park Municipal Golf Course with its view across the city skyline, Spokane's **Indian Canyon Golf Course** (West 4304 West Drive; 509-747-5353) will seem familiar. Set on a hillside that undulates downward toward Spokane, the 18-hole course is well known throughout the region.

GOING TO HELL'S CANYON

*One of the most important Columbia River basin areas to escape damnation by the U.S. Army Corps of Engineers is **Hell's Canyon**. America's deepest gorge (with an average depth of 6000 feet), this wild and scenic 20-mile stretch of the Snake River is accessible from Clarkston, Washington, and neighboring Lewiston, Idaho. It was saved from flooding after conservationists blocked a frightening proposal to dam this scenic region popular with anglers, rafters and jet boat operators. Visitors from all over the world make the pilgrimage to eastern Washington just to see Hell's Canyon. In fact, this scenic treasure is one of the most popular whitewater-rafting trips in the United States. The gorge is part of the Hell's Canyon National Recreation Area (88401 Route 82, Enterprise, OR; 503-426-4978), which encompasses three mountain ranges in Washington, Idaho and Oregon.*

*On your trip you're likely to spot bighorn sheep, elk, deer and bald eagles, as well as Native American petroglyphs and Nez Perce tribal landmarks. You'll also see old mining townsites and the site of one of the region's great tragedies, the Deep Creek Massacre of 1887, which took the lives of 32 Chinese gold miners. The **Clarkston Chamber of Commerce** (502 Bridge Street; 509-758-7712) can provide the names of many other jet boat and rafting operators. Overnight fishing trips can also be arranged with convenient stays at rustic Hell's Canyon lodges.*

The Tri-Cities area has seven courses, two of which are private clubs that honor reciprocal agreements. Courses include **Sun Willows Municipal Golf Course** (2535 North 20th Avenue, Pasco; 509-545-3440); **Canyon Lakes Golf Course** (3700 Canyon Lakes Drive, Kennewick; 509-582-3736); and **Sham-Na-Pum Golf Course** (72 George Washington Way, Richland; 509-946-1914).

The Yakima Valley has at least half a dozen courses, including the **Suntides Golf Course** (231 Pence Road, Yakima; 509-966-9065).

HORSEBACK RIDING

Most guest ranches and riding stables in Washington are located along the Cascade Range. The **Blue Mountain Outfitting** (88229 Bartlett Road, Enterprise, OR; 503-828-7878) offers deer and elk hunting trips in the Blue Mountains.

BICYCLING

For the most part, automobile traffic is so sparse that bicyclists have little difficulty finding lonesome roads that are both challenging and rewarding. More and more cross-country bicyclists are seen along the smaller highways, especially Route 20. Also, in the cities you'll find some bicycle routes that double as hiking trails (see "Hiking" below).

The **Snake River Bikeway** runs six miles between Clarkston and Asotin along both the Clearwater and Snake rivers, and a 24-mile route from **Palouse** leads south on Route 27 to Clear Creek Road to Route 272 back to Palouse.

BIKE RENTALS   Because of the remoteness of the trails here, it's a good idea to bring your own gear. Otherwise, see if rentals are available at bicycle shops in cities and towns along your route.

WHERE WATER WORKS

You may think of Washington as a rainy place, but without Grand Coulee Dam and the string of smaller dams that came along later to turn the Columbia and Snake rivers into a series of lakes, eastern Washington would be barren. Instead, in this part of the state one of the most common scenes is an irrigation sprinkler going about its business of turning the sand into a rich soil that grows wheat, wine grapes, fruit, soybeans, barley, oats, rape, grass seed, corn, alfalfa, potatoes, peas and a host of other crops.

In winter, Banks Lake, near Grand Coulee, is a popular place to ice fish.

HIKING

OKANOGAN HIGHLANDS TRAILS   Backpackers and day hikers alike enjoy this area because the weather is often clear and dry and the forest is more open than in the Cascades and Olympics. A number of established hiking trails are shown on Forest Service maps and in free brochures given out at the ranger station in Okanogan (509-826-3275).

A good walk for a family with smaller children is the 1.5-mile trail leading from Bonaparte Campground just north of the one-store town of Wauconda to the viewpoint overlooking the lake. Another easy one is the 7-mile loop **Big Tree Trail** from Lost Lake Campground, which is only a short distance north of Bonaparte. This one goes through a signed botanical area.

One of the most ambitious of the highlands trails is the **Kettle Crest Trail** (13 miles). The trek begins at the summit of Sherman Pass on Route 20 and winds southward past Sherman Peak and several other mountains. The trail is through mostly open terrain, and you'll have great views of the mountains and Columbia River valley.

GRAND COULEE AREA TRAILS   A system of paths and trails connects the four towns clustered around Grand Coulee Dam. The Bureau of Reclamation built a paved route about 2 miles long called the **Community Trail**, which connects Coulee Dam and Grand Coulee. An informal system of unpaved paths connects these two towns to Elmer City and Electric City.

A walking-biking trail called the **Down River Trail** (6.5 miles) runs north along the Columbia River from Grand Coulee, beginning in the Coulee Dam Shopping Center. It is wheelchair accessible.

The **Bunchgrass Prairie Nature Trail** (.5 mile loop) begins in the Spring Canyon Campground (which is three miles up Roosevelt Lake by water and two miles from Grand Coulee), and goes through one of the few remaining bunchgrass environments here. Self-guided booklets are at the trailhead. Information: 509-633-9441.

SOUTHEASTERN WASHINGTON TRAILS   **Cowiche Canyon** (3 miles) starts five miles from Yakima. The trail is actually an old railroad bed that ran through the steep canyon. The canyon has unusual rock formations, and you can expect to see at least some wildlife.

Noel Pathway is a 4.6-mile trail inside the city limits of Yakima that follows the Yakima River. The pathway is used by bicyclists, too.

Transportation

BY CAR

Eastern Washington is served by a network of roads that range from interstates to logging roads that have been paved by the Forest Service. **Route 97** serves as the north-south dividing line between the Cascade Mountains and the arid, rolling hills undulating to the eastern boundaries of the state.

Route 90 runs through the center of the Washington, from Spokane southwest through Moses Lake, George and across the Columbia River at Vantage where the highway turns almost due west for its final run to Puget Sound.

Route 5 bisects Portland, Oregon, and provides access from the north via Vancouver, Washington. This same highway also is the main line from points south like the Willamette Valley and California.

Route 82 begins near Hermiston, Oregon, crosses the Columbia River to the Tri-Cities (Richland, Kennewick and Pasco) and runs on up the Yakima Valley to join Route 90 at Ellensburg.

Another major highway is **Route 395**, which starts in Lakeview, Oregon, and continues into Washington at the Tri-Cities to Ritzville. There it disappears into Route 90 at Ritzville only to emerge again at Spokane, where it continues north into British Columbia.

Smaller but important highways include **Route 12**, between Clarkston and Walla Walla, and **Route 195**, between Pullman and Spokane.

Perhaps the most beautiful of all the highways in Washington is **Route 20**, which starts at Whidbey Island and continues to the North Cascades, through the Methow Valley, then straight through the Okanogan Highlands to Kettle Falls, where it merges with Route 395.

BY AIR

Spokane International Airport is by far the busiest in eastern Washington, with seven airlines serving the area: Delta Airlines, Empire Airlines, Horizon Air, Morris Air, Northwest Airlines, United Airlines and United Express. Taxis and a shuttle service offer transportation from the Spokane airport downtown. **Airport Shuttle Service** (509-535-6979) offers transportation from your door to the airport by appointment.

Other airports with scheduled service in Washington are **Moses Lake**, **Pullman**, **Wenatchee**, **Yakima**, **Tri-Cities** and **Walla Walla**. All these smaller cities are served by either Horizon Air or United Express or both. In addition, Delta Air Lines serves Tri-Cities. Empire Air serves Tri-Cities and Yakima.

In northern Oregon, **Portland International Airport** is a major gateway. Located ten miles northeast of downtown Portland, it is served by Air B.C., Alaska Airlines, American Airlines, America West Airlines, Continental Airlines, Delta Air Lines, Horizon Air, Northwest Airlines, Trans World Airlines and United Airlines.

BY BUS

Three bus lines operate throughout the region. From the Spokane terminal (1125 West Sprague Avenue) are **Empire Lines** (509-624-4116), **Greyhound Bus Lines** (509-624-5255) and **Northwestern Stage Lines** (509-838-4029). Greyhound also serves Yakima at the depot at 602 East Yakima Avenue.

BY TRAIN

Washington is one of the few states to have two **Amtrak** (800-872-7245) routes. Both start in Spokane. The first route runs from Spokane due west with stops in Wenatchee, Monroe, Everett and Edmonds before arriving in Seattle. The other route runs southwest from Spokane to Portland, Oregon with stops in Ritzville and the Tri-Cities.

CAR RENTALS

Rental agencies in Spokane include **Budget Rent A Car** (800-527-0700), **Practical All Star Rent A Car** (800-772-9732), **National Interrent** (800-328-4567), **Thrifty Car Rental** (800-367-2277) and **U-Save Auto Rental** (800-272-8728).

Agencies in the Tri-Cities include **Avis Rent A Car** (800-331-1212), **Budget Rent A Car** (800-527-0700), **Hertz Rent A Car** (800-654-3131) and **National Interrent** (800-328-4567). Walla Walla is served by **Budget Rent A Car** (800-527-0700).

PUBLIC TRANSPORTATION

The Tri-Cities area (Pasco, Kennewick and Richland) has **Ben Franklin Transit** (509-735-5100). **Valley Transit** (509-525-9140) serves Walla Walla and College Place, and Prosser has its own **Rural Transit** (509-786-1707). Pullman has **Pullman Transit** (509-332-6535). Yakima has **Yakima Transit** (509-575-6175), which also runs a 25¢ shuttle service that uses cable car–style trolleys through the downtown business district.

TAXIS

The major taxi companies in the Spokane area are **Inland Taxi** (509-326-8294) and **Spokane Cab** (509-535-2535).

TEN

The Columbia River Gorge

The Columbia River cuts an 80-mile swath through the Cascade Mountains on its way to the Pacific, leaving in its wake a magnificent region of towering basalt cliffs, waterfalls and forested bluffs known as the Columbia River Gorge. Because it forms a natural border between Oregon and Washington, exploring the Gorge is a two-state proposition, with a lot to see and do on both sides of the river.

Since long before the two states existed, the Gorge has both fascinated and terrified travelers. For centuries the region was a major trading ground for Native Americans who came from as far away as Northern California and British Columbia to meet, talk and barter. Lewis and Clark marveled at the Gorge as they journeyed down the Columbia on the last stretch of their westward trek. Less captivated were the Oregon Trail immigrants of the 1840s who had to detour south around Mt. Hood or else mount their wagons on homemade rafts for a treacherous ride through the rocks and rapids west of The Dalles.

Today, visitors have it a lot easier. On the Washington side, Route 14 follows a mostly water-level route through the Gorge on the north bank, providing good views of the Oregon shore and such river traffic as tugboats pushing grain-laden barges downstream. Frequently sighted at the eastern edge of the Gorge are the bright sails of windsurfers attracted to some of the best conditions for their sport in North America. On the Oregon side, Route 84 follows the Columbia River from Portland through such prime Gorge sightseeing areas as Cascade Locks and The Dalles. Although it's possible to tour the Gorge in a loop drive, taking Route 14 one way and Route 84 the other, we recommend crisscrossing it at various points in between. Declared a national scenic area by Congress

Opened in 1905, the strip at Pearson Air Museum is the oldest operating airfield in the United States.

in 1986, the Columbia Gorge, less than an hour east of Portland, has been a busy area for tourism development during the past few years. Although most hotels and restaurants are still concentrated on the Oregon side, it is the Washington side around Stevenson, with its new interpretive center and deluxe resort, where the most recent activity has taken place. Fortunately, the region is still largely unspoiled and provides much to keep waterfall lovers, windsurfers, hikers and history buffs enthralled for days.

A logical starting point for touring the Columbia Gorge region is at the western end in the historic city of Vancouver. Don't miss **Fort Vancouver** (East Evergreen Boulevard, Vancouver; 360-696-7655; admission May to September). Located across the Columbia River from Portland, this National Historic Site is a cornerstone of Pacific Northwest history. Organized by the Hudson's Bay Company in 1825, the fort was a British fur-trading post and focal point for the commercial development of a region extending from British Columbia to Oregon and from Montana west to the Hawaiian Islands.

Nine structures have been reconstructed on their original fort locations. Collectively, they give a feel for life prior to the arrival of the first white settlers. Start your tour at the visitors center with the introductory video. On your tour you'll see the re-created **Chief Factor's House**, once home to Dr. John McLoughlin, the chief factor who befriended American settlers and is remembered as the "Father of Oregon." The phenomenal ability of the British to instantly gentrify the wilderness is reflected in the fine china and elegant furniture of this white clapboard home wrapped with a spacious veranda.

Also worth a visit are the blacksmith's shop, bakery, kitchen, washroom, fur warehouse, stockade and bastion. At the **Indian Trade Shop and Dispensary**, you'll learn how Native Americans bartered skillfully with the British. Because most of the items were imported, there was a two-year hiatus between ordering goods and receiving them.

On nearby **Officer's Row**, you'll see 21 grand homes built for American Army leaders who served here during the latter half of the 19th and the early part of the 20th century. These charming Victorians are the focus of a rehabilitation program combining interpretive and commercial use. Among the residences are the **Grant House** (360-694-5252) and the **George C. Marshall House**, an imposing Queen Anne. Both are open for tours (360-693-3103).

Next to Fort Vancouver is **Pearson Air Museum** (1105 East 5th Street, Vancouver; 360-694-7026; admission). Exhibits feature a dis-

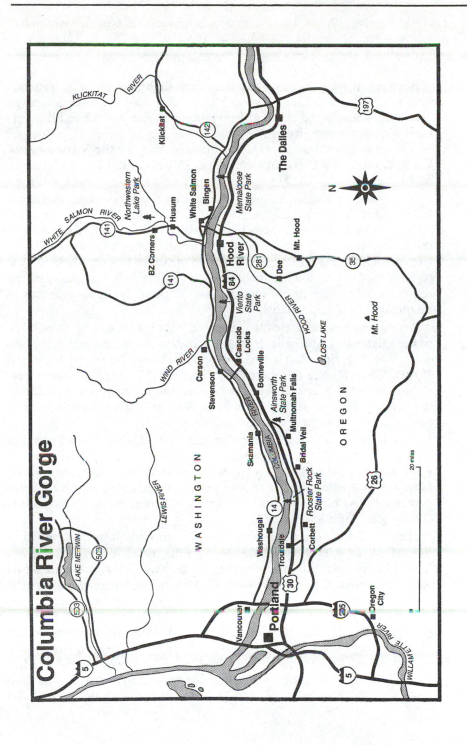

Columbia River Gorge

At the Bonneville Dam fish ladders, professional fish counters keep their eyes on the salmon swimming upstream to spawn, counting up to 80,000 fish on a busy day.

---

play on the world's first nonstop transpolar flight (Moscow to Vancouver) in 1937. The Soviet aviators were greeted by General George Marshall, who hosted them at his residence. The airpark exhibit features flyable vintage aircraft.

To see more of Vancouver, Washington, stop by the **Vancouver/Clark County Visitors and Convention Bureau** (404 East 15th Street, Suite 111; 360-693-1313) to pick up the handy heritage tour brochure.

Originally a Carnegie Library, **Clark County Historical Museum** (1511 Main Street, Vancouver; 360-695-4681) has a better than good regional collection—from the Native American artifacts and handicrafts to the historical doctor's office, general store and type shop. The doll collection includes everything from Eskimo creations to early Barbies. Not to be missed is the downstairs train room with a Pullman unit, railway telegram office, dining car china, a model train layout and photos of memorable local derailments.

From the Oregon side of the river, take Route 84 east up the Gorge to the **Historic Columbia River Highway**. Beginning east of Troutdale (Exit 17), this road ascends the bluff above the river to **Crown Point/Vista House** (Corbett, OR; 503-695-2240), a must-see viewpoint. Descending east toward the Gorge, you'll find yourself in one of the loveliest regions in the Northwest. With more than 70 waterfalls in the area, it's easy to have one to yourself.

Among the highlights are **LaTourell Falls**, **Bridal Veil Falls** and **Coopey Falls**. Perhaps the most popular destination is the **Multnomah Falls region**. Falls in this area include **Mist Falls**, **Wahkeena Falls**, **Necktie Falls**, **Fairy Falls** and, of course, the Gorge's majestic **Multnomah Falls**. Near the base of Lower Multnomah Falls is a visitors center, gift shop and restaurant.

The taming of the Columbia River to provide low-cost power is one of the most controversial stories in the evolution of this region. You'll get the pro side of the picture at **Bonneville Lock and Dam** (Cascade Locks, OR; 503-374-8820), which is reached by taking Exit 40 off Route 84. At the **Bradford Island Visitors Center**, extensive interpretive displays provide an overview of the dam operation and history. You can also learn how the dam operates, see the fish ladders and visit the **Fort Cascades National Historic Site** on the Washington shore. To get there, cross the Columbia River on the **Bridge of the Gods**, named for a natural bridge famous in Indian legend, and head west three miles on Route 14. The 59-acre historic site includes part of the old Portage Railroad, a one-time Chinook Indian village and an old military fort.

Retrace your route across the Bridge of the Gods to the Oregon side and stop at the **Cascade Locks Museum** (Marine Park, Cascade Locks, OR; 503-374-8535) to see exhibits on Native Americans, the first Columbia River locks, the portage road, logging and fishwheels. Water powered, these rotating devices scooped so many salmon from the river that they were banned by the state in 1926. The sternwheeler **Columbia Gorge** (503-374-8619) is docked in Cascade Locks from June through September. The multidecked old paddlewheel steamboat can be boarded for daytime and dinner cruises through the Gorge.

On the Washington side of the bridge in Stevenson is the spacious new **Columbia Gorge Interpretive Center** (150 Northwest Loop Road, Stevenson; 509-427-8211), where the focus is on the cultural and natural history of the Gorge. Located on a ten-acre site overlooking the river, the center includes a 37-foot-high replica of a 19th-century fishwheel, a restored Corless Steam Engine, a theater with a nine-projector slide show re-creating the cataclysmic formation of the Gorge and several exhibits drawn from the oral histories of Native Americans and pioneer settlers in the region. The interpretive center is also the new home of the **Skamania County Historical Museum**, which includes Native American artifacts and the world's largest rosary collection.

Farther east on Route 14 in Washington is **Carson Hot Mineral Springs Resort** (Carson; 509-427-8292). On the Wind River, this resort is known for its mineral baths, massages, beautiful hiking trails, fishing and 18-hole golf course, and includes a hotel, rustic cabins and restaurant. From here, you can drive east along Route 14 to Route 141, which leads north along the White Salmon River valley to Trout Lake. Then return to Route 14 and the town of White Salmon.

Just east of White Salmon in the small town of Bingen is the **Gorge Heritage Museum** (202 East Humboldt Street; 509-493-3573), where you can view old photographs of the region and Native American artifacts, including tools, arrow points and beadwork.

THE MT. HOOD RAILROAD

*A scenic excursion train that links the Gorge with Mt. Hood, the **Mt. Hood Railroad** (110 Railroad Avenue, Hood River, OR; 503-386-3556) meanders along a route pioneered in 1906. The trip climbs up the Hood River valley through steep canyons, orchards and forests. You'll enjoy the views of the Cascades from the restored coaches on a 44-mile roundtrip journey. Special fall foliage trips are well worth your while.*

From White Salmon, cross back to the Oregon side of the Columbia River, where your next stop should be the **Hood River**. Stop at the **Hood River County Visitors Center** (Port Marina Park, OR; 503-386-2000) for information on this scenic hub. Nearby is the **Hood River County Historical Museum** (Port Marina Park; 503-386-6772), featuring exhibits on Native American culture, the westward migration, pioneer farming, logging and the Columbia River. Also found here is an extensive collection of period furniture and early 20th-century artifacts.

One of the prettiest drives in the area is the 27-mile trip from Hood River to **Lost Lake**. Take Route 281 south to Dee and then follow the signs west to this pristine mountain lake where motorized boats are forbidden. Do keep an eye out for logging trucks en route.

We strongly recommend a visit to **The Dalles**. Near the end of the Oregon Trail, where emigrants boarded vessels to float down the Columbia (the Barlow Trail later made it possible to complete the overland journey), this city has an excellent old-town walking tour. Pick up a copy of the route map at **The Dalles Convention and Visitors Bureau** (404 West 2nd Street; 503-296-6616). Highlights on this walk include one of Oregon's oldest bookstores, **Klindt's** (315 East 2nd Street), and the circa-1863 **Waldron Brothers Drugstore** nearby. If you're traveling with children, it's worth checking out **Wonder Works A Children's Museum** (419 East 2nd Street; 503-296-2444; admission). A storefront gem, this volunteer organization has hands-on exhibits for kids, a dress-up area, stage, puppeteer area and crafts. Youngsters will love it.

A favorite stop in town is the **Fort Dalles Museum** (15th and Garrison streets; 503-296-4547; admission). Only one fort building, the Surgeon's Quarters, remains today. But the museum does preserve an excellent

---

SEEING STARS

*Although most are built with public funds, astronomical observatories are seldom accessible to the general public. One exception is the **Goldendale Observatory State Park Interpretive Center** (1602 Observatory Drive, Goldendale; 509-773-3141). Just 11 miles north of the popular Maryhill Museum and the Columbia River, this gem was created by four amateur astronomers with the help of the city of Goldendale in 1973 and taken over by the state in 1980. Instructional tours begin with a visit to the Astro Theater and feature an opportunity to observe the heavens through a 24-inch reflecting telescope, ideal for public viewing of the moon, the planets and the stars. Resident astronomer and ranger Stephen R. Stout also shows visitors how to safely observe the sun through a special eight-inch telescope. Be sure to call first for the observation schedule.*

collection of pioneer artifacts, rifles, quilts and historic photographs. Much of the memorabilia focuses on the lives of early settlers.

During your visit you'll want to see **The Dalles Dam**. Take Route 30 east to Route 197 north. Cross the freeway to Northeast Frontage Road and follow the signs to the dam. Perhaps the saddest part of this story, the downside of that pro-dam story you saw at the Bonneville visitors center, focuses on the demise of the region's best-known Native American fishing grounds. Wherever you go along this part of the Columbia River, in coffee shops, hotel lobbies and visitors centers, you're likely to see classic photographs of Native Americans dipping their nets into the river at heavenly Celilo Falls. To get the full picture, leaf through the scrapbook of Celilo Falls fishing pictures at the Fort Dalles Museum.

If you continue on Route 84 east of The Dalles for 18 miles, you'll come to a small **Celilo Falls Marker**, which indicates where these bounteous fishing waters prospered before being destroyed by the dam in the late 1950s.

A few miles farther east, on the Washington side, is one of the most isolated museums in America. **Maryhill Museum of Art** (35 Maryhill Museum Drive, Maryhill; 509-773-3733; admission) was designed in 1914 as the mansion residence of eccentric millionaire Sam Hill, and was supposed to oversee a Quaker agricultural town. But the plan for a new town flopped and the house on the hill eventually became a museum. This eclectic collection was dedicated in 1926 by Queen Marie of Romania, which helps explain the presence of treasures from that nation's royal collection. Also here are Russian icons, Rodin's *The Man with a Broken Nose*, *Indian Buffalo Hunt* by Charles M. Russell, French decorative arts, a good display of Native American handicrafts and artifacts, as well as one of the world's great chess collections. Views of the Columbia Gorge are spectacular, as are the sunsets. Three miles east of Maryhill is Stonehenge, Sam Hill's memorial to local soldiers who died in World War I.

COLUMBIA RIVER GORGE LODGING

Much of the lodging available in the Gorge area is on the Oregon side of the Columbia River in Hood River or The Dalles.

The Columbia Gorge Hotel (4000 Westcliff Drive, Hood River, OR; 503-386-5566, 800-345-1921, fax 503-387-5414) is a 42-room landmark where strains of Bach waft through the halls, sculptured carpets highlight the public areas and the fireplace is always roaring. This Mediterranean-style hotel tucks guests into wicker, brass, canopy or hand-carved antique beds. The dining room, home of a four-course farm breakfast, offers splendid riverfront dining. Relax in the Valentino Lounge or take a walk through the manicured gardens. Ultra-deluxe.

The chandeliered **Hood River Hotel** (102 Oak Street, Hood River, OR; 503-386-1900, 800-386-1859, fax 503-386-6090) is special. Forty rooms and suites offer a wide range of accommodations in this restored brick landmark. Brightly painted rooms are appointed with oak furniture, four-poster beds, casablanca fans, wing chairs and antiques. Some offer views of the Columbia River. Comfortable sitting areas, a lounge offering jazz and a cheery café are all part of the charm. Kitchenette suites are available. Ultra-deluxe.

Beautifully located overlooking the Columbia River Gorge, **Vagabond Lodge** (4070 Westcliff Drive, Hood River, OR; 503-386-2992) offers spacious, carpeted rooms—some opening right onto the riverfront. All feature contemporary furniture, double or queen-size beds and a secluded garden setting. For the budget-to-moderate price, it's hard to beat this motel.

Located just above the Columbia Gorge Interpretive Center in Stevenson is the **Skamania Lodge** (1131 Skamania Lodge Way; 509-4270-7700, 800-221-7117, fax 509-427-2547), a modern resort built in the tradition of the grand mountain lodges of a century ago. Guests can congregate in the wood-paneled Gorge Room with its deep sofas and three-story river-rock fireplace. Public areas and the 195 guest rooms are handsomely decorated with mission-style furniture, Pendleton fabrics, petroglyph rubbings and Native American–inspired rugs. The grounds include an 18-hole golf course, fitness center, whirlpools, swimming pool, riding trails and more. Deluxe to ultra-deluxe.

Five miles east of Stevenson, the **Sojourner Inn** (142 Lyons Road, Home Valley; 509-427-7070) is a shake-roofed, tri-level contemporary inn nestled into a ridge that faces both the Columbia and Wind rivers. Of the five attractive rooms, the choicest is the Travelers Room, which has a deep-green four-poster bed with down comforter, overstuffed chairs, plants and best of all, a river view. The inn offers a library and patio area and is frequently the scene of art exhibits, informal concerts and other events. The moderate-to-deluxe rates include a full breakfast.

If you crave country living, incomparable views of the Mt. Hood region and horseback riding, check into the **Fir Mountain Ranch** (4051 Fir Mountain Road, Hood River, OR; 503-354-2753). Hidden on a secluded ridge, this lodge-style home offers cozy, countrified lodgings, trail rides and easy access to both the Hood River valley and Mt. Hood itself. A great escape, this isolated bed and breakfast is ideal for families as well. Deluxe.

Across from Hood River on the Washington side of the Columbia River, the **Inn of the White Salmon** (172 West Jewett Boulevard, White Salmon; 509-493-2335, 800-972-5226) is a lovely bed and breakfast that offers brunch seven days a week. All you need to do is check in to one of the inn's countrified rooms featuring brass beds and antiques, and

Much of Vancouver was built with Hidden bricks from the Lowell M. Hidden factory, still in operation today.

this splendid feast is yours. This moderate-to-deluxe-priced inn also features a comfortable parlor.

Offering whitewater access to the White Salmon River, **Orchard Hill Inn** (Husum; 509-493-3024) is the place for cozy country lodging at budget-to-moderate prices. Wicker, antiques, quilted bedspreads, oak floors, kerosene lamps and a fireplace will make you feel right at home in your gabled room. You can enjoy a full breakfast, explore the apple and pear orchards, play volleyball and soak in the whirlpool. Near White Salmon and Hood River, this secluded setting offers views of Mt. Adams and features its very own beer garden.

Williams House Inn (608 West 6th Street, The Dalles, OR; 503-296-2889) is a picturesque Victorian on a wooded hilltop. Adjacent to an arboretum and a creek, the home is furnished with Georgian and Victorian antiques as well as Asian art. Upstairs rooms in the moderate-price range feature canopied beds, a chaise lounge and writing desk. From your balcony, you'll enjoy a view of the Columbia River Gorge and the Klickitat Hills. The three-room main floor suite is a best buy in the moderate range.

For contemporary motel accommodations, try the **Quality Inn** (2114 West 6th Street, The Dalles, OR; 503-298-5161, 800-848-9378, fax 503-298-6411). The fully carpeted rooms offer queen beds featuring pink spreads with seashell designs and oak tables. There's a pool on the premises, as well as Cousins, the only restaurant we know featuring a John Deere tractor in the middle of the dining room. Moderate.

COLUMBIA RIVER GORGE RESTAURANTS

With a name like **Hidden House** (100 West 13th Street, Vancouver; 360-696-2847), you'd think it would be hard to find. But this structure and the adjacent residence (now a retail business) at 110 West 13th Street were built by Lowell M. Hidden and his son Foster. Once the home of Clark College, this handsome red brick Victorian offers dining upstairs and down. Antiques are an integral part of the decor that includes three fireplaces, the original stained glass, ash and black walnut woodwork and a covered veranda ideal for outside dining. The menu features steaks, seafood, chicken Kiev and veal dishes served with homemade poppyseed bread. Northwest wines are featured. Moderate to deluxe.

When it's time for pasta or pizza, head for **Theo's** (109 West 15th Street, Vancouver; 360-694-0300). You can take a seat in the brick-walled dining room at one of the tables illuminated by lead glass lamps and order up Theo's lasagna, manicotti or fettuccine with pesto. The Greek and veggie pizzas are popular here. An extensive sandwich menu is also available. Budget.

In business for nearly 70 years, **The Holland Restaurant** (Main and McLoughlin streets, Vancouver; 360-694-7842) must be doing something right. Once a creamery, now a family-style restaurant with a contemporary look, this spacious establishment serves generous portions at budget prices. American cuisine is the keynote here, with offerings ranging from macaroni and cheese to tenderloin and prawns. The on-premises bakery is known for its strudel, pumpkin muffins and florentines.

Located in a beautiful Victorian, **The Grant House Café** (1101 Officer's Row, Vancouver; 360-699-1213) serves fine Northwest cuisine in a pleasant setting. Named for the president who served at the Fort here as a young quartermaster, it is the oldest Vancouver Barracks residence. Steak and seafood dishes are good and prices are moderate. There is also an extensive wine list highlighting regional varietals.

After a visit to Multnomah Falls, it makes sense to dine at **Multnomah Falls Lodge** (Bridal Veil, OR off Route 84; 503-695-2376). The smoked-salmon-and-cheese platter, stew served in a hollowed-out loaf of french bread, and generous salads are all recommended. The beautiful lodge building with a big stone fireplace, scenic paintings of the surroundings and picturesque views will add to your enjoyment of the Gorge. Moderate.

In Stevenson, **Skamania Lodge** (1131 Skamania Lodge Way; 509-427-7700) has a grand dining room with massive wooden ceiling beams and superb views of the Gorge. The specialties are Northwest-inspired dishes prepared in a woodburning oven, including gourmet pizzas and roasted wild game, meats and seafood. Deluxe.

The **Big River Grill** (192 Southwest 2nd Avenue; 509-427-4888) in downtown Stevenson is a convivial place with wooden booths and old photographs on the walls. Both locals and visitors come here to enjoy salmon chowder in bread bowls, pasta specials, salads topped with grilled meats and such vegetarian entrées as pasta primavera and nutty garden burgers. Moderate.

Almost smack dab on the railroad tracks in Stevenson is the **Crossing Café** (127 Russell Street; 509-427-8097), a tiny wood-framed cottage across from the Columbia Gorge paddlewheeler landing. Along with deli sandwiches and hearty soups, the Crossing offers changing ethnic-inspired lunch specials such as beef burritos and vegetable curries. The budget-priced café is open for lunch only.

Just east of Stevenson, **Sojourner Inn** (142 Lyons Road; 509-427-7070) serves cuisine prepared by a French-trained chef in an intimate dining room with fireplace, pine tables and a 17-mile view of the Gorge.

Menu specials change nightly, but may include Cajun chicken breast in lime beurre blanc served over couscous or shellfish in puff pastry. Because of the restaurant's small capacity, menu orders must be placed at the time of reservation. With enough advance notice, the chef will create a customized menu. Deluxe.

Tucked away in the woods, **Stonehedge Inn** (3405 Cascade Drive, Hood River, OR; 503-386-3940) is an antique-filled home offering country dining at its finest. Set in a garden, this paneled restaurant has a tiny mahogany bar and a roaring fireplace. Entrées include scallop sauté, veal chanterelle, jumbo prawns and filet of salmon. Light entrées, such as a seafood platter, are also recommended. Moderate to deluxe.

Hood River Hotel Café (102 Oak Street, Hood River, OR; 503-386-1900) has pleasant indoor and sidewalk seating in the center of this resort town. The heart of the dining room is a handcrafted bar with an etched glass mirror. Moderate-priced entrées include filet of salmon, spaghetti bolognese and lamb tenderloin.

An elegant dining room overlooking the Gorge, **Columbia River Court** (4000 Westcliff Drive, Hood River, OR; 503-386-5566) is a romantic place to dine on specialties like roast pheasant with sage and pumpkin risotto, fresh Oregon salmon or medallions of fallow venison. Done in an Early American design with oak furniture and candlelit tables, this establishment is well known for its lavish farm breakfast. Deluxe.

Located in one of the most historic buildings in town, the **Baldwin Saloon** (1st and Court streets, The Dalles, OR; 503-296-5666) was built in 1876 and has an 18-foot-long mahogany back bar and turn-of-the-century oil paintings on the brick walls. The restaurant is known for its oyster dishes, baked and on the half shell, and also serves thick sandwiches and burgers, soups and desserts. Moderate.

An A-frame tucked away in an industrial area, **Ole's Supper Club** (2620 West 2nd Street, The Dalles, OR; 503-296-6708) proves that

---

DOWN-HOME DINNERS

*About 20 minutes north of the Columbia Gorge, and well worth the trip, is one of the region's most intriguing restaurants, **The Logs** (Route 141, White Salmon, WA; 509-493-1402). You'll be impressed by the broasted chicken, hickory-smoked ribs, giant fries and fresh fruit pies served in this log-cabin setting. The battered and deep-fried chicken gizzards and cheese sticks are a big hit with the regular clientele, which includes locals, rafters, skiers and devotees of the peppermint fudge ice cream pie. In business for six decades, this is the place where city slickers will come face to face with their first jackalope, safely mounted on the wall. Budget.*

location isn't everything in the restaurant business. The candlelit dining room with oak tables and floors, red plastic chairs, casablanca fans and western paintings is jammed with locals who swear by the prime rib, baked ham lorraine and Pacific salmon fresh from the nearby Columbia. Dinners, complete with fresh-baked bread, vegetables, salad and soup, include chicken piccata and fettuccine with fresh scallops. Moderate.

To the people at **Johnny's Café** (408 East 2nd Street, The Dalles, OR; 503-296-4565), cordon bleu sounds like something you use to tint your fireplace. This temple of American cuisine has made few concessions to the trends of the 1990s. Lit with fluorescent bulbs, furnished in formica and vinyl and kept in sync with Top-40 tunes from the jukebox, this eatery is big on macaroni and cheese. For decades, locals have been coming here to feast on broasted chicken, salmon steak, fish and chips, liver and onions, pies and puddings. Here's home cooking to write home about. Budget.

COLUMBIA RIVER GORGE SHOPPING

Fort Vancouver Gift Shop (East Evergreen Boulevard, Vancouver; 206-696-7655) is the place to go for books and pamphlets on Pacific Northwest history. Souvenir maps will add to your appreciation of the region's heritage. We recommend picking up a copy of the *Fort Vancouver National Historic Site Handbook 113*.

Aviation buffs will want to stop by the gift shop at **Pearson Air Museum** (1105 East 5th Street, Vancouver; 360-694-7026). The shop has a good collection of memorabilia and souvenirs for adults and juniors alike.

Pendleton Woolen Mills and Outlet Store (2 17th Street, Washougal; 360-835-1118) offers big savings on irregulars. Tours of the mill, in operation since 1912, are available, but call first for schedule information.

Stevenson's small, walkable downtown has a number of distinctive art galleries and gift shops, among them: **River House Art Gallery and Studio** (Seymour and 1st streets; 509-427-5930) offers original watercolors; **The Three Magpies** (Russell and Second streets; 509-427-4377) features crafts by Northwest artisans; **North Bank Gallery and Art Supplies** (62 Russell Street; 509-427-7100) specializes in fine art by Gorge artists; and **Indian Heaven** (280 West 2nd Avenue; 509-427-7754) sells Native American arts and crafts.

Carson has a few sources for antique collectors, including the **Old Carson School House Antique Mall** (Wind River Highway; 509-427-7727) and **Wind River Trading Post** (Wind River Highway; 509-427-4766).

A good place to select a fine Oregon white or red is **The Wine Sellers** (514 State Street, Hood River, OR; 503-386-4647). Fresh french bread, cheese and souvenirs round out the offerings.

The only sound of civilization you're likely to hear in Ainsworth State Park is from passing trains.

Fruit makes a great present for the folks back home. If you're looking for a spot to purchase Hood River apples, comice pears and cherries, try **Rasmussen Farms** (3020 Thomsen Road off Route 35 south of Hood River, OR; 503–386–4622). They can all be shipped as gift packs.

Columbia Art Gallery (207 2nd Street, Hood River, OR; 503–386–4512) represents 150 artists, primarily from the Columbia Gorge region. Featured are the works of photographers, printmakers, potters, glassblowers, weavers and painters.

The Dalles Art Center (220 East 4th Street, The Dalles, OR; 503–296–4759), located in the historic Carnegie Library, exhibits work by local and regional artists. Much of this fine art is available for purchase. Both galleries showcase pottery, jewelry, paintings, beadwork, calligraphy, wearable art and baskets.

COLUMBIA RIVER GORGE NIGHTLIFE

On weekends, a deejay plays danceable oldies in the **Whistle Stop Lounge** (900 West 7th Street, Vancouver; 360–695–3374). Filled with railroad memorabilia and movie posters, the lounge offers booth and table seating. With 29 trains a day passing the premises, rail fans are guaranteed plenty of action. There's a full bar on the premises.

A popular gay and lesbian nightspot in Vancouver is **North Bank Tavern** (106 West 6th Street; 509–695–3862), which offers a video area, dancefloor and outdoor patio.

The **Power Station** (2126 Southwest Halsey Street, Troutdale, OR; 503–492–4686) is a theater and pub located in the former Multnomah County poor farm. The theater, which presents movies and occasional special events, is in the farm's former boiler room. The pub serves a full menu and is in the converted laundry building. Also on the premises is the Edgefield Brewery and Winery.

The **River Rock Lounge** at the Skamania Lodge (1131 Skamania Lodge Way, Stevenson; 509–427–7700) features live acoustic music on weekends before a woodburning fireplace.

Full Sail Brew Pub (506 Columbia Street, Hood River, OR; 503–386–2247) offers tastings of their very popular microbrewed beers, as well as a pub-style menu. There is outside deck seating with fine views of the Columbia.

Scootie's Bungalow Tavern (Wind River Highway, Carson; 509–427–4523) has TV with sports channels, pool table and dart boards.

Memaloose State Park is named for an offshore Columbia River island that was once a Native American burial ground.

COLUMBIA RIVER GORGE PARKS

Offering more than three miles of sandy Columbia River frontage, the 872-acre **Rooster Rock State Park** (503-695-2261) is near the Gorge's west end. The rock, named for a towering promontory, is adjacent to a camping site chosen by Lewis and Clark in 1805. Popular for swimming and windsurfing, Rooster Rock also has hiking trails, a small lake and forested bluff. The park is wheelchair accessible and sports picnic tables, a boat ramp and a boat basin. Fishing is good for salmon. The park is 22 miles east of Portland on Route 84 at Exit 25.

Originally a rest stop on the old Columbia River Highway, the 247-acre **Viento State Park** (503-374-8811) includes a riverfront and Viento Creek forest section. Stellar views of the Columbia River make this a popular camping and picnicking facility. It can get very windy, however. You'll find the park on Route 84, eight miles west of Hood River in Oregon.

Ranking high among the treasures of the Columbia River Scenic Highway is **Ainsworth State Park** (503-695-2301), a 156-acre refuge. Near the bottom of St. Peter's Dome, the forested park has a beautiful hiking trail that connects with a network extending throughout the region. A serene getaway. Facilities include picnic tables and campsites. The park is east of Portland on Route 30.

Northwestern Lake Park is a little Washington jewel located on the White Salmon River north of the Columbia. This is a great destination for a day trip where you can swim, fish, hike or just loaf. There are also summer cabins nearby for those who want to stay a little longer. Picnic tables and a boat launch are available; restaurants and groceries are found in Husum or BZ Corners. To get there, head west from White Salmon on Route 14 to Route 141, then continue north five miles to the park.

A 336-acre site, **Memaloose State Park** (503-478-3008), located on the old Columbia River Highway, spreads out along a two-mile stretch of riverfront and is forested with pine, oak and fir. There are campsites and restrooms, but much of the park is steep and rocky. It can also be very windy. In case you were wondering, "Memaloose" is a Chinook word linked to the sacred burial ritual. The park is located off Route 84, about 11 miles west of The Dalles in Oregon; westbound access only.

The Sporting Life
FISHING

To land a salmon, steelhead, walleye or sturgeon, head to the Columbia River area. **Green's Fish On Charter Service** (1206 West 2nd Street, The Dalles, OR; 503-296-4652) can help you find the big ones. Also offering guided fishing trips in the Gorge area is **Northwest Guide Service** (Woodard Creek Road, Skamania; 509-427-4625).

The art of flyfishing abounds on rivers in the Gorge region. Providing flyfishing lessons and excursions is **The Wild Side Outdoor Adventures** (P.O. Box 973, Hood River, OR 97031; 503-354-3112) and **The Gorge Fly Shop** (416 Oak Street, Hood River, OR; 503-386-9234).

RIVER RAFTING

The White Salmon River north of the Columbia is a popular rafting spot. **Phil Zoller's Guide Service** (1244 Route 141, White Salmon; 509-493-2641), **White Water Adventure** (38 Northwestern Lake, White Salmon; 509-493-3121) and **Renegade River Rafters** (P.O. Box 263, Stevenson, WA 98648; 509-427-7238) offer trips here. Another often-rafted river in the Gorge is the Klickitat. Outfitters to contact are **River Recreation** (13 211th Place Southeast, Redmond; 206-392-5899), **North Cascades River Expeditions** (P.O. Box 116, Arlington, WA 98223; 206-435-9548) and **All River Adventures** (P.O. Box 12, Cashmere, WA 98815; 509-782-2254).

WINDSURFING

One of the world's best windsurfing areas, the Columbia River Gorge is *the* place to learn this exciting sport. **Rhonda Smith Windsurfing Center** (Port Marina Park, Hood River, OR; 503-386-9463) is the place to go for equipment rentals, lessons, kids camps and racing lessons. **Big Winds** (505 Cascade Street, Hood River, OR; 509-386-6086) offers rentals and instruction for children and adults. **Gorge Windsurfing** (420 East 1st Street, The Dalles, OR; 503-298-8796) has sailboard equipment and instructions. Lessons, rentals and demo equipment are arranged at The Dalles Riverfront Park.

GOLF

If you are interested in teeing off in Hood River, Oregon, try the **Hood River Golf and Country Club** (1850 Country Club Road; 503-386-3009). In Stevenson, the Skamania Lodge offers the 18-hole **Bridge of the Gods Golf Course** (1131 Skamania Lodge Way; 509-427-7700).

Hood River has become a windsurfing capital thanks to the strong breezes there.

In Carson, Washington, head for the **Hot Springs Golf Course** (Hot Springs Avenue and St. Martins Road; 509-427-5150). Located on Route 14 between Beacon Rock and North Bonneville is **Beacon Rock Public Golf Course** (509-427-5730).

HORSEBACK RIDING

For equestrians, the Gorge area has two options: in Hood River, horseback riding on mountain trails is offered by **Fir Mountain Ranch** (4051 Fir Mountain Road; 503-354-2753); in Stevenson, **Skamania Lodge** (1131 Skamania Lodge Way; 509-427-7700) offers trail rides in hills above the Gorge.

BICYCLING

The Columbia River Gorge along Route 84 is prime cycling territory. Any portion of the 62-mile route between Portland and Hood River is worth your time. You can also turn this into an ambitious 158-mile loop around Mt. Hood by returning to Portland on Routes 35 and 26.

BIKE RENTALS   If you're planning to bicycle in the Columbia River Gorge region, in Hood River you can try **Discover Bicycles** (1020 Wasco Street; 503-386-4820). In The Dalles, rent from **Life Cycles** (418 East 2nd Street; 503-296-9588).

HIKING

Latourell Falls Trail (2 miles), on the Old Columbia Gorge Scenic Highway three miles east of Crown Point, is a moderately difficult walk leading along a streambed to the base of the upper falls. To extend this walk another mile, take a loop trail beginning at the top of lower Latourell Falls and returning to the highway at Talbot Park.

Near the Bridal Veil Exit off Route 84 is **#415 Angels Rest Trail** (2 miles), an easy hike leading to an overlook. This route can be extended another 15 miles to Bonneville Dam by taking the **#400 Gorge Trail**.

Eagle Creek Campground at Exit 40 on Route 84 is the jumpoff point for the easy hike to **Punch Bowl Falls** (2 miles) or the far more challenging trip to **Wahtum Lake** (13 miles). The latter trail leads up through the Columbia Wilderness and is part of the Pacific Crest Trail.

On the Washington side of the river, west of Bonneville Dam, is the one-mile trail leading to the top of **Beacon Rock**, an 800-foot monolith noted by Lewis and Clark. Ascended by a series of switchbacks guarded by railings, this trail offers great views of the Gorge.

East of Home Valley on Route 14 is the **Dog Mountain Trail**, a three-and-a-half-mile climb up 2900 feet for impressive views of Mt. Hood, Mt. St. Helens and Mt. Adams. The trail is especially lovely during May and June when the surrounding hills are covered with wildflowers.

Transportation

BY CAR

From Seattle, **Route 5** heads south toward Portland and the roads that lead eastward toward the Columbia River Gorge. **Route 84** runs the length of the Columbia River Gorge on the Oregon side and just east of the town of Troutdale is paralleled by the **Historic Columbia River Highway**, a windy road that offers beautiful views of the Gorge. **Route 14** travels along the river's Washington side. **Route 35** heads south from Hood River on the Oregon side toward Mt. Hood.

BY AIR

If you plan on flying to the Columbia River Gorge area, Portland and the Tri-Cities are the closest airports that serve major airlines. (See Chapter Nine). However, both Hood River and The Dalles have small airports for charter airlines.

BY BUS

Greyhound Bus Lines stops at several locations along the Gorge. In Oregon, there are stations in Hood River (1203 B Street; 503-386-1212) and The Dalles (201 East Federal Street; 503-296-2421).

BY TRAIN

Amtrak (800-872-7245) offers service to the Columbia River Gorge area on two trains. The "Empire Builder" runs from Spokane to Portland while the "Mount Rainier" travels from Seattle to Eugene, both stopping in Vancouver.

PUBLIC TRANSPORTATION

The town of Hood River is served by **Hood River County Transit** (503-386-4202).

Index

HIDDEN GUIDES

Adventure travel or a relaxing vacation?—"Hidden" guidebooks are the only travel books in the business to provide detailed information on both. Aimed at environmentally aware travelers, our motto is "Adventure Travel Plus." These books combine details on unique hotels, restaurants and sightseeing with information on camping, sports and hiking for the outdoor enthusiast.

ULTIMATE GUIDES

These innovative guides present the best and most unique features of a destination. Quality is the keynote. They are as likely to cover a mom-and-pop café as a gourmet restaurant, a quaint bed and breakfast as a five-star tennis resort. In addition to thoroughly covering each destination, they feature short articles and one-line "teasers" that are both fun and informative.

THE NEW KEY GUIDES

Based on the concept of ecotourism, The New Key Guides are dedicated to the preservation of Central America's rare and endangered species, architecture and archaeology. Filled with helpful tips, they give travelers everything they need to know about these exotic destinations.

ULYSSES PRESS To order direct, send a check or money order to:
Ulysses Press, P.O. Box 3440, Berkeley, CA 94703-3440;
to charge by credit card, call 800/377-2542 or 510/601-8301.

TRAVEL

_____ Hidden Boston and Cape Cod, $9.95
_____ Hidden Carolinas, $15.95
_____ Hidden Coast of California, $15.95
_____ Hidden Colorado, $12.95
_____ Hidden Florida, $14.95
_____ Hidden Florida Keys and Everglades, $9.95
_____ Hidden Hawaii, $15.95
_____ Hidden Idaho, $12.95
_____ Hidden New England, $14.95
_____ Hidden Oregon, $12.95
_____ Hidden Pacific Northwest, $14.95
_____ Hidden Rockies, $16.95
_____ Hidden San Francisco and Northern California, $14.95
_____ Hidden Southern California, $14.95
_____ Hidden Southwest, $15.95
_____ Disneyland and Beyond: The Ultimate Family Guidebook, $9.95
_____ Disney World & Beyond: The Ultimate Family Guidebook, $12.95
_____ The Maya Route: The Ultimate Guidebook, $14.95
_____ Ultimate Arizona, $12.95
_____ Ultimate California, $14.95
_____ Ultimate Las Vegas and Beyond, $11.95
_____ Ultimate Maui, $11.95
_____ Ultimate Santa Fe and Beyond, $11.95
_____ Ultimate Washington, $13.95
_____ The New Key to Belize, $14.95
_____ The New Key to Cancún and the Yucatán, $13.95
_____ The New Key to Costa Rica, $14.95
_____ The New Key to Ecuador and the Galápagos, $14.95
_____ The New Key to Guatemala, $14.95
_____ The New Key to Panama, $14.95

FREE SHIPPING!

Total cost of books   = _____
Book rate shipping   = __FREE__
California residents add 8% sales tax.   = _____
                                  Total enclosed = _____

NAME _____PHONE _____
ADDRESS_____
CITY _____STATE ____ZIP _____

About the Authors

Maria Lenhart has been a freelance writer specializing in travel for 15 years. She has contributed to *Travel/Holiday, Travel & Leisure, Odyssey, Business Travel News,* Fodor's Travel Guides, *Boston Globe, Washington Post, Christian Science Monitor* and many other publications.

Marilyn McFarlane, a member of the Society of American Travel Writers, contributed to the chapters on Seattle and Southern Puget Sound. A Northwest native, she is the author of *Best Places to Stay in the Pacific Northwest, Quick Escapes in the Pacific Northwest* and *Northwest Discoveries.*

Jim Poth is a native of the Northwest who spent 21 years reporting in the region for *Sunset Magazine,* where he became both bureau chief and senior editor. Jim now runs Easy Going Outings, Inc., a recreational guide service in Washington's Skagit Valley.

Roger Rapoport has written many travel guides including *Great Cities of Eastern Europe.* He has written extensively on the Pacific Northwest for *Outside* and the *Oregonian.* Formerly a travel writer at the *Oakland Tribune,* he is now publisher of RDR Books.

John Gottberg has penned eight travel books. The former chief editor of the Insight Guide series and the travel news and graphics editor for the *Los Angeles Times,* he has been published in such magazines as *Travel & Leisure* and *Islands.* He currently resides in Boise, Idaho.

Melissa Rivers has collaborated on numerous guidebooks including *The Wall Street Journal Guides to Business Travel, Fodor's Best Bed and Breakfasts and Country Inns: The Pacific Northwest, Fodor's Canada* and *Fodor's Caribbean.*

Archie Satterfield, a member of the Society of American Travel Writers, resides in Edmonds, Washington. He has authored two dozen books, including *Country Roads of Washington.* He has also written for *Motorland, Pacific Northwest Magazine* and the *Chicago Sun-Times.*

About the Illustrator

Glenn Kim is a freelance illustrator residing in San Francisco. His work appears in numerous Ulysses Press titles, including *Hidden Southwest, The New Key to Belize* and *Ultimate Santa Fe and Beyond.* He has also done illustrations for the National Forest Service, SEGA, a variety of magazines, book covers and greeting cards.